CONTESTED REGIME

This collection of innovative contributions to the study of legal pluralism in international and transnational law focuses on collisions and conflicts between an increasing number of institutional and legal orders, which can manifest themselves in contradictory decisions or mutual obstruction. It combines theoretical approaches from a variety of disciplines with theoretically informed case studies in order to further our understanding of the phenomenon of regime collisions. By bringing together scholars of international law, legal philosophy, the social sciences and post-colonial studies from Latin America, the United States and Europe, the volume demonstrates that collisions between various institutional and legal orders affect different regions in different ways, highlights some of their problematic consequences and identifies methods of addressing such collisions in a more productive manner.

KERSTIN BLOME was a post-doctoral researcher at the University of Bremen and is now a mediator and communication trainer based in Bremen, Germany.

ANDREAS FISCHER-LESCANO is Professor for Public Law, European and International Law and Managing Director of the Centre of European Law and Politics at the University of Bremen, Germany.

HANNAH FRANZKI is reading for a PhD in Law at Birkbeck College, University of London.

NORA MARKARD is Junior Professor for Public Law, International Law and Global Constitutionalism at the University of Hamburg, Germany.

STEFAN OETER is Professor for Public Law, International Law and Foreign Public Law at the University of Hamburg, Germany.

CONTESTED REGIME COLLISIONS

Norm Fragmentation in World Society

Edited by

KERSTIN BLOME

ANDREAS FISCHER-LESCANO

HANNAH FRANZKI

NORA MARKARD

and

STEFAN OETER

CAMBRIDGE
UNIVERSITY PRESS

CAMBRIDGE
UNIVERSITY PRESS

University Printing House, Cambridge CB2 8BS, United Kingdom

One Liberty Plaza, 20th Floor, New York, NY 10006, USA

477 Williamstown Road, Port Melbourne, VIC 3207, Australia

314-321, 3rd Floor, Plot 3, Splendor Forum, Jasola District Centre, New Delhi - 110025, India

79 Anson Road, #06-04/06, Singapore 079906

Cambridge University Press is part of the University of Cambridge.

It furthers the University's mission by disseminating knowledge in the pursuit of education, learning and research at the highest international levels of excellence.

www.cambridge.org
Information on this title: www.cambridge.org/9781107565593

First published 2016
First paperback edition 2018

A catalogue record for this publication is available from the British Library

Library of Congress Cataloging in Publication data
Names: Blome, Kerstin, editor.
Title: Contested regime collisions : norm fragmentation in world society / edited by Kerstin Blome, Andreas Fischer-Lescano, Hannah Franzki, Nora Markard, and Stefan Oeter.
Description: New York : Cambridge University Press, 2016. | Includes bibliographical references and index.
Identifiers: LCCN 2015040825 | ISBN 9781107126572 (Hardback)
Subjects: LCSH: International and municipal law. | Law–Interpretation and construction. | Conflict of laws. | Legal polycentricity. | International law.
Classification: LCC K302 .C66 2016 | DDC 341–dc23 LC record available at http://lccn.loc.gov/2015040825

ISBN 978-1-107-12657-2 Hardback
ISBN 978-1-107-56559-3 Paperback

CONTENTS

CONTRIBUTORS

LARRY CATÁ BACKER is the W. Richard and Mary Eshelman Faculty Scholar & Professor of Law and Professor of International Affairs at Pennsylvania State University.

KERSTIN BLOME is a former post-doctoral researcher at the University of Bremen, a mediator and communication trainer based in Bremen, Germany.

SONJA BUCKEL is Professor of Political Theory at the University of Kassel, Germany.

JEFFREY L. DUNOFF is the Laura H. Carnell Professor of Law at Temple University Beasley School of Law.

SEBASTIAN EICKENJÄGER is a doctoral researcher in the Faculty of Law at the University of Bremen.

ANDREAS FISCHER-LESCANO is Professor of Public Law, European Law and International Law and Managing Director of the Centre of European Law and Politics at the University of Bremen, Germany.

HANNAH FRANZKI is reading for a PhD in Law at Birkbeck, University of London.

ISABELL HENSEL is a doctoral researcher in the Faculty of Law at the European University Viadrina in Frankfurt (Oder), Germany.

JOHAN HORST is a doctoral researcher in the ERC project 'Transnational Force of Law' at the University of Bremen, Germany.

Nora Markard is Junior Professor of Public Law, International Law and Global Constitutionalism at the University of Hamburg, Germany.

Christoph Menke is Professor of Political and Legal Philosophy at the Goethe University of Frankfurt, Germany.

Kolja Möller is a post-doctoral researcher in the 'Normative Orders' research programe at the Goethe University of Frankfurt, Germany.

Marcelo Neves is Professor of Public Law and Legal Theory in the Faculty of Law, University of Brasilia, Brazil.

Sebastian Oberthür is Professor of Environment and Sustainable Development at the Institute for European Studies at the Vrije Universiteit Brussel, Belgium.

Stefan Oeter is Professor of Public Law, International Law and Foreign Public Law at the University of Hamburg, Germany.

Gunther Teubner is Professor Emeritus of Private Law and Sociology of Law at the Goethe University of Frankfurt, Germany.

Lars Viellechner is Associate Professor of Constitutional Law, Constitutional Theory, Legal Philosophy and Transnational Law at the University of Bremen, Germany.

PREFACE

This volume is based on a three-day conference held in Bremen, Germany, in January of 2014. The conference served to present the findings of a long-term research project on 'The Juridification of Dispute Settlement in International Law', which was part of the Collaborative Research Centre 597 'Transformations of the State' at the University of Bremen.

Supported by the University of Bremen, Jacobs University Bremen and the University of Oldenburg, this Collaborative Research Centre (CRC) brought together scholars from political science, law, sociology, economics and communication studies to analyse whether and how globalisation has changed the core institutions und functions of the democratic constitutional and interventionist state of the late twentieth and early twenty-first century. The first phase of the CRC (2003–2006) traced a diffusion of statehood along the spatial (national-international) and modal (public-private) axis with regard to the four main dimensions of statehood: law, legitimacy, welfare and security. The reasons for the varying degrees of diffusion were addressed in the second phase (2007–2010), while the third and final phase (2011–2014) dealt with the impact of this transformation on the provision of the normative goods rule of law, democratic legitimacy, welfare and security.

In this context, the research project on 'The Juridification of Dispute Settlement in International Law', situated in the CRC's 'Rule of Law' pillar, focused on different degrees of juridification of international dispute settlement in a fragmented legal order. Supervised by Michael Zürn und Bernhard Zangl, the first project phase pursued the question whether and to what degree the national rule of law was supplemented by an international rule of law. It found an uneven juridification in terms of the establishment and recognition of international dispute settlement bodies in the fields of international trade, security, human rights, labour standards and the protection of endangered species. These findings were the starting point for the project's second phase, relying on prominent theoretical approaches of international relations (realism, institutionalism and liberalism) to explain the differences in dispute settlement design, usage and acceptance.[1]

The concluding project phase, supervised by Andreas Fischer-Lescano in co-operation with Stefan Oeter of the University of Hamburg, dealt with collisions between regimes with different degrees of juridification. In many ways, this research project was a continuation of Andreas Fischer-Lescano's and Gunther Teubner's work on 'Regime Collisions', drawing the 'bigger picture' of regime collisions and outlining ways to manage them in a heterarchic network of regimes. This project phase was designed to apply this approach to case studies on regime collisions in different areas of international law, such as WTO law and social human rights, or the UN security system and international criminal law, and to further develop the concept of regime collisions.

Many have contributed to the success of this project. Kerstin Blome, Achim Helmedach, Aletta Mondré, Gerald Neubauer and Lars Viellechner were involved in writing the funding proposal for the final project phase. Moreover, without the work of Sarah Ehlers, Sebastian Eickenjäger, Hannah Franzki, Johan Horst, Nora Markard, Kolja Möller and all student assistants, the project would not have been implemented and completed successfully in its final phase. We would also like to give our thanks to the German Research Foundation (DFG) for funding the project and thus making this work possible; to the project managers of the CRC, Stefan Leibfried and Dieter Wolf; and to Dörthe Hauschild and Monika Hobbie from the administrative team who impeccably managed all things administrative and financial and helped to make the conference go smoothly. Thanks are also due to all those who participated in the conference, who shared with us their insights on the topic of regime collisions and who critically discussed with us the main findings of our research project.

Kerstin Blome, Andreas Fischer-Lescano, Hannah Franzki,
Nora Markard, Stefan Oeter

[1] For the main findings of the project's first two phases see, e.g., A. Mondré, G. Neubauer, A. Helmedach and B. Zangl, 'Uneven Judicialization: Comparing International Dispute Settlement in Security, Trade, and the Environment', *New Global Studies*, 4 (2010), pp. 1–32, and B. Zangl, A. Helmedach, A. Mondré, A. Kocks, G. Neubauer and K. Blome, 'Between Law and Politics: Explaining International Dispute Settlement Behavior', *European Journal of International Relations*, 18 (2012), pp. 369–401.

Contested collisions

An introduction

KERSTIN BLOME, ANDREAS FISCHER-LESCANO,
HANNAH FRANZKI, NORA MARKARD AND STEFAN OETER

Regime collisions

International law has come a long way. The total number of international treaties in force today is near impossible to determine, and even multilateral treaties open for general signature have multiplied at a rate that would have been hard to imagine even sixty years ago.[1] International organizations have proliferated, and so have international courts and tribunals, charged with adjudicating conflicts arising under such treaties.[2] What is more, states have long ceased to be the only actors on the international stage. Not only have individuals been assuming their own position in international law as human rights continued to develop;[3] corporate actors, also, have carved out a place for themselves in the international legal arena. Transnational law, as it is called, has become one of the most dynamic areas of law beyond the nation-state.[4]

Crucially, these developments have involved the formation of a plethora of international regimes, which the Study Group of the International Law Commission on Fragmentation has defined as 'combination[s] of rules which [lay] down specific rights, obligations, competences, and

[1] There are over 50,000 treaties registered in the UN system, and of the 6,000 multilateral treaties concluded in the twentieth century, 30 per cent were open for all states to participate: Final report of the Study Group of the International Law Commission: Fragmentation of International Law: Difficulties arising from the diversification and expansion of international law (ILC A/CN.4/L.682, 13 April 2006), para. 7.

[2] See, e.g., Mackenzie et al., *The Manual on International Courts and Tribunals.*

[3] Peters, 'Humanity as the A and Ω of Sovereignty', even argues that this is part of a radical shift in the perspective on international law.

[4] See, e.g., Teubner (ed.), *Global Law Without a State.*

rules on the administration of such rules, in particular including rules on the reaction to violations'.[5] This process has been described as 'fragmentation' of international law,[6] an uncoordinated growth, as each regime is created to address a specific problem or set of issues. No systematic efforts are made to make sure a new or developing regime fits into the order of existing regimes. As a result, regimes often overlap, containing different rules for the same issue.[7]

This is not just a technical matter that is only of concern to order-loving lawyers. Overlapping regimes often represent quite different sets of interests, or systemic rationalities.[8] For example, it makes a big difference whether shrimp fishing is approached from a market-oriented perspective geared toward securing the global free flow of goods, or within the framework of sustainable management of aquatic resources, or from the perspective of the conservation of endangered species.[9] Or, to use an example from the ILC Report on the Fragmentation of International Law, are the conflicts over a nuclear power plant at the shores of the North Sea, simultaneously brought before an Arbitral Tribunal under the UN Convention on the Law of the Sea, an OSPAR[10] dispute settlement mechanism, and the European Court of Justice, 'principally about the law of the sea, about (possible) pollution of the

[5] Outline of the Chairman of the ILC Study Group on Fragmentation of International Law: The Function and Scope of the lex specialis rule and the question of 'self-contained regimes' (2003), http://untreaty.un/ilc/sessions/55/fragmentation_outline.pdf. This concept is similar to the one dominant in international relations theory, referring to 'a set of implicit or explicit principles, norms, rules, and decision-making procedures around which actors' expectations converge in a given area of international relations'; Krasner, 'Structural Causes and Regime Consequences', p. 185.

[6] Final report of the Study Group of the International Law Commission: Fragmentation of International Law: Difficulties arising from the diversification and expansion of international law (ILC A/CN.4/L.682, 13 April 2006). See also: Koskenniemi, 'Legal Fragmentation(s)'; Koskenniemi and Leino, 'Fragmentation of International Law?'.

[7] See, e.g., Pulkowski, *The Law and Politics of International Regime Conflict*, on the trade, culture and human rights regimes; see also the contributions in Young, *Regime Interaction in International Law*. For a perspective on the relationship between two different economic regimes (trade and investment), see Puig, 'International Regime Complexity and Economic Law Enforcement'.

[8] Even if they involve similar sets of state parties, they will have been negotiated at different times, by different departments, in different bargains: Simma and Pulkowski, 'Of Planets and the Universe', p. 489.

[9] See Joyner and Tyler, 'Marine Conservation versus International Free Trade'.

[10] 1992 Convention for the Protection of the Marine Environment of the North-East Atlantic, combining two earlier instruments named after Oslo (OS) and Paris (PAR).

North Sea, or about inter-EC relationships?'[11] There is no inbuilt priority of one regime over the other(s), in the sense that one systemic perspective is more valid and thus might normatively trump the other. In the absence of an established hierarchy of norms in the international sphere – apart from some *ius cogens* norms – there is no pre-defined institutional mechanism that secures consistent decisions.[12] Such different systemic rationalities, different perceptions of what the matter is 'really' about, may therefore lead to irreconcilably different outcomes in judicial or arbitral procedures.

A contested matter: interdisciplinary perspectives

In a systems theoretic account, such fraught constellations can be described as 'regime collisions',[13] which are much more than mere legal conflicts to be resolved by legal rules. Systems theory describes global society as functionally differentiated into 'social systems', such as the political or the economic system, the ecological system, and so on. Operating on a binary code, such as 'pay/don't pay', in the case of the economic system, each of these systems pursues its own rationality (*Eigenrationalität*). At their intersections, these autonomous systems seek to integrate the other system's operations into their own coded logic. In that very manner, the legal system forms legal regimes around other social systems, subjecting them to its particular binary code of 'law/illegality'. As a result, global law is necessarily and irreversibly fragmented into different legal regimes that follow different normative logics, such as trade, security, environmental protection, and so on. Just like the social systems underlying them, each of these regimes seeks to universalize its *Eigenlogik*[14] at the expense of the others. It is thus not only normative orders that collide, but also underlying conflicting

[11] Final report of the Study Group of the International Law Commission: Fragmentation of International Law: Difficulties arising from the diversification and expansion of international law (ILC A/CN.4/L.682, 13 April 2006), para. 10.

[12] See, e.g. de Wet and Vidmar (eds.), *Hierarchy in International Law*, in particular the 'Introduction', but also Vidmar 'Norm Conflicts and Hierarchy', pp. 13–40. On the relationship between specialized regimes and general international law, see Simma and Pulkowski, 'Of Planets and the Universe'.

[13] First published in 2004 as: Fischer-Lescano and Teubner, 'Regime-Collisions'; expanded to book length in German: Fischer-Lescano and Teubner, *Regime-Kollisionen*.

[14] Fischer-Lescano and Teubner, 'Regime-Collisions', p. 1006 ff.

societal goals and interests:[15] 'At core, the fragmentation of global law is not simply about legal norm collisions or policy-conflicts, but rather has its origin in contradictions between society-wide institutionalized rationalities, which law cannot solve.'[16]

Regime collisions, of course, are not just a topic for legal scholars or even systems theorists. Regime theory, for example, a neo-institutionalist theory of international relations, is also concerned with 'overlaps' between different regimes. Using terms such as 'institutional linkage',[17] 'institutional interaction',[18] 'regime overlap',[19] 'regime interplay',[20] or 'regime complexes',[21] these approaches focus on identifying the positive (synergetic) or negative effects of different types of interaction on the efficiency of the interacting institutions.[22] In the case of 'regime overlaps', where 'the functional scope of one regime protrudes into the functional scope of others',[23] conflicts tend to arise where the overarching goals and norms of the regimes or the concrete rules on the attainment of these goals diverge, or are even mutually exclusive,[24] as in the case of the WTO free trade regime and international environmental regimes.[25]

Not only do the perspectives on regime collisions vary, though. Approaches also differ in whether such overlaps are necessarily to be seen as problematic. Thus, in their contributions to this volume, *Jeffrey Dunoff* and *Sebastian Oberthür* argue that most regime interactions actually work out well, and that a focus on collisions tends to reduce the larger picture of different interactions to the pathological cases. *Stefan Oeter* even points out that collisions and the contestations they entail can contribute to a promotion of the larger project of constitutionalizing the global order. *Kolja Möller* cautions against this optimism; in this struggle for hegemony between different regime rationalities, he argues, there is no space to question the very existence of a regime and its logic, rather than to merely manage its expansionist tendency.

15 Ibid., p. 1017. 16 Ibid., p. 1004.
17 Young, 'Institutional Linkages in International Society'.
18 Gehring and Oberthür, 'Causal Mechanisms of Interaction'.
19 Rosendal, 'Impacts of Overlapping International Regimes'.
20 Stokke, 'The Interplay of International Regimes'.
21 Gehring and Faude, 'Dynamics of Regime Complexes'.
22 Gehring and Oberthür, 'Causal Mechanisms of Interaction', pp. 135ff.
23 Rosendal, 'Impacts of Overlapping International Regimes', p. 96, following Young.
24 Ibid., p. 100–01.
25 Gehring and Oberthür, 'Causal Mechanisms of Interaction', p. 137; see also Gehring and Faude, 'Dynamics of Regime Complexes', p. 125.

From yet another angle, it could be asked whether the focus on collisions between *legal* regimes might be too narrow, and whether collisions between the legal system and other spheres should not also be taken into account. Thus, *Christoph Menke* examines the conflictual relationship between law and the non-legal sphere, while *Sonja Buckel* more specifically looks into law's relationship with the economic system. In his case study on whistle blowing, *Andreas Fischer-Lescano* shows how the legal system must secure spaces in the political system for democratic deliberation by ensuring autonomy.

Finally, the solutions proposed are quite different. Assuming that overlapping legal regimes are not a mere consistency problem, but a reflection of underlying conflicting societal goals and interest, this casts doubt on 'one-dimensional solutions'.[26] Given the nature of fragmentation of international law, the hope for normative unity must be seen as illusory, a paradise lost[27] – especially since the involvement of autonomous private regimes in the 'interlegality' or heterarchical co-existence of such regimes brings down any hope for a classic hierarchy of norms.[28] From a systems theory point of view, regime collisions can therefore only be resolved via 'heterarchical forms of law that limit themselves to creating loose relationships between the fragments of law'.[29] Such network structures function by means of mutual observation and mutual irritation: Systems and regimes interact with and react to one another, each in their own logic but responding to the other's logic, in order to establish compatibility between different rationalities.[30] Formulating a common good in this process, even in the specific terms and norms of the respective regime – for example in the way that *Stefan Oeter* describes – promotes an alterity orientation, a responsiveness or *comitas*[31] to the *Eigenrationalität* of the other regime. Regime collisions therefore require a legal form for autonomous regimes to reflect other regimes' interests. In this vein, *Lars Viellechner* proposes a 'duty to consider' or deference clauses on both sides, which will secure a default deference to another regime's decisions in order to prevent clashes, and

[26] Fischer-Lescano and Teubner, 'Regime-Collisions', pp. 1003–04.

[27] Ibid., p. 1007. Tomuschat, 'International law as a coherent system', pp. 323–30, points out that international law has no 'golden past'; to the contrary, it was always fragmented and has only recently started growing together to some extent.

[28] Fischer-Lescano and Teubner, 'Regime-Collisions', pp. 1007ff.

[29] Ibid., p. 1017.

[30] Ibid., pp. 1018, 1024, 1030. This responsive interaction is described as 're-entry' of another system's logic into the first system.

[31] Teubner and Korth, 'Two Kinds of Legal Pluralism', p. 37.

a duty to take the other regime's solutions into account and to integrate them as much as possible.[32]

As Viellechner demonstrates, such horizontal, network-like structures have already developed between different courts charged with securing constitutional and human rights in different settings, such as a constitutional system, a regional human rights regime, and the European Union. Other, more recent regimes have sought to actively address possible collisions by incorporating collision norms. For example, the 1998 Rome Statute (RS) governing the work of the International Criminal Court (ICC) contains clauses on its relationship to the UN Security Council. Both the ICC and the Security Council deal with international crimes: The ICC was established to prosecute 'the most serious crimes of concern to the international community as a whole' (Article 5 RS), and the Security Council addresses them with diplomatic means or forceful measures, as part of its 'primary responsibility for the maintenance of international peace and security' (Article 24 of the UN Charter). This is particularly obvious in the case of the future crime of aggression.[33] Often, these legal and political concerns will go hand in hand, as transitional justice is usually seen as promoting a stable peace. Therefore, the UN Security Council can charge the Court with investigations under Article 13 RS, even if the state concerned has not acceded to the Statute. However, criminal investigations can also be seen as threatening a peace process. For example, this was a criticism of the African Union (AU)[34] in the case of Sudan, where an ICC arrest warrant was issued against the Acting Head of State, Omar Al-Bashir[35] (the investigations have recently been put on hold[36]). As the ICC is not a UN organ but an independent international organization of its own, Security Council resolutions as

[32] Viellechner, 'Berücksichtigungspflicht als Kollisionsregel'.

[33] The definition of the crime of aggression and its 'trigger mechanism' were adopted at the first Review Conference in Kampala in 2010 and cannot enter into force before 2017; ICC Res. RC/Res.6 of June 11, 2010.

[34] AU Peace and Security Council, Communiqué PSC/MIN/Comm(CXLII), Rev. 1, July 21, 2008; reports on the Arab League Council's statement of July 19, 2008 available at www.iccnow.org/?mod=newsdetail&news=2783. The AU subsequently pushed for a reform of Article 16: AU Executive Council, 16th Ordinary Session, January 25–29, 2010, Report on the Ministerial Meeting on the Rome Statute, EX.CL/568 (XVI) Annex 1.

[35] The warrant was issued in March 2009 for crimes against humanity and war crimes, a second one was issued for genocide in 2010 (*Prosecutor* v. *Omar Hassan Ahmad Al Bashir*, ICC-02/05-01/09).

[36] OTP, Statement to the United Nations Security Council on the Situation in Darfur, pursuant to UNSCR 1593 (2005), December 12, 2014.

such have no binding effect on the Court. In its Article 16, the Rome Statute therefore provides for a possibility for the Security Council to request a (renewable) six-month deferral of investigations in the interest of international peace and security. By preventing clashing decisions or regime logics, such collision norms can prevent threats to the legitimacy and effectiveness of either regime. On the other hand, arguably, this effect will only be achieved if such norms and the solutions they prescribe are themselves perceived as legitimate.[37]

The law can, however, also take the back seat and merely secure the conditions for collision management within the regimes on their own terms. Thus, the contributions of *Isabell Hensel* and *Gunther Teubner*, *Larry Catá Backer* and *Sebastian Eickenjäger* explore ways of self-regulation that are merely structured by law. Hensel and Teubner propose the registration of medical trials as a way to secure the integrity of the scientific system against the pressures of the economic system, while securing the fundamental rights of patients. At the intersection of the economic system and the human rights regime, Backer looks at governance mechanisms and Eickenjäger at non-financial reporting as ways to make sure competing regime logics are taken into account.

From a more radical theoretical perspective, however, such efforts at managing collisions can be seen as 'creeping managerialism'. Instead of just accepting the different regime logics and merely seeking to work out a stable balance, *Kolja Möller* asks how destituent constituencies can establish a sustainable counterweight to hegemonic regimes and challenge their logics from below. Meanwhile, it should be borne in mind that, given that regime collisions are expressions of larger systemic interactions, solutions must not necessarily be legal, but might equally validly occur in other social systems. Thus, Fischer-Lescano and Teubner also consider 'giving back' decisions to the political system.[38]

While talk of the fragmentation of international law and of 'regime collisions' has therefore spread to an extent that it can be considered a matter of common concern, the descriptions, analyses and solutions proposed remain contested. This volume therefore unites theoretical approaches from a variety of disciplines as well as theoretically informed case studies in order to push our understanding of this phenomenon further, to highlight some of their problematic consequences, but also to examine possibilities of addressing them in a productive way.

[37] See Blome and Markard, 'Contested Collisions'.

[38] Fischer-Lescano and Teubner, *Regime-Kollisionen*, p. 130.

The organization of this volume

In taking up the phenomenon of 'contested collisions' from an interdisciplinary perspective, this volume seeks to illuminate aspects thus far neglected by the literature on fragmentation and to initiate a shift in the terms of debate that characterize the field. The contributions to this volume therefore present a combination of theoretical approaches to the phenomenon of regime collisions, and case studies that illustrate the value of the theoretical reflections for understanding what is at stake in these collisions. The collection unites a group of international scholars who impart approaches from international law, legal philosophy, the social sciences, and postcolonial studies to the volume. By bringing together contributions from Latin America, the United States and Europe, we seek to attend to the fact that collisions between various institutional and legal orders can affect world regions in different ways.

The contributions in this volume are clustered into three main parts, according to the perspective they take on the phenomenon of regime collisions. Each part combines theoretical explorations as well as theoretically informed and/or theory-generating case studies that demonstrate the relevance and implications of the adopted perspective.

Part I Between collisions and interaction

The first part of this book critically examines the phenomenon of regime collisions and puts it into perspective. The chapters point out potentialities produced by collisions and highlight instances of productive regime interaction in a fragmented legal order, thereby challenging the prevailing assumption that the emergence of transnational legal regimes, and the lack of a hierarchical order in the international sphere, is inherently problematic.

In the first chapter, *Stefan Oeter* brings to bear debates from the field of global constitutionalism on the problem of regime collision, arguing that such a perspective allows us to see in which way regime collisions actually enable debates about fundamental norms. He points out that the mobilization of the public in favour of competing regime logic in cases of collision can create a counterweight to the institutional asymmetries generated by uneven judicialization. Oeter starts from the observation that the term 'constitutionalism' does not merely describe processes of constitutionalization but also refers to the legitimacy of a legal order. Merely observing processes of constitutionalization does not yet impart information about the constitutional *quality* of the emerging order. Such legitimacy, Oeter argues, is subject to struggles of contestation – and it is here that regime collisions can be brought into the project of global constitutionalism, by providing a decisive source of principled contestation. Actors that feel threatened with 'colonisation' by an alien regime raise principled objections against the legitimacy of the hegemonic regime invoking what they consider to be fundamental values and basic principles of the global community. The public contestation of these values forces stronger regimes to take into account arguments and/or values of the weaker institutionalized regime. In so far as regime collisions promote contestations in support of fundamental values, Oeter argues, they should be not perceived as a problem, but as a possibility to question the constitutional quality of the global order.

In a more practical vein, *Jeffrey L. Dunoff* develops a typology of positive regime interactions, which, in his view, have been under-theorized thus far. His contribution shifts the focus away from conflicts or collisions to regime interactions more generally, emphasizing that collisions between legal orders represent only a small slice of the universe of regime overlaps and interactions. He argues that the literature on regime collisions has emphasized normative conflict at the expense of the study of institutional interaction. Dunoff draws on the concept of relational interactions to develop a typology of regime interactions. In particular, he identifies two different axes by which regime interactions can be categorized. The first one focuses on the various forms that regime interactions assume, namely operational, regulatory, and conceptual interactions. The second axis focuses on the nature of the interaction, which spans a continuum from rationalization of parallel or overlapping efforts, expansions of powers or jurisdiction, to conflictual interactions. Considered together, these axes can be conceptualized as a three-by-three matrix, which captures much of the universe of regime interaction.

This line of argument is taken up in the third chapter of this part, in which *Sebastian Oberthür* draws on his extensive research in the field of global environmental policy to show that international organizations have been effectively creating synergies through regime interplay. Looking into the mechanisms designed to collectively shape institutional interplay and regime complexes, Oberthür asks what they have delivered so far and how their potential may be further enhanced and exploited. His answer consists of six theses: He argues that (1) discussions about conflict and 'collisions' in the fragmented world of international law and politics should be balanced by attention to the potential for synergy; (2) the fragmented world of international law and institutions is characterized by a significant degree of order; (3) this order is shaped and advanced by collective interplay management that has become the 'daily bread' of international law makers; (4) this interplay management itself is shaped and constrained significantly by international power and interests as well as normative mechanisms that privilege status quo forces and path-dependent developments over fundamental change; (5) It is in principle possible to devise international (meta-)norms that could significantly strengthen and substantiate the international legal framework of regime interplay, but such an effort may not be politically feasible and (6) Advances can and have to be made on the basis of the existing interplay management structures that can be developed gradually/incrementally.

Finally, *Lars Viellechner* introduces a theory of responsive legal pluralism that takes active care of mutual adaptation, by means of a horizontal coordination of the different legal orders, through which the negative consequences of the fragmentation of law could be remedied. Viellechner puts forward a theory of responsive legal pluralism that guarantees the coherence and legitimacy of law in the face of collisions provoked by the fragmentation of law. Such a responsive legal pluralism would be characterized by a horizontal coordination among the different legal orders that open themselves for each other by internally reflecting their mutual impact. Indeed, he observes, a new kind of conflict law required to this end is already gradually evolving. In accordance with the spirit of some express provisions in treaties and constitutions, courts and tribunals are dialectically developing rules of complementarity and subsidiarity without however relinquishing their own identity. A 'responsive legal pluralism' of this kind offers a promising fourth way to overcome both the out-dated dualist doctrine of sovereigntism and the unattainable monist vision of universalism, while at the same time avoiding radical legal pluralism.

Part II Addressing collisions: regulation and self-regulation

The second part of this collection aims to deepen our understanding of existing regime collisions. While engaging with judicial or quasi-judicial mechanisms, all four contributions break with the assumption that regime collisions could be solved through a centralized or hierarchically organized court order. Instead, they look into legal mechanisms that resolve regime collisions either through meta-collision norms or by rules created on a case-by-case basis.

In their case study on the manipulation of scientific publications by pharmaceutical companies, *Isabell Hensel* and *Gunther Teubner* examine the collisions between the pharmaceutical industry's interest in positive research results, the interest of the science community in non-censored publishing, and the health interest of patients. Against this backdrop, they show how horizontal fundamental rights could operate as collision-rules that would allow each system to reaffirm its identity and own values. These rights, they argue, should be understood as collective institutions to account for the dual character of the fundamental rights as both a social and a legal process. Instead of individual rights claims, they argue, a collective-institutional protection of fundamental rights is needed that would guarantee the autonomy of societal processes (in this case publication in the sciences and health protection) against the totalizing tendencies of other societal processes (profit-oriented censoring by the pharmaceutical industry). The law needs to be sensitive to the societal potential of dealing with rationality collisions and also has to maintain areas for self-regulation by providing organization and procedures. In the case under scrutiny, trial registration is put forward as a viable institutional alternative to an individual rights approach, as it is especially attuned to the inherent logic of science and public health.

Drawing on various examples from Latin America, *Marcelo Neves* argues that we should understand the legal conflicts that emerge between local, national, transnational, and international legal orders as a problem of 'trans-constitutionalism', which can be solved only if the different legal orders observe their own limits in dealing with certain problems. From his point of view, only constructive transversal networks could be a solution, stimulating reciprocal learning processes. Neves sees collisions as a trans-constitutional problem because they may involve national, international, supra-national, and transnational courts or arbitration tribunals, as well as native local legal institutions. Based on the analysis of several cases, Neves infers that trans-constitutionalism in a 'multi-level' or multicentric global legal system usually concerns an infringement of 'fundamental rights' or 'human rights'. But rather than an ultimate decision-making instance, trans-constitutionalism requires a method for interaction: trans-constitutionalism entails the recognition that the legal orders entangled in the search for a solution to a constitutional problem that is concomitantly relevant to all of them must pursue transversal forms of articulation. This, he argues, can only be achieved if each legal order observes the others in an effort to understand its own limits and possibilities for contributing to the solution.

The last two contributions to this part of the volume pursue two different mechanisms of self-regulation in the area of corporate governance. *Larry Catá Backer* starts with the observation that regime collisions over the negative human rights impact of economic activities by states, enterprises, and individuals are increasingly resolved through non-legal mechanisms, in particular by the elaboration of governance frameworks. The development of such governance regimes for the human rights impacts of economic activity suggests the way in which non-legal approaches play a crucial role in the creation of structures within which the collisions of polycentric governance can be managed (but not ordered). Law remains an important element, but is no longer the sole ordering principle of a unified system within which rule collisions may be resolved. Of course, the elaboration of governance frameworks, too, can produce collisions between the state and international public and private organizations (enterprises and civil society actors), each of which have their distinct governance regimes. The most useful means for providing collision-management structures, Catá Backer argues, may be sought within public international organizations that provide an arena within which such collisions may be made predictable and their results more certain.

Sebastian Eickenjäger's case study also concerns the collision of the legal and the economic spheres. While usually business operations' negative impacts on human rights are addressed by forging corporate accountability, Eickenjäger explores the potential of Non-financial Reporting (NfR), a non-legal mechanism to address collisions between human rights and business interests. The chapter gives a brief overview on current practices of NfR and introduces the most common reporting standard in this area, the Global Reporting Initiative (GRI). Eickenjäger then examines its potential to effectively curb financial speculations with food crops, which have a devastating impact on food security in many countries. Specifically, he discusses the case of the Allianz Group as an example of current GRI practice, which epitomises the collisions between the economic system on the one hand, and social, economic, and cultural rights on the other. Based on this analysis, Eickenjäger outlines potentials and shortcomings of NfR as a mechanism to deal with collisions between the two legal fields.

Part III Collisions otherwise: law and the collision with non-legal spheres

The contributions in the foregoing part address the problem of regime collisions through a predominantly legal framework. They suggest legal mechanisms to prevent one system from imposing its own logic onto another system, and to secure a solution that respects both regime rationalities. To what extent, however, is the law itself involved in imposing its own logic onto other systems, onto the non-legal spheres? The third part of this volume therefore seeks to reflect on the implications of making the law the guardian over collisions between different social spheres.

In the first contribution, *Kolja Möller* observes a 'creeping managerialism' in dealing with regime collisions and argues that a more radical theoretical perspective is needed. In his view, constitutional reflexivity may tame the expansionist tendencies of regimes, but it provides hardly any space for a fundamental debate over the necessity of a regime in the first place. Instead, Möller proposes to understand differentiation itself as a part of hegemonic conditions. Drawing on the theory of Ernesto Laclau and Chantal Mouffe, he suggests that fragmentation is part of contested social change, that the relationship of hegemony between regimes reflects the deep asymmetries between world social systems, and that dominance is not awarded to a regime as such, but to specific programmes and projects, such as free trade, which are subject to hegemonic struggles *within* the regimes. Constitutionalization of such regimes then seals these specific programmes off from potential alternatives and allows participation only in strictly regulated, legitimacy-enhancing fora. In response to such post-democratic conditions, Möller retrieves the 'destituent' element from the *pouvoir constituant*, which, however, will itself have to go through a process of constitutionalization in order to become effective.

The second contribution of this part offers a philosophical reflection on the relationship between law and its constitutive outside. Drawing on Walter Benjamin's critique of violence, *Christoph Menke* offers an innovative reading of the destiny of law, doomed to imprint its own logic onto non-legal spheres and conflicts when turning a conflict into a legal dispute. Any act of legal judgment is guided not only by law's pretension to validity, which is to say, it not only seeks to combat what is unlawful; it also seeks to prevail over the non-legal. Yet the law cannot abdicate its pretension to prevail over the non-legal. It can only reflect this tendency. Menke points out the conditions for the possibility of a 'self-reflection of the law', that is, a reflection of the law as something that is different from the non-legal. The result of this self-reflection is (merely) to highlight this quality, and to show how the law in its ordinary operation introduces the very distinction between law and non-law. It is only by highlighting this operation that the self-reflection of the law changes the law. Menke thus concludes with some reflections on a law that would approximate doing justice to its outside by reflecting its own violence.

Sonja Buckel explores the role of the juridico-political system in relation to the economic system from a materialistic perspective, developing a more dynamic picture of this relationship than the image of 'collisions' suggests. She starts from the observation of a major crisis of capitalist socialization, in which the maximization of the inherent rationalities of global functional systems have generated severe hazards for their human environments. As Niklas Luhmann observes, in such situations of crisis, law is unable to withstand political pressure – demonstrated by the new economic governance mechanisms, which the Member States of the European Union adopted in contravention of the EU's democratic safety guarantees. However, this relationship, Buckel argues, is to be seen not so much as a collision of logics, but rather as a dialectical relationship. On the basis of Marx's *Eighteenth Brumaire*, she unfolds this dialectical relationship in four steps: (1) the universalizing potential of democracy as a condition of bourgeois rule, (2) the threat posed by democracy's egalitarianism to class rule, (3) anti-democratic involution as a reaction to this threat, at the risk of eroding democratic interest mediation, and (4) the continuous strengthening of executive power throughout this dialectical process. Buckel applies this analysis to the developments from the interwar period to the founding phase of the Federal Republic of Germany, and to the crisis of Fordism in the mid-1970s. Returning to the current crisis situation, Buckel observes the lack of a transnational hegemonic project and a strengthening not of 'the' executive, but of particular exclusionary configurations of state apparatuses, resulting in fragmented hegemony. The dialectic will remain at work, she claims, unless its cause, the lack of a societal democracy, is addressed.

The relevance of such philosophical reflections for the study of regime collisions is demonstrated by two case studies that question the potential of law for resolving regime collisions and the limits inherent in primarily understanding regime collisions as legal collisions. *Andreas Fischer-Lescano's* case study shows how the usual legal framing of whistle blowing, namely a balancing between individual rights and issues of state security, misses the central point, namely that whistle blowing is not so much about the rights of individuals, but about enabling a democratic debate over the limits that security services should respect. His contribution thus challenges conventional approaches that portray the conflict over whistleblowing as one between individual liberties on both sides – those protected by freedom of speech vs. those protected by security policy. Instead, he argues, the underlying conflict is one between impersonal autonomous spaces: whistle blowing defends basic forms of democratic participation and control against the encroachments of a transnational security apparatus that resorts to unlawful practices and renders invisible those who are responsible for them. For Fischer-Lescano, balancing proportionality and practical concordance to address this conflict, common in (particularly German) legal discourse, constitutes a subtle instrument of repression. To disrupt the repressive operation of this legal method, he suggests that the principle of proportionality needs to be put in proportion. Only a tempered proportionality can facilitate rather than repress the exercise of liberties.

In the second case study, *Johan Horst* and *Hannah Franzki* examine the on going litigation for compensation initiated by indigenous communities affected by the environmental pollution produced by Texaco's (now Chevron) oil-drilling activities in Ecuador. In their view, this case epitomises the complexities of collisions between the social, economic, cultural, and environmental rights of indigenous communities on the one hand and the law of investment protection on the other. Crucially, Horst and Franzki observe, it offers insight into the ways in which the double fragmentation of the transnational sphere – into different legal regimes, but also into different social systems – limits the emancipatory potential of human rights litigation to address the detrimental impacts of large-scale foreign investment. In relation to the first fragmentation, the authors caution against the incorporation of human rights into investment law, as the latter would merely subject human rights to the logic of investment law. With regard to the second fragmentation into different social spheres, they highlight how a difference between the indigenous population and modern law is created in which the indigenous population is not perceived as a conflicting jurisdiction – capable of producing its own law – but as mere receivers of rights within the structure of a national state. Horst and Franzki thus draw attention to the danger of creating an image of the underlying conflict that reproduces colonial representations when invoking human rights law to protect those negatively affected by large-scale investment projects.

Bibliography

Blome, K., and N. Markard, '"Contested Collisions": Conditions for a Successful Collision Management – The Example of Article 16 of the Rome Statute', *Leiden Journal of International Law*, 29 (2016 forthcoming).

Fischer-Lescano, A., and G. Teubner, 'Regime-Collisions: The Vain Search for Legal Unity in the Fragmentation of Global Law', *Michigan Journal of International Law*, 25 (2004), pp. 999–1045.

Regime-Kollisionen (Frankfurt a.M.: Suhrkamp-Verlag, 2006).

Gehring, T., and B. Faude, 'The Dynamics of Regime Complexes: Microfoundations and Systemic Effects', *Global Governance*, 19 (2013), pp. 119–30.

Gehring, T., and S. Oberthür, 'The Causal Mechanisms of Interaction between International Institutions', *European Journal of International Relations*, 15 (2009), pp. 125–56.

International Law Commission, *Final report of the Study Group: Fragmentation of International Law: Difficulties arising from the diversification and expansion of international law*, ILC A/CN.4/L.682, April 13, 2006.

Joyner, C. C., and Z. Tyler, 'Marine Conservation versus International Free Trade: Reconciling Dolphins with Tuna and Sea Turtles with Shrimp', *Ocean Development and International Law*, 31 (2000), pp. 127–50.

Koskenniemi, M., *Outline of the Chairman of the ILC Study Group on Fragmentation of Inter-national Law: The Function and Scope of the lex specialis rule and the question of 'self-contained regimes'* (2003), http://legal.un.org/ilc/sessions/55/fragmentation_outline.pdf.

'Legal Fragmentation(s): An Essay on Fluidity and Form' in G-P. Calliess et al. (eds.), *Soziologische Jurisprudenz: Festschrift für Gunther Teubner* (Tübingen: Mohr Sie-beck, 2009), pp. 795–810.

Koskenniemi, M. and P. Leino, 'Fragmentation of International Law? Postmodern Anxieties', *Leiden Journal of International Law*, 15 (2002), pp. 553–79.

Krasner, S., 'Structural Causes and Regime Consequences: Regimes as Intervening Variables', *International Organization*, 36 (1982), pp. 185–205.

Mackenzie, R., C. Romano and Y. Shany, *The Manual on International Courts and Tribunals*, 2nd edn. (Oxford University Press, 2010).

Peters, A., 'Humanity as the A and Ω of Sovereignty', *European Journal of International Law*, 20 (2009), pp. 513–44.

Puig, S., 'International Regime Complexity and Economic Law Enforcement', *Journal of International Economic Law*, 17 (2014), pp. 491–516.

Pulkowski, D., *The Law and Politics of International Regime Conflict* (Oxford University Press, 2014).

Rosendal, G. K., 'Impacts of Overlapping International Regimes: The Case of Biodiversity', *Global Governance*, 7 (2001), pp. 95–117.

Simma, B., and D. Pulkowski, 'Of Planets and the Universe: Self-contained Regimes in International Law', *European Journal of International Law*, 17 (2006), pp. 483–529.

Stokke, O. S., 'The Interplay of International Regimes: Putting Effectiveness Theory to Work', *Fridtjof Nansen Institute Report* 14/2001.

Teubner, G. (ed.), *Global Law Without a State* (Dartmouth: Aldershot, 1997).

Teubner, G., and P. Korth, 'Two Kinds of Legal Pluralism: Collision of Transnational Regimes in the Double Fragmentation of World Society' in M. A. Young (ed.), *Regime Interaction in International Law: Facing Fragmentation* (Cambridge University Press, 2012), pp. 23–54.

Tomuschat, C., 'International Law as a Coherent System: Unity or Fragmentation?' in M. H. Arsanjani et al. (eds.), *Looking to the Future: Essays on International Law in Honour of W. Michael Reisman* (Leiden: Martinus Nijhoff, 2011), pp. 323–54.

Viellechner, L., 'Berücksichtigungspflicht als Kollisionsregel', *Europäische Grundrechte-Zeitschrift*, 38 (2011), pp. 203–07.

de Wet, E., and J. Vidmar (eds.), *Hierarchy in International Law* (Oxford University Press, 2012).

Young, O. R., 'Institutional Linkages in International Society: Polar Perspectives', *Global Governance*, 2 (1996), pp. 1–24.

Young, M. A. (ed.), *Regime Interaction in International Law: Facing Fragmentation* (Cambridge University Press, 2012).

PART I

Between collisions and interaction

1

Regime collisions from a perspective of global constitutionalism

STEFAN OETER[1]

Introduction

At first sight, it seems strange to put the two (seemingly competing) paradigms of 'regime collisions' and 'global constitutionalism' in one intellectual box. The research on 'regime collisions'[2] is based upon and inspired by the debates on 'fragmentation' of international law.[3] The fragmentation debate has seen its monistic temptations, attempts to restore a (perceived lost) 'unity' of the international legal order. Most scholars involved in the fragmentation debate, however, are of a decidedly pluralist orientation – and this is particularly true for the scholars dealing in detail with 'regime collisions'.[4] The debate on global constitutionalism, on the other hand, seems (at least to the outsider) inspired by an ambition to achieve something like a 'constitution' for the global community – and a 'constitution' in a genuine sense seems to contain (at least in principle) an orientation towards the construction of a 'unified' legal order.

However, the image of competing paradigms, going into completely opposite directions – which would make them irreconcilable – is a fatal misunderstanding, as I will try to elaborate in the following pages. It rests on a false perception of what the theoretical strand of global constitutionalism wants to achieve, or even what its primary research object is.

[1] This text partly draws on a draft proposal for a Collaborative Research Centre (CRC) on 'Constitutionalism Unbound' prepared by Antje Wiener and Stefan Oeter.

[2] See Fischer-Lescano and Teubner, *Regime-Kollisionen*, pp. 7ff., but also Young (ed.), *Regime Interaction in International Law*, pp. 1–19.

[3] See only Pellet, 'Notes sur la "fragmentation" du droit international'; Webb, *International Judicial Integration and Fragmentation*, pp. 4–9, 145–201; Howse, 'Fragmentation and Utopia'; Trachtman, 'Fragmentation, Coherence and Synergy in International Law'; Koskenniemi, 'Legal Fragmentation(s)'; Benvenisti and Downs, 'The Empire's New Clothes'.

[4] See e.g., Teubner and Korth, 'Two Kinds of Legal Pluralism'.

Most writings on global constitutionalism are not on the question how we can achieve a 'global constitution', in the sense of a written document constituting a global polity with a uniform institutional system[5] – a dream that for some scholars is more a nightmare than positive utopia.[6] Global constitutionalism starts from a different angle. It starts from the observation of 'public authority' evolving 'beyond the nation-state',[7] where states delegate parts of their powers to international institutions beyond the reach of national parliaments and national systems of checks and balances, a kind of new 'Global Administrative Law' developing in its wake.[8] But if we are in a process of shifting public authority from the state to the global realm – and there are more than enough indicators that such a global power shift is happening – then we are confronting a serious constitutional problem.[9] The traditional set-up at the state level, where the constitution creates institutions, competences and procedures that constitute the power structure of a certain polity, while at the same time also deliberately limiting the power of the institutional system by a set of fundamental rights granted to the individual members of society, has no corresponding solution at the global level. The various forms of public authority beyond the nation-state are not disciplined by any kind of constitutional framing (at least in a traditional sense). Accordingly we are facing a constitutional question in the global realm today, without having clear-cut answers.[10]

One answer to this challenge is the debate on 'constitutionalization'. Admittedly, there is no overarching, uniform 'constitution' of the international community. But is it impossible to say that a number of international documents fulfil functions of a constitutional document (at least in a wider sense), not only by organising the power structures, the institutions and procedures of global governance, but also (in codifying catalogues of fundamental human rights) by limiting the exercise of

[5] See e.g., Schwöbel, *Global Constitutionalism in International Legal Perspective*, pp. 11–49.

[6] See as a bibliographical survey on global constitutionalism Wiener, 'Global Constitutionalism'; see in addition Diggelmann and Altwicker, 'Is There Something Like a Constitution of International Law?', and Kjaer, *Constitutionalism in the Global Realm*, pp. 1–13.

[7] See von Bogdandy, Wolfrum, von Bernstorff, Dann and Goldmann (eds.), *The Exercise of Public Authority by International Institutions*, in particular pp. 3–32, as well as von Bogdandy and Venzke, *In wessen Namen?*, pp. 29–30, 136–60.

[8] See Kingsbury, Krisch and Stewart, 'The Emergence of Global Administrative Law'; see also Kuo, 'Between Fragmentation and Unity'.

[9] See e.g., Peters, 'Conclusions'.

[10] See also von Bogdandy and Venzke, 'In Whose Name?'.

public authority 'beyond the nation-state'? A growing body of literature deals with identifying and describing such multi-faceted phenomena – and such 'constitutionalization' usually is seen as a progress towards a more just world order.[11]

The question remains, however, what we gain by detecting more and more phenomena of 'constitutionalization'. Firstly, given the fuzzy use of the concept, we do not exactly know what characteristics really make up 'constitutionalization', and, secondly, we do not know for sure that every kind of 'constitutionalization' really carries moral progress with it. In other words, this descriptive category does not tell us anything about 'constitutional quality' in a normative sense, about the legitimacy of a normative order and its 'justness' in terms of moral philosophy.[12] Depending on the use of the term and the phenomena described with it, 'constitutionalization' may also be seen in the mere institutional hardening of legal regimes that consolidate a set-up that was unjust from the outset, characterized by asymmetries of power, oppression of the powerless, ruthless exploitation and unacceptable distributional inequalities.[13] An academic study of 'global constitutionalism' thus requires more than just an empirical analysis; it requires a closer look at normative issues of 'legitimacy' and 'justness', with a need to discuss the normative assumptions and implications in its own terms.

Taking up themes, assumptions and first insights from an on-going collective research project at Hamburg under the title 'Constitutionalism Unbound', the following reflections will outline not only the challenges that result from this observation, sketching out the possible pitfalls, but also the potential of a research program that combines empirical research with normative questions. They will then demonstrate that constellations of 'regime collisions' constitute extremely interesting cases for any research on global constitutionalism, while at the same time research on regime collisions might profit quite a lot from global constitutionalism studies.

[11] See the literature reviews by Peters, 'Global Constitutionalism', pp. 2ff.; see in addition Brown, 'The Constitutionalization of What?'; Wiener, Lang, Tully, Poiares Maduro and Kumm, 'Why a New Journal on Global Constitutionalism?'; Klabbers, Peters and Ulfstein (eds.), *The Constitutionalization of International Law*, pp. 1–44.

[12] See only Cohen, *Globalization and Sovereignty*, pp. 21–78, as well as Nardin, 'International Ethics and International Law'.

[13] See e.g., Brunkhorst, *Legitimationskrisen*, pp. 173–226.

Phenomena of 'constitutionalization'

As already mentioned, an abounding strand of literature is looking for phenomena of 'constitutionalization' across the entire range of international law.[14] There is, however, neither a clear definition nor a robust consensus of what constitutes 'constitutionalization'. The use of the term varies a lot, and its meanings are far from evident. Only the starting-point of the debate seems beyond dispute: International law has not only undergone a process of rapid expansion into practically all areas of social practice, but has at the same time entered into a process of strong institutionalization also.[15] The decades since 1945 have seen an enormous growth of international organizations;[16] indeed, there is practically no body of (sectorial) international legal rules that is not linked to some kind of an international organization to further develop and implement these rules. While international organizations are creatures of states, they cannot be modelled in simple terms of a principal-agent relationship. Even very traditional strands of (state-centred) rational choice theory admit that they are actors on its own terms, actors that shape international law, bypass states, pursue their own agendas and coalesce with a variety of actors in order to overcome blockades in the diplomatic set-up.[17]

At the same time, it seems clear that 'constitutionalization' is more than mere 'legalization'. Legal regimes still can serve as strategic tools for state actors, manipulated and exploited for the selfish interests of powerful actors.[18] 'Constitutionalization' is used mostly where a claim might legitimately be made that law is gaining a systemic autonomy that allows it to put limits to political practice.[19] Such a systemic 'hardening' of legal into constitutional regimes means that certain types of political action

[14] See O'Donoghue, *Constitutionalism in Global Constitutionalisation*, in particular pp. 14–52; Peters, 'Are We Moving Towards Constitutionalization of the World Community?'; Fassbender and Siehr (eds.). *Suprastaatliche Konstitutionalisierung*, in particular pp. 23–52; Pernice (ed.), *Konstitutionalisierung jenseits des Staates*, in particular pp. 45–70; Kleinlein, *Konstitutionalisierung im Völkerrecht*, in particular pp. 5–97, 617–84; Habermas, *Zur Verfassung Europas*, pp. 39–96; Frowein, 'Konstitutionalisierung des Völkerrechts'.

[15] See Oeter, 'Theorising the Global Legal Order'.

[16] See e.g., Klabbers, *An Introduction to International Institutional Law*, pp. 14–37.

[17] See e.g., Collins and White (eds.), *International Organizations and the Idea of Autonomy*, in particular pp. 63–86, 120–40, 213–29.

[18] See Oeter, 'Chancen und Defizite internationaler Verrechtlichung'.

[19] See Peters, 'Global Constitutionalism', p. 2.

must be justified in terms of legal discourse – and that political actors cannot evade such 'justification discourse' in legal terms, but are forced into it, like political actors inside the nation-state cannot avoid justifying their actions in constitutional terms.[20] A decisive step towards such systemic autonomy is the creation of mechanisms of obligatory judicial dispute settlement, or of other authoritative dispute resolution by third organs. The success story of its dispute settlement has made the World Trade Organization (WTO) a candidate for 'constitutionalization' talk,[21] and the sweeping powers of authoritative decision-making at the hands of the UN Security Council have induced many authors to perceive the United Nations (UN) in a constitutionalist perspective.[22]

The UN Security Council with its broad powers and its byzantine decision-making, however, illustrates at the same time the dangers inherent in such a model of 'constitutionalization'.[23] It is far from clear that the Security Council, as the supreme organ for the maintenance of peace, is itself bound by the same values and fundamental norms that it purportedly seeks to impose on states. Gross and consistent patterns of human rights violations are now generally perceived as a 'threat to international peace' in the sense of Article 39 of the UN Charter, justifying a military intervention mandated by the Security Council.[24] But at the same time, the Security Council does not accept being bound in its own operations by human rights standards. The notorious *Kadi* case[25] on human rights limits to UN sanctions as well as the appalling lack of judicial remedies for victims of human rights violations in cases of UN-directed interim administrations (like in Kosovo) illustrate these imbalances.[26]

As a consequence, we are confronted with some challenging questions. Does 'constitutionalization' empower the *addressees* of global governance

[20] See Thornhill, 'Contemporary Constitutionalism and the Dialectic of Constituent Power'.

[21] See Cass, *Constitutionalization of the World Trade Organization*, in particular pp. 5–18, 97–205. See also Petersmann, 'From State-Centered towards Constitution "Public Reason"'; Petersmann, 'Human Rights, Constitutionalism, and the World Trade Organization'.

[22] See e.g., Fassbender, *The United Nations Charter as the Constitution of the International Community*, in particular pp. 1–9, 77–158; Fassbender, 'We the Peoples of the United Nations'.

[23] See Krisch, 'International Law in Times of Hegemony'.

[24] See only Krisch, 'Article 39 UN Charter', pp. 1284–93.

[25] Case C-402/05 P and C-415/05 P, *Kadi and Al Barakaat International Foundation* v. *Council and Commission*, [2008] ECR I-6351.

[26] See only Moos, *Individualrechtsschutz gegen menschenrechtswidrige hoheitliche Maßnahmen*, pp. 55–65, 311–60.

norms? For example, is the protection of fundamental rights improved as a result of changing the rules of procedure of the WTO or the UN? Given the reference to 'constitutionalization', we would expect that the 'publics' potentially perceive these processes of 'hardening' of legal regimes as positive steps towards 'peace through law' and global justice – but there are quite a number of examples where the contrary seems true.

The three schools of 'global constitutionalism'

The authors dealing with these challenging issues[27] are usually categorized as belonging to the new academic current of 'global constitutionalism'. But this term, too, is rather fuzzy, and used for a variety of authors that have different academic interests and work with different paradigms and methodologies.

In a rough generalization, one might distinguish three schools of thought: normative, functionalist, and pluralist.[28] A common feature of all strands of global constitutionalism is a multi-disciplinary perspective in a discourse that bridges social sciences and law. While they also share the assumption that we can observe a qualitative shift from globalization towards constitutionalization, the concept of 'global constitutionalism' that each applies reflects different perceptions.[29] Leading questions address the purpose and possibilities of constitutionalism 'beyond the state', that is, the most feasible approach they think should be taken with regard to justice and legitimacy in the global realm.

The normative school considers constitutionalization 'beyond the state' as a strategic move towards establishing a global constitution or, at least, compensating for constitutional loss at the national or subnational level.[30] The authors of this school agree on the preference of shaping the world order according to modern principles of constitutional law and justice; they disagree decidedly, however, between supporters and contenders of a global constitution in the narrow sense of the word.[31]

[27] See as recent examples Fassbender and Siehr (eds.), *Suprastaatliche Konstitutionalisierung*, pp. 23–53; Pernice (ed.), *Konstitutionalisierung jenseits des Staates*, pp. 129–59; Kleinlein, *Konstitutionalisierung im Völkerrecht*, pp. 511–615.

[28] Concerning the distinction of the three mentioned schools see Wiener, 'Global Constitutionalism', pp. 9–11.

[29] See Peters, 'Global Constitutionalism', pp. 1–2.

[30] See e.g., Peters, 'Compensatory Constitutionalism'.

[31] See O'Donoghue, *Constitutionalism in Global Constitutionalisation*, pp. 200–48.

The key conceptual approach of this group rests on the extension of principles, norms and rules of modern constitutionalism beyond the modern state with the goal of constructing a global order with a constitutional character, as a surrogate for the vanishing power of national constitutionalism. As an example one might refer to Jürgen Habermas who, in his 2011 essay, puts forward his long-time argument that while a global constitution (in a narrow sense) is neither necessary nor desirable, a neo-Kantian politically constituted world society definitely is.[32] There are joint enterprises by lawyers and political scientists making a comparable point.[33] One of the boldest examples of such a normative approach is Bardo Fassbender's argument that the UN Charter should today already be considered a global constitution – not in the making, but in existence.[34]

The functionalist school, on the other hand, studies processes of constitutionalization in a strictly empirical, descriptive perspective. The authors of this school attempt to map the various processes of constitutionalization and the bits and pieces of a 'constitutionalized' global legal order, to be found in rather different segments of international law and institutions. Their perspective on constitutionalism is dominated by observations of a growing autonomy of global legal institutions and of a 'hardened' institutional set-up that limits the direct control of politics over legal operations, with a specific emphasis on new standardized procedures and regulatory agreements.[35]

The pluralist school takes a critical approach to the universalist assumptions advanced by the normative school. Pluralist authors, although differing a lot in the detail of their argumentation, would typically question the uncritical reference to the regulative ideal of neo-Kantian federalism, or liberal community ideals as stable regulative frames for constitutional change in the global realm. Instead, they theorize constitutional change as contextualized, contingent, and constitutive, taking a reflexive approach that relates the process of structured observation (mapping processes of constitutionalization) with that of normative construction (shaping the global sphere according

[32] See Habermas, *Zur Verfassung Europas*, pp. 39–96.

[33] See e.g., Peters and Armingeon, 'Global Constitutionalism from an Interdisciplinary Perspective'.

[34] Fassbender, *The United Nations Charter as the Constitution of the International Community*, pp. 77–114.

[35] See e.g., as a paradigmatic example, Dunoff and Trachtmann (eds.), *Ruling the World.*

to constitutionalism). Prominent examples of the pluralist school are Nico Krisch as well as Daniel Halberstam and James Tully.[36]

Of course, this description works with ideal types; the boundaries between the schools are not quite as clear-cut in reality. Often, a scholarly perspective is developed from a two-tiered perspective combining approaches of different schools. Examples of such a fusion of perspectives and approaches are Anne Peters's call for purposeful constitutionalization to compensate for normative deficits following globalization,[37] Mattias Kumm's functionalist distinction between small and large 'c' constitutionalism,[38] or Nico Krisch's combination of the functionalist and pluralist schools in developing the concept of postnational constitutionalism.[39]

Importantly, the perspectives of different schools of thought also tend to combine their perspectives in a shared focus on the way non-state actors are able to exercise agency in constitutional discourse 'beyond the nation-state' – an agency that attempts (and to a certain degree also manages) to shape the development and modification of constitutional norms in the global realm.[40] 'State-plus' actorship is a decisive feature for global constitutionalism: the state as exclusive actor of traditional international relations has been dethroned, a number of other actors – international organizations, NGOs, civil society movements, advocacy groups – have become important players in normative discourses of a global character.

Bearing in mind the relative novelty of the emerging field of global constitutionalism, some further clarifications are needed in order to avoid misunderstandings. In accordance with the leading literature on European constitutionalism,[41] one should define the term constitutionalism as a theoretical framework (rather than a phenomenon). As such, constitutionalism guides research on constitutionalization. Accordingly, *global constitutionalism* may be defined as a framework approach to study constitutionalization in the global realm. Following the law-in-context

[36] See Krisch, *Beyond Constitutionalism,* in particular pp. 3–26; Halberstam, 'Constitutional Heterarchy'; Tully, 'On Local and Global Citizenship'.

[37] See Peters, 'The Merits of Global Constitutionalism'.

[38] See Kumm, 'How Does European Union Law Fit into the World of Public Law?'.

[39] See Krisch, *Beyond Constitutionalism,* in particular pp. 69–108, 225–307.

[40] See Forst, *Kritik der Rechtfertigungsverhältnisse*, in particular pp. 53–92; Wiener, *The Invisible Constitution of Politics,* pp. 21–58.

[41] See e.g., Walker, 'Flexibility Within a Metaconstitutional Frame'; Weiler and Wind (eds.), *European Constitutionalism beyond the State,* pp. 1–5; De Burca and Weiler (eds.), *The Worlds of European Constitutionalism,* pp. 8–18.

approach,[42] one should define constitutionalization as *a practice category* and therefore a phenomenon to be assessed through empirical observation. In turn, global constitutionalism is understood as a theoretical framework including different cultural and temporal contexts, an academic 'artefact' that comprises the stipulation of constitutional norms, principles and procedures in other than state-bound environments. It examines unbound constitutionalization from a comparative perspective that takes into account cultural diversity as a formative and distinctive dimension of constitutionalism. Rather than applying a 'Westphalian discourse' of state-bound constitutional communities, an enlightened version of global constitutionalism therefore encourages alternative visions of community.

The role of contestation in 'global constitutionalism'

The different schools of thought on global constitutionalism share a common assumption: normative discourses and processes at global level have (at least) a potential to develop constitutional features. Approaches focused on mapping detect constitutional traits in 'emerging' elements of the global legal order, whereas adherents of shaping follow a vision of deliberately developing such constitutional elements.

But what makes such constitutional elements 'constitutional' in the proper sense of the word? That is, what characteristics constitute the constitutional dimension in the various processes of constitutionalization? This is far from clear, one must admit. But some basic core elements of such 'constitutional nature' nevertheless seem to be beyond dispute. It does not make sense to talk about the 'constitutional' nature of norms, principles and institutions if they are not more than the product of '*pouvoirs constitués*', set in a given institutional framework by constituted actors without any participation of society at large. Constitutional norms and principles derive their dignity and force – if they deserve the expression in a genuine sense – from the overall normative consensus that underpins them. In a model type situation, constitutional norms constitute shared ground rules, the basic 'rules of the game' shared by all actors involved. This does not mean that all actors involved share the same understanding in operational detail,

[42] See e.g., Kratochwil, *Rules, Norms, and Decisions*, in particular pp. 1–20; Onuf, 'The Constitution of International Society'; Kratochwil, *The Status of Law in World Society*, pp. 26–49.

agree on a shared meaning-in-use.[43] Meaning-in-use will usually remain in dispute, even in the case of constitutional norms. But what distinguishes constitutional norms and principles from ordinary legal provisions is the basic consensus on the rule as such. The competing actors all invoke the constitutional norm, even as they claim different – and often very contradictory – concepts of concrete meaning-in-use.

The consequences of these basic insights are far-reaching. The emerging global legal order is of an essentially contested nature.[44] It is impossible to design a suitable global constitution in an air-conditioned conference room, as a deduction from overarching normative principles assumed to be beyond dispute. If such a constitution were to be imposed by a coalition of powerful states, it would be contested at its roots. Indeed, there are few fundamental norms of global law that are so settled that no contestation of the rule as such takes place – and if so, 'meaning-in-use' usually tends to remain contested.

Contestation, however, has two sides. A strong degree of contestation may generally be perceived as an indicator of problems of legitimacy – and international law in its fundamental emanations is quite strongly contested.[45] The state-centred international legal process is obviously not capable of securing legitimacy of its normative output any more. Individuals and civil society actors do not feel adequately represented by states and their organs, and demand their own voice in global norm-setting.[46] Studies of contested compliance suggest that the legitimacy problem of global governance not only persists, but also is becoming ever stronger.[47] In a traditional perspective, this seems to contradict the parallel increase of constitutionalization.

If, however, we conceptualize contestation as indicative of the constitutionally warranted right of (non-state) actors to voice in the global legal process and as a major driving force of constitutional discourse in general, the relationship between contestation and constitutionalization loses its paradoxical character. This means that our traditional understanding of

43 On the concept of 'meaning-in-use', see Milliken, 'The Study of Discourse in International Relations'.

44 On the theoretical concept of 'contestation', see Wiener, *A Theory of Contestation*, pp. 1–16, 45–54, 79–84.

45 See on the (contested) legitimacy of international law Franck, *The Power of Legitimacy*, pp. 3–26, 41–9, 183–207.

46 See e.g., Peters et al. (eds.), *Non-State Actors as Standard Setters*, pp. 1–26.

47 See e.g., Kingsbury, Krisch and Stewart, 'Global Administrative Law', pp. 15–20, 27–37; Slaughter, *A New World Order*, pp. 8–33, 216–59.

constitutionalization' is too limited to traditional modes of 'inter-national' (i.e., inter-state) law-making, whereas the paradigm of constitutionalism – if taken seriously – forces us to look to the perceptions, practices and reactions of societies as the basic level of normative discourses and any process of emerging constitutional patterns and practices. In particular when we ask the additional question about constitutional quality, and focus on the range of social practices affected by such a question, the civil society addressees of constitutional policies must be included. This requires an analytical perspective that is able to conceptualize the emergence (or change) of constitutional quality both from a top-down and a bottom-up perspective.

A series of problems remains. The relation between the constituent power and the constituted power has always remained mystical to a large degree because it has always rested on the paradoxical assumption of a constitutional moment,[48] a notion that has proven difficult to conceptualize in an analytical perspective.[49] Instead, questions of legitimacy usually take the place. Research needs to focus on the diversity of groups that raise constitutional claims – a perspective that might help to generate knowledge about the presence or absence of shared validation of constitutional norms in the global realm. The legitimacy of any claim of global public authority depends on such shared validation. Accordingly, what is needed in research on global constitutionalism is an attempt to identify the degree of such shared validation. Global regimes develop 'constitutional scripts', but the legitimacy of such 'scripts' remains open to dispute.

The question of 'constitutional quality'

The legitimacy of the 'constitutional scripts' underlying global regimes is an open issue that needs further research. The following remarks will address this issue under the heading of 'constitutional quality'. In principle, according to constitutional theory, a constitution serves to check societal actors in their interrelation, warrant access to the protection of rights and entitles the governing institutions, the '*pouvoir*

[48] See Thornhill, 'Contemporary Constitutionalism', pp. 369–91; Loughlin and Walker (eds.), *The Paradox of Constitutionalism*, pp. 1–8; Möllers, 'We Are (Afraid of) the People'.

[49] See in particular the seminal book by Ackerman, *We the People, Vol. II: Transformations*, as well as Kotzur, '"Constitutional Moments" in globaler Perspektive'.

constitué', to act on behalf of the community of citizens, the '*pouvoir constituant*'.[50] A constitution keeps law and politics 'in check'.[51] The relations between the constitution and the political community organized by such constitution are guided by a set of constitutional principles and norms. Given that a constitution's substance is stable, and that its principles, norms and procedures remain valid over time, the *reference to the citizenry* as the constituent power is a necessary condition for a text to be 'of constitutional quality'. The (assumed) existence of a constituent power beyond the *pouvoir constitué* of public authority is therefore the first indicator of constitutional quality. However, it is important to note that – whether written or unwritten – a constitution derives its authority from sources that are external to the constitutional text. That is, a constitution's legitimation stems from normative foundations that are socially constructed in an interplay of normative claims and various acts of contestation that either lead to a shared understanding or end up in normative dissent. Such normative foundation underpins the validity of the formal constitutional document[52] – a normative foundation that shines up also in the Kelsenian quest for a 'Grundnorm' that bases the validity claim of a legal order.[53] This *external source of authority* is contingent on the larger historical context in which a political community is constituted. This external source of authority is the second indicator of constitutional quality.

As outlined earlier, the different schools of thought on global constitutionalism refer to distinct implicit logics. According to one school, constitutionalization in the global realm is based on a functionalist rationale. This school employs 'taxonomic' rather than 'normative' criteria[54] to enhance the legitimacy of global governance institutions.[55] The second takes the opposite view, arguing that global constitutionalization is a necessary normative corrective for the loss of normative quality of

[50] See the contributions in Loughlin and Walker (eds.), *Paradox of Constitutionalism*, in particular the contribution of Möllers, 'We Are (Afraid of) the People'.

[51] See Oeter, 'Verkoppelung von Recht und Politik im europäischen Verfassungsdenken'.

[52] See Reus-Smit, 'The Constitutional Structure of International Society'.

[53] See in this regard the recent book of Kammerhofer, *Uncertainty in International Law*, as well as Bongiovanni, 'Rechtsstaat and Grundnorm in the Kelsenian Theory'.

[54] See Dunoff and Trachtman (eds.), *Ruling the World*, p. 4.

[55] See Buchanan and Keohane, 'The Legitimacy of Global Governance Institutions', and Slaughter, *A New World Order*, pp. 230–59, as well as a critical note by Cohen, *Globalization and Sovereignty*, pp. 58–79.

state-bound constitutionalization.[56] The third school takes a pluralist view that expects, and endorses, the parallel existence of different types and degrees of constitutionalization:[57] it conceptualizes *constitutional quality* as socially constituted rather than meta-theoretically given. In taking such a perspective, one might develop an analytical approach that allows one to uncover 'invisible' normative structures of meaning-in-use.[58]

In sum, *constitutional quality* is indicated by two criteria, if we want to look at it from an analytical angle: First, it requires a reference to an imagined community of citizens, e.g., to 'humankind' as the potential constitutional community of the entire globe; second, it must facilitate access to contestation to its constituents, thus alluding to the process of self-constituting community in a recursive process. Even though each serves as an indicator of constitutional quality, both are necessary criteria. For example, in the global context, the reference to 'mankind' as the external source of authority in the UNCLOS serves as an indicator for constitutional quality, while the existence of the constituent power is less clearly identifiable, given that UNCLOS is negotiated, signed and ratified by states, which means that the reference group of legitimation is a group of states rather than citizens.[59]

In this critical perspective of an enlightened paradigm of global constitutionalism there is no normative reason to expect that constitutionalization will automatically generate constitutional quality – by all means and on all accounts. It could just be the contrary – and in some cases we can empirically demonstrate that the result in practice is the contrary. Whether or not unbound constitutionalization is actually constitutive for constitutional quality needs to be proven empirically, given the change of context that constitutionalism experiences in the shift from the familiar national or domestic political realm towards the global realm.

A global constitutionalism perspective on regime collisions

If we want to approach constitutional quality from an empirical perspective, we must look at processes of contestation in normative discourses. In contestation, the reference group changes from state agents, as agents

[56] See Peters, 'Merits of Global Constitutionalism'; Habermas, *Zur Verfassung Europas*, pp. 39–96.
[57] See Walker, 'Flexibility Within a Metaconstitutional Frame'; Poiares Maduro, 'Courts and Pluralism'.
[58] See Wiener, *The Invisible Constitution of Politics*, pp. 59–86.
[59] See also Kratochwil, 'Leaving Sovereignty Behind?'.

of the 'constituted powers', that is, the '*pouvoir constitué*', to a broader reference group encompassing societal actors. References to alternative visions of community, going beyond state-bound constellations of actors, might develop in processes of contestation – and the resulting normative discourse might validate such alternative visions of community. The (potential) validation depends on shared meanings common to all actors involved – be it state-bound actors or be it non-state actors. Only if they share the meaning ascribed to a norm as being a fundamental norm of a constitutional character can we assume the external source of authority a constitutional set-up needs. The constitution does not carry its own source of validity within, but it is validated by the community to which it refers as a document of constitutional character, laying down the fundamental rules of the game that are thus set out of dispute.

How does all that help us in dealing with regime collisions? A lot, I argue. We use the concept of 'regime collisions' to describe the fact that fragmentation into an increasing number of international regimes with overlapping areas of competence can lead to contradictory decisions or mutual obstruction.[60] The evolution of more and more fragmented international regimes is a result of functional differentiation in modern societies. Each functional sub-system develops its own set of legal rules mirroring the functional logic of the relevant sub-system (and describing it in legal code). With growing global interdependence, and the phenomena usually called 'globalization', these functional sub-systems come under pressure to develop their own modes of international and/or transnational coordination.[61] Such coordination might happen by transnational administrative networks[62] (as the 'light' form in coordination in the global realm), but might also develop harder forms of institutional arrangements, as happens in the typical forms of international treaty regimes with a set of legally binding rules enacted in international treaties and an international organization entrusted with the task of taking care of the further development of such rules as well as their implementation in administrative and judicial practice at national level.[63]

[60] See e.g., Webb, *International Judicial Integration*, pp. 4–9; Young (ed.), *Regime Interaction*, in particular her 'Introduction' and her article 'Regime Interaction in Creating, Implementing and Enforcing International Law'; Trachtman, 'Fragmentation, Coherence and Synergy'.

[61] See Calliess and Zumbansen, *Rough Consensus and Running Code*, pp. 96–122.

[62] See e.g., Oeter, 'Vom Völkerrecht zum transnationalen Recht'.

[63] See Oeter, 'The Openness of International Organisations for Transnational Public Rule-Making'.

Such regimes are driven by radically different rationalities. The results of such radical differences in rationalities, however, are not just a technical problem. The segments of social life covered by the output of norms and decisions that are produced by the regimes are not neatly separated. It might easily happen that different regimes cover the same social practices, albeit from rather different perspectives mirroring completely different systemic rationalities.[64] There is no inbuilt systemic priority, in the sense that one systemic perspective is more valid and thus might normatively trump the other. In the absence of an established hierarchy of norms – and such a hierarchy definitely does not exist, beyond the shallow category of '*ius cogens*' – there is no pre-defined institutional mechanism that secures consistent decision.[65]

Contestation: going public as constitutionalization strategy

Such a result is unwanted, although it constitutes to a certain degree an unavoidable result of a 'heterarchic' and pluralist set-up.[66] The described 'regime collisions' typically give rise to processes of contestation, at least as far as issues of public concern are at stake. Such contestation easily creeps over into the societal realm and cannot be confined to the arenas of mere diplomacy and/or technocratic expert discourse.[67] The ensuing mobilization of (at least partial) publics shifts the level of normative discourse. You cannot argue the case of free trade in shrimp caught somewhere in violation of conservation rules protecting an endangered species like turtles simply by insisting on the systemic rationality of free trade – at least not if you want to make your case in a broader public.[68] The way out is usually a recourse to the fundamental principles that might be useful in arguing the decision taken to be 'valid' on a more principled level. The shift to the level of more principled arguments has its discursive costs, however. If you want to sell to an international public the argument that the shrimp caught under dubious circumstances should benefit from free trade nevertheless, you cannot argue it by merely referring to 'national interests', that is, a particular concern. You must

64 See Fischer-Lescano and Teubner, *Regime-Kollisionen*, pp. 10–24, 34–40.
65 See e.g., de Wet and Vidmar (eds.), *Hierarchy in International Law*, in particular the 'Introduction', but also Vidmar 'Norm Conflicts and Hierarchy'.
66 See Krisch, *Beyond Constitutionalism*, pp. 263–96.
67 See e.g., Willets, *Non-Governmental Organizations in World Politics*, pp. 32–63, 114–43; MacDonald, *Global Stakeholder Democracy*, pp. 62–82.
68 See Joyner and Tyler, 'Marine Conservation versus International Free Trade'.

discursively appeal to a common good of 'humankind', be it free trade as a value in itself, or be it enlightened interests of conservation of stocks or of sustainable management of resources.[69] Otherwise you have lost the discursive battle from the outset.

'Contested collisions' thus force the actors concerned to refer to fundamental values and basic principles if they want to make an impact on public discourse. A precondition, I admit, is that contested collisions become an issue of public debate – but the implicit logic of regime collisions tends to induce the actors towards 'going public'. The public nature of the discourse also forces dispute settlement bodies to enter in a discourse based on principled arguments. Simply insisting on the technical rationality of your specific regime has proven to be a hazardous strategy when dealing with the public at large. This is clearly visible in constellations of asymmetric judicialization. The mobilization of publics in favor of regime rationalities that are not as strongly institutionalized as the one governing the judicial dispute settlement called upon to judge the regime collision might create a counterweight to the institutional asymmetries generated by uneven 'judicialization'.[70]

An alternative option to heterarchic 'collision rules', at least in theory, would be an open strategy of hegemony, converting institutional dominance into strategies of epistemic exclusion. At least in terms of institutional architecture, a judicial dispute resolution body in the framework of an institutionally dominant regime could simply insist on its bounding to the systemic rationality of the regime it belongs to. The cost of such a strategy, however, would be to openly repress the concerns linked to the systemic rationalities of the competing regimes. In institutional terms, there might not exist a counter-balance forcing the dispute settlement body to take into consideration the concerns embodied by the other regimes. But as soon as the decision of the dispute settlement is exposed to public scrutiny, with a public mobilized already in the course of the initial regime collision, this strategy of exclusion tends to become a dangerous path. You may manage to insist upon the sectorial rationality inside the institutional architecture of the specific regime, but you will be in a severe danger of losing the discursive battle in a broader public. A clever body of judges/arbitrators will anticipate that risk and will try to take on board – at least in rhetorical terms – the competing concerns

[69] Regarding the paradigm of 'sustainable management' of resources, see Hambler and Canney, *Conservation*, pp. 237–69.

[70] Compare in this regard also the contribution of Marcelo Neves in this volume.

underlying the systemic rationalities of the other regimes in collision. To a certain degree that might work without affecting the 'inner' rationality of the dominant regime; but admitting the validity of an 'external' concern (or rationality) is never completely without costs. Admitting its validity at least potentially means being forced to take it seriously and compromising with it, if you do not want to end up in shallow façades of mere rhetorical gestures (which might become counterproductive if its mere rhetorical character becomes too obvious).

The logic of public contestation thus delivers an answer to the challenging question why judicial dispute settlement bodies in instances of asymmetric 'judicialization' tend to take on board competing concerns (beyond the systemic rationality of their regime) at all. The pressure towards including such competing regime rationalities and – in serious cases – even compromising with them does not derive from the inner logic of the regimes, but is an outflow of the intrinsic dynamics of processes of public contestation. The consequences of such insight are of a serious nature. If there exists a counter-strategy in cases of uneven 'judicialization', it is the emergency exit to mobilization of the public, converting the (at the outset more or less technical) regime collision into a contestation of the regime as such with reference to fundamental values and basic principles shared by the overall public.

Constitutionalization by compensatory judicialization

The perspectives become grim if the potential of public mobilization and the institutional imbalance go hand in hand. There exists a recent example for such pitfalls. Historically, human rights and the rules of the law of armed conflicts have been perceived as completely separate regimes following completely different systemic rationalities.[71] The purpose of human rights was the protection of the liberty, dignity and property of human beings against unfair interference by state organs. The laws of armed conflict traditionally were dominated by calculations of military utility, a logic of reciprocity that created the basis of a set of mutual obligations disciplining military organizations in the exercise of armed force in situations of armed conflict.[72] The values of basic human

[71] See e.g., Kolb and Gaggioli (eds.), *Research Handbook on Human Rights and Humanitarian Law*, in particular pp. 77–103; Ben-Naftali (ed.), *International Humanitarian Law and International Human Rights Law*, in particular pp. 1–10, 95–126.

[72] See Heldmann, *Das Reziprozitätsprinzip im Humanitären Völkerrecht*, pp. 98–156.

rights and the dictates of public conscience and humanity, however, are much more appealing to a modern public than crude calculations of reciprocity argued by military professionals. The result is a gradual, but powerful process of 'humanization' of the laws of armed conflict, which found its expression in the terminological shift to the notion 'humanitarian law'. The price of such 'humanization', however, was by and large the repression of mechanisms of reciprocity.[73] The body of rules still is administered by an 'epistemic community' of military experts and military lawyers, despite the change in substance, which takes care of the essential issue that the changed set of rules must still be sold to the military as being a meaningful restraint on the battlefield.

The fragile balance just described has come under extreme pressure during the last few years. Humanitarian law has practically no institutional arrangements of compliance management. The International Fact-Finding Commission instituted under the Additional Protocol I has never been used by member states.[74] The ICRC acts as a guardian of the Geneva Convention system, but its activities are largely limited to quiet diplomacy.[75] To the contrary, the human rights regimes have experienced a strong institutionalization, with the system of specific treaty bodies, the UN Human Rights commissioner and – in political terms most important – the Human Rights Council with its system of special rapporteurs and commissions of inquiry.[76] The last several years have shown more and more activities of human rights bodies dealing with human rights in situations of armed conflict, thus filling the institutional void left by the (deficient) institutional structures of humanitarian law. One may welcome this development as a victory for human rights – but the replacement of the codified rules of military ethics laid down in the regulations of humanitarian law by a simple extension of human rights norms at its origin drafted for peacetime situations brings an unhappy epistemic bias with it as an unavoidable side cost.[77] It is difficult to bring the systemic rationalities of military operations in armed conflict on board in human rights discourse – if you do not want

[73] See Greenwood, 'Human Rights and Humanitarian Law'.
[74] See e.g., Kalshoven, 'The International Humanitarian Fact-Finding Commission'.
[75] See Forsythe and Rieffer-Flanagan, *The International Committee of the Red Cross*, pp. 38–53.
[76] See e.g., Kälin and Künzli, *The Law of International Human Rights Protection*, pp. 206–38, 240–53, 267–8; see also – as far as the overlap with IHL is concerned – Kälin, 'Universal Human Rights Bodies and International Humanitarian Law'.
[77] See Oeter, 'Fortschrittsnarrative im Humanitären Völkerrecht'.

to resort to the emergency brake of derogations in times of public emergency (and such a state of emergency is usually not formally declared in the needed procedural terms in situations of armed conflicts, which makes the emergency clauses technically inapplicable). The result is a 'colonization' of humanitarian law by the logic of human rights. Military lawyers complain about this phenomenon, but it is an uphill struggle to defend the systemic rationality of the laws of armed conflict against the pathetic appeals used by human rightists in a broader public. And even in an analytical perspective I am not that sure that this is a victory for the noble cause of humanity. As long as there is no strong implementation mechanism for human rights standards, the effectiveness of human rights in operational practice depends very much on tools like 'socialization' and 'internalization', the conviction that the standards make sense and must be observed at all costs. This worked to a certain degree with the traditional standards of humanitarian law, which mirrored (and described) the inner rationality of the military system – it does not really work with human rights up to now, however.

There is probably only one way out – and this is the way towards a strengthened institutionalization of compliance management.[78] As soon as a regime has its own international institutions that can give a strong voice to the internal logic, that is, the systemic rationalities of the regime, it can make its cause heard – and defend its own rationalities against the hegemonic onslaughts of other regimes.[79] If you do not go that way, the actors will have to accept that their systemic rationalities will be brushed aside and colonized by the rationalities of the colliding, but institutionally stronger competitor regime.

Conclusion

In an ironic way, 'contested collisions' prove to be an important part of the social processes that are of utmost interest for global constitutionalism research. Regime collisions are a decisive source of principled contestation, where actors that feel threatened by 'colonization' by an alien regime raise principled objections against the legitimacy of the hegemonic regime, objections based on fundamental values and basic principles of the global community. Institutional asymmetry, which is

[78] As to the functional role of monitoring arrangements and compliance mechanisms see Dai, *International Institutions and National Policies*, pp. 33–68, 69–99.

[79] See Oeter, 'Fortschrittsnarrative im Humanitären Völkerrecht', pp. 1024–6.

often at the roots of such regime collisions, thus gives rise to two sorts of reaction that both are of utmost interest for research on global constitutionalism.

The first type of reaction is the typical reaction of 'underdog' regimes that – due to uneven 'judicialization' – cannot defend its systemic rationalities by responding in terms of an opposing judicial decision (or a comparable institutional response by a treaty body or an analogous institution). If you cannot fight on equal footing, you have to mobilize your 'hidden' reserves – which means in these cases a strategy of 'going public', mobilizing sympathetic publics with an appeal to the noble values and principles put on the banner of the respective regime. Such a strategy of forcing the other side to argue its case in a wider public on a principled level transforms the collision from an inner-systemic expert discourse to public contestation and the ensuing normative discourses in terms of fundamental values and basic principles. Such contestation (and the resulting normative discourses) constitutes an important source of processes of 'constitutionalization'. State-bound expert discourse transforms into a public discourse with multiple actorship, and the implicit legitimization strategies tend to shift from the particularism of 'state interests' to common goods of humankind.

The other type of reaction is at least as interesting in terms of global constitutionalism. Uneven 'judicialization' with its resulting institutional asymmetry might also induce the actors represented in the 'inferior' regime to struggle for an improved, 'hardened' institutional set-up. It might lead to compensatory 'judicialization' as a strategy to keep pace with the competitors and regain institutional balance.

We are facing here an interesting dialectics of global constitutionalism. International law will not get rid of contestation as a normative challenge pointing to its underlying fundamental values and principles. But there are different avenues how this contestation is framed. There exist two 'ideal types' of institutional framing of patterns of contestation. It can happen as a principled contestation to specific normative regimes and its practices raised from the outside, from the general public and/or advocacy groups representing such public. This type of external, public contestation forces state actors operating inside the regime to shift the level of argumentation and to develop discursive strategies of defence taking up the principled objections. The other 'ideal type' of a framing of contestation is the option to 'institutionalize' contestation inside the regimes. Judicial institutions and/or independent monitoring bodies incorporated in a specific regime are the typical institutional emanation of such an institutionalist strategy. Such an institutional incorporation has its costs, but it clearly also has its advantages, because it has an inherent potential to keep contestation more limited, to channel it in an institutional framework.

A last remark in order to conclude these reflections: The paper should have demonstrated that – contrary to a first intuition – there is quite a close relationship between studies on 'regime collisions' and global constitutionalism research. I wanted to demonstrate that the study of regime collisions could benefit a lot from incorporating models and tools of global constitutionalism. But also, the other way round, research of global constitutionalism can profit a lot by focusing on regime collisions. Contested collisions' constitute one of the prime objects of research from which global constitutionalism will profit a lot in future.

Bibliography

Ackerman, B. A., *We the People ,Vol. II: Transformations.* (Cambridge, Mass.: Belknap Press, 1998).

Ben-Naftali, O. (ed.), *International Humanitarian Law and International Human Rights Law* (Oxford University Press, 2011).

Benvenisti, E., and G. W. Downs, 'The Empire's New Clothes: Political Economy and the Fragmentation of International Law', *Stanford Law Review*, 60 (2007), pp. 595–631.

von Bogdandy, A., and I. Venzke, *In wessen Namen? Internationale Gerichte in Zeiten globalen Regierens* (Frankfurt am Main: Suhrkamp, 2014).

'In Whose Name? An Investigation of International Courts' Public Authority and Its Democratic Justification', *European Journal of International Law*, 23 (2012), pp. 7–41.

von Bogdandy, A., R. Wolfrum, J. von Bernstorff, P. Dann, and M. Goldmann (eds.), *The Exercise of Public Authority by International Institutions* (Heidelberg et al.: Springer, 2010).

Bongiovanni, G., 'Rechtsstaat and Grundnorm in the Kelsenian Theory', *Archiv für Rechts- und Sozialphilosophie,* 70 Beiheft (1997), pp. 93–102.

Brown, G. W., 'The Constitutionalization of What?', *Global Constitutionalism*, 1 (2012), pp. 201–28.

Brunkhorst, H., *Legitimationskrisen. Verfassungsprobleme der Weltgesellschaft* (Baden-Baden: Nomos, 2012).

Brunnée, J., and S. J. Toope, 'Constructivism and International Law' in J. L. Dunoff and M. A. Pollack (eds.), *Interdisciplinary Perspectives on International Law and International Relations: The State of the Art* (Cambridge University Press, 2013), pp. 119–45.

Legitimacy and Legality in International Law: An Interactional Account (Cambridge University Press, 2010).

Buchanan, A., and R. O. Keohane, 'The Legitimacy of Global Governance Institutions', *Ethics and International Affairs*, 20 (2006), pp. 405–37.

Calliess, G.-P., and P. Zumbansen, *Rough Consensus and Running Code. A Theory of Transnational Private Law* (Oxford: Hart, 2010).

Cass, D. Z., *Constitutionalization of the World Trade Organization* (Oxford University Press, 2005).

Cohen, H., 'Book Review – Eric A. Posner's The Perils of Global Legalism (2009)', *German Law Journal*, 13 (2012), pp. 67–75.

Cohen, J. L., *Globalization and Sovereignty. Rethinking Legality, Legitimacy, and Constitutionalism* (Cambridge University Press, 2012).

Collins, R., and N. D. White (eds.), *International Organizations and the Idea of Autonomy: Institutional Independence in the International Legal Order* (London: Routledge, 2011).

Dai, X., *International Institutions and National Policies* (Cambridge University Press, 2007).

De Búrca, G., and J. H. H. Weiler (eds.), *The Worlds of European Constitutionalism* (Cambridge University Press, 2012).

Diggelmann, O., and T. Altwicker, 'Is There Something Like a Constitution of International Law? A Critical Analysis of the Debate on World Constitutionalism', *Zeitschrift für ausländisches öffentliches Recht und Völkerrecht*, 68 (2008), pp. 623–50.

Dobner, P., and M. Loughlin (eds.), *The Twilight of Constitutionalism* (Oxford University Press, 2010).

Dunoff, J. L., and J. P. Trachtmann (eds.), *Ruling the World? Constitutionalism, International Law, and Global Governance* (Cambridge University Press, 2009).

Fassbender, B., *The United Nations Charter as the Constitution of the International Community* (Leiden: Martinus Nijhoff, 2009).

'We the Peoples of the United Nations: Constituent Power and Constituent Form in International Law' in N. Walker and M. Loughlin (eds.), *The Paradox of Constitutionalism: Constituent Power and Constitutional Form* (Oxford University Press, 2007), pp. 269–90.

Fassbender, B., and A. Siehr (eds.), *Suprastaatliche Konstitutionalisierung: Perspektiven auf die Legitimität, Kohärenz und Effektivität des Völkerrechts* (Baden-Baden: Nomos, 2012).

Fischer-Lescano, A., and G. Teubner, *Regime-Kollisionen: Zur Fragmentierung des globalen Rechts* (Frankfurt am Main: Suhrkamp, 2006).

Forst, R., *Kritik der Rechtfertigungsverhältnisse. Perspektiven einer kritischen Theorie der Politik* (Frankfurt am Main: Suhrkamp, 2011).

Das Recht auf Rechtfertigung – Elemente einer konstruktivistischen Theorie der Gerechtigkeit (Frankfurt am Main: Suhrkamp, 2007).

Forsythe, D. P., and B. Rieffer-Flanagan, *The International Committee of the Red Cross: A Neutral Humanitarian Actor* (London: Routledge, 2007).

Franck, T. M., *The Power of Legitimacy Among Nations* (Oxford University Press, 1990).

Frowein, J. A., 'Konstitutionalisierung des Völkerrechts' in K. Dicke et al. (eds.), *Völkerrecht und Internationales Privatrecht in einem sich wandelnden internationalen System, Berichte der Deutschen Gesellschaft für Völkerrecht* Vol. XXXIX (Heidelberg: C. F. Müller, 2000), pp. 427–47.

Greenwood, C., 'Human Rights and Humanitarian Law: Conflict or Convergence', *Case Western Reserve Journal of International Law*, 43 (2010), pp. 491–512.

Habermas, J., *Zur Verfassung Europas. Ein Essay* (Frankfurt am Main: Suhrkamp, 2011).

Halberstam, D., 'Constitutional Heterarchy: The Centrality of Conflict in the European Union and the United States' in J. L. Dunoff and J. B. Trachtman (eds.), *Ruling the World?* (Cambridge University Press, 2009), pp. 326–55.

Hambler, C., and S. M. Canney, *Conservation* (Cambridge University Press, 2013).

Heldmann, S., *Das Reziprozitätsprinzip im Humanitären Völkerrecht* (Berlin: Duncker & Humblot, 2015).

Howse, R., 'Fragmentation and Utopia: Towards an Equitable Integration of Finance, Trade, and Sustainable Development' in A. Cassese (ed.), *Realizing Utopia. The Future of International Law* (Oxford University Press, 2012), pp. 427–41.

Joyner, C. C., and Z. Tyler, 'Marine Conservation versus International Free Trade: Reconciling Dolphins with Tuna and Sea Turtles with Shrimp', *Ocean Development and International Law*, 31 (2000), pp. 127–50.

Kälin, W., 'Universal Human Rights Bodies and International Humanitarian Law' in R. Kolb and G. Gaggioli (eds.), *Research Handbook on Human Rights and Humanitarian Law* (Cheltenham, Edward Elgar, 2013), pp. 441–65.

Kälin, W., and J. Künzli, *The Law of International Human Rights Protection* (Oxford University Press, 2009).

Kalshoven, F., 'The International Humanitarian Fact-Finding Commission – a Sleeping Beauty?', *Humanitäres Völkerrecht – Informationsschriften*, 15 (2002), pp. 213–16.

Kammerhofer, J., *Uncertainty in International Law: A Kelsenian Perspective* (London: Routledge, 2011).

Kingsbury, B., N. Krisch, and R. B. Stewart, 'The Emergence of Global Administrative Law', *Law & Contemporary Problems*, 68 (2005), pp. 15–61.

Kjaer, P. F., *Constitutionalism in the Global Realm: A Sociological Approach* (London: Routledge, 2014).

Klabbers, J., *An Introduction to International Institutional Law*, 2nd edn (Cambridge University Press, 2009).

Klabbers, J., A. Peters, and G. Ulfstein (eds.), *The Constitutionalization of International Law* (Oxford University Press, 2009).

Kleinlein, T., *Konstitutionalisierung im Völkerrecht: Konstruktion und Elemente einer idealistischen Völkerrechtslehre* (Heidelberg et al.: Springer, 2012).

Kolb, R., and G. Gaggioli (eds.), *Research Handbook on Human Rights and Humanitarian Law* (Cheltenham: Edward Elgar, 2013).

Koskenniemi, M., 'Legal Fragmentation(s)' in G.-P. Calliess et al. (eds.), *Soziologische Jurisprudenz. Festschrift für Gunther Teubner* (Berlin: De Gruyter, 2009), pp. 795–810.

Kotzur, M., '"Constitutional Moments" in globaler Perspektive', *Jahrbuch des öffentlichen Rechts der Gegenwart*, 62 (2014), pp. 445–58.

Kratochwil, F., *The Status of Law in World Society: Meditations on the Role and Rule of Law* (Cambridge University Press, 2014).

'Leaving Sovereignty Behind? An Inquiry into the Politics of Post-Modernity' in R. Falk, M. Juergensmeyer and V. Popovski (eds.), *Legality and Legitimacy in Global Affairs* (Oxford University Press, 2012), pp. 127–48.

Rules, Norms, and Decisions. On the Conditions of Practical and Legal Reasoning in International Relations and Domestic Affairs (Cambridge University Press, 1989).

Krisch, N., 'Article 39 UN Charter' in B. Simma, G. Nolte, D.-E. Khan and A. Paulus (eds.), *The United Nations Charter: A Commentary*, 3rd edn, 2 vols. (Oxford University Press, 2012), pp. 1272–96.

Beyond Constitutionalism: The Pluralist Structure of Postnational Law (Oxford University Press, 2010).

'International Law in Times of Hegemony: Unequal Power and the Shaping of the International Legal Order', *European Journal of International Law*, 16 (2005), pp. 369–408.

Kumm, M., 'How Does European Union Law Fit into the World of Public Law? Costa, Kadi and Three Conceptions of Public Law' in J. Neyer and A. Wiener (eds.), *Political Theory of the European Union* (Oxford University Press, 2011), pp. 111–38.

Kuo, M.-S., 'Between Fragmentation and Unity: The Uneasy Relationship between Global Administrative Law and Global Constitutionalism', *San Diego International Law Journal*, 10 (2009), pp. 439–67.

Loughlin, M., and N. Walker (eds.), *The Paradox of Constitutionalism: Constituent Power and Constitutional Form* (Oxford University Press, 2007).

MacDonald, T., *Global Stakeholder Democracy: Power and Representation Beyond Liberal States* (Oxford University Press, 2008).

McLaughlin, R., 'The Law of Armed Conflict and International Human Rights Law: Some Paradigmatic Differences and Operational Implications', *Yearbook of International Humanitarian Law*, 13 (2011), pp. 213–43.

Milliken, J., 'The Study of Discourse in International Relations: A Critique of Research and Methods', *European Journal of International Relations*, 5 (1999), pp. 225–54.

Möllers, C., '"We Are (Afraid of) the People". Constituent Power in German Constitutionalism' in M. Loughlin and N. Walker (eds.), *The Paradox of Constitutionalism: Constituent Power and Constitutional Form* (Oxford University Press, 2007), pp. 87–105.

Moos, L., *Individualrechtsschutz gegen menschenrechtswidrige hoheitliche Maßnahmen von Übergangsverwaltungen der Vereinten Nationen am Beispiel der United Nations Interim Administration Mission in Kosovo* (Berlin: Duncker & Humblot, 2013).

Nardin, T., 'International Ethics and International Law' in M. Frost (ed.), *International Ethics, Vol. III: The Changing Constitution of Global Politics – Ethical Issues* (Los Angeles: Sage, 2011), pp. 43–58.

Niesen, P. (ed.), *Transnationale Gerechtigkeit und Demokratie* (Frankfurt am Main: Campus, 2012).

O'Donoghue, A., *Constitutionalism in Global Constitutionalisation* (Cambridge University Press, 2014).

Oeter, S., 'Fortschrittsnarrative im Humanitären Völkerrecht – Vom Kriegsvölkerrecht zu Menschenrechten in bewaffneten Konflikten' in C. Calliess (ed.), *Liber amicorum für Torsten Stein* (Baden-Baden: Nomos, 2015), pp. 1002–26.

'Vom Völkerrecht zum transnationalen Recht – "Transnational Administrative Networks" und die Bildung hybrider Akteursstrukturen' in G.-P. Calliess (ed.), *Transnationales Recht* (Tübingen: Mohr Siebeck, 2014), pp. 387–402.

'The Openness of International Organisations for Transnational Public Rule-Making' in O. Dilling, M. Herberg and G. Winter (eds.), *Transnational Administrative Rule-Making: Performance, Legal Effects, and Legitimacy* (Oxford: Hart, 2011), pp. 235–51.

'Verkoppelung von Recht und Politik im europäischen Verfassungsdenken' in C. Franzius, F. Mayer and J. Neyer (eds.), *Strukturfragen der Europäischen Union* (Baden-Baden: Nomos, 2010), pp. 67–85.

'Theorising the Global Legal Order – An Institutionalist Perspective' in A. Halpin and V. Roeben (eds.), *Theorising the Global Legal Order* (Oxford: Hart, 2009), pp. 61–83.

'Chancen und Defizite internationaler Verrechtlichung: Was das Recht jenseits des Nationalstaates leisten kann' in B. Zangl and M. Zürn (eds.), *Verrechtlichung – Baustein für Global Governance?* (Bonn: Dietz, 2004), pp. 46–73.

Onuf, N., 'The Constitution of International Society', *European Journal of International Law*, 5 (1994), pp. 1–19.

Pellet, A., 'Notes sur la "fragmentation" du droit international' in D. Alland (ed.), *Unité et diversité du droit international* (Leiden: Martinus Nijhoff, 2014), pp. 757–84.

Pernice, I. (ed.), *Konstitutionalisierung jenseits des Staates: Zur Verfassung der Weltgemeinschaft und den Gründungsverträgen internationaler Organisationen* (Baden-Baden: Nomos, 2012).

Peters, A., 'Global Constitutionalism' in M. Gibbons (ed.), *The Encyclopedia of Political Thought* (Chichester: Wiley-Blackwell, 2014), Online resource, available at http://onlinelibrary.wiley.com/doi/10.1002/9781118474396.wbept0421/pdf, accessed on 6 February 2015.

'Are We Moving towards Constitutionalization of the World Community?' in A. Cassese (ed.), *Realizing Utopia: The Future of International Law* (Oxford University Press, 2012), pp. 118–35.

'Conclusions', in J. Klabbers, A. Peters and G. Ulfstein (eds.), *The Constitutionalization of International Law* (Oxford University Press, 2009), pp. 342–51.

'The Merits of Global Constitutionalism', *Indiana Journal of Global Legal Studies*, 16 (2009), pp. 397–411.

'Compensatory Constitutionalism', *Leiden Journal of International Law*, 19 (2006), pp. 579–610.

Peters, A., L. Koechlin, T. Förster, and G. Fenner Zinkernagel (eds.), *Non-State Actors as Standard Setters* (Cambridge University Press, 2009).

Peters, A., and K. Armington, 'Global Constitutionalism from an Interdisciplinary Perspective', *Indiana Journal of Global Legal Studies*, 16 (2009), pp. 385–95.

Petersmann, E.-U., 'From State-Centered towards Constitution "Public Reason" in Modern International Economic Law' in G. Bongiovanni (ed.), *Reasonableness and Law* (Dordrecht and Heidelberg: Springer, 2009), pp. 421–58.

'Human Rights, Constitutionalism, and the World Trade Organization: Challenges for World Trade Organization Jurisprudence and Civil Society', *Leiden Journal of International Law*, 19 (2006), pp. 633–67.

Poiares Maduro, M., 'Courts and Pluralism: Essay on a Theory of Judicial Adjudication in the Context of Legal and Constitutional Pluralism' in J. L. Dunoff and J. B. Trachtman (eds.), *Ruling the World?* (Cambridge University Press, 2009), pp. 356–80.

Posner, E. A., *The Perils of Global Legalism* (University of Chicago Press, 2009).

Reus-Smit, C., 'The Constitutional Structure of International Society and the Nature of Fundamental Institutions', *International Organization*, 51 (1997), pp. 555–89.

Schwöbel, C., *Global Constitutionalism in International Legal Perspective* (Leiden: Martinus Nijhoff, 2011).

Slaughter, A.-M., *A New World Order* (Princeton University Press, 2004).

Teubner, G., and P. Korth, 'Two Kinds of Legal Pluralism: Collision of Transnational Regimes in the Double Fragmentation of World Society' in M. A.

Young (ed.), *Regime Interaction in International Law* (Cambridge University Press, 2009), pp. 23–54.

Thornhill, C., 'Contemporary Constitutionalism and the Dialectic of Constituent Power', *Global Constitutionalism*, 1 (2012), pp. 369–404.

Trachtman, J. P., 'Fragmentation, Coherence and Synergy in International Law', *Transnational Legal Theory*, 2 (2011), pp. 505–36.

Tully, J., 'On Local and Global Citizenship: An Apprenticeship Manual' in J. Tully, *Public Philosophy in a New Key*, 2 vols. (Cambridge University Press, 2008), Vol. II, pp. 243–309.

Strange Multiplicity: Constitutionalism in an Age of Diversity (Cambridge University Press, 1995).

Vidmar, J., 'Norm Conflicts and Hierarchy in International Law: Towards a Vertical International Legal System?' in E. de Wet and J. Vidmar (eds.), *Hierarchy in International Law* (Oxford University Press, 2012), pp. 13–40.

Walker, N., 'Flexibility within a Metaconstitutional Frame: Reflections on the Future of Legal Authority in Europe' in G. De Burca and J. Scott (eds.), *Constitutional Change in the EU: From University to Flexibility?* (Oxford: Hart, 2000), pp. 9–30.

Webb, P., *International Judicial Integration and Fragmentation* (Oxford University Press, 2013).

Weiler, J. H. H., and M. Wind (eds.), *European Constitutionalism Beyond the State* (Cambridge University Press, 2003).

de Wet, E. and J. Vidmar (eds.), *Hierarchy in International Law* (Oxford University Press, 2012).

Wiener, A., *A Theory of Contestation* (Heidelberg: Springer, 2014).

The Invisible Constitution of Politics: Contested Norms and International Encounters (Cambridge University Press, 2008).

'Global Constitutionalism' in *Oxford Bibliographies Online: International Relations*, available at www.oxfordbibliographies.com/view/document/obo-9780199743292/obo-9780199743292-0092.xml?rskey=CnfQ7M&result=1&q=antje%20wiener#firstMatch.

'Contested Compliance: Interventions on the Normative Structure of World Politics', *European Journal of International Relations*, 10 (2004), pp. 189–234.

Wiener, A., A. F. Lang, J. Tully, M. P. Maduro, and M. Kumm, 'Why a New Journal on Global Constitutionalism? Editorial', *Global Constitutionalism*, 1 (2012), pp. 1–15.

Willets, P., *Non-Governmental Organizations in World Politics: The Construction of Global Governance* (London, Routledge, 2011).

Young, M. A. (ed.), *Regime Interaction in International Law: Facing Fragmentation* (Cambridge University Press, 2012).

'Introduction' in M. A. Young, (ed.), *Regime Interaction in International Law: Facing Fragmentation* (Cambridge University Press, 2012), pp. 1–20.
'Regime Interaction in Creating, Implementing and Enforcing International Law' in M. A. Young, (ed.), *Regime Interaction in International Law: Facing Fragmentation* (Cambridge University Press, 2012), pp. 85–110.

2

How to avoid regime collisions

JEFFREY L. DUNOFF*

As this paper was being drafted, a disagreement over fishing quotas for herring stock in the Northeast Atlantic improbably catapulted the issue of "regime collisions" back to the center of international legal discourse. The underlying facts are unremarkable: The relevant coastal states – including Iceland, Norway, the Russian Federation, and the European Union (EU), agree that the total allowable catch (TAC) of the stock should be based on international scientific advice, and in accordance with an agreed long-term management plan. Pursuant to this plan, these states have from time to time adjusted the TAC among themselves. However, in recent years, the Faroe Islands, a self-governing nation within the territory of Denmark, has become increasingly dissatisfied with its allocation. In 2013, it set a higher catch limit for its own herring fisheries.

This decision triggered an intricate set of legal responses. First, following inconclusive negotiations among coastal states, in August 2013 the European Commission adopted a ban on imports of herring and mackerel that were caught under the control of the Faroe Islands (as well as fishery products containing or made of such fish). The measure also includes restrictions on the use of EU ports by vessels fishing for the herring and mackerel stocks under the control of the Faroe Islands.[1]

The Faroe Islands responded with a double-barreled litigation strategy. In August 2013, the Kingdom of Denmark, in respect of the Faroe Islands, initiated arbitration proceedings under Annex VII of the United Nations Convention on the Law of the Sea (UNCLOS), claiming that the

* I am grateful to Andreas Fischer-Lescano, Nora Markard, and Kerstin Blome for the opportunity to participate in this project, and to participants at a conference on "Contested Collisions" at the University of Bremen in January 2014 and an anonymous external reviewer for thoughtful comments on earlier drafts.

[1] See European Commission, "Commission Adopts Trade Measures Against Faroe Islands to Protect the Atlanto-Scandian Herring Stock," Commission Press Release (August 20, 2013) IP/13/785, http://europa.eu/rapid/press-release_IP-13-785_en.htm.

EU actions violated UNCLOS article 279.[2] Several months later, in November 2013, the Faroe Islands, acting with full powers granted by the Government of Denmark, and acting as "Denmark in respect of the Faroe Islands," sought consultations with the EU at the World Trade Organization (WTO) regarding its "use of coercive economic measures in relation to Atlanto-Scandian herring."[3] This request – the first step in the formal initiation of a WTO dispute – alleges that the EU measure violates articles I, V, and XI of the General Agreement on Tariffs and -Trade (GATT).[4]

The initiation of parallel proceedings in different international fora involving the same fact pattern and the same parties is reminiscent of other high-profile disputes, such as the Swordfish case and the MOX Plant dispute. The Swordfish case involved a Chilean law prohibiting the landing in Chilean ports of swordfish caught on the high seas. The EU claimed that this measure violated international trade law, and initiated dispute settlement proceedings against Chile at the WTO.[5] Simultaneously, Chile instituted an action against the EU before the International Tribunal for the Law of the Sea (ITLOS), claiming that EU fishing practices violated UNCLOS.[6] The MOX Plant case, involving a dispute over radioactive discharge by a UK nuclear facility into the Irish Sea, prompted parallel litigations before a Convention for the Protection of the Marine Environment of the North-East Atlantic (OSPAR) Arbitral Panel, an UNCLOS Arbitral Tribunal, and the European Court of Justice.

These and other disputes implicating potentially conflicting rules from different legal regimes have, in turn, attracted substantial academic attention, and the trajectory of this scholarship captures many of the

[2] See Government of the Faroe Islands, "The Faroe Islands takes the EU to international tribunal over intended economic measures" (August 16, 2013), www.government.fo/news/news/the-faroe-islands-takes-the-eu-to-international-tribunal-over-intended-economic-measures/.

[3] See "European Union – Measures on Atlanto-Scandian Herring – Request for Consultations by Denmark in Respect of the Faroe Islands" (November 7, 2013) WT/DS469/1, http://docsonline.wto.org.

[4] The dispute represents the first time that an individual EU member state has requested consultations under the WTO's dispute settlement understanding with another WTO member. The unusual party alignment is possible because the Faroe Islands is covered by Denmark's membership of the WTO, but is not covered by the Denmark's membership of the EU.

[5] "Chile – Measures Affecting the Transit and Importation of Swordfish, Request by the European Communities" (November 7, 2000) WT/DS193/2, http://docsonline.wto.org.

[6] ITLOS, *Conservation and Sustainable Exploitation of Swordfish Stocks in the South-Eastern Pacific Ocean* (*Chile* v. *European Community*) (2000) 40 ILM 475.

most significant debates in international law over the past two decades. One early strand of writings focused on the "trade and" issues, such as "trade and environment" or "trade and human rights," which explored real or perceived collisions between trade norms embedded in WTO treaties and rules from other international law regimes.[7] Several years later, Martti Koskenniemi's writings, as both a scholar and International Law Commission (ILC) member, triggered a flurry of writings on "the fragmentation of international law."[8] Much of this scholarship highlights concerns that international law's decentralized processes of law-making, institution-building, and dispute resolution risks inconsistent judgments, conflicting jurisprudence, and legal uncertainty.[9]

A related literature explores the dynamics behind "regime complexes," formed when different international legal regimes intersect and overlap in non-hierarchical relationships. While the phrase was developed in relation to plant genetic resources – which are subject to rules from the trade, intellectual property, environment, and agriculture regimes[10] – regime complexes are found in a variety of policy domains, including human rights, climate change, refugees, and intellectual property.[11] The regime complex literature develops theories intended to explain variation in levels of regime integration,[12] and highlights the prevalence and significance of regime complexity.[13]

[7] For a sense of the structure of the "trade and" debates, Dunoff, "The Death of the Trade Regime"; Howse, "From Politics to Technocracy – and Back Again."

[8] See, e.g., United Nations (UN) General Assembly, "Fragmentation of International Law: Difficulties Arising From the Diversification and Expansion of International Law, Finalized by Martti Koskenniemi" (April 13, 2006) UN Doc A/CN.4/L.682, http://legal.un.org/ilc/documentation/english/a_cn4_l682.pdf, as corrected (August 11, 2006) UN Doc. A/CN.4/L.682/Corr.1; Koskenniemi and Leino, "Fragmentation of International Law?". For papers that examine the relationship between the positions of Koskenniemi the scholar and Koskenniemi the ILC member, see Broude, "Keep Calm and Carry On:"; Murphy, "Defragmenting International Law."

[9] The fragmentation literature, in turn, helped spark a large debate over the conceptual coherence and normative desirability of global constitutionalism. See generally, Dunoff and Trachtman (eds.), *Ruling the World?*; Klabbers, Peters, and Ulfstein, *The Constitutionalization of International Law*; Stefan Oeter's contribution to this volume thoughtfully explores the relationship between fragmentation and global constitutionalism.

[10] Raustiala and Victor, "The Regime Complex for Plant Genetic Resources."

[11] Helfer, "Regime Shifting"; Alter and Meunier, "The Politics of Regime Complexity"; Oberthür and Gehring (eds.), *Institutional Interaction in Global Environmental Governance*; Keohane and Victor, "The Regime Complex for Climate Change."

[12] See, e.g., Johnson and Urpelainen, "A Strategic Theory of Regime Integration and Separation."

[13] Raustiala, "Institutional Proliferation and the International Legal Order."

A more recent literature focuses on "regime interactions."[14] While this literature purports to examine a broad range of ways that regimes can overlap and interact, in fact many of these writings foreground regime collisions.[15] For example, in a contribution to a leading volume on regime interactions, Gunther Teubner and Peter Korth explored the "collision of transnational regimes in the double fragmentation of world society,"[16] and James Crawford and Penelope Nevill highlighted the various technique courts use when asked to resolve conflicts generated by regime collisions.[17]

As this outpouring of writings suggests – and as the chapters in this volume confirm – regime collisions, and the doctrinal, institutional, and jurisprudential issues they raise, continue to captivate international lawyers. Regime collisions raise difficult issues concerning the resolution of normative conflict in a legal environment marked by non-hierarchical relations, the "systemic" nature of international law, and how different actors strategically create and exploit regime conflict. Writings in this area offer any number of "solutions" aimed at reconciling formally disparate international legal norms through strategies such as normative hierarchy, inter-institutional comity, margins of appreciation, *lex posterior*, *lex specialis*, subsidiarity, and systemic integration – among others.

However, given the amount of scholarly attention lavished on these issues, and the frustratingly inconclusive nature of the proposed solutions, it is appropriate to ask whether the continued fascination with regime collisions is likely to generate a productive research agenda – or to lead international lawyers into conceptual cul-de-sacs, diverting them from deeper understandings of the determinants of and dynamics behind regime interactions? The burden of this paper – part of an ongoing project on the entire range of regime interactions – is to suggest that the intensive focus on regime *collisions* threatens to lead international lawyers astray. The focus on collisions rests upon an incomplete and misleading model of regime interactions. It leads into doctrinal quagmires that admit of no obvious or satisfying exit. And perhaps most importantly, it deflects scholarly attention from more important and

[14] See, e.g., Young (ed.), *Regime Interaction in International Law.*

[15] There are exceptions that adopt broader perspectives on regime interaction similar to that urged in this paper. See, e.g., Oberthür and Gehring (eds.), *Institutional Interaction*; Young, *Trading Fish, Saving Fish*; Kelly, "Institutional Alliances and Derivative Legitimacy."

[16] Teubner and Korth, "Two Kinds of Legal Pluralism."

[17] Crawford and Nevill, "Relations between International Courts and Tribunals."

more common forms of regime interaction. In short, the turn to regime collisions leads to jurisprudential dead ends.

To be sure, these are large claims, and they cannot be fully defended in this brief chapter. Instead, I will explicate a few elements of these larger claims. Following this introduction, the paper provides a brief explanation of why an undue focus on regime collisions misleads. In particular, I argue that the focus on regime collisions rests on a conceptualization of regime interactions in terms of discrete *transactions* or *disputes*. However, the much more common and more important forms of regime interactions consist of ongoing relationships between actors in different regimes. This argument is intended to demonstrate that regime collisions are just part – an important part, no doubt – of a much larger universe of regime interactions. The paper then uses the lens of relational interactions to develop a typology of regime interactions. In particular, it identifies two different axes by which we can categorize regime interactions. One focuses on the various *forms* that regime interactions can take, including operational, regulatory, and conceptual regime interactions. The second axis focuses on the *nature* of the interaction, which spans a continuum from rationalization of parallel or overlapping efforts, and expansions of powers or jurisdiction, to conflictual interactions. Considered together, these axes capture much of the universe of regime interaction. Finally, having identified understudied and undertheorized categories of regime interactions, I very briefly offer the outlines of a future research agenda in this area.

The heart of this paper consists of a reconceptualization followed by a mapping exercise. It is intended to contribute to the existing literature in several different ways. First, by emphasizing that "regime collisions" represent only a small slice of the universe of regime overlaps and interactions, the paper opens up the conceptual and analytic space for the study of various types of relational interactions among regimes that, until now, have been largely overlooked by legal and international relations scholars. Moreover, the focus on regime collisions has emphasized *normative conflict* at the expense of attention to *institutional interaction*. For example, the ILC report at the heart of the fragmentation literature explicitly focused on the "substantive question" of relationships among legal rules, and "decided to leave . . . aside" questions related to "the competence of various institutions applying legal rules and their hierarchical relations *inter se*."[18] This paper thus addresses questions of

[18] ILC, "Fragmentation of International Law: Difficulties Arising from the Diversification and Expansion of International Law" (July 18, 2006) UN Doc A/CN.4/L.702, para. 13.

institutional collaboration that to date have been largely unexplored. This shift in focus will enable scholars to discover new patterns of regime cooperation and conflict.

The shift in focus urged here likewise suggests a richer understanding of international regimes than that offered by dominant approaches. In particular, the approach developed here permits us to see regimes as more than constellations of rules and institutions[19] and highlights the ways in which regimes are purposeful actors in their own right with independent interests, capabilities, and agendas. Finally, the approach developed here suggests that the boundaries between regimes are virtually always ambiguous, frequently porous, and increasingly fluid. As a result, the significance of the borders traditionally considered to distinguish between regimes can diminish in importance in the course of regime interactions. Moreover, relationships among regimes are highly dynamic, and can shift from collaborative to competitive to conflictual as different issues emerge, or as relationships evolve over time. This paper thus offers an approach designed to provide greater analytical traction to the study of regime interaction than dominant approaches do, and thereby advance our understandings of how, why, and when international legal regimes intersect and interact.

Who – or what – is colliding?

This volume addresses "contested collisions." This phrasing – no doubt intentionally – leaves open precisely *who* or *what* is colliding. Broadly speaking, the diverse papers in this volume reveal at least two ways to conceptualize the actors or entities that collide. Building on pioneering work by Gunther Teubner and Andreas Fischer-Lescano,[20] several of the contributions to this volume envision the collisions at issue as taking place between conflicting *rationalities*. The basic claim, drawn from systems theory, is that "at [its] core, the fragmentation of global law is

[19] See generally Barnett and Finnemore, *Rules for the World* (arguing that regimes can develop dominant frameworks for understanding certain phenomena, as International Monetary Fund (IMF) did with exchange rate policies, can set the terms of debate, generate schemes of classification and definition, and set norms and standards). Although scholars have focused on the relative autonomy of particular international organizations, such as the World Bank, IMF, UN, and EU, the approach set out in this paper is the first to examine regimes as autonomous actors in the context of ongoing interactions with other regimes.

[20] Fischer-Lescano and Teubner, "Regime Collisions."

not simply about legal norm collisions or policy-conflicts, but rather has its origins in contradictions between society-wide institutionalized rationalities, which law cannot solve . . ."[21] From this perspective, legal fragmentation "is merely an ephemeral reflection of a more fundamental, multi-dimensional fragmentation of global society itself."[22]

While the systems theory conceptualization of fragmentation has considerable power, for the purposes of this paper I adopt a competing understanding, and foreground collisions between *international legal regimes*. In the international relations literature, the notion of an international regime is broadly defined as a constellation of governing arrangements constructed by states to coordinate their expectations and organize international behavior in various issue areas.[23] As Friedrich Kratochwil and John G. Ruggie noted, regimes "comprise a normative element, state practice, and organizational roles."[24] International legal regimes are typically centered upon a treaty text, as well as associated institutional bodies, mechanisms, and practices.[25] Thus, international lawyers often speak of, for example, the trade regime or the human rights regime. As noted earlier, in recent years this literature has evolved to address issues of regime complexity and interaction that are the focus of this paper.

It is worth noting that these two conceptualizations overlap, but are not congruent. For example, it makes sense to claim that the trade regime embeds a different logic than does the human rights regime, or that the nature and structure of the UN's collective security system embeds a different logic than the international criminal law regime.[26] But many regimes themselves contain conflicting logics; for example, elsewhere I've described three different logics that purport to explain the multilateral trade system.[27]

From a transactional to a relational approach to regime interaction

The herring dispute between the Faroe Islands and the EU illustrates many features of the "transactional model" that underlies most

[21] Ibid. [22] Ibid.

[23] The locus classicus remains Krasner (ed.), *International Regimes* (most of which was first published in a special issue of *International Organization* in 1982).

[24] Kratochwil and Ruggie, "International Organization," p. 759.

[25] For an analysis of how treaties lie at the center of international legal regimes, see Chayes and Chayes, *The New Sovereignty*.

[26] See Blome and Markard, "Contested Collisions."

[27] Dunoff, "The Death of the Trade Regime."

approaches to regime collisions. Thus, as typically conceptualized, these disputes share a number of common structural elements.

First, these disputes are typically understood as being essentially bilateral in nature. Hence, although vessels from many states fish the Northeast Atlantic, and catch from this area is purchased and consumed by parties in numerous states across the globe, analysis of the mackerel dispute centers upon legal claims between the Faroe Islands and the EU.

Second, these disputes are typically understood as arising out of a discrete event or series of events that can be localized in time and space. The mackerel dispute was triggered by a decision by the Faroe Islands to triple its mackerel catch in certain waters. Similarly, the swordfish dispute arises out of specific Spanish fishing practices in particular waters near Chile where swordfish spawn, and the MOX Plant litigation involves the construction and operation of a particular facility that recycles specific materials (plutonium) produced during nuclear fuel reprocessing.

Third, these disputes are largely conceived in state- and court-centric terms. As noted earlier, the mackerel wars implicate many actors, including private parties engaged in fishing practices and individual consumers in many different states – not to mention the populations of cod and mackerel (assuming they have cognizable interests). Nevertheless, the moving party behind the UNCLOS and WTO complaints is the Kingdom of Denmark, and the WTO dispute is brought by "Denmark acting in respect of the Faroe Islands" (although the litigation will be conducted by the government of the Faroe Islands).[28] Moreover, although the mackerel dispute involves complex negotiations in multiple forums, the regime "collision" is seen as manifesting and playing itself out before international tribunals, in this case a WTO panel and, potentially, Appellate Body, and an UNCLOS Arbitral Tribunal and, potentially, the ITLOS. Analysis of the swordfish and MOX Plant disputes likewise focused on activities at various international tribunals.

Fourth, regime collisions are typically understood to have a retrospective focus. That is, the collision is understood to arise out of a discrete event that took place in the past. The goal of the litigation arising out of this event is to clarify the legal rights and obligations of the states party to the litigation.

[28] It follows that the relevant international regimes are seen as largely passive, in the sense that they are forums for the resolution of the dispute between the parties.

Fifth, and finally, the litigations arising out of regime collisions are thought to involve potential or actual conflicts between applicable legal norms found in two or more international legal regimes. As a result, in its determination of legal rights of the parties, the tribunal will be asked to address the relationship of the conflicting rules, and typically seek either to harmonize these norms or to privilege one set of norms and subordinate others.

Thus, the structure of regime collisions resembles nothing so much as a classic problem of private international law, or conflict of laws. That is, a fact pattern involving two actors embedded within two different legal jurisdictions – say, a buyer in state A and a seller in state B whose deal goes awry – with litigation raising threshold issues of where the dispute should be heard, and which jurisdiction's substantive rules will be considered controlling.

It is therefore not surprising that many scholars invoke classic conflict of laws approaches to resolve regime collisions. For example, writing in the 1950s, both Wilfred Jenks and Philip Jessup explicitly analogized the problem of conflicting treaty norms to that of conflicts of laws.[29] In the early 2000s, similar ideas would recur. For example, in a widely cited article Andreas Fischer-Lescano and Gunther Teubner suggested that regime conflicts should be addressed through conflict of laws strategies.[30] More recently, private international law scholar Ralf Michaels and public international law scholar Joost Pauwelyn have attempted to identify both the strengths and the limits of conflict of laws approaches to address regime collisions.[31]

However, while it is true that international legal regimes do sometimes overlap and collide with respect to discrete events, this "transactional" approach to regime overlaps is partial and therefore potentially misleading. In fact, just as a vanishingly small percentage of legal undertakings on the domestic plane lead to litigation, the discrete fact patterns that give rise to regime "collisions" and litigations are far from the primary occasion for different international legal regimes to overlap or intersect. Instead, international legal regimes much more frequently interact in

[29] Jenks, "The Conflict of Law-Making Treaties," p. 403 ("some of the problems which [conflicts between treaties] involve may present a closer analogy with the problem of conflict of laws than with the problem of conflicting obligations within the same legal system"); Jessup, *Transnational Law*, pp. 72–113.

[30] Fischer-Lescano and Teubner, *Regime Collisions*.

[31] Michaels and Pauwelyn, "Conflict of Norms or Conflict of Laws?"

ongoing and continuous relationships. Indeed, the volume and intensity of these "relational" interactions swamp the paradigmatic litigations that typically capture scholarly attention.

As described more fully later, these "relational" interactions possess several features that sharply distinguish them from the transactional interactions at issue in most litigation. International litigation is largely about the narrowing of issues for authoritative resolution by an international tribunal. The relational interactions that highlighted here, in contrast, have a highly dynamic character that often expands the range of issues under consideration and frequently involves multiple non-judicial forums. In addition, international litigations involving multiple regimes are typically state-centric; states are virtually always parties and often the only parties. The relational interactions, in contrast, often involve a more diverse set of actors. In particular, there is frequently significant participation by non-state actors, including a diverse mix of international organizations, non-governmental organizations, regional bodies, and informal networks.

International litigations are necessarily reactive; they center upon a discrete event in the past and the determination of whether one party's actions during that event violated international legal norms. Moreover, to the extent they involve conflicting rules found in different legal regimes, international litigations often revolve around efforts to harmonize norms, or to privilege one set of international legal norms and subordinate others. Relational interactions, in contrast, are typically forward looking. Moreover, instead of searching for *the* governing norm, relational interactions explicitly acknowledge that multiple regimes often can and do exercise concurrent authority over actions or events. Hence, relational interactions are often directed toward the articulation of new international norms to prospectively govern behavior within a particular area of international relations. Thus these interactions are often "jurisgenerative," or law-creating. To better understand these claims about the ubiquity and importance of relational interactions, it will be useful to identify the various categories of interactions. I turn now to this task.

A typology of regime interactions

As suggested, regime interactions can be productively analyzed along two different axes. One highlights the *form* of the interaction. A second axis highlights the *nature* of the interaction. Each is explored in more detail in the next section.

The conventional focus on regime collisions misleadingly suggests that most regime interactions involve potentially conflicting legal norms that are resolved in formal legal proceedings at international tribunals. However, shifting attention to the wide variety of interactions that take place in ongoing relationships between and among regimes reveals a much wider array of interactions.

Operational interactions

Lawyers often focus on law-making, law-interpretation, and law enforcement within international regimes. Important as these activities are, they are hardly the only undertakings that international bodies engage in; in particular, international organizations undertake a wide variety of operational activities. At times, these activities have great political salience and high visibility; the Organisation for the Prohibition of Chemical Weapons (OPCW) recently supervised and verified the destruction of chemical weapons and chemical weapons production facilities in Syria and the International Atomic Energy Agency conducts inspections of and issues reports on Iran's nuclear facilities. Studies of operational activities typically focus on a single body or regime, and to date have not explored how actors from different international legal regimes interact in the course of conducting their operational activities.

A handful of examples from a diverse array of issue areas will provide a sense of these operational activities. In the public health field, perhaps the best known example is UNAIDS, a joint venture involving ten "cosponsors" from a broad spectrum of international legal regimes, including the Office of the High Commissioner for Refugees (UNHCR); United Nations Children's Fund (UNICEF); World Food Programme (WFP); United Nations Development Programme (UNDP); United Nations Population Fund (UNPF); United Nations Office on Drugs and Crime (UNODC); International Labour Organization (ILO); United Nations Educational, Scientific and Cultural Organization (UNESCO); World Health Organization (WHO); and World Bank. Each organization had historically been active in combating AIDS, and in an effort to minimize duplication and maximize the impact of finite international resources, the ten organizations entered into both a partnership and an agreed-upon "division of labor."

The environment is another area where actors from different international legal regimes often partner to rationalize and enhance efforts. For example, the Global Environment Facility (GEF) was created as a partnership among the UNDP, United Nations Environment Programme (UNEP), and World Bank. As originally conceived, the GEF was designed to capitalize on the expertise and comparative advantages of each agency. UNDP brought a global network of country offices and an expertise in development; UNEP was the only UN organization whose core focus was the environment; and the World Bank brought extensive experience in lending focusing on investment, infrastructure development, and policy reform. The GEF serves as the designated financial mechanism for international agreements on biodiversity, climate change, and persistent organic pollutants, and supports the work of international agreements to combat desertification, manage international waters and protect the ozone layer. Since 1991, it has provided over $10.5 billion in grants for over 2,700 projects in over 165 states.

In the trade area, a number of collaborations among international bodies are intended to build local capacity. To mention just a few, the WTO, United Nations Conference on Trade and Development (UNCTAD), and the International Trade Centre (ITC) created the "Joint Integrated Technical Assistance Programme," to help African states adapt national trading systems to the obligations and disciplines of the then-new WTO; the IMF, ITC, UNCTAD, UNDP, World Bank, and the WTO partnered to create the Enhanced Integrated Framework, which assists least developed states set up structures needed to coordinate the delivery of trade related assistance and build capacity to trade;[32] and the Food and Agricultural Organization (FAO), World Organization for Animal Health (OIE), World Bank, WHO, and WTO partnered to create the Standards and Trade Development Facility, which supports developing states build capacity to implement international sanitary and phytosanitary standards; it acts as both a coordinating and financing mechanism.

While many additional examples could be offered, these brief descriptions should be sufficient to suggest that these partnerships are ubiquitous in international affairs – even among international bodies that are not commonly thought of as "operational" organizations.[33] However, apart from a handful of well-known examples like UNAIDS,

[32] On December 17, 2013, the World Tourism Organization became the eighth organization to join this partnership.

[33] The WTO's website offers a "non-exhaustive list" of approximately 200 international organizations that the WTO's secretariat has working relations with: www.wto.org/english/thewto_e/coher_e/igo_divisions_e.htm.

nternational lawyers and international relations scholars tend to overlook these efforts. These initiatives thus constitute sites of global governance that are "hidden in plain sight," and whose significance has been underexplored. For current purposes, it will be useful to mention a few salient characteristics of these efforts.

First, these partnerships frequently exhibit forms of organizational creativity and dynamism that is often lacking in the partner institutions. The original UNAIDS Programme Coordinating Board included various IGOs, donor states, and recipient governments. Thereafter, the Economic and Social Council (ECOSOC) also provided for five civil society organizations to sit on the Board, with three from developing states. UNAIDS thus became the first UN program to include civil society representatives on its governing body.

Second, these initiatives tend to evolve, and quite often, to expand in scale, scope, and number of participants over time. For example, when originally launched in 1991, the GEF consisted of three implementing agencies, UNEP, UNDP, and the World Bank; today the GEF partnership has grown to include ten agencies: the original three plus FAO, United Nations Industrial Development Organization (UNIDO), African Development Bank (AfDB), Asian Development Bank (ADB), European Bank for Reconstruction and Development (EBRD), Inter-American Development Bank (IADB), and the International Fund for Agricultural Development (IFAD).

Efforts to combat environmental crime exhibit a similar pattern. In the mid-1990s, the secretariats of the Convention on International Trade in Endangered Species (CITES) and the World Customs Organization (WCO) began to collaborate in developing training materials and seminars for customs officials. More recently, CITES, Interpol, United Nations Office on Drugs and Crime (UNODC), the World Bank, and the WCO created the "International Consortium on Combating Wildlife Crime" (ICCWC). The consortium, created in response to the increasing sophistication of wildlife crime, has provided enforcement-related guidance to the Global Tiger Initiative; developed an analytic toolkit for analyzing domestic preventive and criminal justice responses; and launched "Project Predator," a major initiative addressing illegal trade in Asian big cats.

Third, efforts to coordinate or harmonize operational efforts enjoy variable levels of success. For example, in its earliest days, UNAIDS confronted enormous difficulties in attempting to meld the diverse missions, cultures, expertise, and bureaucratic structures of its partner agencies.[34] While inter-agency collaboration at UNAIDS improved over time, other initiatives to coordinate never become operational.

For example, following a major accident and oil spill in the Atlantic off the Spanish coast in 2002, the UN Secretary General convened a Consultative Group on Flag State Implementation, which included officials from the International Maritime Organization (IMO), ILO, FAO, UNEP, UNCTAD, and the Organization for Economic Co-operation and Development (OECD).[35] Substantial differences of opinion among members of the Consultative Group quickly emerged however,[36] and efforts to coordinate operational activities sparked strong resistance. The IMO, in particular, argued that with respect to flag state implementation of safety and anti-pollution standards, "[t]he role of the IMO in this regard should be seen as pre-eminent."[37] In a letter to the UN Secretary General, the IMO's Secretary General tartly observed that issues related to state compliance with "IMO Conventions and regulations are not subjects which need additional coordination at inter-agency meetings," and that the "IMO does not see the need for any further meetings of the inter-agency Consultative Group."[38]

Fourth, there are substantial variations in the actors that initiate operational interactions. Sometimes, the impetus for new activities, governance structures, or international bodies comes from IOs themselves. For example, the creation of the WFP, the world's largest humanitarian agency fighting hunger, was primarily driven by the FAO, working together with officials from the United Nations.[39] Significantly, creation of the WFP came only after an earlier, unsuccessful FAO effort to create a body like the WFP, and a sophisticated, multi-year effort by the FAO to cultivate support within the UN and other IOs for the creation of such an entity.

Other times the impetus comes from states. As a formal matter, the Intergovernmental Panel on Climate Change (IPCC) was jointly established by the World Meteorological Organization (WMO) and UNEP. However, the political push for the IPCC came largely from a wary US Administration, among others, who did not want potentially contentious

[34] Knight, *UNAIDS*.

[35] UN General Assembly, "Oceans and the Law of the Sea: Report of the Secretary-General" (March 3, 2003) UN Doc A/58/65.

[36] UN General Assembly, "Oceans and the Law of the Sea, Consultative Group on Flag State Implementation: Report of the Secretary-General" (March 5, 2004) UN Doc A/59/63.

[37] Ibid. at p. 5. [38] Ibid. at Annex III.

[39] For a fuller review of WFP's creation, see Johnson, *Organizational Progeny*.

scientific findings on climate issues to be under the control of the WMO or other IOs with substantial bureaucracies, but rather under the control of a body of representatives appointed by each government.[40] In practice, the "intergovernmental" dimension of the IPCC has proven to be a double-edged sword. On the one hand, the intergovernmental nature of the IPCC was largely responsible for educating many domestic officials about the problem of climate change and made them more willing to negotiate.[41] On the other hand, IPCC reports are sometimes discounted as the product of the political negotiations associated with an intergovernmental body.[42]

At times, the push for new collaborative undertakings comes from non-state actors. For example, the unsuccessful suggestion to coordinate on the enforcement of international shipping standards originated in a joint initiative of Greenpeace International, the International Transport Workers' Federation, and the World Wide Fund for Nature.

Fifth, and most significantly for current purposes, initiatives focused on operational activities, virtually always generate normative standards. Summarizing a study of operational activities undertaken by a single international body, Ian Johnston explains that

> [the normative] evolution proceeds as follows: operational activities occur against the backdrop of widely acknowledged but not well-specified norms; in carrying out those activities, international organizations do not seek to enforce the norms per se but typically act in a manner that conforms to them; these activities generate friction, triggering bouts of legal argumentation; the reaction of affected governments – and the discourse that surrounds the action and reaction – can cause the law to harden . . .[43]

These dynamics are only heightened when actors from multiple regimes, with different normative standards, collaborate in operational activities. Again, UNAIDS is illustrative. When UNAIDS was founded, the different partner agencies had different procurement policies. Some partner agencies, like UNICEF, emphasized supplier compliance with the Convention on the Rights of the Child; others, like UNHCR, had certain

[40] See, e.g., Bolin, *A History of the Science and Politics of Climate Change*.

[41] Agrawala, "Context and Early Origins of the Intergovernmental Panel on Climate Change," p. 611 (citing an interview with Jean Rippert, former Chair of climate negotiations).

[42] Ibid.

[43] Johnstone, "Law-Making Through the Operational Activities of International Organizations."

preferences for local suppliers; and virtually all employed different rules depending on the size of the purchase. Collaboration among agencies required extensive negotiations to harmonize, or at least coordinate, the normative standards applicable to procurement.

Moreover, experience demonstrates the practical reality that any one set of interactions – say, over coordinating funding mechanisms in HIV/AIDS prevention – in turn invariably gives rise to a new set of issues – say, ensuring integrity in the use of these funds. Thus, over time UNAIDS has spearheaded efforts by its co-sponsoring agencies not only to harmonize the rules governing procurement policies but also to adopt a common "zero tolerance" approach to corruption in the use of financial resources.

Normative output associated with collaborative initiatives in one set of operational activities often influence related initiatives elsewhere. After the various UNAIDS agencies were able to agree to common standards in procurement and anti-fraud efforts, in January, 2006, the Global Fund to Fight AIDS, Tuberculosis and Malaria, the World Bank, and the Office of the Global AIDS Coordinator created the "Coordinated Procurement Planning Initiative." The initiative was designed to improve procurement coordination for HIV/AIDS commodities among multilateral institutions and international donors. In 2008, WHO and the United Nations International Drug Purchase Facility joined the initiative, and in 2009 UNAIDS joined. These efforts, in turn, have raised new questions about project management, transparency, and accountability that will require the development of principles and policies to address corruption, fraud, and integrity in procurement.

Regulatory interactions

In addition to operational interactions, actors from different international legal regimes often engage in regulatory interactions. To date, international lawyers have tended to focus on regime collisions and on the regulatory overlaps that manifest themselves when one treaty explicitly references legal norms from another regime, such as when WTO legal texts defer to IMF determinations regarding exchange restrictions,[44] adopt standards of intellectual property protection set out in the Paris Convention on Industrial Property, the Berne Convention for the

[44] General Agreement on Tariffs and Trade (January 1, 1948) LT/UR/A-1A/1/GATT/2, art. XV:2, http://docsonline.wto.org.

Protection of Literary and Artistic Works, the Rome Convention (on performers, phonogram producers, and broadcasters), and the Washington Treaty (on integrated circuits),[45] or encourage use of standards developed by the Codex Alimentarius Commission, the International Plant Protection Committee, and the International Office of Epizootics.[46] However, to focus exclusively on collisions and treaty clauses that delineate relationships with other treaties is to overlook the many ways that international legal regimes often engage in lengthy consultations or negotiations that generate international legal standards. Several examples will illustrate how international regulatory standards arise out of iterative collaborations among actors from different regimes.

International efforts to control hazardous substances and activities have, for many years, been marked by collaboration among international organizations that cross regimes. In 1995, the WHO, OECD, FAO, ILO, UNEP, and UNIDO jointly created the Inter-Organization for the Sound Management of Chemicals (IOMC), with the World Bank and UN Development Programme participating in an observer capacity. The IOMC's regulatory undertakings include the establishment of a globally harmonized system for the classification and labeling of chemicals and efforts to regulate obsolete and unwanted pesticides in Africa.[47]

While IOMC addresses a diverse set of issues, developments related to the Stockholm Convention on Persistent Organic Pollutants (POPs Convention) illustrate regulatory interactions on a relatively narrow topic. This treaty, which entered into force in 2004, bans the use of certain

45 Agreement on Trade-Related Aspects of Intellectual Property Rights, Marrakesh Agreement Establishing the World Trade Organization, Annex 1C (April 15, 1994) LT/UR/A-1C/IP/1, http://docsonline.wto.org.

46 Agreement on the Application of Sanitary and Phytosanitary Measures art 12(3), Marrakesh Agreement Establishing the World Trade Organization, Annex 1A (April 15, 1994) LT/UR/A-1A/12, http://docsonline.wto.org.

47 More recently, a new effort to coordinate work on chemical management across international bodies was launched. In February 2006, IOMC, UNEP, and the Intergovernmental Forum on Chemical Safety (IFCS) convened the International Conference on Chemicals Management. Three other organizations – the GEF, the UNDP, and the World Bank – joined the co-conveners in adopting an overarching policy strategy and a Global Plan of Action that together constitute the Strategic Approach to International Chemicals management (SAICM). An explicit goal of this initiative is to "strengthen the coherence and the synergies that exist" between existing efforts to manage dangerous chemicals and to address "existing gaps in the framework of international chemicals policy." Although thus far this initiative has not produced any legally binding instruments, it is not difficult to envision this collaborative effort, like previous collaborative efforts among international bodies in this area, producing new regulatory instruments in the future.

pesticides and chemicals. A central issue during treaty negotiations was whether to ban DDT. A broad coalition of environmental groups advocated for the elimination of this pesticide, but many developing states and public health advocates argued that DDT was a highly effective tool against malaria, and no feasible alternative for malaria control existed. The WHO, which formally participated in the negotiations, argued that a ban would be premature given the lack of cost-effective substitutes. The WHO position ultimately prevailed, and the POPs Convention restricts, but does not ban, use of DDT.

Moreover, the POPs Convention expressly contemplates a continuing series of interactions between actors from the chemicals regime and the international public health regime. First, the treaty provides that parties may produce and use DDT only in accordance with WHO recommendations and guidelines. Thus, any changes in guidelines for DDT use produced within the public health regime automatically produce regulatory changes within the chemicals regime. In addition, the POPs Convention expressly provides that every three years the treaty parties will consult with the WHO to determine whether there is still a need to permit the use of DDT for vector control. The clear expectation is that if and when the WHO determines that there is no longer a need to use DDT for malarial control, the chemicals regime will be changed to ban DDT.[48] Thus, the treaty explicitly structures an ongoing series of interactions between the POPs secretariat and the WHO over global efforts to regulate DDT.

The interactions between FAO and the CITES Secretariat provide another example of inter-regime regulatory interactions.[49] Historically, the FAO has taken the lead in developing standards for the protection of endangered marine species, including particularly the Code of Conduct for Responsible Fisheries. However, as implementation of FAO norms

48 As of May 2011, the WHO still recommended the use of DDT in malaria vector control, provided WHO guidelines are followed. See WHO, "The Use of DDT in Malaria Vector Control: WHO Position Statement" (2011), WHO/HTM/GMP/2011. In June 2013, the conference of the parties to the Stockholm Convention adopted a decision concluding that states that rely upon DDT for disease vector control "may need to continue such use until locally safe, effective, affordable, and environmentally sound alternatives are available for a sustainable transition away from DTT." Stockholm Convention on Persistent Organic Pollutants, "Decision Adopted by the Conference of the Parties to the Stockholm Convention at its sixth meeting" (Spring 2013) SC-6/1:DDT.

49 The description that follows draws largely from Margaret Young's highly detailed account of FAO-CITES interactions: Young, "Protecting Endangered Marine Species."

has traditionally been weak, over time pressures developed to address trade in endangered marine species through CITES. Although there was some question whether CITES covered marine species,[50] in 2002 a CITES Conference of Parties agreed to list several commercially-exploited marine species. However, the decision was controversial, given questions about the scope of CITES's mandate, its expertise, a supposed bias in favor of conservation and against economic development, and concerns over creating norms potentially inconsistent with FAO norms.[51]

CITES includes a provision requiring consultation with the FAO when a proposal regarding marine species is submitted, and the FAO Code of Conduct encourages states to cooperate in complying with treaties that regulate the trade of endangered species.[52] These provisions lead to efforts to formalize these interactions and, eventually, to lengthy and contentious efforts to negotiate of a memorandum of understanding.

In 2002, a FAO meeting addressed the relationship between FAO and CITES. A meeting summary states:

> The view was expressed that CITES should be seen as a complementary instrument . . . and that a CITES listing should be limited to exceptional cases only and when all relevant bodies associated with the management of the species in question agreed that a listing would be advantageous. Some countries expressed support for the role of CITES in fisheries management . . .

The first quoted sentence reflects the view of some states that the FAO could effectively veto efforts in CITES to list marine species; the next sentence reflects that not all FAO members shared this view.[53]

In 2003, the CITES Secretariat produced a draft MOU that emphasized the coordination of work and shared reporting. In response the FAO produced a draft MOU that sought to narrow CITES jurisdiction in several ways, although given the lack of consensus at FAO these provisions were placed in brackets. The CITES Secretariat then made slight changes to its draft, and forwarded it to the FAO's Director-General for FAO consideration. A FAO working group then prepared a new draft

[50] See, e.g., CITES, "Travaux Preparatoires, Summary Record – Tenth Plenary Session, 10 February 1973" (March 5, 1973) CITES Doc SR/10 (Final), p. 3.

[51] Young, "Protecting Endangered Marine Species," pp. 540–58.

[52] Convention on International Trade in Endangered Species of Wild Fauna and Flora (March 3, 1973), art XV(2)(b) www.cites.org/sites/default/files/eng/disc/E-Text.pdf; FAO, "Code of Conduct for Responsible Fisheries" (1995), art 11.2.9, www.fao.org/3/a-v9878e .pdf.

[53] Young, "Protecting Endangered Marine Species," p. 465.

MOU, which modified some of the efforts to limit CITES jurisdiction, and which became the basis for negotiations between the FAO and the CITES secretariat. Once again, disagreement emerged over FAO's role in CITES listing decisions, including debates over whether CITES would merely "consider" or "incorporate to the extent possible" FAO input into listing decisions.

The final text provides for a complex process for the FAO to consult with CITES when it considers proposals to list marine species.[54] First, the CITES Secretariat will inform FAO of relevant proposals; FAO will then undertake a scientific and technical review and transmit the results to the CITES Secretariat; the CITES Secretariat will make "its own findings and recommendations, taking due account of the FAO review"; to ensure "maximum coordination of conservation measures, the CITES Secretariat will respect, to the greatest extent possible, the results of the FAO [review]." This text diverges from earlier CITES drafts which did not envision a process for consultations over CITES listings, and from earlier FAO drafts which would have listings contingent upon agreement from all relevant organizations (i.e., provide the FAO a veto).

The procedures set forth in the MOU have since been operationalized – although not without controversy. For example, in 2007, Germany proposed the listing of two shark species. A FAO expert panel concluded that the available scientific evidence did not support the proposed listing,[55] and the CITES parties did not approve the German proposals.

Proposals to list a number of species were made in advance of a 2013 CITES Conference of the Parties. FAO expert panels recommended that some of these proposals be adopted (including the shark species rejected in 2007). On one species, the porbeagle shark, the FAO panel

[54] "Memorandum of Understanding between the Food and Agriculture Organization of the United Nations (FAO) and the Secretariat of the Convention on International Trade in Endangered Species (CITES)" (2006), www.cites.org/eng/disc/sec/FAO-CITES-e.pdf.

[55] See FAO, "Fisheries Report No 833: Report of the Second FAO Ad Hoc Expert Advisory Panel for the Assessment of Proposals to Amend Appendices I and II of CITES concerning Commercially-Exploited Aquatic Species" (2007) CITES Doc COP14 Inf 38, www.cites.org/eng/cop/14/inf/E14i-38.pdf. Germany critiqued the methodology used by the FAO panel, "Comments on the FAO Assessment of the CITES Amendment" (June 7, 2007) CITES COP14 Inf 48; and the FAO responded with a defense of its methodology. COP to CITES, "The Interpretation of Annex 2a (Criteria for the Inclusion of Species in Appendix II in accordance with Article II, Paragraph 2(a), of the Convention) and Annex 5 (Annex 5 Definitions, Explanations and Guidelines) of Resolutions Conf 9.24 (Rev COP13) in relation to Commercially-Exploited Aquatic Species" (June 3–15, 2007) CITES Doc COP14 Inf 64.

was split, with a majority recommending listing, and for some species, such as the Ceja River stingray, the FAO panel recommended against listing. In each case, the FAO's recommendations were followed. Thereafter, the CITES Secretariat and FAO developed a joint plan of action to implement these listings, and delegations from the FAO and CITES secretariat have met to discuss collaboration opportunities in the implementation of shark protection projects.

Continuing and iterative regulatory interactions between actors from different international regimes are found in numerous other areas of international law and policy. For example, the IMO and ILO have collaborated to establish a number of joint working groups and expert groups, which have produced various guidelines, including: the ILO/IMO Code of Practice on Security in Ports[56]; ILO/IMO Guidelines on Provision of Financial Security in case of Abandonment of Seafarers[57]; ILO/IMO Guidelines on Shipowner's Responsibilities in respect to Contractual Claims for Personal Injury or Death of Seafarers[58]; and the ILO/IMO Guidelines on the Medical Examinations of Seafarers.[59] The WTO, CITES, UNCLOS, regional fisheries organizations, and FAO have engaged in continuing and iterative interactions over WTO negotiating texts on fisheries subsidies.[60] The International Hydrographic Organization has collaborated with the IMO to develop joint measures for the transition to electronic nautical charts. The International Civil Aviation Organization(ICAO), which sets standards for aviation safety, and the International Telecommunication Union (ITU), which allocates global radio spectrum and satellite orbits, have worked collaboratively on issues of mutual concern over the years, including particularly over avoiding

[56] This code was approved by the ILO's Governing Body at its 289th Session in March 2004, and was approved by the IMO Maritime Safety Committee at its seventy-eighth session.

[57] IMO, "Guidelines on Provision of Financial Security in Case of Abandonment of Seafarers" (December 17, 2001) A 22/Res.930, adopted on November 29, 2001.

[58] IMO, "Guidelines on Shipowners' Responsibilities in Respect to Contractual Claims for Personal Injury to or Death of Seafarers" (December 17, 2001) A22/Res.931, adopted November 29, 2001.

[59] These guidelines have been endorsed by the ILO Governing Body and the IMO Maritime Safety Committee. Notably, the guidelines supersede guidelines developed by the ILO and the WHO in 1997. By their terms, the ILO/IMO guidelines are not legally binding; but they do strongly influence domestic legislation and "provide an example of an international instrument that has been drafted through a cooperative process that takes into account the values and objectives of both international organizations with an interest in the subject matter"; Harrison, *Making the Law of the Sea*, p. 252.

[60] See Young, *Trading Fish, Saving Fish*; Stokke and Coffey, "Institutional Interplay and Responsible Fisheries."

interference with essential aeronautical radio-communication and radio-navigation systems. They are now starting to work on regulatory issues raised by civilian automated pilotless aircraft (drones).

Many other examples could be provided, but the general point should be clear. The ongoing dialogue between experts from the chemicals regime with their counterparts from public health regimes over when and how to regulate continued use of DDT; the ongoing exchanges between FAO and CITES over listing decisions; the continuing joint working groups created by ILO and IMO; the ongoing exchanges between the international civil servants from the Law of the Sea regime with their counterparts from the Food and Agriculture Organization and the WTO over the nature and content of new rules on fisheries subsidies; and the iterative interactions among specialists from the ITU and the ICAO over the allocation of radio frequencies illustrate, by way of example, the underappreciated fact that international regimes frequently collaborate in various formats and forums to produce international legal standards.

Conceptual interactions

The most intriguing and potentially most powerful regime interactions are conceptual interactions. International legal regimes are more than clusters of rules, principles, institutions, and practices that regulate behavior within an issue area. And legal regimes do not simply produce rules and standards. They also create knowledge. Specifically, the activities of international legal regimes constitute part of "the processes by which we collectively come to know, describe, and imagine the world in which we live."[61] As a result, when international actors embedded within an international regime create rules or engage in operational activities, they simultaneously create social knowledge. They do so by, for example, "defin[ing] shared international tasks (like "development"), creat[ing] and defin[ing] new categories of actors (like "refugee"), creat[ing] new interests for actors (like "promoting human rights"), and transfer[ing] models of organization around the world (like markets and democracy)."[62]

Scholarship exploring these issues has tended to focus on developments in specific regimes, such as international trade or international

[61] Lang, "Legal Regimes and Professional Knowledges."

[62] Barnett and Finnemore, "The Politics, Power and Pathologies of International Organizations." See also Barnett and Finnemore, *Rules for the World.*

humanitarian law.[63] Once again the analytic road not yet taken in legal scholarship would expand this focus and examine the ways that knowledge production through international regimes results from interactions *among*, as opposed to *within*, international legal regimes.

By way of illustration, let us return to "trade and environment" debates, one of the earliest sites of perceived regime collision. WTO panels and the Appellate Body have continued to struggle with perceived conflicts between liberalized trade norms and environmental protection efforts.[64] At the same time, the WTO Secretariat has been engaged in an ongoing set of conceptual interactions with actors from international environmental regimes. For example, in 2009, the WTO and UNEP jointly published a report addressing the linkages between trade and climate change. Issued at a critical time in the ongoing negotiations over a post-Kyoto climate change treaty, the joint WTO/UNEP report challenges the conventional wisdom that views trade liberalization as in tension with efforts to combat climate change. The report argues that trade liberalization can have a positive effect on greenhouse gas emissions by, inter alia, accelerating the transfer of clean technologies. The report also discusses, at length, two controversial pricing mechanisms that can be used to control greenhouse gas emissions, taxes and emissions trading systems. Like a similar joint study between the WTO and ILO on globalization,[65] the joint WTO/UNEP report does not purport to dispense policy advice. Rather it is designed to introduce new concepts and to shift the debate over the relationship between trade and climate change; in the report's own words, its "aim is to promote greater understanding of [the interaction between trade and climate change policies] and to assist policy-makers in this complex policy area."[66]

[63] Drake and Nicolaides, "Ideas, Interests and Institutionalization"; Lang, "Legal Regimes and Professional Knowledges"; Kennedy, *The Dark Side of Virtue*; Kennedy, "Challenging Expert Rule."

[64] See, e.g., WTO, "European Communities – Measures Prohibiting the Importation and Marketing of Seal Products" (November 25, 2013) WT/DS400/R, www.wto.org/english/tratop_e/dispu_e/400_401r_e.pdf; WTO, "Canada – Certain Measures Affecting the Renewable Energy Generation Sector" (May 6, 2013) WT/DS412/AB/R www.wto.org/english/tratop_e/dispu_e/412_426abr_e.pdf; WTO, "United States – Measures Concerning the Importation, Marketing and Sale of Tuna and Tuna Products" (May 16, 2012) WT/DS381/AB/R, www.wto.org/english/tratop_e/dispu_e/381abr_e.pdf.

[65] See, e.g., World Trade Organization and International Labour Organization, *Trade and Employment*.

[66] Ibid.

The WTO/UNEP collaboration was focused upon a relatively well-defined set of issues. Other conceptual interactions address a more diffuse set of issues. Consider, for example, the emerging relationship between the climate change and human rights regimes. For nearly two decades, the climate debate has focused on the nature, causes, and consequences of climate change. However, in recent years a potentially significant effort has been launched by human rights bodies to change the terms of climate discourse. An important element of this strategy is the instigation of multiple interactions between the climate regime and the human rights regime by human rights bodies.

These efforts began in December 2005 when an alliance of Inuit from Canada and the United States filed a petition with the Inter-American Commission on Human Rights. The petition alleged that global warming caused substantially by the United States has negatively impacted the rights of indigenous peoples of the Arctic. The petition exemplifies the "transactional" and litigation-centered approach to regime interactions. In a two-paragraph response in November 2006, the Commission rejected without prejudice the petition, stating that "the information provided does not enable us to determine whether the alleged facts would tend to characterize a violation of the rights protected by the American Declaration [of the Rights and Duties of Man]."[67] Although the Commission eventually held a hearing on the linkages between human rights and climate change in March 2007, the litigation strategy has had little practical impact.

Thereafter, certain parts of the human rights community pursued a different strategy. Specifically, these actors have sought to trigger a series of regime interactions in non-judicial forums. For example, in 2007, the UN Deputy High Commissioner for Human Rights addressed the Bali Conference and urged the need to use a human rights perspective when discussing environmental issues. At roughly the same time, a diverse range of international actors, ranging from the UNDP and the Organization of American States to Oxfam International and Kofi Annan's Global Humanitarian Forum, began to explore the interface between climate change and human rights. In 2008, the Human Rights Council asked the Office of the High Commissioner for Human Rights (OHCHR) to prepare a "detailed analytical study of the relationship between climate change and human rights." In undertaking the study, the OHCHR opened up a

[67] See, e.g., Osofsky, "The Inuit Petition as a Bridge?"; Hohmann, "Igloo as Icon."

dialogue with a variety of other UN bodies, international organizations, national human rights institutes, non-governmental organizations, and academic experts. In January 2009, the OHCHR released a study concluding that climate change interferes with a wide range of human rights and that states have an obligation under international human rights law to protect those rights from the adverse effects of climate change, including in particular through international cooperation.[68]

As a result of these, and other, initiatives, actors from the human rights and climate change regimes have engaged in an extended dialogue and exchange of information. Moreover, the climate/human rights dialogue is now starting to migrate into other fora. For example, the Special Rapporteur on adequate housing has addressed how climate change challenges the right to housing. In August 2012, the UN High Commissioner for Human Rights appointed an Independent Expert on Human Rights and the Environment.[69]

These initiatives are best understood as a successful effort to spark a normative dialogue between the human rights and climate regimes. In the words of a prominent advocate, the goal of this effort is to transform "how climate change is perceived"; to date, climate change "has been viewed as a scientific projection, 'a kind of line graph stretching into the future with abstract measurements based on parts per million, degrees centigrade or centimeters . . . '"[70] But the introduction of "human rights thinking" is intended to change this conceptualization by "supplying a set of internationally agreed values around which policy responses can be negotiated and motivated" and hence "contribute, qualitatively, to the construction of better policy responses at both the national and international level."[71] In short, actors in the human rights community are provoking an ongoing set of conceptual interactions intended to change how we understand the problem of climate change, and therefore the range of appropriate responses.

These efforts also help to highlight the difference between a focus on "transactional" and "relational" regime interactions. The various activities described earlier are not intended to be one-off interactions. Rather,

68 UN Human Rights Council, "Report of the Office of the High Commissioner for Human Rights on the Relationship Between Climate Change and Human Rights" (January 15, 2009) UN Doc A/HRC/10/61.

69 UN Human Rights Council, "Human Rights and the Environment" (April 19, 2012) UN Doc A/HRC/RES/19/10.

70 Limon, "Human Rights and Climate Change," p. 451 (citation omitted).

71 Ibid. at pp. 451–2.

various actors inside the human rights community are attempting to initiate precisely the type of ongoing, iterative relationship between regimes that falls outside the ambit of the transactional model but is at the heart of the relational interactions this paper highlights.

Moreover, the purpose of these relational interactions differs fundamentally from the purposes of transactional interactions. Unlike the litigations at the heart of the transaction model, the interactions between human rights and climate are not intended to settle jurisdictional boundaries, to identify conflicts of law principles, or to privilege or subordinate one norm or another. There is much more going on here than forum shopping or regime shifting; no one involved in these efforts harbors the illusion that human rights bodies will replace the IPCC and UN Framework Convention on Climate Change as the locus of climate debates.

While conceptual interactions between and among regimes no doubt involve the politics of redefinition,[72] it is clear that much more is at stake. The overtures from the human rights regime represent a new way to think about the climate change issue, and a new framework for criticizing or justifying international efforts in this area. The human rights advocates are offering new doctrinal and operational approaches to climate change that focuses on the vulnerable and marginalized. At a more fundamental level, the human rights regime is seeking a conceptual interaction that is ultimately over the conceptualization, or the social meaning, of climate change.

Nature of regime interaction

In addition to distinguishing among the form of regime interaction, it is useful to distinguish among the nature of regime interactions. For current purposes, regime interactions can be characterized as focused on "rationalization," on the "expansion" of jurisdiction or authority, or as "conflictual."

Rationalization

As noted earlier, many regime interactions are triggered by the empirical reality that multiple international bodies exercise authority over the same set of individuals or activities, or address the same issues. For example,

[72] The phrase is borrowed from Koskenniemi, "The Politics of International Law – 20 Years Later."

while the international response to AIDS was slow to develop, by the late 1980s the WHO had developed an active AIDS program and, by the early 1990s, a number of other IOs, including the World Bank, UNDP, and UNICEF, were likewise actively engaged. Donors were soon to complain about the "inefficiency of coordination between different UN agencies," and that "duplication of effort and territorial rivalries threaten to weaken the global response to AIDS."[73] Thus, the original motivation behind UNAIDS was the desire to coordinate disparate international responses, and one of UNAIDS's organizational accomplishments was the negotiation of a "division of labor" among all of the partner agencies.

Similar dynamics can be seen in the area of humanitarian aid. Due to the ad hoc and unpredictable nature of emergencies, international responses were traditionally highly disorganized. In 2005, a UN Emergency Response Coordinator introduced an Agenda for Reform, which eventually led to the formation of groups of organizations organized by "cluster." The WFP is designated lead agency of the "logistics cluster," meaning that it is responsible for coordination, information management, and, where necessary, logistics service provision to ensure effective and efficient logistics response in every operation. In this role, WFP has worked with the WHO, International Organization for Migration, United Nations Relief and Works Agency, and other international organizations in Syria, and facilitated cargo operations on behalf of thirty-two different international organizations in the Philippines in the aftermath of Typhoon Haiyan.

Rationalization logics are also one motivation that drives some regulatory interactions. For example, a key threshold issue in the CITES/FAO regulatory interactions discussed earlier, was who should be the lead agency with respect to protecting marine species, and what, exactly, was the division of labor between the two agencies. In part, this involved a dialogue over the threshold issue of clarifying CITES authority over marine species, and over how most appropriately to utilize FAO's scientific expertise.

Rationalization logics are present in some conceptual interactions as well. For example, the WTO/UNEP report on trade and climate contains analysis of existing and proposed cooperation mechanisms and efforts to strengthen cooperation between "the trade and climate change regimes ... in a mutually supportive manner, within their respective

[73] Knight, *UNAIDS*, p. 20.

spheres of competence."[74] In this context, the WTO Secretary General expressed the view that the issues of competitiveness and technology transfer were better addressed by the climate regime than the WTO.

Expansion

Some regime interactions result in an expansion of the scope of agency operations, even if on topics already within an agency's ambit. On the operational side, the early CITES/WCO interactions provide a good illustration. CITES was centrally concerned with trade in wildlife and understood that customs officials worldwide were a key to effective enforcement. However, while CITES had good relationships with officials in environment ministries, it had little contact with customs officials. The WCO had traditionally been focused on issues like harmonized commodity descriptions and tariff codes. By collaborating together, the two entities were able to expand their operations and elevate wildlife among the myriad forms of contraband that customs officials watch for. The two bodies thereafter worked extensively in developing and applying new technologies that more effectively and efficiently regulate trade in wildlife.

Likewise, in the regulatory context, regime interactions permit international bodies to expand their footprint. For example, the POPs/WHO interactions provide actors from the public health regime direct and ongoing influence in the chemicals regime. The interaction similarly holds the potential to strengthen the environmental regime, in that the POPs Convention may soon more strictly regulate a probable carcinogen.

Some conceptual interactions lead regimes into areas not traditionally considered within their ambit. For example, the WTO, World Intellectual Property Organization (WIPO), and WHO recently released a joint study on "Promoting Access to Medical Technologies: Intersections between public health, intellectual property and trade." Like other conceptual interactions discussed earlier, it does not prescribe how to address particular health problems, but rather examines how to tailor systems to encourage innovation and how to ensure sustainable and equitable access to innovations. The focus on innovation and accessibility pulls each of the three partners outside of its core areas of expertise.

[74] United Nations Environment Programme and the World Trade Organization, *Trade and Climate Change*, p. 83.

Conflictual

As this volume's focus on regime collisions suggests, regime interactions are sometimes conflictual. The early experience of UNAIDS illustrates how this can happen in operational contexts. Under pressure from donors, different international agencies with different views of how best to address the AIDS epidemic were forced to work together, sparking intense debates over how to prioritize and allocate resources. Other times the conflicts preclude any collaboration at all, as happened when the UN Secretary General attempted to get IMO and other bodies to cooperate on flag state implementation of international maritime safety standards.

Regulatory interactions can likewise trigger and/or reproduce regime conflict. By way of example, consider inter-regime efforts to address shipbreaking. A number of legal instruments – all adopted within months of each other – touch on this activity, including IMO Guidelines on Ship Recycling,[75] ILO Guidelines on Safety and Health in Shipbreaking,[76] and Technical Guidelines for the Environmentally Sound Management of the Full and Partial Dismantling of Ships, adopted by the Conference of Parties to the Basel Convention.[77] But this highly fragmented approach quickly raised concerns over regulatory gaps, overlaps, and potential inconsistencies, and the IMO, ILO, and Basel Secretariats formed a Joint Working Group to study the relationship among the various instruments.[78] The three bodies agreed to work on the drafting of a new treaty to be concluded under IMO auspices.

Thereafter, officials from the three organizations were deeply involved in drafting what eventually became the Hong Kong International Convention for the Safe and Environmentally Sound Recycling of Ships. Members of the Joint Working Group were invited to comment on early treaty drafts,[79] the Joint Working Group offered recommendations on provisions to be included in the treaty, and members of the ILO and Basel Convention secretariats attended treaty negotiations. The Hong

[75] IMO, "IMO Guidelines on Ship Recycling" (March 4, 2004) IMO Doc A 23/Res.962, amended by IMO, "Amendment to the IMO Guidelines on Ship Recycling" (December 1, 2005) IMO Doc A 24/Res.980.

[76] 289th Session of the ILO Governing Body.

[77] UNEP, Basel Convention Compilation of Decisions (December 9–13, 2002) Decision VI/24.

[78] See ILO/IMO/BC Working Group on Ship Scrapping, "Report of the Working Group" (February 18, 2005) ILO/IMO/BC WG 1/8, para 3.8.

[79] ILO/IMO/BC Working Group on Ship Scrapping, "Report of the Joint Working Group" (December 14, 2005) ILO/IMO/BC WG 2/11, paras 4.10–4.12.

Kong Convention, adopted in 2009, clearly shows the results of the inter-agency collaboration as it expressly incorporates many of the principles set forth in the documents prepared by the three institutions. For example, the treaty's preamble expressly notes the ILO's and Basel Convention's role respecting ship recycling and cites the instruments already adopted on the topic; the treaty states that it shall not prejudice the rights and obligations of parties under other agreements, which clearly contemplates ILO and Basel instruments; and the Annex creates a process of continuing regime interactions in the promulgation of regulations under the treaty. Although the treaty has not yet entered into force, the ILO and Basel Secretariats have been involved in the development of draft regulations under the treaty.

On the other hand, the process of negotiating the Hong Kong Convention has also given rise to inter-regime controversy. In particular, critics have claimed that the Hong Kong Convention is weaker than the Basel Convention in several respects, including that the Basel Convention covers a broader range of ships and recycling facilities; that the Basel Convention's technical guidelines (like the EU's waste shipment regulation) rejects "beaching" as a dismantlement method, while the question is open under the Hong Kong Convention (at least until the IMO adopts guidelines); and that the enforcement mechanisms under the Basel Convention are functioning relatively well for most wastes, while the practical effectiveness of the Hong Kong Convention's enforcement mechanisms will depend on many factors and are at present unknown.[80] A UN Special Rapporteur on the adverse effects of the movement and dumping of toxic and hazardous products and wastes on the enjoyment of human rights issued a report concluding that the Hong Kong Convention failed to provide a level of control and enforcement equivalent to that established under the Basel Convention.[81]

Against the backdrop of these critiques, the Basel Convention parties commenced an examination of whether the Hong Kong Convention

[80] For an analysis of these, and other differences by the EU, see European Commission, "Communication from the European Commission to the Council" (December 3, 2010) COM(2010) 88 final.

[81] Georgescu, Special Rapporteur on the Adverse Effects of the Movement and Dumping of Toxic and Dangerous Products and Wastes on the Enjoyment of Human Rights, "Preliminary assessment of whether the Hong Kong Convention establishes an equivalent level of control and enforcement as that established under the Basel Convention," www.shipbreakingplatform.org/shipbrea_wp2011/wp-content/uploads/2011/12/UN-special-rapporateur-on-Basel-IMO-conventions-comparison.doc.

rovides "an equivalent level of control and enforcement as that estab-
shed under the Basel Convention."[82] An Open Ended Working Group rovided an assessment to the Conference of the Parties,[83] which ebated the issue at an October 2011 meeting. The discussion revealed sharp split among Basel parties, with the EU, United States, Japan, hina, and others arguing that the Hong Kong Convention provided level of control and enforcement at least equal to the Basel Conven-ion, while other states, including Mexico, Nigeria, for the African roup, and NGOs argued to the contrary. Despite extensive discussion, onsensus could not be reached. The Conference of the Parties adopted decision explicitly noting this ongoing disagreement. The decision lso encourages states to ratify the Hong Kong Convention (suggesting quivalence), but at the same time acknowledged that the Basel onvention Secretariat should continue to assist countries to apply he Basel Convention as it relates to ships (suggesting a lack of quivalence).[84]

As the dispute over the compatibility and equivalence of the Hong ong Convention and Basel Convention suggests, iterative interactions lo not inevitably lead to substantive agreement, and actors from different egimes may continue to view issues through different perspectives lespite ongoing interactions. In the ship-breaking context, the ongoing lisagreement whether the Hong Kong Convention supports or under-nines the Basel Convention has likely contributed to the very low rate of atification – at this point in time, only one state has ratified – and may esult in the Convention never entering into force.

82 Conference of the Parties to the Basel Convention on the Control of Transboundary Movements of Hazardous Wastes and Their Disposal, "Report of the Conference of the Parties to the Basel Convention on the Control of Transboundary Movements of Hazardous Wastes and their Disposal on its Ninth Meeting" (June 27, 2008) UNEP/CHW.9/39, Dec IX/30 on Dismantling of Ships, http://archive.basel.int/meetings/cop/cop9/docs/39e-rep.pdf.

83 Open-ended Working Group of the Basel Convention on the Control of Transboundary Movements of Hazardous Wastes and their Disposal, Cooperation between the Basel Convention and the International Maritime Organization (April 14, 2010) UNEP/CHW/OEWG-7/12, http://archive.basel.int/meetings/oewg/oewg7/docs/12r.pdf.

84 Conference of the Parties to the Basel Convention on the Control of Transboundary Movements of Hazardous Wastes and Their Disposal, "Cooperation between the Basel Convention and the International Maritime Organization" (July 5, 2011) UNEPCHW.10/28/BC-10/17, http://archive.basel.int/meetings/cop/cop10/documents/17e.pdf. The decision also underscored the importance of continued cooperation between the ILO, IMO, and the Basel Convention on the issue of ship recycling.

Looking ahead

It is of course true that international regimes sometimes collide, and the thoughtful contributions to this volume do much to advance our understanding of these phenomena. But, as the aforementioned analysis suggests, it is also true that actors from different international regimes interact in a variety of non-conflictual ways – and that international lawyers who seek to understand the workings of the contemporary international legal order ignore these interactions at their peril.

The analysis and typology of these other interactions developed in this paper can be understood as a prolegomenon to a rich research agenda. While it is not possible to identify all of the different directions that future research might take, as a start future scholarship could explore how institutional design, procedural rules, bureaucratic resources, and discursive practices can facilitate or impede non-conflictual regime interactions. Thus, by way of example, future inquiries might examine issues such as:

Institutional design: International relations scholars have begun to analyze institutional design as a function of the underlying cooperation problem that states seek to solve. These scholars suggest that when states face uncertainty about the behavior of other actors, they create centralized monitoring systems; when they face defection problems, they create enforcement mechanisms, and so forth.[85] But this literature has not examined how institutional design can induce or frustrate regime interactions. The organizations at the heart of most international regimes can be designed with more or less powerful or autonomous secretariats; constituent instruments can expressly require dialogue with other international bodies or not; treaty provisions can expressly address whether norms from one body are hierarchically superior or hierarchically inferior to norms from other regimes; provisions can consciously be designed to incorporate norms from other regimes. Rational design scholars can systematically investigate both the environmental conditions that give rise to use of these design provisions, and to their consequences.

For example, one likely fruitful line of inquiry would explore the institutional mechanisms to address non-compliance. As noted, the WTO has a frequently utilized dispute settlement mechanism. This highly legalized mechanism is designed to depoliticize trade disputes, and resolve them in a rule-based system. Many other international

[85] Koremenos, "Institutionalism and International Law."

bodies, in contrast, adopt much less legalized approaches. For example, in the Montreal Protocol, parties to the ozone regime famously developed a "non-compliance" procedure that adopted a "managerial," as opposed to an "enforcement," approach to non-compliance.[86] Over time, the Montreal Protocol's non-compliance mechanism developed strong working relationships with the GEF, the World Bank, and other international bodies, and these various entities collaborated closely across a range of issues in ways that effectively constituted a system of integrated institutions. As these examples suggest, the design of compliance mechanisms is suggestive of how institutional design features can facilitate or impede regime interactions.

Jurisdictional grants can likewise be viewed through the lens of institutional design. For example, when concerns over the proliferation of international tribunals arose in the late 1990s, a variety of institutional proposals surfaced which sought to place the International Court of Justice (ICJ) more clearly at the apex of a hierarchy of international courts, including proposals authorizing referrals from specialized tribunals to the ICJ, increasing the number of actors empowered to request ICJ advisory opinions, or even granting the ICJ a generalized appellate jurisdiction. Advocates of these ideas invariably argued that such mechanisms would permit the ICJ to address cases involving potentially conflicting norms from different regimes. In light of the analysis presented in this paper, however, one might wish to consider whether proposals to enhance the ICJ's ability to resolve conflicts in international law would act as a complement to, or as a substitute for, the various forms of institutional interactions outlined earlier.

Procedural rules: Likewise, procedural rules can do much to facilitate or impede regime interactions. The WTO considers controversies over food safety standards in at least two different institutional settings, WTO dispute settlement proceedings and the Sanitary and Phytosanitary Standards (SPS) Committee. The SPS Committee provides a forum for consultations about food safety measures, which affect trade and makes decisions by consensus. The SPS Committee has agreed to invite representatives from Codex Alimentarius Commission, Office Internationale des Epizooties, the Secretariat of the International Plant Protection Convention, WHO, UNCTAD, and the International Standards Organization, among other international bodies, to its meetings.

[86] The terminology is drawn from Chayes and Chayes, *The New Sovereignty*.

The decision to invite these representatives has created an institutional structure that encourages precisely the sort of ongoing, constructive inter-regime dialogue highlighted in this paper. Empirical work has shown that disputes considered in the SPS Committee are far more likely to be resolved than are disputes considered in WTO dispute settlement.[87]

Procedural rules can be designed to encourage these forms of interactions. For example, although no such rule currently exists, one could imagine a WTO rule requiring that SPS matters be raised in the SPS Committee as a condition precedent to the initiation of a WTO dispute over an SPS measure. Such an "exhaustion" rule would provide the opportunity for regime interactions in a relational setting that has proven to be effective in advancing mutually beneficial outcomes, and would divert SPS matters from being heard in the dispute settlement system, where cooperative regime interactions are much less likely and which necessarily adopts more of a "transactional" approach to disputes.

Other procedural rules would have more ambiguous effects. Consider, for example, challenges to Australia's plain packaging legislation regarding cigarettes at the WTO. Can WTO panels take account of non-WTO law, such as the WHO's Framework Convention on Tobacco Control (FCTC), which arguably addresses the issue of cigarette packaging? While the issue is perhaps not entirely free from doubt,[88] most agree that the law applicable in WTO proceedings consists solely of WTO law.[89] On the one hand, this approach means that WTO panels would not have jurisdiction to consider whether a relevant conflict exists between FCTC and WTO norms and, if so, which provision takes priority. From one perspective, the WTO's "choice of law" rules can be seen as requiring WTO panels to refrain from opining on potential conflicts of norms. On the other hand, by looking only at WTO law, a panel could more easily find against Australia – setting up a potential conflict between a trade regime antagonistic to plain packaging laws and a public health regime that encourages such laws.

Bureaucratic structures* and *resources: International bureaucrats are central players in the regime interactions detailed earlier. Scholars have already examined the tools international bureaucrats use to create and

[87] Dunoff, "Lotus Eaters." [88] Pauwelyn, *Conflict of Norms in Public International Law.*
[89] Dunoff, "The WTO in Transition."

expand their powers.[90] More recently, attention has been devoted to understanding the role of international bureaucrats in the creation and design of international bodies.[91] But this literature has not investigated the role of international bureaucrats in triggering or avoiding regime interactions. The discussion of FAO/CITES interactions – and of the IMO's reluctance to engage in regime interactions over flag state implementation – illustrate just some of the different positions bureaucrats can adopt. The anecdotal accounts presented earlier can be expanded into a systematic research inquiry.

Bureaucratic resources are, of course, critical to the number and nature of regime interactions. Consider, for example, an international body that wishes to track the work of the WTO. To do so, it would be crucial for that body to have a presence at the meetings of relevant WTO committees. A partial list of the WTO committees that are open to representatives of other international bodies includes the committee on anti-dumping practices, committee on subsidies and countervailing measures, committee on safeguards, committee on agriculture, committee on balance of payments restrictions, committee on regional trade agreements, committee on trade and development, committee on trade and environment, committee on market access, committee on import licensing, committee on rules of origin, committee on technical barriers to trade, committee on trade-related investment measures, committee on trade in financial services, committee on government procurement, and the committee on specific commitments (not to mention a similar number of WTO working groups). As this incomplete list suggests, it would be difficult for all but the most well-resourced and technically adept regimes to be able to send representatives to follow, let alone participate in, the work of these various committees.

To be sure, the brief mention of these issues does nothing more than scratch the surface of a productive research agenda. Related lines of inquiry could explore which factors determine whether any particular interaction will be cooperative or conflictual? What are the power dynamics in play in different types of interactions? Which actors are advantaged, and which disadvantaged, by different types of regime interactions? How much are outcomes a function of the type of problem at issue, and how much are they a function of which regimes are involved?

[90] Barnett and Finnemore, *Rules for the World.* [91] Johnson, *Organizational Progeny.*

Conclusion

In short, in a highly legalized but deeply fragmented international order, it is necessary to understand the "contested collisions" that sometimes arise when regimes overlap and come into contact with one another. The burden of this contribution has been to suggest that it is just as important to understand that not all interactions are collisions, and that regimes interact in a variety of non-conflictual ways. To do so, it has developed an analytic typology that captures a larger universe of regime interactions than scholars usually consider, and has briefly outlined a research agenda designed to advance our understanding of this universe.

Bibliography

Agrawala, S., "Context and Early Origins of the Intergovernmental Panel on Climate Change," *Climatic Change*, 39 (1998), pp. 605–20.

Alter, K. J., and S. Meunier, "The Politics of Regime Complexity," *Perspectives on Politics*, 7 (2009), pp. 13–24.

Barnett, M., and M. Finnemore, *Rules for the World: International Organizations in Global Politics* (Cornell University Press, 2004).

Barnett, M. N., and M. Finnemore, "The Politics, Power and Pathologies of International Organizations," *International Organization*, 53 (1999), pp. 699–732.

Blome, K., and N. Markard, "'Contested Collisions': Conditions for a Successful Collision Management – The Example of Article 16 of the Rome Statute," *Leiden Journal of International Law*, 29 (2016), forthcoming.

Bolin, B., *A History of the Science and Politics of Climate Change: The Role of the Intergovernmental Panel on Climate Change* (Cambridge University Press, 2007).

Broude, T., "Keep Calm and Carry On: Martti Koskenniemi and the Fragmentation of International Law," *Temple International and Comparative Law Journal*, 27 (2013), pp. 279–92.

Chayes, A., and A. Chayes, *The New Sovereignty: Compliance with International Regulatory Agreements* (Harvard University Press, 1996).

Crawford, J., and P. Nevill, "Relations between International Courts and Tribunals: The 'Regime Problem'" in M. Young (ed.), *Regime Interaction in International Law: Facing Fragmentation* (Cambridge University Press, 2012), pp. 235–60.

Drake, W., and K. Nicolaides, "Ideas, Interests and Institutionalization: 'Trade in Services' and the Uruguay Round," *International Organization*, 46 (1992), pp. 37–100.

)unoff, J. L., "Lotus Eaters: Reflections on the *Varietals* Dispute, the SPS Agreement and WTO Dispute Resolution" in G. Berman and P. Mavroidis (eds.), *Trade and Human Health and Safety* (Cambridge University Press, 2006), pp. 153–89.

"The WTO in Transition: Of Constituents, Competence and Coherence," *George Washington International Law Review*, 33 (2001), pp. 979–1013.

"The Death of the Trade Regime," *European Journal of International Law*, 10 (1999), pp. 733–62.

)unoff, J. L., and J. P. Trachtman (eds.), *Ruling the World? Constitutionalism, International Law, and Global Governance* (Cambridge University Press, 2009).

'ischer-Lescano, A., and G. Teubner, "Regime Collisions: The Vain Search for Legal Unity in the Fragmentation of Global Law," *Michigan Journal of International Law*, 25 (2004), pp. 999–1046.

Iarrison, J., *Making the Law of the Sea: A Study in the Development of International Law* (Cambridge University Press, 2013).

Helfer, L. R., "Regime Shifting: The TRIPs Agreement and New Dynamics of International Intellectual Property Lawmaking," *Yale Journal of International Law*, 29 (2004), pp. 1–83.

Hohmann, J., "Igloo as Icon: A Human Rights Approach to Climate Change for the Inuit?" *Transnational Law and Contemporary Problems*, 18 (2009), pp. 295–316.

Howse, R., "From Politics to Technocracy – and Back Again: The Fate of the Multilateral Trading Regime," *American Journal of International Law*, 96 (2002), pp. 94–117.

Jenks, C. W., "The Conflict of Law-Making Treaties," *British Year Book of International Law*, 30 (1953), pp. 401–53.

Jessup, P., *Transnational Law* (Northford, CT: Elliots Books, 1956).

Johnson, T., *Organizational Progeny: Why Governments are Losing Control over the Proliferating Structures of Global Governance* (Oxford University Press, 2014).

Johnson, T. and J. Urpelainen, "A Strategic Theory of Regime Integration and Separation," *International Organization*, 66 (2012), pp. 645–77.

Johnstone, I., "Law-Making Through the Operational Activities of International Organizations," *George Washington International Review*, 40 (2008), pp. 87–122.

Kelly, C. R., "Institutional Alliances and Derivative Legitimacy," *Michigan Journal of International Law*, 29 (2008), pp. 609–64.

Kennedy, D., "Challenging Expert Rule: The Politics of Global Governance," *Sydney Journal of International Law*, 27 (2005), pp. 5–28.

The Dark Side of Virtue: Reassessing International Humanitarianism (Princeton University Press, 2005).

Keohane R. O., and D. Victor, "The Regime Complex for Climate Change," *Perspectives on Politics*, 9 (2011), pp. 7–23.

Klabbers, J., A., Peters and G. Ulfstein, *The Constitutionalization of International Law* (Oxford University Press, 2009).

Knight, L., *UNAIDS; The First 10 Years, 1996–2007* (Geneva: UNAIDS, 2008).

Koremenos, B., "Institutionalism and International Law" in J. Dunoff and M. Pollack (eds.), *Interdisciplinary Perspectives on International Law and International Relations* (Cambridge University Press, 2013), pp. 59–82.

Koskenniemi, M., "The Politics of International Law – 20 Years Later," *European Journal of International Law*, 20 (2009), pp. 7–19.

Koskenniemi, M., and P. Leino, "Fragmentation of International Law? Postmodern Anxieties," *Leiden Journal International Law*, 15 (2002), pp. 553–79.

Krasner, S. D. (ed.), *International Regimes* (Ithaca: Cornell University Press, 1983).

Kratochwil, F., and J. G. Ruggie, "International Organization: A State of the Art on an Art of the State," *International Organization*, 40 (1986), pp. 753–75.

Lang, A. T. F., "Legal Regimes and Professional Knowledges: The Internal Politics of Regime Definition" in M. Young (ed.), *Regime Interaction in International Law: Facing Fragmentation* (Cambridge University Press, 2012), pp. 113–35.

Limon, M., "Human Rights and Climate Change: Constructing a Case for Political Action," *Harvard Environmental Law Review*, 33 (2009), pp. 339–476.

Michaels, R., and J. Pauwelyn, "Conflict of Norms or Conflict of Laws? Different Techniques in the Fragmentation of Public International Law," *Duke Journal of Comparative and International Law*, 22 (2012), pp. 349–76.

Murphy, S. D., "Defragmenting International Law: The Significance of Koskenniemi's 2006 ILC Project," *Temple International and Comparative Law Journal*, 27 (2013), pp. 293–308.

Oberthür, S., and T. Gehring (eds.), *Institutional Interaction in Global Environmental Governance: Synergy and Conflict among International and EU Policies* (Cambridge: MIT Press, 2006).

Osofsky, H., "The Inuit Petition as a Bridge? Beyond Dialectics of Climate Change and Indigenous Peoples' Rights," *American Indian Law Review*, 31 (2006–07), pp. 675–97.

Pauwelyn, J., *Conflict of Norms in Public International Law: How WTO Law Relates to Other Rules of International Law* (Cambridge University Press, 2003).

Raustiala, K., "Institutional Proliferation and the International Legal Order" in J. L. Dunoff and M. A. Pollack (eds.), *Interdisciplinary Perspective on International Law and International Relations: The State of the Art* (Cambridge University Press, 2013), pp. 293–320.

Raustiala K., and D. Victor, "The Regime Complex for Plant Genetic Resources," *International Organization*, 15 (2004), pp. 277–309.

Stokke, O. S., and C. Coffey, "Institutional Interplay and Responsible Fisheries: Combating Subsidies, Developing Precaution" in S. Oberthür and

T. Gehring (eds.), *Institutional Interaction in Global Environmental Governance: Synergy and Conflict among International and EU Policies* (Cambridge: MIT Press 2006), pp. 127–55.

Teubner, G., and P. Korth, "Two Kinds of Legal Pluralism: Collision of Transnational Regimes in the Double Fragmentation of World Society" in M. Young (ed.), *Regime Interaction in International Law: Facing Fragmentation* (Cambridge University Press, 2012), pp. 23–54.

United Nations Environment Programme and World Trade Organization, *Trade and Climate Change* (World Trade Organization, 2009).

World Trade Organization and International Labour Organization, *Trade and Employment: Challenges for Policy Research* (International Labour Office, 2007).

Young, M. A. (ed.), *Regime Interaction in International Law: Facing Fragmentation* (Cambridge University Press, 2012).

Trading Fish, Saving Fish: The Interaction between Regimes in International Law (Cambridge University Press, 2011).

"Protecting Endangered Marine Species: Collaboration Between the Food and Agriculture Organization and the CITES Regime," *Melbourne Journal International Law*, 11 (2010), pp. 441–90.

3

Regime-interplay management

Lessons from environmental policy and law

SEBASTIAN OBERTHÜR

Introduction

This chapter explores the governance of the interface between different international institutions and regimes. In this context, I use the terms 'international institution' and 'international regime' quasi interchangeably. International institutions/regimes are understood as negotiated dynamic sectoral legal systems consisting of sets of rules and practices, including decision-making procedures, that prescribe behavioural roles, constrain activity and shape actors' expectations.[1] The analysis thus zooms in on the relationship between different international regimes, which has become an increasingly prominent topic of investigation in both political science (especially its sub-discipline of International Relations) and international law under headlines such as 'institutional/regime interaction' or 'interplay', 'institutional/regime complexes', 'fragmentation' or 'governance architectures'.[2] The analysis remains limited to the international level ('horizontal interaction') and does not extent to 'vertical interaction' across different levels of governance.[3]

This chapter is based on a broad and relatively comprehensive understanding of 'regime interaction' or 'interplay'. It includes, first, specific

1 See Gehring, *Dynamic International Regimes*; Keohane, 'Neoliberal Institutionalism'.

2 E.g., Biermann, Pattberg, van Asselt, and Zelli, 'The Fragmentation of Global Governance Architectures'; Oberthür and Gehring, *Institutional Interaction in Global Environmental Governance*; Oberthür and Stokke, *Managing Institutional Complexity*; Raustiala and Victor, 'The Regime Complex for Plant Genetic Resources'; M. Young, *Regime Interaction in International Law.*

3 On horizontal and vertical interaction, see Young, *The Institutional Dimensions*, chapters 4 and 5.

action that may be taken within institutions to cooperate with or directly address other institutions. For example, international regimes may pursue 'interlinkages' amongst each other, in particular by advancing cooperation in reporting and implementation.[4] They may also ask each other for assistance, be it in terms of implementation or rule development. This kind of direct interaction involves direct communication between the regimes involved. Beyond that, regime interaction, second, also includes rather indirect inter-institutional influence that materialises at the rule or behavioural implementation levels without direct inter-institutional communication. For example, the World Trade Organization's (WTO) free-trade disciplines may *de facto* affect the ability of other multilateral agreements to devise trade restrictions, and the implementation of one international agreement may well affect the problem area regulated by another one.[5]

Specifically, I aim to explore the status and potential of collective governance of the inter-relationship and interaction between international institutions/regimes, coined as 'interplay management'.[6] Which mechanisms exist to collectively shape institutional interplay and regime complexes? What have these mechanisms of interplay management delivered so far (achievements and limitations)? And how may their potential be further enhanced and more fully exploited?

In the following, I approach these questions by drawing primarily on research conducted in the field of environmental policy and law. Environmental policy and law has indeed been a particularly prominent field of research regarding institutional interaction, regime complexes and interplay management. At the same time, there is reason to suggest that the findings should also be applicable more generally. They are to a large degree based on or linked to general insights on the functioning and operation of international regimes/institutions, which would suggest their relevance for other areas of policy and law. Where generalizability may be more limited because of the specific characteristics of the empirical field, the insights may best inspire further enquiry to investigate the extent to which the picture differs in other areas of policy and law.

[4] E.g., Chambers, *Interlinkages*.

[5] See, also for further examples, Oberthür and Gehring, *Institutional Interaction in Global Environmental Governance*; Gehring and Oberthür, 'The Causal Mechanisms of Interaction'.

[6] Stokke, *The Interplay of International Regimes*; Oberthür, 'Interplay Management'.

I develop my argument in the form of six theses. I thus argue that:

(1) Discussions about conflict and 'collisions' in the fragmented world of international law and politics should be balanced by attention to the potential for synergy.
(2) The fragmented world of international law and institutions is characterized by a significant degree of order.
(3) This order is shaped and advanced by collective interplay management that has become the 'daily bread' of international law makers.
(4) This interplay management is itself shaped and constrained significantly by international power and interests as well as normative mechanisms that privilege status quo forces and path-dependent developments over fundamental change and innovation.
(5) It is in principle possible to devise international (meta-)norms that could significantly strengthen and substantiate the international legal framework of regime interplay, but such an effort may not be politically feasible.
(6) Advances can and have to be made on the basis of the existing interplay management structures that can be developed gradually and incrementally.

Normative conflict is overrated – synergy neglected

Parts of the relevant literature seem to put too much of an emphasis on regime conflicts or collisions when investigating the consequences of an increasingly fragmented international governance and thinking about interplay management, at the cost of the potential for synergy. Much of the existing literature focuses on conflicts and problems. In the field of environmental governance, for example, the largest literature regarding inter-institutional relations has addressed the problematic relationship between multilateral environmental agreements (MEAs) and the WTO.[7] Also beyond environmental governance, it is evident that much of the literature and the predominant part of scientific attention have explored problematic conflicts and 'collisions' arising out of an increasingly fragmented international order.[8]

[7] See Gehring and Oberthür, 'Institutional Interaction', pp. 26–8.

[8] E.g., Wolfrum and Matz, *Conflicts in International Environmental Law*; Fischer-Lescano and Teubner, 'Regime-Collisions'; see also Blome and Markard, 'Contested Collisions'.

In contrast, available empirical research – that is still limited – suggests that synergy may be a more frequent result of institutional overlap than conflict. Systematic explorations of phenomena of regime interaction that do not have an *ex ante* selection bias focusing on conflict remain rare. One existing study of more than 160 cases of inter-institutional influence in global environmental governance found that a majority of these cases resulted in synergy, whereas only about a quarter resulted in disruption. To be sure, the field studied may not be representative of international law and politics in general. Also, these numbers are based on the numbers of instances of inter-institutional influence without weighing the seriousness of the effects observed. However, they provide an indication that synergy may actually be more prominent than is usually assumed in studies focusing on conflict and collisions.[9]

This indication correlates with the potential for positive effects of fragmented governance structures that has been highlighted in the growing literature on 'regime complexes'. Thus, Robert Keohane and David Victor have argued that a regime complex – understood as a loosely coupled set of regimes – can have a particular governance potential (and may, under certain conditions, be preferable to a comprehensive, unified regime).[10] In a similar vein, the late Elinor Ostrom argued that a polycentric, complex, and multilevel governance structure might best fit complex and multilevel problem structures.[11] The emerging discussion about the 'orchestration' of and by institutions in global governance hits a related cord, as it implies that complexes of institutions and actors can be coordinated so as to contribute to governance in a complementary way.[12]

These findings and debates face an uphill battle, however, including when it comes to political attention. The aforementioned empirical study of institutional interaction in global environmental governance also found that policy-making was much more likely to respond to conflictive than to synergistic cases, irrespective of the potential to enhance such synergistic effects.[13] That people generally react more strongly to the risk of losses entailed in conflict than to the possibility of additional benefits[14]

9 See Gehring and Oberthür, 'Comparative Empirical Analysis', pp. 316–21.
10 Keohane and Victor, 'The Regime Complex for Climate Change'.
11 Ostrom, 'A Polycentric Approach'.
12 Abbott, Genschel, Snidal, and Zangl, *International Organizations as Orchestrators*.
13 Gehring and Oberthür, 'Comparative Empirical Analysis', pp. 321–5; see also Johnson and Urpelainen, 'A Strategic Theory'.
14 Tversky and Kahnemann, 'The Framing of Decision' and 'Choices, Values, and Frames'.

may help us explain and understand the higher political salience of problematic cases, but it cannot serve to justify the neglect of the synergistic potential of institutional overlap.

The overall lesson from these findings is that (1) we should not equate fragmentation of governance regimes with conflict and dysfunctionality, and (2) when thinking about political management of such fragmentation, we should not only consider how to prevent and address conflict but also how to enhance synergies.[15]

There is a significant degree of order in the fragmented world of international law and institutions

When thinking about regime-interplay management, we should also not start from the false pretence that the fragmentation of international governance automatically means chaos or disorder. Fragmentation in this context means the existence of a large and, in the process dimension of the term, increasing amount of formally unconnected, non-hierarchical and differentiated governance institutions. Such fragmentation may, especially where it is considered problematic, easily be equated with a lack of order and the occurrence of regime collisions and conflicts resulting in heightened regulatory uncertainty. However, the existence of a 'patchwork'[16] of institutions does not necessarily mean that the components or fragments would need to relate to each other without order or that they would need to collide and create uncertainty. While it can hardly be denied that these dangers exist, multiple parts can still be arranged to form an order and can complement each other rather than collide.[17]

There are some reasons to assume that the fragmentation of international governance and law as a process follows systematic patterns and results in a systematically patterned 'patchwork'. In a social systems perspective, the fragmentation of international law and governance may reflect, and be the result of, broader dynamics of more general processes of functional differentiation. As such, fragmentation is not

[15] See also Dunoff in this volume.

[16] Biermann, Pattberg, van Asselt, and Zelli, 'The Fragmentation of Global Governance Architectures', p. 16.

[17] See e.g. discussion in Biermann, Pattberg, van Asselt, and Zelli, 'The Fragmentation of Global Governance Architectures', pp. 15–21.

chaotic but a process that follows a social and systemic logic. In particular, it results from competing societal rationalities of different subsystems and the interests and power structures underlying them, which drive a process of ever-deeper differentiation. The resulting fragmented structures are an expression of this differentiation process and thus reflect its logic.[18] In this logic of differentiation, it may be considered consequential that collisions of the emerging subsystems or fragments are not lasting and will rarely erupt into open conflict as this might endanger and question the continuation of the process of differentiation. Instead, differentiation entails a logic of emerging complementarity and divisions of labour.[19]

In line with such a logic, existing research on global environmental governance suggests that the relationship between different overlapping regimes may best be understood as an inter-institutional equilibrium that, over time, forms and deepens specific divisions of labour. Any inter-institutional disorder is not lasting. For example, the problematic relationship between MEAs and the WTO referred to earlier has in several steps developed into a division of labour in which the WTO and MEAs fulfil different and largely complementary functions (despite the persistence of the underlying societal conflict). Whereas the WTO defines the general parameters of exemptions from free trade disciplines for environmental purposes, MEAs define the concrete form of environmental trade restrictions within the confines of WTO law.[20] In Arctic governance, different governance functions (knowledge creation, regulation, capacity building, etc.) are distributed among various institutions around the Arctic Council.[21] In the governance of access to and benefit-sharing from genetic resources, the Convention on Biological Diversity (CBD) and its 2010 Nagoya Protocol on Access to Genetic Resources and the Fair and Equitable Sharing of Benefits Arising from their Utilization have a general and central role that has been complemented by sectorally specialised regimes that are recognised by the central CBD/Nagoya Protocol on the condition that they are in line with its objectives. In this regime complex, a latent conflict with international intellectual property rights (IPRs) protected under the WTO remains unmitigated with a

[18] Fischer-Lescano and Teubner, 'Regime-Collisions'; Buzan and Albert, 'Differentiation'.
[19] Buzan and Albert, 'Differentiation'.
[20] Gehring, 'The Institutional Complex of Trade and Environment'.
[21] Stokke, 'Interplay Management, Niche Selection'; Humrich, 'Fragmented International Governance'.

fragile division of labour between the CBD in charge of access and benefit-sharing regulation and the WTO regulating trade-related IPRs.[22]

This is not to say that all would be idyllic in fragmented governance architectures and that all underlying *societal* conflicts would have been resolved. These societal conflicts remain very much virulent. The aforementioned tensions between free trade and environmental protection or between the international protection of intellectual property and the striving for economic development by developing countries have persisted alongside many others. They arise from 'clashes of rationalities' and tensions immanent in competing objectives pursued in different policy domains.[23] It might even to some extent be naïve to think that international institutions built around these competing rationalities could themselves resolve the underlying societal conflicts at all levels.

Even with societal conflict and contestation continuing, the point here is that, in most (if not all) cases, a relatively stable balance or equilibrium between the underlying competing objectives is enshrined in the relevant international governance architecture. While the existing inter-institutional equilibria may not be socially unproblematic or uncontested, they have significantly contained the underlying conflicts *for the purposes of the relationship between the relevant international regimes*. Few inter-regime conflicts have become 'manifest', most have stayed 'latent'[24] – not least as a result of the emergence of inter-institutional divisions of labour reflecting a relatively stable balance between the regimes involved. Many of the most serious regime 'conflicts' rooted in widely diverging institutional policy objectives have thereby over time been significantly diffused for the purposes of international regimes so that states do not have to choose between abiding by one or the other. Even where this equilibrium is rudimentary, the search for inter-institutional order does therefore not start from a clean slate. As a result, 'solving' perceived problems arising from the aforementioned clashes of rationalities does not entail *creating* order, but *changing* or *deepening* it. This finding is not trivial but has consequences for the prospects of further regime-interplay management, as further discussed later.

This bears asking why fragmented governance architectures would tend to form relatively stable inter-institutional equilibria and divisions of labour. Interestingly, it is the aforementioned danger of disorder,

22 Oberthür and Pozarowska, 'Managing Institutional Complexity'.
23 Fischer-Lescano and Teubner, 'Regime-Collisions', especially pp. 1005–7.
24 On the distinction, see Zelli, 'Regime Conflicts', pp. 200–2.

conflicts and regulatory uncertainty between legal systems that points to the likely most convincing response. Where actors belong to both/all institutions involved, they share an interest in preventing incompatible commitments that would force them to choose between complying with one or the other institution. Such incompatible commitments would not only undermine actors' credibility as consistent and reliable international partners,[25] but it would also erode cooperative gains of all institutions involved. Actors may differ in their preferences as to the accommodation of two or more institutions, but as members of these institutions they have an interest in avoiding inconsistencies that may jeopardise related cooperation gains, including in the institution more highly valued by them. In addition, Jean-Frédéric Morin and Amandine Orsini have argued that feedback effects between the international and national levels support augmented inter-regime integration over time (while incentivising increased policy coherence nationally).[26] All this is not to say that actors could or would not at times stoke inter-institutional conflict and create 'strategic inconsistency'[27] to pursue their policy goals and influence the inter-institutional equilibrium. However, there are strong forces driving actors towards accommodating different international sectoral legal systems even where their objectives diverge substantially – forces that significantly temper and counterbalance actors' interest in fuelling inter-institutional conflict.[28]

The inter-institutional order is significantly shaped and governed by collective interplay management

Interplay management refers to deliberate efforts by relevant actors to address and improve institutional interaction and its effects, usually in pursuit of collective objectives as enshrined in the institutions in question. Whereas inter-institutional influence may occur 'behind the backs' of the actors involved, interplay management requires that actors are aware of and reflect upon this inter-institutional influence. In short, interplay management thus refers to the governance of inter-institutional relations and influence.[29]

25 See Keohane, *After Hegemony*.
26 Morin and Orsini, 'Regime Complexity and Policy Coherency'.
27 Raustiala and Victor, 'The Regime Complex', p. 301.
28 Oberthür and Stokke, 'Conclusions', pp. 326–31; Gehring and Oberthür, 'The Causal Mechanisms'.
29 See, also for the following, Oberthür, 'Interplay Management', pp. 373–8.

We can distinguish three levels of collective interplay management. At the first and highest level, interplay management could rely on overarching institutional and legal frameworks, which requires decision-making beyond the interacting institutions. Given the absence of a world government, such overarching interplay management could occur through sectoral institutions such as specialised international organisations and programmes, the United Nations at large or general rules of international law, as for example reflected in the 1969 Vienna Convention on the Law of Treaties. Overarching interplay management has so far played a rather secondary role.[30]

Second, interplay management can be based on targeted efforts to coordinate the activities of the specific institutions involved, possibly including the creation of joint rules governing their specific relationship. Such 'joint interplay management' involves the conscious creation of horizontal structures for coordination between formally independent sectoral regimes. Some efforts at such coordination have been made in global environmental governance.[31] However, their effectiveness has remained limited. In particular, there is limited prospect that coordination without the shadow of hierarchy could effectively address tensions between different regimes that are rooted in diverging objectives.

The central place of the governance of inter-institutional relations has so far been the 'unilateral interplay management' by the individual institutions involved through their independent action and decision-making. It is the formally independent decisions in individual institutions that shape the relationship with other institutions and thus bring about conflict or synergy with them in the first place. Thus, the conflict between MEAs and the world trade system emerged when members of some MEAs (prominently, the 1987 Montreal Protocol on Substances That Deplete the Ozone Layer) decided to employ trade restrictions to implement and enforce their institution's environmental objectives.[32] Similarly, the aforementioned tension between the international IPR system regulated under the WTO (and the World Intellectual Property Organization, WIPO) and benefit-sharing pursued under the CBD and its Nagoya Protocol emanates from their respective decisions: While the

[30] See also discussion at notes 53 to 55.

[31] See e.g., Chambers, *Interlinkages*; van Asselt *The Fragmentation of Global Climate Governance*.

[32] Gehring, 'The Institutional Complex of Trade and Environment'.

WTO and WIPO grant IPR protection according to general criteria, the CBD and its Nagoya Protocol have passed regulations to ensure benefit-sharing from the use of genetic resources with the providers of these resources.[33] The inter-institutional equilibria have subsequently also been further developed and formed through unilateral decisions within each of the institutions involved. The claim of MEAs regarding environmentally motivated trade restrictions has subsequently been accepted and curtailed especially through decisions of the dispute settlement mechanism within the WTO.[34] As regards the governance of genetic resources, the relationship between the CBD system and other relevant international institutions has been significantly further developed through the 2010 Nagoya Protocol.[35]

Both the original decisions establishing the conflictive (or synergistic) inter-institutional relationship and the subsequent decision-making can be understood as interplay management. As mentioned earlier, in order to qualify as interplay management these decisions must have been pursued with the awareness of their inter-institutional effects and, at least in part, in order to shape these effects. As this eventually is an empirical question, it is beyond the scope of this article to investigate conclusively to what extent relevant decisions thus amount to interplay management. However, it may be instructive to note that even some of the earlier cases of inter-institutional tension display elements of such interplay management in their emergence. For example, MEAs consciously designed their environmentally motivated trade restrictions in a way that would minimise the potential for conflict with the world trade system (e.g., minimising discrimination by exempting non-parties that implement equivalent measures).[36] With the increasing proliferation of international institutions and the growing awareness of their interlinkages, decision-makers have since become increasingly aware of inter-institutional effects and conscious 'unilateral' interplay management has become the 'daily bread' of institutional decision-making. The relationship with other international organisations/institutions has become a standard agenda item for most/many international forums and is explored in some depth for most relevant

33 Rosendal, 'The Convention on Biological Diversity'.

34 Gehring, 'The Institutional Complex of Trade and Environment'.

35 Oberthür and Pozarowska, 'The Impact of the Nagoya Protocol'.

36 Gehring 'The Institutional Complex of Trade and Environment', pp. 235–8; see also Eckersley, 'The Big Chill'.

decisions. In the case of the 2010 Nagoya Protocol, it was even one of the major issues in the negotiations.[37]

It follows that the governance of regime complexes and inter-institutional relations can and does occur in clearly identifiable political arenas that allow allocation of political responsibility and accountability. Admittedly, there is no dedicated forum to address institutional interaction as such (overarching interplay management) so that the nevertheless emerging inter-institutional order may be considered to arise 'spontaneously' from collective but independent action within and by the elemental institutions of a regime complex.[38] However, this order and its effects do not emerge from the proverbial 'invisible hand'; the number of relevant institutions is generally not (yet) so high that the effects of the decisions taken within them on the overall inter-institutional relationship could not be anticipated. In contrast to what a purely 'spontaneous' order might lead us to suggest, regime complexes thus do possess forums for the purposeful and deliberate collective governance of their inter-institutional relationships and the resulting effects: the elemental institutions of the complex. This includes the possibility of direct communication between relevant institutions, for example by one institution requesting assistance from another one.[39] Overall, it is thus possible to allocate political responsibility for the management of inter-institutional relations to the members of, and the decision-makers within, the elemental institutions who can be held accountable.

A further relevant distinction refers to two ideal-typical principal modes of interplay management that can be labelled 'regulatory' and 'enabling'. Regulatory interplay management focuses on prescribing, proscribing or permitting certain behaviour, ascribing regulatory authority as well as implementing and enforcing measures. It can be both substantive and procedural. The creation of meta-norms governing regime interplay may qualify as regulatory interplay management. Enabling interplay management employs cognitive elements (communication, information, knowledge) and the allocation of resources, aiming at inter-institutional learning and capacity building. It may thus be considered a 'softer', non-hierarchical governance type. Both principal interplay management modes are not mutually exclusive, but can generally work in tandem. For example, regulatory instruments may be employed to

[37] Wallbott, Wolff and Pożarowska, 'The Negotiations of the Nagoya Protocol'.
[38] Gehring and Faude, 'The Dynamics of Regime Complexes'.
[39] Gehring and Oberthür, 'The Causal Mechanisms', pp. 134–5.

advance inter-institutional learning and exchange of information. However, enabling interplay management alone may have a limited potential in the case of inter-institutional conflict and collision that result from divergent institutional objectives. Effectively addressing such conflict or collision may require regulatory delimitation.[40]

Interplay management is constrained so that radical change of and innovation in inter-institutional orders faces an uphill struggle

Whereas collective governance of inter-institutional relations is thus possible and is indeed happening, its structures are such that fundamental change of existing equilibria is unlikely and innovation difficult due to strong status-quo forces. Two such forces deserve particular mentioning here: (1) the international constellation of power and interests against the backdrop of prevailing consensus decision-making in international institutions and (2) the commitments that members of existing institutions have engaged, which limit the room for manoeuvre. Whereas the former is common to international decision-making in general, the latter strengthens the status quo forces in particular in decision-making on inter-institutional relations (i.e., interplay management).

Decision-making within international institutions in general does not facilitate change. It may be considered to be to a large extent driven by interests and the distribution of power of relevant actors (as perceived, constructed and reproduced by these actors). Change requires significant members of an institution to be dissatisfied with the status quo and to advocate change. In addition, it requires that such advocates of change build a winning coalition of sufficiently powerful and influential actors that can overcome the resistance of 'veto players'. The international constellation of interests and power is further mediated by decision-making rules. The default decision-making rule in multilateral forums is consensus, which tends to empower status quo interests (although significant exceptions from consensus decision-making do exist[41]). Multilateral decision-making thus usually (save for the exceptions) establishes a high hurdle for institutional change in general, including

[40] See Oberthür, 'Interplay Management', pp. 377–81.

[41] On the repertoire of how to overcome the lowest-common denominator rule in international environmental decision-making, see, as a classic, Sand, *Lessons Learned*; also Gehring, *Dynamic International Regimes*.

through interplay management. Overall, these factors already make changing existing inter-institutional equilibria a challenging and demanding endeavour.[42]

In the particular case of inter-institutional orders and divisions of labour, the commitments of parties under the institutions involved frequently even further strengthen the status quo forces, however. Where change would require escalating inter-institutional conflict and challenging the turf of an existing institution, parties face a significant disincentive to engage in such an escalation if they are member to both/all institutions implicated. As mentioned earlier, in this case they share an interest in avoiding serious rule collisions that would make it impossible for them to honour existing commitments. Status quo forces may be less pronounced in the case of complementary international regimes, but are still strong because of the energy and initiative required to question the status quo.[43]

Under these circumstances, fundamental change faces important impediments and path dependence is privileged in inter-institutional relations. Existing, incumbent institutions and commitments possess a 'first-mover advantage' so that path-dependent developments (e.g., the deepening of an existing inter-institutional division of labour or the incorporation of new concerns into existing institutional logics) may trump more fundamental change.[44] The inroads MEAs were able to make into free-trade doctrine regarding environmentally motivated trade restrictions were thus limited by the first-mover advantage of the WTO that limited the room for manoeuvre of MEAs.[45] It has thus been argued that the inertia inherent in institutional complexes may lead to a pattern of 'punctuated equilibrium' in which far-reaching changes are rare and involve moving between relatively stable balances.[46]

Interests that are not reflected by and not involved in existing institutions may thus have to create their own institutions in order to make themselves heard. New societal concerns may face serious difficulties in being reflected, in particular if and when they (appear to) collide with existing institutionalised commitments, as in the aforementioned case of MEAs and the WTO. The story of the creation of the International

[42] See Oberthür and Pozarowska, 'Managing Institutional Complexity and Fragmentation'.
[43] See Oberthür and Stokke, 'Conclusions', pp. 331–4.
[44] Oberthür and Pozarowska, 'Managing Institutional Complexity and Fragmentation'.
[45] See, for example, Eckersley, 'The Big Chill'.
[46] Colgan, Keohane and Van de Graaf, 'Punctuated Equilibrium'; see also Young, *Institutional Dynamics*, p. 10 and pp. 53–82.

Renewable Energy Agency next to the incumbent International Energy Agency provides an example of the establishment of a new institution that complemented rather than competed with existing institutions and served to give newly emerging renewable energy interests their own forum and voice.[47] Interests outside the existing patchwork of institutions have few options in addition to creating their own institution, thus fuelling functional differentiation through fragmentation.[48]

The evolution of the division of labour between MEAs and the WTO also demonstrates that adaptations can nevertheless be significant – but we should also be careful not to overlook the special circumstances of the case that facilitated the achievements. The inroads MEAs were able to make were comparatively far-reaching, as MEAs were, as already noted, able to carve out authority to define environmental trade restrictions within the confines of WTO law. In analysing the broader relevance of this achievement, we should not forget the rather special facilitative circumstances. First of all, environmental protection constituted a particularly prominent, broad and strong new societal concern so that completely neglecting it in the WTO context could have (further) undermined the legitimacy of the WTO. Furthermore, adaptations within the WTO could occur through its dispute settlement mechanism, so that one of the major impediments of change, namely political consensus decision-making, was circumvented and did not determine the outcome.[49] Although the institutional evolution of a regime complex may be somewhat easier to achieve in the case of complementary developments, the example of MEAs and the WTO may thus have exceptional features that confirm the general rule that achieving far-reaching change faces high hurdles.

Relevant international legal norms could be developed significantly in order to provide more substantive guidance to ongoing interplay management (including the balancing of competing objectives)

The current international legal framework of regime interplay remains sharply limited and may best be understood as framing, but not guiding, the largely political process of interplay management. A few meta-norms

[47] Van de Graaf, 'Fragmentation in Global Energy Governance'.

[48] This mechanism can be understood as one of the drivers of fragmentation as an expression of 'an accelerated differentiation of society into autonomous social systems'; see Fischer-Lescano and Teubner, 'Regime-Collisions', p. 1006.

[49] Gehring, 'The Institutional Complex of Trade and Environment'.

exist in the form of priority rules, including *lex superior*, *lex posterior* and *lex specialis*. However, these only address the issue of norm collision, while failing to cover other areas of interplay management aiming at enhancing synergy. *Lex posterior* and *lex specialis* remain formal-procedural with very limited value for the settling of specific cases because it is not necessarily clear-cut which rule or law was earlier or is more specialised. Because of the limited amount of normative hierarchy in international law, *lex superior* bears very limited relevance in practice. Most importantly, however, the capacity of the international legal system to authoritatively apply these priority rules to particular cases remains low in the absence of a judiciary or other central institution with related authority. As a result, the aforementioned rules mainly serve as an ingredient in the political debate on normative priorities that informs decisions in individual institutions affecting inter-institutional relations ('unilateral interplay management', whether taking the form of treaty interpretation or treaty design, including possible conflict clauses).[50]

Other forms of interplay management within and between international institutions have so far proceeded with little guidance by general international law. Harro van Asselt discusses a number of institutional coordination activities, especially entailing exchange of information, the establishment of inter-institutional coordination mechanisms, joint programming of implementation activities and the like. These coordination activities can be more or less formalised (e.g., through inter-institutional memoranda), but are generally pursued without much resort to legal means.[51] These activities generally appear to advance interplay management in its enabling mode. This mode has so far primarily been advanced on a case-by-case basis, but has hardly been addressed or even promoted in substance in general public international law.[52]

There is scope for further developments and strengthened international legal interplay management. For example, as regards the environment, I have argued elsewhere that: (1) competent international secretariats or experts could be mandated to collect relevant information in proper assessments and to feed it into political decision-making in order to more systematically support inter-institutional learning; (2) international institutions could be instructed to provide, to the extent

[50] See the discussion of legal techniques of interplay management in van Asselt, 'The Fragmentation of Global Climate Governance', pp. 62–71 and 137–41.

[51] See van Asselt, 'The Fragmentation of Global Climate Governance', pp. 71–8.

[52] See Oberthür, 'Interplay Management'.

ossible, assistance to environmental institutions; (3) such institutions ould also be required to base their relevant decisions on environmental npact assessments and to consult with competent environmental instiutions prior to taking relevant decisions; and (4) international instiutions could in general be required to respect certain core objectives nshrined in environmental institutions.[53] Similar substantive rules could robably be elaborated for other crosscutting policy areas (and may ventually require a weighing exercise itself).

Since establishing such substantive guidance in a centralised or hierrchical way may not be feasible, it could in principle be incorporated n a decentralised way in the statutes of relevant international institu-ions. The chances of establishing such general meta-norms in overarch-ng international legal instruments such as the Vienna Convention on he Law of Treaties or the UN Charter, a decision of the UN General ssembly and/or the UN Security Council may be considered low.[54] ttempting to change the UN Charter or the Vienna Convention on he Law of Treaties for this purpose may equal opening Pandora's box. It nay also be questionable whether the issue possesses sufficient political alience to be addressed in a comprehensive way by bodies such as the JN General Assembly or the UN Security Council. Under the circum-tances, the most realistic way of strengthening interplay management nay thus be through incrementally developing the norms and practices of relevant international regimes.[55]

Conclusion: advances can and have to be made on the basis of current interplay management structures

Since fundamental/radical change is notoriously difficult to achieve in the world of international law and institutions, regime-interplay management will in all likelihood have to build on the existing structures. Immanent in this finding is the positive message that interplay management does not need to be developed from scratch but can indeed build on existing structures, instruments and mechanisms (and an increasing knowledge about their operation). The decision-making bodies and bureaucracies/secretariats of existing institutions can be used to pursue 'unilateral interplay management' within individual institutions and to

[53] Ibid. [54] Ibid.

[55] For a similar result, see Fischer-Lescano and Teubner, 'Regime-Collisions', especially pp. 1022 and 1037.

engage in and advance 'joint interplay management' (involving coordination between institutions) where feasible and advantageous. So-called 'bridge' or 'boundary institutions' may specifically focus on linking and coordinating other institutions. In this way, concrete cases of inter-regime conflict can be addressed and the exploitation of potential for inter-regime synergy be promoted. We thus do not need to wait for major reform before we can start making progress in shaping inter-institutional relations and regime complexes or governance architectures.

What are the main strengths and weaknesses of the existing system of interplay management and what are the major needs for strengthening this system? On the positive side, as argued earlier, the existing system of governing inter-institutional relations has been reasonably successful in managing, containing and diffusing inter-regime conflict and collision so that manifest conflict has remained the exception. On the more problematic side, interplay management has not only been unable to dissolve latent conflict and underlying societal tensions, but the system has also displayed little capability to reap and enhance inter-institutional synergy. With respect to both synergy and conflict, there is also scope for addressing inter-institutional relations more systematically, rather than on an ad-hoc basis, in relevant political forums. It can also be noted that the emergence of (accepted) inter-institutional divisions of labour has at times taken significant amounts of time. For example, the aforementioned 'interlocking governance structure' between the WTO and MEAs has taken more than a decade to mature. The resulting divisions of labour have been closely related to existing constellations of power and interest with an in-built status quo bias. As a result, some actors may have been left aggrieved so that underlying value conflicts remain virulent.

Interplay management may contribute to addressing the underlying societal issues, but can hardly be expected to fully resolve them. After all, this management as conceived of here only addresses one level, the international level, in the more complex system of multi-level governance. Tensions between economic development and environmental objectives have a much broader and wider reach than the conflict between the WTO and MEAs that is at stake as regards the management of the trade-environment interface at the international level. They involve a broader set of issues and other levels of governance. As such, it may be unrealistic or even naïve to expect the management of the interplay of relevant international institutions to be able to settle this conflict or even only the tension between trade and the environment, which is embedded in this broader conflict. It may be more appropriate to expect interplay management to contain and defuse the relevant international tensions at stake and to contribute its share to addressing the broader underlying societal conflict.

To this end, developing regime-interplay management incrementally and bottom up in individual institutions, as outlined, may over time bring about broader normative change. Solutions found in such a decentralised way for specific issues of regime interaction – that also allows for experimentation – can create important precedents for addressing issues of a similar type on other occasions.[56] These precedents can, once diffusing more broadly, constitute (best) practice and become customary rules with broader normative force. International secretariats and organisations can facilitate such norm diffusion by spreading knowledge on such evolving best practice. For example, the UN Environment Programme is already mandated to facilitate/promote coherence within the environment field. In this way, some of the aforementioned potential for a further development of legal interplay management might be incrementally realised and normative change initiated step by step.[57]

Such normative change growing from evolving practice may pave the way to a more explicit codification of related meta-norms. Such meta-norms hold the promise of a systematic approach to managing inter-institutional conflict and synergy, but their codification seems hardly feasible at present. The diffusion of best practice that over time turns into a soft normative standard may allow for experience to grow and may eventually facilitate the design of explicit meta-norms that capture, systematise and advance this best practice.

References

Abbott, K. W., P. Genschel, D. Snidal, and B. Zangl (eds.), *International Organizations as Orchestrators* (Cambridge University Press, 2015).

Axelrod, M., 'Savings Clauses and the "Chilling Effect": Regime Interplay as Constraints on International Govenance' in S. Oberthür and O. S. Stokke (eds.), *Managing Institutional Complexity. Regime Interplay and Global Environmental Change* (Cambridge, MA: MIT Press, 2011), pp. 87–114.

[56] For example, Mark Axelrod has shown that so-called savings clauses explicitly countering the *lex posterior* rule have become a quite general practice in international environmental law; Axelrod, 'Savings Clauses'.

[57] See text accompanying note 53.

Blome, K., and N. Markard, '"Contested Collisions": Conditions for a Successful Collision Management – The Example of Article 16 of the Rome Statute', *Leiden Journal of International Law*, Available on CJO 2015 doi:10.1017/S0922156515000783.

Biermann, F., P. Pattberg, H. van Asselt, and F. Zelli, 'The Fragmentation of Global Governance Architectures: A Framework for Analysis', *Global Environmental Politics*, 9 (2009) (4), pp. 14–40.

Buzan, B., and M. Albert, 'Differentiation: A Sociological Approach to International Relations Theory', *European Journal of International Relations*, 16 (2010), pp. 315–37.

Chambers, W. B., *Interlinkages and the Effectiveness of Multilateral Environmental Agreements* (Tokyo: United Nations University Press, 2008).

Colgan, J. D., R. O. Keohane, and T. Van de Graaf, 'Punctuated Equilibrium in the Energy Regime Complex', *The Review of International Organizations*, 7 (2012), pp. 117–43.

Eckersley, R., 'The Big Chill: The WTO and Multilateral Environmental Agreements', *Global Environmental Politics*, 4 (2004) 2, pp. 24–50.

Fischer-Lescano, A., and G. Teubner, 'Regime-Collisions: The Vain Search for Legal Unity in the Fragmentation of Global Law', *Michigan Journal of International Law*, 25 (2004), pp. 999–1046.

Gehring, T., *Dynamic International Regimes. Institutions for International Environmental Governance* (Frankfurt: Peter Lang, 2004).

'The Institutional Complex of Trade and Environment: Toward an Interlocking Governance Structure and a Division of Labor' in S. Oberthür and O. S. Stokke (eds.), *Managing Institutional Complexity. Regime Interplay and Global Environmental Change* (Cambridge, MA: MIT Press, 2011), pp. 227–54.

Gehring, T., and B. Faude, 'The Dynamics of Regime Complexes: Microfoundations and Systemic Effects', *Global Governance: A Review of Multilateralism and International Organizations*, 19 (2013), pp. 119–30.

Gehring, T., and S. Oberthür, 'Comparative Empirical Analysis and Ideal Types of Institutional Interaction' in S. Oberthür and T. Gehring (eds.), *Institutional Interaction in Global Environmental Governance. Synergy and Conflict among International and EU Policies* (Cambridge, MA: MIT Press 2006), pp. 307–71.

'The Causal Mechanisms of Interaction between International Institutions', *European Journal of International Relations*, 15 (2009), pp. 125–56.

'Institutional Interaction: Ten Years of Scholarly Development' in S. Oberthür and O. S. Stokke (eds.), *Managing Institutional Complexity. Regime Interplay and Global Environmental Change* (Cambridge, MA: MIT Press, 2011), pp. 25–58.

Humrich, C., 'Fragmented International Governance of Arctic Offshore Oil: Governance Challenges and Institutional Improvement', *Global Environmental Politics*, 13 (2013), pp. 79–99.

Johnson, T., and J. Urpelainen, 'A Strategic Theory of Regime Integration and Separation', *International Organization*, 66 (2012), pp. 645–77.

Keohane, R. O., *After Hegemony: Cooperation and Discord in the World Political Economy* (Princeton University Press, 1984).

'Neoliberal Institutionalism: A Perspective on World Politics' in R. O. Keohane (ed.), *International Institutions and State Power: Essays in International Relations Theory* (Boulder, Col.: Westview, 1989), pp. 1–20.

Keohane, R. O., and D. G. Victor, 'The Regime Complex for Climate Change', *Perspectives on Politics*, 9 (2011), pp. 7–23.

Morin, J.-F., and A. Orsini, 'Regime Complexity and Policy Coherency: Introducing a Co-adjustments Model', *Global Governance: A Review of Multilateralism and International Organizations*, 19 (2013), pp. 41–51.

Oberthür, S., 'Interplay Management: Enhancing Environmental Policy Integration among International Institutions', *International Environmental Agreements: Politics, Law and Economics*, 9 (2009), pp. 371–91.

Oberthür, S. and T. Gehring (eds.), *Institutional Interaction in Global Environmental Governance. Synergy and Conflict among International and EU Policies* (Cambridge, MA: MIT Press, 2006).

Oberthür, S., and O. S. Stokke, 'Conclusions: Decentralized Interplay Management in an Evolving Interinstitutional Order' in S. Oberthür and O. S. Stokke (eds.), *Managing Institutional Complexity. Regime Interplay and Global Environmental Change* (Cambridge, MA: MIT Press, 2011), pp. 313–41.

Oberthür, S., and J. Pozarowska, 'Managing Institutional Complexity and Fragmentation: The Nagoya Protocol and the Global Governance of Genetic Resources', *Global Environmental Politics*, 13 (2013), pp. 100–18.

'The Impact of the Nagoya Protocol on the Evolving Institutional Complex of ABS Governance' in S. Oberthür and G. K. Rosendal (eds.), *Global Governance of Genetic Resources: Access and Benefit Sharing after the Nagoya Protocol* (Abingdon: Routledge, 2014), pp. 178–95.

Ostrom, E., 'A Polycentric Approach for Coping with Climate Change', *Policy Research Working Paper* 5095 (The World Bank, October 2009).

Raustiala, K., and D. G. Victor, 'The Regime Complex for Plant Genetic Resources', *International Organization*, 58 (2004), pp. 277–309.

Rosendal, G. K., 'The Convention on Biological Diversity: Tensions with the WTO TRIPS Agreement over Access to Genetic Resources and the Sharing of Benefits' in S. Oberthür and T. Gehring (eds.), *Institutional Interaction in Global Environmental Governance. Synergy and Conflict among International and EU Policies* (Cambridge, MA: MIT Press, 2006), pp. 79–102.

Sand, P. H., *Lessons Learned in Global Environmental Governance* (Washington, D.C.: World Resources Institute, 1990).

Stokke, O. S., *The Interplay of International Regimes: Putting Effectiveness Theory to Work*, Report No. 14 (Lysaker, Norway: Fridtjof Nansen Institute, 2001).

'Interplay Management, Niche Selection and Arctic Environmental Governance' in S. Oberthür and O. S. Stokke (eds.), *Managing Institutional Complexity. Regime Interplay and Global Environmental Change* (Cambridge, MA: MIT Press, 2011), pp. 143–70.

Tversky, A., and D. Kahnemann, 'The Framing of Decision and Rational Choice', *Science*, 211 (1981), pp. 453–8.

'Choices, Values and Frames', *American Psychologist*, 39 (1984), pp. 341–50.

van Asselt, H., *The Fragmentation of Global Climate Governance: Consequences and Management of Regime Interactions* (Cheltenham: Edward Elgar, 2014).

Van de Graaf, T., 'Fragmentation in Global Energy Governance: Explaining the Creation of IRENA', *Global Environmental Politics*, 13 (2013), pp. 14–33.

Wallbott, L., F. Wolff, and J. Pożarowska, 'The Negotiations of the Nagoya Protocol: Issues, Coalitions and Process' in S. Oberthür and G. K. Rosendal (eds.), *Global Governance of Genetic Resources: Access and Benefit Sharing after the Nagoya Protocol* (Abingdon: Routledge, 2014), pp. 33–59.

Wolfrum, R., and N. Matz, *Conflicts in International Environmental Law* (Berlin: Springer, 2003).

Young, M. A. (ed.), *Regime Interaction in International Law: Facing Fragmentation* (Cambridge University Press, 2012).

Young, O. R., *The Institutional Dimensions of Environmental Change: Fit, Scale and Interplay* (Cambridge, MA: MIT Press, 2002).

Institutional Dynamics: Emergent Patterns in International Environmental Governance (Cambridge, MA: MIT Press, 2010).

Zelli, F., 'Regime Conflicts and Their Management in Global Environmental Governance' in S. Oberthür and O. S. Stokke (eds.), *Managing Institutional Complexity. Regime Interplay and Global Environmental Change* (Cambridge, MA: MIT Press, 2011), pp. 199–226.

4

Responsive legal pluralism

The emergence of transnational conflicts law[*]

LARS VIELLECHNER

Introduction

The debate on the evolution of law in world society[1] is still trapped in between the outworn theories of 'monism'[2] and 'dualism'[3] that once defined the relationship between national and international law. Admittedly, the terms as such are rarely, if ever, employed in the current discussion. Moreover, in contemporary legal thinking, the concepts of the constitution and democracy are substituting those of the state and sovereignty. For all intents and purposes, however, familiar arguments from the earlier debate are being resurrected and, today as in the past, descriptive and normative perspectives cannot easily be disentangled.

Appearances of neo-monism shine through certain theories of 'global constitutionalism'[4] that try to transfer the model of the national constitution to the context of world society. Different proposals range from interpreting the charter of the United Nations as the constitution of an international community[5] to constructing a vision of multilevel

* Reprinted from *Transnational Legal Theory*, 6 (2015), pp. 312–32, with permission by Taylor & Francis. All websites last accessed 28 February 2015.

1 For the notion of 'world society' in systems theory, see Luhmann, *Theory of Society*, vol. 1, pp. 83–99. For the concurring notion of 'globalisation' in the social sciences, see, e.g., Giddens, *Consequences of Modernity*, pp. 63–78; Sassen, *Sociology of Globalization*, pp. 11–44.

2 For monism with primacy of national law, see Jellinek, *Staatenverträge*, pp. 46–66. For monism with primacy of international law, see Kelsen, *Souveränität*, pp. 204–41; Scelle, *Droit des gens*, vol. 1, pp. 32–3.

3 Triepel, *Völkerrecht und Landesrecht*, pp. 7–10; Anzilotti, *Diritto internazionale*, vol. 1, pp. 47–61.

4 Falk, 'Global Constitutionalism', p. 13; Peters, 'Global Constitutionalism', p. 397.

5 See Fassbender, 'United Nations Charter as Constitution', p. 529.

constitutionalism that encompasses different legal orders.[6] Occurrences of neo-dualism, by contrast, come to the fore in some theories of 'national constitutionalism'[7] that seek to seal off the constitution of the nation-state from foreign influence.

From a normative perspective, however, both approaches equally meet objections. While convincing concepts of democracy beyond the nation-state have not yet been developed,[8] retreating to popular sovereignty fails to take into account the concerns of foreigners in cross-border affairs.[9] Apart from that, both approaches encounter factual hurdles. While establishing a global constitution seems almost impossible given the heterogeneity of world society,[10] even the legal orders of the most powerful nation-states may no longer avoid the influence of foreign norms due to the increase of social relations across borders.[11]

On a descriptive account, it thus appears most accurate to identify 'pluralism'[12] as the essential characteristic of the law in world society. Pluralism in this sense does not only refer to the coexistence of national and international law. Rather, it points to the overlapping and intertwinement of a plurality of partly territorially confined, partly functionally oriented legal orders without any overarching unity or clear hierarchy (Part II). Under these conditions, it is here argued from a normative point of view, the legitimacy and coherence of the law may only be guaranteed through horizontal coordination. The different legal orders must show themselves 'responsive'[13] towards their counterparts, mutually taking each other into account by developing a new kind of conflicts law that follows the model of private international law. Indeed, legal

[6] See Pernice, 'Global Dimension of Multilevel Constitutionalism', p. 973; Habermas, 'Political Constitution for Pluralist World Society', p. 312.

[7] Rubenfeld, 'Unilateralism and Constitutionalism', p. 1971; Rabkin, *Law without Nations?*.

[8] For some notable attempts, see Held, *Democracy and the Global Order*; Bohman, *Democracy across Borders*; Archibugi, *Global Commonwealth of Citizens*.

[9] See Joerges and Neyer, 'Constitutionalisation of Comitology', p. 294; Kumm, 'Cosmopolitan Turn in Constitutionalism', pp. 612–21.

[10] See Kennedy, 'Legal Pluralism and Cosmopolitan Dream', p. 641; Teubner, *Constitutional Fragments*, pp. 13–14.

[11] See Nye, *Paradox of American Power*; Jackson, *Constitutional Engagement in a Transnational Era*.

[12] For some concurring accounts, see Teubner, 'Global Bukowina', p. 3; Krisch, *Beyond Constitutionalism*; Berman, *Global Legal Pluralism*.

[13] The term is borrowed from Nonet and Selznick, *Law and Society in Transition*, pp. 14–15, who employ it in a different sense, though: 'law as a facilitator of response to social needs and aspirations'.

practice already reflects such a conception. In accordance with the spirit of some express provisions in treaties and constitutions, courts and tribunals dialectically formulate rules of complementarity and subsidiarity without relinquishing their own identity (Part III). A responsive legal pluralism of this kind offers a promising fourth way to overcome both the outdated dualist doctrine of sovereigntism and the unattainable monist vision of universalism while at the same time avoiding the perils of radical legal pluralism. It may even amount to an adequate reconfiguration of the modern concept of constitutionalism in the current context (Part IV).

Plurality

Legal pluralism on the global scale (Section 1) still takes a rather radical shape (Section 2) that bears some normative problems on its part (Section 3).

Description

More than forty years ago, German sociologist Niklas Luhmann suspected that cognitive patterns of behaviour would supersede normative structures in the evolution of world society.[14] According to his findings, there has long been a preference for normative mechanisms of orientation that maintain expectations even in the case of disappointment because of their stabilising function. For this reason, he claimed, such social systems as religion, politics and law had assumed a predominant role in the past. By contrast, he found that those social systems that open up and support worldwide social relations, such as the economy, science and technology, clearly show a cognitive style of orientation, which is capable of learning and willing to adapt. A 'shift of evolutionary primacy from normative to cognitive mechanisms'[15] of orientation therefore appeared obvious to him. Nevertheless, there is no evidence for an atrophy of law. The emerging world society rather reveals an urgent need for conventional means to stabilise expectations and to resolve disputes that is satisfied in two ways.

On the one hand, international law intrudes into those subject matters that used to be reserved as the internal affairs of the states, especially the economy and the ecology, but also the domains of human rights and

[14] See Luhmann, *Sociological Theory of Law*, pp. 255–64. [15] Ibid., p. 262.

criminal law.[16] Multilateral treaties have created several international organisations for this purpose. Some of them even dispose of their proper dispute settlement mechanisms. The World Trade Organisation, including its Dispute Settlement Understanding, counts among the most prominent examples on the global scale.[17] The study group of the International Law Commission, entrusted with investigating the recent evolution of international law, observes both its expansion and its fragmentation into several legal orders. It recognises the functional differentiation of society, as described by the sociological theory of social systems, reflected within international law: 'The fragmentation of the international social world has attained legal significance especially as it has been accompanied by the emergence of specialized and (relatively) autonomous rules or rule-complexes, legal institutions and spheres of legal practice.'[18] Pursuant to the report, the partial legal orders of international law, designated as 'regimes',[19] differ from each other by their specialisation:

> What once appeared to be governed by 'general international law' has become the field of operation for such specialist systems as 'trade law', 'human rights law', 'environmental law', 'law of the sea', 'European law' and even such exotic and highly specialized knowledges as 'investment law' or 'international refugee law' etc. – each possessing their own principles and institutions.[20]

For this reason, allegedly, the different regimes of international law are able to follow their own intrinsic logic. It should be noted, however, that some of them resist functional confinement. This holds true for international human rights regimes such as the International Covenant on Civil and Political Rights with its Human Rights Committee[21] and

[16] See Simma, 'From Bilateralism to Community Interest', p. 217; Trachtman, *Future of International Law*.

[17] See Cass, *Constitutionalization of World Trade Organization*; Jackson, *Sovereignty, WTO, and Changing Fundamentals*.

[18] Fragmentation of International Law: Difficulties Arising from the Diversification and Expansion of International Law: Report of the Study Group of the International Law Commission, 13 April 2006, UN Doc A/CN.4/L.682, para. 8. See also Koskenniemi and Leino, 'Fragmentation of International Law', p. 553; Hafner, 'Fragmentation of International Law', p. 849.

[19] Fragmentation of International Law (n. 18), para. 15. See also Fischer-Lescano and Teubner, 'Regime-Collisions', p. 999.

[20] Fragmentation of International Law (n. 18), para. 8.

[21] See Buergenthal, 'International Human Rights System', p. 783; McGoldrick, *Human Rights Committee*.

egimes of regional integration such as the European Union with its Court of Justice.[22]

On the other hand, if international law fails to regulate cross-border issues due to a lack of consent or pace among states, 'transnational governance arrangements'[23] are emerging, constituted by contracts of private law. Similar to the regimes of international law, these arrangements are characterised by their functional specialisation. The Internet Corporation for Assigned Names and Numbers (ICANN), which distributes domains on the Internet, may be mentioned as the most developed instance.[24] It is a non-profit public benefit corporation, established according to Californian law, which maintains contractual relations with the government of the United States of America. In order to settle disputes between holders of rights in names or trademarks and registrants of corresponding domain names, it has even institutionalised a special dispute settlement mechanism, based on the Uniform Domain Name Dispute Resolution Policy (UDRP), which figures as general terms and conditions of each domain name registration agreement.[25] In their capacity as dispute resolution service providers, the ICANN recognises both private institutions, such as the National Arbitration Forum based in Minneapolis, and an international organisation, the World Intellectual Property Organisation.[26]

Interpretation

According to some observers, the law of the emerging world society is thus marked by a 'new legal pluralism'[27] that corresponds with earlier conceptions of the law. Legal historians use to consider the competing authorities in the Middle Ages as legal pluralism.[28] Legal anthropologists and sociologists thereby understand the coexistence of state law and the law of the indigenous populations in former colonies.[29]

22 See Stein, 'Transnational Constitution', p. 1; Weiler, 'Transformation of Europe', p. 2403.
23 Teubner, 'Global Private Regimes', p. 71; Calliess, 'Transnational Civil Regimes', p. 215.
24 See Froomkin, 'Cyberspace', p. 17; Crawford, 'ICANN Experiment', p. 409.
25 See Helfer and Dinwoodie, 'Non-National Systems', p. 141; Froomkin, 'Uniform Dispute Resolution Policy', p. 605.
26 See Internet Corporation for Assigned Names and Numbers, List of Approved Dispute Resolution Service Providers, www.icann.org/en/help/dndr/udrp/providers.
27 Berman, 'New Legal Pluralism', p. 225; Santos, *New Legal Common Sense*, p. 92: 'post-modern legal plurality'.
28 See Berman, *Law and Revolution*, p. 10; Grossi, *Ordine giuridico medievale*, pp. 223–35.
29 See Pospíšil, *Anthropology of Law*, pp. 97–126; Hooker, *Legal Pluralism*.

For some authors, legal pluralism even existed in the modern nation-state. On the one hand, certain early theories of federalism assumed that sovereignty might be divided. For example, Alexis de Tocqueville claimed that there are 'two governments between which sovereignty was going to be apportioned' in the United States of America.[30] Alexander Hamilton had already defended this view in the debate on the establishment of the federal constitution.[31] Similarly, the Supreme Court of the United States had stated in an early decision: 'Every State in the Union, in every instance where its sovereignty has not been delegated to the United States, I consider to be as completely sovereign, as the United States are in respect to the powers surrendered.'[32] After the failed revolution of 1848, Georg Waitz adopted Tocqueville's notion of divided sovereignty to underscore the possibility of establishing a federal state from sovereign monarchies in Germany. In his view, both the central state and the individual states were considered to be sovereign with regard to their respective spheres of authority.[33] Carl Schmitt later developed a conception of the federation in which the question of sovereignty, that is, the question of the ultimate authority to decide an existential conflict, 'always remains open'[34] unless the association is to dissolve. The essence of a federation in this sense thus resides in 'an intermediary condition'[35] between unity and pluralism of several political entities.

On the other hand, corporatist theories of the state granted each social association its own law-making power. Thus, in Germany, Otto von Gierke identified a social law that regulated the internal affairs of associations such as unions, syndicates and clubs.[36] Subsequently, some Anglo-American authors derived various theories of the 'pluralist state'[37] and 'private government'[38] from this way of thinking about the law. Thus, for Harold Laski, the state was only 'one of the groups to which the individual belongs'.[39] In his view, sovereignty meant 'no more than the ability to secure assent'.[40] In France and Italy, the corporatist theory

30 Tocqueville, *Democracy in America*, p. 107.
31 See Hamilton, 'Federalist No. 9', p. 50. See also Madison, 'Federalist No. 39', p. 250.
32 *Chisholm* v. *Georgia*, (1793) 2 U.S. 419, 435.
33 See Waitz, 'Wesen des Bundesstaates', p. 501.
34 Schmitt, *Constitutional Theory*, p. 390. 35 Ibid., p. 389.
36 See von Gierke, *Political Theories of the Middle Age*.
37 Barker, *Political Thought*; Cole, *Social Theory*; Laski, 'Personality of Associations', p. 404.
38 Selznick, *Industrial Justice*, pp. 259–76; Macaulay, 'Private Government', p. 445.
39 Laski, 'Sovereignty of the State', p. 90. 40 Ibid., p. 92.

ound an equivalent in the institutionalist theory of law, which regarded ach social institution as a distinct legal order.[41]

Regarding federalism, however, the conviction that in a confederation he individual states remain fully sovereign whereas in a federal state he state collective as such gains sovereignty has eventually taken hold. n the United States of America, the civil war settled the issue.[42] In ontinental Europe, constitutional theory accounted for that view by istinguishing sovereign and non-sovereign states, the latter disposing f their own competences but not of the competence-competence, that is, he power to allocate competences.[43] Schmitt, for his part, stressed that he antinomy of a federation rests upon the homogeneity of its members s an essential presupposition, which ensures that the extreme case of an xistential conflict does not occur.[44]

Regarding corporatism, Gierke, although identifying a structural ongruence of the state and other social associations, recognised a relationhip of subordination between them.[45] Even the fiercest advocates of the luralist theory of the state later changed their minds. Thus, Laski, who had nitially contended that 'the State does not enjoy any necessary pre-eminence or its demands',[46] in hindsight conceded that the state has always had 'to laim an indivisible and irresponsible sovereignty because there was no other vay in which it could define and control the legal postulates of society'.[47]

In accordance with its occurrence in the Middle Ages, the legal pluralsm in modern times hence presented itself in a 'weak'[48] form only: there as always been a strong belief in the unity of the law, first grounded on eligion, then on the state. Concordantly, the International Law Commission insists on the fact that general international law still constitutes and omplements the special regimes of international law.[49] Yet the question rises whether general international law today includes any rules and rinciples other than those enshrined in the Vienna Convention on the Law of Treaties. And the transnational governance arrangements, which rest upon private law contracts, even elude general international law.

41 See Hauriou, 'Théorie de l'institution', p. 1; Romano, *Ordinamento giuridico*.
42 See Amar, 'Sovereignty and Federalism', p. 1425.
43 See Laband, *Staatsrecht*, vol. 1, pp. 55–88; Jellinek, *Staatenverbindungen*, pp. 36–58.
44 See Schmitt, *Constitutional Theory*, p. 392.
45 See von Gierke, *Wesen der menschlichen Verbände*, p. 29.
46 Laski, 'Sovereignty of the State', p. 92. 47 Laski, *Grammar of Politics*, pp. xi–xii.
48 Griffiths, 'Legal Pluralism', p. 5.
49 See Fragmentation of International Law (n. 18), paras. 172–85. See also Simma and Pulkowski, 'Self-Contained Regimes', p. 483.

Apart from that, each legal order attains a relative autonomy by exclusively following its proper 'secondary rules'[50] as understood by H. L. A. Hart. Such secondary rules do not only include rules of recognition, which allow for the conclusive identification of the primary rules of obligation to be applied, but also rules of adjudication, which empower courts to ascertain whether a primary rule of obligation has been violated on a particular occasion.[51] In many instances, it is only 'the proliferation of international courts and tribunals'[52] that brings about the very legal pluralism to which it owes its own existence. In this way, the different legal orders may operate self-referentially. Thus, the Court of Justice of the European Union, for example, solely decides according to 'the law stemming from the treaty, an independent source of law', and therefore maintains that it has constituted 'its own legal system'.[53] Similarly, any dispute resolution service provider approved by the ICANN, pursuant to Paragraph 15(a) of the procedural rules of the UDRP, shall decide a complaint 'in accordance with the Policy, these Rules and any rules and principles of law that it deems applicable'.[54] In the parlance of systems theory, the various legal orders hence belong to a single legal system, but they reconnect to the same legal code by different programmes in the form of constitutions or foundational treaties.[55] Consequently, transnational legal pluralism takes a more 'radical'[56] form than its predecessors both before and after the formation of the modern nation-state, which dispenses with any unity or hierarchy.

Investigation

A radical legal pluralism of this kind provokes objection because it curbs participation in the formation of law as well as legal certainty and equality.[57] From the perspective of the modern concept of

50 Hart, *Concept of Law*, p. 91.

51 See Wellens, 'Diversity in Secondary Rules', p. 3; Schultz, 'Secondary Rules of Recognition', p. 59.

52 Romano, 'Proliferation of International Judicial Bodies', p. 709; Alford, 'Proliferation of International Courts and Tribunals', p.160.

53 ECJ, Judgment of 15 July 1964, Case 6/64, *Costa* v. *ENEL*, (1964) ECR 585, 593–4.

54 Internet Corporation for Assigned Names and Numbers, Rules for Uniform Domain Name Dispute Resolution Policy, 30 October 2009, www.icann.org/en/help/dndr/udrp/rules.

55 For the distinction between 'code' and 'programme' in systems theory, see Luhmann, *Law as a Social System*, pp. 173–210.

56 MacCormick, 'Constitutional Collision', p. 528; Krisch, 'Radical Pluralism', p. 386.

57 See Eleftheriadis, 'Pluralism and Integrity', p. 365; Letsas, 'Harmonic Law', p. 77.

constitutionalism,[58] each partial legal order, taken separately, suffers from a particular normative deficit.

The special regimes of international law, such as the World Trade Organisation and the European Union, lack democratic legitimacy because executive agents dominate their law-making processes.[59] The legal orders of the several nation-states, by contrast, appear as undemocratic as long as they disregard the concerns of foreigners in regulating cross-border affairs.[60] Finally, the transnational governance arrangements, which rest upon private law contracts even though they fulfil quasi-public functions, such as the ICANN, in general neither grant participation and nor do they protect fundamental rights and freedoms.[61] In cases of 'cybergriping' in which domain names reproduce trademarks or names of celebrities, supplemented by critical suffixes such as 'sucks', for example, both freedom of speech and property rights must be reconciled.[62]

Moreover, if the different legal orders overlap in their scopes of application, conflicts of norms may arise.[63] At times, different secondary rules provide for the application of contradictory primary rules of obligation. More frequently, different courts interpret identical norms divergently. Thus, the German Federal Constitutional Court and the European Court of Human Rights fundamentally disagreed about how to reconcile the right of privacy with the freedom of the press in a case concerning the publication of celebrity photos in tabloid newspapers.[64]

Conversely, some special regimes of international law may ignore norms following a rationality that is foreign to their own.[65] Thus, in a case concerning an import prohibition of certain shrimp products

[58] See Michelman, 'W(h)ither the Constitution', p. 1063; Grimm, 'Achievement of Constitutionalism', p. 3.

[59] See Dahl, 'Can International Organizations Be Democratic', p. 19; Eriksen, *Unfinished Democratization of Europe*.

[60] See n. 9.

[61] See Teubner, 'Anonymous Matrix', p. 327; Viellechner, 'Constitution of Transnational Governance Arrangements', pp. 449–55.

[62] See Teubner and Karavas, 'www.CompanyNameSucks.com', p. 262.

[63] See Pauwelyn, *Conflict of Norms in Public International Law*; Teubner and Korth, 'Two Kinds of Legal Pluralism', p. 23.

[64] See, on the one hand, German Federal Constitutional Court, Judgment of 15 December 1999, Case 1 BvR 653/96, *Caroline von Monaco II*, 101 *Entscheidungen des Bundesverfassungsgerichts* 361; on the other hand, ECtHR, Judgment of 24 June 2004, Application 59320/00, *Von Hannover* v. *Germany*.

[65] See Charnovitz, 'Free Trade, Fair Trade, Green Trade', p. 621.

harvested by means that threaten sea turtles, the appellate body of the World Trade Organisation had to decide whether a special regime of international law promoting free trade must also take into account ecological concerns.[66] While both the establishment of a universal legal order and the fall-back to the national constitution may be impossible to realise irrespective of normative objections, the persistence of radical legal pluralism, therefore, appears undesirable.

Responsivity

The practice of horizontal coordination among the different legal orders (Section 1) that is recently emerging (Section 2) may however offer a solution to the normative deficiencies of legal pluralism if it manages to further improve and consolidate (Section 3).

Foundation

For lack of any superior authority, the recognition and reconciliation of the different legal orders cannot be imposed from above. Hence, under conditions of legal pluralism, the legitimacy and coherence of the law may only be guaranteed through a horizontal coordination among the different legal orders, taking each other into account by internally reflecting their mutual impact. The founding principle animating such practice, which could replace outdated notions of sovereignty, may be called 'responsivity'.[67] By way of self-restraint, it requires each legal order to open itself for foreign norms. The German Basic Law, for instance, already comprises appearances of responsivity in its principles of 'openness', or 'friendliness', towards both international and European law, which the Federal Constitutional Court deduces from the constitutional provisions on the status of inter-state treaties and customary international law within domestic law and on European integration respectively.[68]

[66] See WTO, Report of the Appellate Body of 12 October 1998, Dispute AB-1998–4, *United States/Import Prohibition of Certain Shrimp and Shrimp Products*, WT/DS58/AB/R.

[67] See n. 13. See also Delmas-Marty, *Ordering Pluralism*, p. 13: 'ordered pluralism'.

[68] For international law, see German Federal Constitutional Court, Judgment of 26 March 1957, Case 2 BvG 1/55, *Reichskonkordat*, 6 *Entscheidungen des Bundesverfassungsgerichts* 309, 362; Lovric, 'Constitution Friendly to International Law', p. 75. For European Law, see German Federal Constitutional Court, Judgment of 30 June 2009, Joined Cases 2 BvE 2/08 *et al.*, *Lisbon*, 123 *Entscheidungen des Bundesverfassungsgerichts* 267, 347; Ziller, 'German Constitutional Court's Friendliness towards European Law', p. 53.

Contrary to what some theories of 'cosmopolitan pluralism' claim, the horizontal coordination of the different legal orders does not require a common commitment to basic constitutional principles'.[69] If a thick substantive congruence of this kind existed, conflicts between them would rarely arise. In any case, they could easily be resolved with regard to the overarching principles, which hence erected a monist-universalist legal order. The horizontal coordination does not even expect the different legal orders to share 'a common set of discursive forms'[70] enabling them to engage with each other. Communication among them is possible from the outset as they concurrently employ the language and forms of law.[71] Yet the ability to communicate with each other does not account for the initial incentive to mutual consideration. In this respect, some more radical versions of legal pluralism inspired by systems theory can do no more than rely on the fact that external pressure will induce self-restraint.[72]

Responsive legal pluralism, by contrast, implies that the different legal orders are both able and willing to take each other into account on their own initiative. It suggests that they constrain themselves because they acknowledge that each of them takes up a regulatory task that none of the others may accomplish on its own. Such structural openness does not merely rest upon perceived self-interest, as rationalist theories of international law and relations suggest.[73] It is much more demanding since it presupposes the different legal orders to develop a capacity of 'reflexion'[74] on their own identity. In this way, it allows them the insight that they form part of a larger legal system in which all of them are torn between independence and interdependence so that they must reassess their effects on their counterparts. More precisely, responsivity combines complementarity and subsidiarity as flipsides of the same coin.[75] On the one hand, the different legal orders may expand their scopes of application if there are gaps in foreign law. On the other hand, they must confine their scopes of application in cases of overlap. On no account, however, may any one of them be compelled to relinquish its proper identity.

[69] Kumm, 'Cosmopolitan Turn in Constitutionalism', p. 271.

[70] Berman, *Global Legal Pluralism*, p. 17.

[71] See n. 55.

[72] See Teubner, *Constitutional Fragments*, pp. 158–62.

[73] See Goldsmith and Posner, *Limits of International Law*, pp. 225–6; Guzman, *How International Law Works*, pp. 211–18.

[74] Teubner, 'Substantive and Reflexive Elements', p. 273.

[75] See also Føllesdal, 'Subsidiarity as a Constitutional Principle', p. 37.

As a matter of fact, it would be hazardous to leave the horizontal coordination of the different legal orders to political negotiation.[76] In this case, the imponderables of happenstance, opportunity and capture could possibly reign. Neither would it suffice to entrust the horizontal coordination of the different legal orders to the informal dialogue of the various courts and tribunals. Even though such networks of courts and tribunals may be emerging,[77] their dialogue remains fragile without express regulation. Responsivity therefore calls for implementation by a new kind of 'conflicts law'[78] that follows the model of private international law. Indeed, private international law usefully lends itself as an archetype here for two reasons. Firstly, it has always assumed that there are several valid legal orders coexisting with each other that might simultaneously claim application to a certain cross-border situation. Secondly, since its inception, it has built on a mechanism of horizontal coordination that concedes that conflicts of norms may only be resolved from within a certain legal order, even though its intrinsic logic might strive for generalisation.[79] At the same time, classical conflict of laws suffers from two shortcomings that need to be overcome with regard to the current context. Firstly, it is traditionally confined to the supposedly unpolitical realm of private law, which allegedly does not touch upon sovereignty.[80] Secondly, it is conventionally based on a principle of comity that grants recognition to foreign law as a courtesy only.[81] Responsivity, by contrast, occurs as a legally actionable principle of openness that may, under certain circumstances, even require the application of foreign public law as well as international and non-state law. According to some commentators, conflict of laws is even particularly well-suited to mitigate highly politicised conflicts that otherwise appear unsolvable because of its intellectual style as 'technique'.[82]

[76] As suggested by Krisch, *Beyond Constitutionalism*, pp. 225–62.

[77] See Slaughter, 'Global Community of Courts', p. 191; Cassese, *Tribunali di Babele*.

[78] For different proposals, see Teubner, *Constitutional Fragments*, pp. 150–74; Joerges, 'New Type of Conflicts Law', p. 465; Berman, 'Conflict of Laws', p. 1105; Knop, Michaels and Riles, 'Conflict of Laws Approach', p. 269.

[79] See Story, *Conflict of Laws*, para. 9; von Savigny, *System des heutigen Römischen Rechts*, vol. 8, para. 348.

[80] See Lowenfeld, 'Public Law in the International Arena', pp. 322–6; Dodge, 'Public-Private Distinction in the Conflict of Laws', p. 371.

[81] See Story, *Conflict of Laws*, paras. 28–38; Yntema, 'Comity Doctrine', p. 9.

[82] Knop, Michaels and Riles, 'Conflict of Laws Style', p. 589.

A horizontal coordination of the different legal orders by such means has good prospects of success. As it only demands agreement on the terms of engagement, but not on substantive norms, the costs are low. At the same time, as the openness towards others in turn allows for exerting influence on external affairs, the gains are high. Responsive legal pluralism thus shares all the virtues of what has been called 'reflexive law'[83] while avoiding most of its inconveniences. Reflexive law, it should be recalled, was once imagined by some strands of legal systems theory within the nation-state as a means to stimulate reflexion processes within other social systems in order to allow for their mutual consideration and hence for social integration in the absence of a central steering agency. Such reconciliation of different social systems by law is much more difficult to attain than the reconciliation of different legal orders among each other. As the rigorous thread of systems theory asserts, it is 'inconceivable that law could control and regulate the autopoiesis of all social systems',[84] even in the extenuated sense of a regulation of self-regulation. By contrast, within the law of world society, none of the different legal orders assumes a superordinate position, not even as a catalyst or moderator. Moreover, as the critique from discourse theory contends, different social systems 'would have to have available an at least partially shared language'[85] in order to understand each other and to take each other into account. In comparison, different legal orders may easily communicate with each other through a 'universal code of legality'[86] without any problem of translation.

Elaboration

Legal practice proves that a transnational conflicts law is gradually evolving. Some conflicts rules are already expressly anchored in the basic charters of particular legal regimes. International criminal law, for example, contains a rule of complementarity.[87] Thus, according to Article 17(1)(a) of the Rome Statute of the International Criminal Court, the court may only try a case if a state which has jurisdiction over it 'is unwilling or unable genuinely to

[83] Teubner, 'Substantive and Reflexive Elements', pp. 266–81; Willke, 'Societal Guidance through Law', p. 353.

[84] Luhmann, 'Reflexive Law', p. 397.

[85] Habermas, *Between Facts and Norms*, p. 347.

[86] Günther, 'Legal Pluralism', p. 16. See also n. 55.

[87] See El Zeidy, 'Principle of Complementarity', p. 869; Burke-White, 'Proactive Complementarity', p. 53.

carry out the investigation or prosecution'.[88] European human rights law, by contrast, contains a rule of subsidiarity.[89] Thus, Article 53 of the European Convention on Human Rights provides that the convention shall not be construed 'as limiting or derogating from any of the human rights and fundamental freedoms which may be ensured under the laws of any High Contracting Party or under any other agreement to which it is a Party'.[90] European Union law, for its part, expresses the conviction that the reconciliation of the different legal orders may not touch upon their identity.[91] Thus, Article 4(2) of the Treaty on European Union prescribes that the Union shall respect 'the equality of Member States before the Treaties as well as their national identities, inherent in their fundamental structures, political and constitutional, inclusive of regional and local self-government'.[92]

However, the reach of these explicit rules remains limited while the relations to regulate are multiple. Therefore, national and international courts and tribunals are called upon to provisionally create the conflicts rules required in a process of dialectical interaction. The 'cooperation of courts'[93], then, is both a precondition for and a corollary of responsivity. Yet the rules of coordination emanating from that practice, albeit judge-made, neither bear upon procedure nor do they regulate the relationships between different institutions. Rather, they turn out to be conflicts rules that determine the relationships between different legal orders. Potential competences of institutions and obligations to abide by precedents may hence only arise from the procedural and substantive law declared applicable by those rules.

Notably the German Federal Constitutional Court has demonstrated much creativity in developing transnational conflicts rules, without employing the term however. Regarding the relationship between the German legal order and European Union law, it has formulated a rule of

88 Rome Statute of the International Criminal Court, 17 July 1998, Article 17, 2187 UNTS 90, 100–1.

89 See Petzold, 'Principle of Subsidiarity', p. 41; Pastor Ridruejo, 'Le principe de subsidiarité', p. 1077.

90 Convention for the Protection of Human Rights and Fundamental Freedoms, 4 November 1950, Article 53, 213 UNTS 221, 249.

91 See Besselink, 'National and Constitutional Identity', p. 36; von Bogdandy and Schill, 'National Identity', p. 1417.

92 Consolidated Version of the Treaty on European Union, 30 March 2010, Article 4, (2010) C83 OJEU 13, 18.

93 Garlicki, 'Cooperation of Courts', p. 509; Voßkuhle, 'Multilevel Cooperation of the European Constitutional Courts', p. 175.

subsidiarity with reservation.[94] According to its 'Solange' decision, it will refrain from deciding on the applicability of European Union law in Germany as long as the European Union generally ensures a protection of fundamental rights 'which is to be regarded as substantially similar to the protection of fundamental rights required unconditionally by the Basic Law'.[95] Subsequently, the European Court of Human Rights has also adopted this idea, transferring it to the relationship between the European Convention on Human Rights and European Union law.[96] According to its 'Bosphorus' judgment, state action taken in compliance with obligations resulting from the membership in an international organisation is 'justified as long as the relevant organisation is considered to protect fundamental rights, as regards both the substantive guarantees offered and the mechanisms controlling their observance, in a manner ... at least equivalent to that for which the Convention provides'.[97] Applying the same logic, but in the opposite direction, the Court of Justice of the European Union has established a rule of complementarity regarding the relationship between European Union law and United Nations law.[98] According to its 'Kadi' decision, it will continue to scrutinise the regulations of the European Union that implement resolutions of the United Nations Security Council requiring member states to sanction persons suspected of terrorism as long as the procedure of re-examination offered by the United Nations Sanctions Committee 'does not offer the guarantees of judicial protection'.[99]

Regarding the relationship between the German legal order and European human rights law as well as other regimes of international law, the German Federal Constitutional Court has developed yet another rule of subsidiarity with reservation.[100] According to its 'Görgülü' decision, the Basic Law's commitment to international law obliges all state authorities 'to take into account' the provisions of international treaties

[94] See Lanier, 'Solange, Farewell', p. 1.

[95] German Federal Constitutional Court, Decision of 22 October 1986, Case 2 BvR 197/83, *Solange II*, 73 *Entscheidungen des Bundesverfassungsgerichts* 339, 387.

[96] See Jacqué, 'Jurisprudence "Solange II"', p. 756; Gaja, '"Solange" Yet Again', p. 517.

[97] ECtHR, Judgment of 30 June 2005, Application 45036/98, *Bosphorus* v. *Ireland*, para. 155.

[98] See Besson, 'European Legal Pluralism after Kadi', p. 237; Halberstam and Stein, 'United Nations, European Union, and King of Sweden', p. 13.

[99] ECJ, Judgment of 3 September 2008, Joined Cases C-402/05 P and C-415/05 P, *Kadi and Al Barakaat* v. *Council and Commission*, (2008) ECR I-6351, para. 322.

[100] See Krisch, 'Open Architecture of European Human Rights Law', p. 183.

to which the Federal Republic of Germany is a Party and the relating decisions of international courts when applying domestic law.[101] This rule requires compliance with international law as long as the result does not violate essential principles of German law. It thus implies a public policy exception familiar to private international law. Conversely, the European Court of Human Rights grants the member states of the European Convention on Human Rights a 'margin of appreciation'[102] when curtailing certain convention rights, thereby respecting national peculiarities in both law and fact.[103] Both conflicts rules are thus mutually reinforcing.

The conflicts rules that are generally recognised as best practices may later qualify for codification. Thus, Article 23(1) of the German Basic Law acknowledges the jurisprudence of the German Federal Constitutional Court regarding the relationship between the German legal order and European Union Law. In its revised form, it provides that the Federal Republic of Germany participates in the development of a European Union 'that guarantees a level of protection of basic rights essentially comparable to that afforded by this Basic Law'.[104]

Evolution

In order to consolidate the burgeoning practice of responsivity among the different legal orders, the various conflicts rules need further refinement and dissemination. On the one hand, some of them require substantive improvement. Thus the rules of complementarity must allow for different 'levels of intensity'[105] when expanding the scope of application of a particular legal order. The distinction between strict scrutiny, intermediate review and rational basis test, familiar to some legal orders in constitutional review of legislation, may serve as a guideline here. For the rules

[101] German Federal Constitutional Court, Decision of 14 October 2004, Case 2 BvR 1481/04, *Görgülü*, 111 *Entscheidungen des Bundesverfassungsgerichts* 307, 315. See also German Federal Constitutional Court, Decision of 19 September 2006, Joined Cases 2 BvR 2115/01 *et al.*, *Vienna Convention on Consular Relations*, 9 *Kammerentscheidungen des Bundesverfassungsgerichts* 174, 191.

[102] ECtHR, Judgment of 7 December 1976, Application 5493/72, *Handyside* v. *United Kingdom*, para. 48.

[103] See Arai-Takahashi, *Margin of Appreciation Doctrine*; Legg, *Margin of Appreciation in International Human Rights Law*.

[104] Basic Law for the Federal Republic of Germany, 23 May 1949, Article 23, as amended by the act of 21 December 1992, www.gesetze-im-internet.de/englisch_gg.

[105] Gerards, 'Margin of Appreciation Doctrine', p. 88.

of subsidiarity, a 'methodology for deference'[106] needs to be worked out. A continuum of recognition discerning in how far foreign law deserves compliance may offer a solution here. Moreover, those conflicts rules that suffer from vagueness, such as the margin of appreciation, require some specification.[107] For example, regarding the protection of fundamental rights in multipolar legal relationships, some authors propose to interpret the European Convention on Human Rights as a common framework endorsing a range of several equally acceptable national solutions to a particular legal problem.[108]

On the other hand, the various conflicts rules need to be mutually established within all partial legal orders with regard to all of their external relations. A more precisely defined margin of appreciation, for example, might be integrated as a general rule of subsidiarity in all international human rights regimes.[109] It might also lend itself as a conflicts rule regarding the relationship between other regimes of international law and national legal orders[110] as well as different regimes of international law between each other.[111]

Appropriate conflicts rules first need to be created when it comes to the relationship between the national legal orders and transnational governance arrangements such as the ICANN. Here as elsewhere, the 'Solange' rule may find another field of application.[112] The national legal orders would then ensure a complementary protection of fundamental rights as long as the transnational governance arrangements failed to provide it.[113] It does not appear appropriate, however, to exclusively apply domestic legal standards in this context. Rather, the courts would be well advised to determine the applicable law in such cross-border issues according to a method called 'substantive law approach'[114] in private international law scholarship. This method suggests composing

[106] Alford, 'Continuum of Deference', p. 682.
[107] See Brauch, 'Margin of Appreciation', p. 113; Letsas, 'Two Concepts of the Margin of Appreciation', p. 705.
[108] See Lübbe-Wolff, 'Role of National Courts in the Convention System', p. 11.
[109] See Carozza, 'Subsidiarity as a Structural Principle', p. 38; Shelton, 'Subsidiarity and Human Rights Law', p. 4.
[110] See Sweeney, '"Margin of Appreciation" in the Internal Market', p. 27.
[111] See Shany, 'General Margin of Appreciation Doctrine', p. 907.
[112] See Lavranos, 'Solange-Method as a Tool', p. 275; Tzanakopoulos, 'Impact of the Solange Argument', p. 185.
[113] See Viellechner, 'Constitution of Transnational Governance Arrangements', pp. 455–9.
[114] Von Mehren, 'Special Substantive Rules', p. 347. See also Dinwoodie, 'Global Norms', p. 469; Berman, 'Cosmopolitan Vision of Conflict of Laws', p. 1819.

a new substantive norm from elements of all legal orders concerned. The national courts would then incur a 'double function',[115] or role splitting, which Georges Scelle once observed with regard to the implementation of international law. On the one hand, they would act as national agents. On the other hand, they would serve a transnational rule of law.[116]

Conclusion

Consequently, in opposition to Luhmann's initial assumption, cognitive patterns of behaviour will not supersede normative mechanisms in the evolution of world society. Rather, both elements will blend into one: the capacity to learn and to adapt is built into the law. By mutual observation and the adoption of foreign norms, the different legal orders are gradually converging. As Luhmann himself later acknowledged:

> The inclusion of cognitive mechanisms in the essentially normative structure of law appears to correspond to the development of a global society. Worldwide structural formations and their consequential problems, contexts of interaction and disequilibria, 'govern' the regionally validated positive law not in the form of an overlapping norming, a higher-level, supra-state and hence supra-positive law, but because of the fact that the dynamism of global society establishes stimuli for learning, perhaps exercising pressures toward learning and drawing up a certain non-arbitrariness of problem solutions.[117]

At the same time, democracy undergoes a deep structural transformation, reconfiguring in the mutual recognition and contestation of the different legal orders.[118] In this process, it is the courts that ensure individual participation in the formation of transnational norms.

Certain theories of 'constitutional pluralism'[119] even detect an adequate reformulation of modern constitutionalism in its inherent tension between universalism and particularism, democracy and the rule of law including fundamental rights protection, epitomised in such state

[115] Scelle, *Droit des gens*, vol. 1, p. 43.

[116] See Berman, 'Judges as Cosmopolitan Transnational Actors', p. 109; Nollkaemper, *National Courts and the International Rule of Law*.

[117] Luhmann, *Sociological Theory of Law*, p. 262.

[118] See Ladeur, 'Globalization and the Conversion of Democracy', p. 89; Krisch, *Beyond Constitutionalism*, pp. 264–76.

[119] Poiares Maduro, 'Three Claims of Constitutional Pluralism', p. 67; Halberstam, 'Local, Global and Plural Constitutionalism', p. 150. See also Walker, 'Idea of Constitutional Pluralism', p. 317.

f the law. On the one hand, legal certainty and equality press for ıe avoidance of conflicting norms as far as possible. On the other hand, emocracy allows for the self-determination of the different legal orders, as ɔng as they do not affect the fundamental rights of outsiders. Responsive ɛgal pluralism thus strikes a balance between the outdated dualist doctrine f sovereigntism and the unattainable monist vision of universalism without falling prey to the perils of radical legal pluralism.

Bibliography

lford, R. P., 'The Proliferation of International Courts and Tribunals: International Adjudication in Ascendance', *American Society of International Law Proceedings*, 94 (2000), pp. 160–5.

'Federal Courts, International Tribunals, and the Continuum of Deference', *Virginia Journal of International Law*, 43 (2003), pp. 675–796.

mar, A. R., 'Of Sovereignty and Federalism', *Yale Law Journal*, 96 (1987), pp. 1425–1520.

nzilotti, D., *Corso di diritto internazionale*, 3rd edn, 3 vols. (Rome: Athenaeum, 1928).

rai-Takahashi, Y., *The Margin of Appreciation Doctrine and the Principle of Proportionality in the Jurisprudence of the ECHR* (Antwerp: Intersentia, 2002).

rchibugi, D., *The Global Commonwealth of Citizens: Toward Cosmopolitan Democracy* (Princeton University Press, 2008).

Barker, E., *Political Thought in England: From Herbert Spencer to the Present Day* (London: Williams and Norgate, 1915).

Berman, H. J., *Law and Revolution: The Formation of the Western Legal Tradition* (Cambridge, MA: Harvard University Press, 1983).

Berman, P. S., 'Judges as Cosmopolitan Transnational Actors', *Tulsa Journal of Comparative and International Law*, 12 (2004), pp. 109–21.

'Conflict of Laws, Globalization, and Cosmopolitan Pluralism', *Wayne Law Review*, 51 (2005), pp. 1105–45.

'Towards a Cosmopolitan Vision of Conflict of Laws: Redefining Governmental Interest in a Global Era', *University of Pennsylvania Law Review*, 153 (2005), pp. 1819–82.

'The New Legal Pluralism', *Annual Review of Law and Social Science*, 5 (2009), pp. 225–42.

Global Legal Pluralism: A Jurisprudence of Law Beyond Borders (Cambridge University Press, 2012).

Besselink, L. F. M., 'National and Constitutional Identity Before and After Lisbon', *Utrecht Law Review*, 6 (2010), pp. 36–49.

Besson, S., 'European Legal Pluralism after Kadi', *European Constitutional Law Review*, 5 (2009), pp. 237–64.

von Bogdandy, A., and S. Schill, 'Overcoming Absolute Primacy: Respect for National Identity under the Lisbon Treaty', *Common Market Law Review*, 48 (2011), pp. 1417–53.

Bohman, J., *Democracy across Borders: From Dêmos to Dêmoi* (Cambridge, MA: MIT Press, 2007).

Brauch, J. A., 'The Margin of Appreciation and the Jurisprudence of the European Court of Human Rights: Threat to the Rule of Law', *Columbia Journal of European Law*, 11 (2005), pp. 113–50.

Buergenthal, T., 'The Evolving International Human Rights System', *American Journal of International Law*, 100 (2006), pp. 783–807.

Burke-White, W. W., 'Proactive Complementarity: The International Criminal Court and National Courts in the Rome System of International Justice', *Harvard International Law Journal*, 49 (2008), pp. 53–108.

Calliess, G.-P., 'Transnational Civil Regimes: Economic Globalisation and the Evolution of Commercial Law' in V. Gessner (ed.), *Contractual Certainty in International Trade: Empirical Studies and Theoretical Debates on Institutional Support for Global Economic Exchanges* (Oxford: Hart Publishing, 2009), pp. 215–38.

Carozza, P. G., 'Subsidiarity as a Structural Principle of International Human Rights Law', *American Journal of International Law*, 97 (2003), pp. 38–79.

Cass, D. Z., *The Constitutionalization of the World Trade Organization: Legitimacy, Democracy, and Community in the International Trading System* (Oxford University Press, 2005).

Cassese, S., *I tribunali di Babele: i giudici alla ricerca di un nuovo ordine globale* (Rome: Donzelli, 2009).

Charnovitz, S., 'Free Trade, Fair Trade, Green Trade: Defogging the Debate', *Cornell International Law Journal*, 27 (1994), pp. 459–525.

Cole, G. D. H., *Social Theory* (London: Methuen, 1920).

Crawford, S. P., 'The ICANN Experiment', *Cardozo Journal of International and Comparative Law*, 12 (2004), pp. 409–48.

Dahl, R. A., 'Can International Organizations Be Democratic? A Sceptic's View' in I. Shapiro and C. Hacker-Cordón (eds.), *Democracy's Edges* (Cambridge University Press, 1999), pp. 19–36.

Delmas-Marty, M., *Ordering Pluralism: A Conceptual Framework for Understanding the Transnational Legal World*, N. Norberg trans. (Oxford: Hart Publishing, 2009).

Dinwoodie, G. B., 'A New Copyright Order: Why National Courts Should Create Global Norms', *University of Pennsylvania Law Review*, 149 (2000), pp. 469–580.

Dodge, W. S., 'The Public-Private Distinction in the Conflict of Laws', *Duke Journal of Comparative and International Law*, 18 (2008), pp. 371–94.

El Zeidy, M. M., 'The Principle of Complementarity: A New Machinery to Implement International Criminal Law', *Michigan Journal of International Law*, 23 (2002), pp. 869–975.

Eleftheriadis, P., 'Pluralism and Integrity', *Ratio Juris*, 23 (2010), pp. 365–89.

Eriksen, E. O., *The Unfinished Democratization of Europe* (Oxford University Press, 2009).

Falk, R. A., 'The Pathways of Global Constitutionalism', in R. A. Falk, R. C. Johansen and S. S. Kim (eds.), *The Constitutional Foundations of World Peace* (Albany: State University of New York Press, 1993), pp. 13–38.

Fassbender, B., 'The United Nations Charter as Constitution of the International Community', *Columbia Journal of Transnational Law*, 36 (1998), pp. 529–619.

Fischer-Lescano, A., and G. Teubner, 'Regime-Collisions: The Vain Search for Legal Unity in the Fragmentation of Global Law', *Michigan Journal of International Law*, 25 (2004), pp. 999–1046.

Føllesdal, A., 'The Principle of Subsidiarity as a Constitutional Principle in International Law', *Global Constitutionalism*, 2 (2013), pp. 37–62.

Froomkin, A. M., 'Wrong Turn in Cyberspace: Using ICANN to Route Around the APA and the Constitution', *Duke Law Journal*, 50 (2000), pp. 17–186.

'ICANN's "Uniform Dispute Resolution Policy": Causes and (Partial) Cures', *Brooklyn Law Review*, 67 (2002), pp. 605–718.

Gaja, G., 'The Review by the European Court of Human Rights of Member States' Acts Implementing European Union Law: "Solange" Yet Again?' in P.-M. Dupuy et al. (eds.), *Common Values in International Law: Essays in Honour of Christian Tomuschat* (Kehl: Engel, 2006), pp. 517–26.

Garlicki, L., 'Cooperation of Courts: The Role of Supranational Jurisdictions in Europe', *International Journal of Constitutional Law*, 6 (2008), pp. 509–30.

Gerards, J., 'Pluralism, Deference and the Margin of Appreciation Doctrine', *European Law Journal*, 17 (2011), pp. 80–120.

Giddens, A., *The Consequences of Modernity* (Stanford University Press, 1990).

von Gierke, O., *Political Theories of the Middle Age*, F. W. Maitland trans. (Cambridge University Press, 1900).

Das Wesen der menschlichen Verbände (Berlin: Schade, 1902).

Goldsmith, J. L., and E. A. Posner, *The Limits of International Law* (Oxford University Press, 2005).

Griffiths, J., 'What Is Legal Pluralism?', *Journal of Legal Pluralism and Unofficial Law*, 24 (1986), pp. 1–55.

Grimm, D., 'The Achievement of Constitutionalism and Its Prospects in a Changed World' in P. Dobner and M. Loughlin (eds.), *The Twilight of Constitutionalism?* (Oxford University Press, 2010), pp. 3–22.

Grossi, P., *L'ordinegiuridico medievale* (Rome: Laterza, 1995).

Günther, K., 'Legal Pluralism or Uniform Concept of Law? Globalisation as a Problem of Legal Theory', *No Foundations*, 5 (2008), pp. 5–21.

Guzman, A. T., *How International Law Works: A Rational Choice Theory* (Oxford University Press, 2008).

Habermas, J., *Between Facts and Norms: Contributions to a Discourse Theory of Law and Democracy*, W. Rehg trans. (Cambridge, MA: MIT Press, 1996).

'A Political Constitution for the Pluralist World Society?' in J. Habermas, *Between Naturalism and Religion: Philosophical Essays*, C. Cronin trans. (Cambridge: Polity Press, 2008), pp. 312–52.

Hafner, G., 'Pros and Cons Ensuing from Fragmentation of International Law', *Michigan Journal of International Law*, 25 (2004), pp. 849–63.

Halberstam, D., 'Local, Global and Plural Constitutionalism: Europe Meets the World' in G. de Búrca and J. H. H. Weiler (eds.), *The Worlds of European Constitutionalism* (Cambridge University Press, 2012), pp. 150–202.

Halberstam, D., and E. Stein, 'The United Nations, the European Union, and the King of Sweden: Economic Sanctions and Individual Rights in a Plural World Order', *Common Market Law Review*, 46 (2009), pp. 13–72.

Hamilton, A., 'The Federalist No. 9' in J. E. Cooke (ed.), *The Federalist* (Middletown: Wesleyan University Press, 1961), pp. 50–6.

Hart, H. L. A., *The Concept of Law* (Oxford: Clarendon Press, 1961).

Hauriou, M., 'La théorie de l'institution et de la fondation: essai de vitalisme social', *Cahiers de la nouvelle journée*, 4 (1925), pp. 1–45.

Held, D., *Democracy and the Global Order: From the Modern State to Cosmopolitan Governance* (Cambridge: Polity Press, 1995).

Helfer, L. R., and G. B. Dinwoodie, 'Designing Non-National Systems: The Case of the Uniform Domain Name Dispute Resolution Policy', *William and Mary Law Review*, 43 (2001), pp. 141–274.

Hooker, M. B., *Legal Pluralism: An Introduction to Colonial and Neo-Colonial Laws* (Oxford: Clarendon Press, 1975).

Jackson, J. H., *Sovereignty, the WTO, and Changing Fundamentals of International Law* (Cambridge University Press, 2006).

Jackson, V. C., *Constitutional Engagement in a Transnational Era* (Oxford University Press, 2010).

Jacqué, J.-P., 'L'arrêt Bosphorus, une jurisprudence "Solange II" de la Cour européenne des droits de l'homme?', *Revue trimestrielle de droit européen*, 41 (2005), pp. 756–67.

Jellinek, G., *Die rechtliche Natur der Staatenverträge: Ein Beitrag zur juristischen Construction des Völkerrechts* (Vienna: Hölder, 1880).

Die Lehre von den Staatenverbindungen (Vienna: Hölder, 1882).

Joerges, C., 'A New Type of Conflicts Law as the Legal Paradigm of the Postnational Constellation' in C. Joerges and J. Falke (eds.), *Karl Polanyi,*

Globalisation and the Potential of Law in Transnational Markets (Oxford: Hart Publishing, 2011), pp. 465–501.

Joerges, C., and J. Neyer, 'From Intergovernmental Bargaining to Deliberative Political Processes: The Constitutionalisation of Comitology', *European Law Journal*, 3 (1997), pp. 273–99.

Kelsen, H., *Das Problem der Souveränität und die Theorie des Völkerrechts: Beitrag zu einer reinen Rechtslehre*, 2nd edn (Tübingen: Mohr, 1928).

Kennedy, D., 'One, Two, Three, Many Legal Orders: Legal Pluralism and the Cosmopolitan Dream', *New York University Review of Law and Social Change*, 31 (2007), pp. 641–59.

Knop, K., R. Michaels, and A. Riles, 'International Law in Domestic Courts: A Conflict of Laws Approach', *American Society of International Law Proceedings*, 103 (2009), pp. 269–74.

'From Multiculturalism to Technique: Feminism, Culture, and the Conflict of Laws Style', *Stanford Law Review*, 64 (2012), pp. 589–656.

Koskenniemi, M., and P. Leino, 'Fragmentation of International Law? Postmodern Anxieties', *Leiden Journal of International Law*, 15 (2002), pp. 553–79.

Krisch, N., 'The Open Architecture of European Human Rights Law', *Modern Law Review*, 71 (2008), pp. 183–216.

Beyond Constitutionalism: The Pluralist Structure of Postnational Law (Oxford University Press, 2010).

'Who Is Afraid of Radical Pluralism? Legal Order and Political Stability in the Postnational Space', *Ratio Juris*, 24 (2011), pp. 386–412.

Kumm, M., 'The Cosmopolitan Turn in Constitutionalism: On the Relationship between Constitutionalism in and beyond the State' in J. L. Dunoff and J. P. Trachtman (eds.), *Ruling the World? Constitutionalism, International Law, and Global Governance* (Cambridge University Press, 2009), pp. 258–324.

'The Cosmopolitan Turn in Constitutionalism: An Integrated Conception of Public Law', *Indiana Journal of Global Legal Studies*, 20 (2013), pp. 605–28.

Laband, P., *Das Staatsrecht des Deutschen Reiches*, 5th edn, 4 vols. (Tübingen: Mohr Siebeck, 1911–1914).

Ladeur, K.-H., 'Globalization and the Conversion of Democracy to Polycentric Networks: Can Democracy Survive the End of the Nation-State?' in K.-H. Ladeur (ed.), *Public Governance in the Age of Globalization* (Aldershot: Ashgate, 2004), pp. 89–118.

Lanier, E. R., 'Solange, Farewell: The Federal German Constitutional Court and the Recognition of the Court of Justice of the European Communities as Lawful Judge', *Boston College International and Comparative Law Review*, 11 (1988), pp. 1–29.

Laski, H. J., 'The Personality of Associations', *Harvard Law Review*, 29 (1916), pp. 404–26.

'The Sovereignty of the State', *Journal of Philosophy, Psychology and Scientific Methods*, 13 (1916), pp. 85–97.

A Grammar of Politics, 4th edn (London: Allen and Unwin, 1938).

Lavranos, N., 'The Solange-Method as a Tool for Regulating Competing Jurisdictions among International Courts and Tribunals', *Loyola of Los Angeles International and Comparative Law Review*, 30 (2008), pp. 275–334.

Legg, A., *The Margin of Appreciation in International Human Rights Law: Deference and Proportionality* (Oxford University Press, 2012).

Letsas, G., 'Two Concepts of the Margin of Appreciation', *Oxford Journal of Legal Studies*, 26 (2006), pp. 705–32.

'Harmonic Law: The Case Against Pluralism' in J. Dickson and P. Eleftheriadis (eds.), *Philosophical Foundations of European Union Law* (Oxford University Press, 2012), pp. 77–108.

Lovric, D., 'A Constitution Friendly to International Law: Germany and Its Völerrechtsfreundlichkeit', *Australian Yearbook of International Law*, 25 (2006), pp. 75–104.

Lowenfeld, A. F., 'Public Law in the International Arena: Conflict of Laws, International Law, and Some Suggestions for Their Interaction', *Recueil des cours de l'Académie de droit international*, 163 (1979-II), pp. 311–445.

Lübbe-Wolff, G., 'How Can the European Court of Human Rights Reinforce the Role of National Courts in the Convention System?', *Human Rights Law Journal*, 32 (2012), pp. 11–15.

Luhmann, N., *A Sociological Theory of Law*, E. King and M. Albrow trans. (London: Routledge and Kegan Paul, 1985).

'Some Problems with "Reflexive Law"' in G. Teubner and A. Febbrajo (eds.), *State, Law, and Economy as Autopoietic Systems: Regulation and Autonomy in a New Perspective* (Milan: Giuffrè, 1992), pp. 389–415.

Law as a Social System, K. A. Ziegert trans. (Oxford University Press, 2004).

Theory of Society, R. Barrett trans., 2 vols. (Stanford University Press, 2012).

Macaulay, S., 'Private Government' in L. Lipson and S. Wheeler (eds.), *Law and the Social Sciences* (New York: Russell Sage Foundation, 1986), pp. 445–518.

MacCormick, N., 'Risking Constitutional Collision in Europe?', *Oxford Journal of Legal Studies*, 18 (1998), pp. 517–32.

Madison, J., 'The Federalist No. 39' in J. E. Cooke (ed.), *The Federalist* (Middletown: Wesleyan University Press, 1961), pp. 250–7.

McGoldrick, D., *The Human Rights Committee: Its Role in the Development of the International Covenant on Civil and Political Rights* (Oxford: Clarendon Press, 1991).

von Mehren, A. T., 'Special Substantive Rules for Multistate Problems: Their Role and Significance in Contemporary Choice of Law Methodology', *Harvard Law Review*, 88 (1974), pp. 347–71.

Michelman, F. I., 'W(h)ither the Constitution?', *Cardozo Law Review*, 21 (2000), pp. 1063–83.

Nollkaemper, A., *National Courts and the International Rule of Law* (Oxford University Press, 2011).

Nonet, P., and P. Selznick, *Law and Society in Transition: Toward Responsive Law* (New York: Harper and Row, 1978).

Nye, Jr., J. S., *The Paradox of American Power: Why the World's Only Superpower Can't Go It Alone* (Oxford University Press, 2002).

Pastor Ridruejo, J. A., 'Le principe de subsidiarité dans la Convention européenne des droits de l'homme' in J. Bröhmer et al. (eds.), *Internationale Gemeinschaft und Menschenrechte: Festschrift für Georg Ress zum 70. Geburtstag* (Cologne: Heymanns, 2005), pp. 1077–83.

Pauwelyn, J., *Conflict of Norms in Public International Law: How WTO Law Relates to Other Rules of International Law* (Cambridge University Press, 2003).

Pernice, I., 'The Global Dimension of Multilevel Constitutionalism: A Legal Response to the Challenges of Globalisation' in P.-M. Dupuy et al. (eds.), *Common Values in International Law: Essays in Honour of Christian Tomuschat* (Kehl: Engel, 2006), pp. 973–1005.

Peters, A., 'The Merits of Global Constitutionalism', *Indiana Journal of Global Legal Studies*, 16 (2009), pp. 397–411.

Petersmann, E.-U., 'Time for a United Nations "Global Compact" for Integrating Human Rights into the Law of Worldwide Organizations: Lessons from European Integration', *European Journal of International Law*, 13 (2002), pp. 621–50.

Petzold, H., 'The Convention and the Principle of Subsidiarity' in R. St. J. Macdonald, F. Matscher and H. Petzold (eds.), *The European System for the Protection of Human Rights* (Dordrecht: Nijhoff, 1993), pp. 41–62.

Poiares Maduro, M., 'Three Claims of Constitutional Pluralism' in M. Avbelj and J. Komárek (eds.), *Constitutional Pluralism in the European Union and Beyond* (Oxford: Hart Publishing, 2012), pp. 67–84.

Pospíšil, L., *Anthropology of Law: A Comparative Theory* (New York: Harper and Row, 1971).

Rabkin, J. A., *Law without Nations? Why Constitutional Government Requires Sovereign States* (Princeton University Press, 2005).

Romano, C. P. R., 'The Proliferation of International Judicial Bodies: The Pieces of the Puzzle', *New York University Journal of International Law and Politics*, 31 (1999), pp. 709–51.

Romano, S., *L'ordinamento giuridico: studi sul concetto, le fonti e i caratteri del diritto* (Pisa: Spoerri, 1918).

Rubenfeld, J., 'Unilateralism and Constitutionalism', *New York University Law Review*, 79 (2004), pp. 1971–2028.

Sassen, S., *A Sociology of Globalization* (New York: Norton, 2007).

von Savigny, F. C., *System des heutigen Römischen Rechts*, 8 vols. (Berlin: Veit, 1849).

Scelle, G., *Précis de droit des gens: principes et systématique*, 2 vols. (Paris: Sirey, 1932–1934).

Schmitt, C., *Constitutional Theory*, J. Seitzer trans. (Durham, NC: Duke University Press, 2008).

Schultz, T., 'Secondary Rules of Recognition and Relative Legality in Transnational Regimes', *American Journal of Jurisprudence*, 56 (2011), pp. 59–88.

Selznick, P., *Law, Society, and Industrial Justice* (New York: Russell Sage Foundation, 1969).

Shany, Y., 'Toward a General Margin of Appreciation Doctrine in International Law?', *European Journal of International Law*, 16 (2005), pp. 907–40.

Shelton, D., 'Subsidiarity and Human Rights Law', *Human Rights Law Journal*, 27 (2006), pp. 4–11.

Simma, B., 'From Bilateralism to Community Interest in International Law', *Recueil des cours de l'Académie de droit international*, 250 (1994-VI), pp. 217–384.

Simma, B., and D. Pulkowski, 'Of Planets and the Universe: Self-Contained Regimes in International Law', *European Journal of International Law*, 17 (2006), pp. 483–529.

Slaughter, A.-M., 'A Global Community of Courts', *Harvard International Law Journal*, 44 (2003), pp. 191–219.

de Sousa Santos, B., *Toward a New Legal Common Sense: Law, Globalization, and Emancipation*, 2nd edn (London: Butterworths, 2002).

Stein, E., 'Lawyers, Judges, and the Making of a Transnational Constitution', *American Journal of International Law*, 75 (1981), pp. 1–27.

Story, J., *Commentaries on the Conflict of Laws, Foreign and Domestic: In Regard to Contracts, Rights, and Remedies, and Especially in Regard to Marriages, Divorces, Wills, Successions, and Judgments* (Boston: Hilliard, Gray and Company, 1834).

Sweeney, J. A., 'A "Margin of Appreciation" in the Internal Market: Lessons from the European Court of Human Rights', *Legal Issues of Economic Integration*, 34 (2007), pp. 27–52.

Teubner, G., 'Substantive and Reflexive Elements in Modern Law', *Law and Society Review*, 17 (1983), pp. 239–85.

'Global Bukowina: Legal Pluralism in the World Society' in G. Teubner (ed.), *Global Law without a State* (Aldershot: Dartmouth, 1997), pp. 3–28.

'Global Private Regimes: Neo-Spontaneous Law and Dual Constitution of Autonomous Sectors?' in K.-H. Ladeur (ed.), *Public Governance in the Age of Globalization* (Aldershot: Ashgate, 2004), pp. 71–87.

'The Anonymous Matrix: Human Rights Violations by "Private" Transnational Actors', *Modern Law Review*, 69 (2006), pp. 327–46.

Constitutional Fragments: Societal Constitutionalism and Globalization (Oxford University Press, 2012).

Teubner, G., and V. Karavas, 'www.CompanyNameSucks.com: The Horizontal Effect of Fundamental Rights on "Private Parties" within Autonomous Internet Law', *Constellations*, 12 (2005), pp. 262–82.

Teubner, G., and P. Korth, 'Two Kinds of Legal Pluralism: Collision of Transnational Regimes in the Double Fragmentation of World Society' in M. A. Young (ed.), *Regime Interaction in International Law: Facing Fragmentation* (Cambridge University Press, 2012), pp. 23–54.

de Tocqueville, A., *Democracy in America*, H. C. Mansfield and D. Winthrop trans. (University of Chicago Press, 2000).

Trachtman, J. P., *The Future of International Law: Global Government* (Cambridge University Press, 2013).

Triepel, H., *Völkerrecht und Landesrecht* (Leipzig: Hirschfeld, 1899).

Tzanakopoulos, A., 'Judicial Dialogue in Multi-Level Governance: The Impact of the Solange Argument' in O. K. Fauchald and A. Nollkaemper (eds.), *The Practice of International and National Courts and the (De-)Fragmentation of International Law* (Oxford: Hart Publishing, 2012), pp. 185–215.

Viellechner, L., 'The Constitution of Transnational Governance Arrangements: Karl Polanyi's Double Movement in the Transformation of Law' in C. Joerges and J. Falke (eds.), *Karl Polanyi, Globalisation and the Potential of Law in Transnational Markets* (Oxford: Hart Publishing, 2011), pp. 435–64.

Voßkuhle, A., 'Multilevel Cooperation of the European Constitutional Courts: Der Europäische Verfassungsgerichtsverbund', *European Constitutional Law Review*, 6 (2010), pp. 175–98.

Waitz, G., 'Das Wesen des Bundesstaates', *Allgemeine Monatsschrift für Wissenschaft und Literatur*, 4 (1853), pp. 494–530.

Walker, N., 'The Idea of Constitutional Pluralism', *Modern Law Review*, 65 (2002), pp. 317–59.

Weiler, J. H. H., 'The Transformation of Europe', *Yale Law Journal*, 100 (1991), pp. 2403–83.

Wellens, K. C., 'Diversity in Secondary Rules and the Unity of International Law: Some Reflections on Current Trends', *Netherlands Yearbook of International Law*, 25 (1994), pp. 3–37.

Willke, H., 'Societal Guidance through Law?' in G. Teubner and A. Febbrajo (eds.), *State, Law, and Economy as Autopoietic Systems: Regulation and Autonomy in a New Perspective* (Milan: Giuffrè, 1992), pp. 353–88.

Yntema, H. E., 'The Comity Doctrine', *Michigan Law Review*, 65 (1966), pp. 9–32.

Ziller, J., 'The German Constitutional Court's Friendliness towards European Law: On the Judgment of Bundesverfassungsgericht over the Ratification of the Treaty of Lisbon', *European Public Law*, 16 (2010), pp. 53–73.

PART II

Addressing collisions

Regulation and self-regulation

5

Horizontal fundamental rights as conflict of laws rules

How transnational pharmagroups manipulate scientific publications

ISABELL HENSEL AND GUNTHER TEUBNER

But where are the pictures of the people who drowned?[1]

Publication bias

Here are three cases of the manipulation of clinical studies in the pharmaceutical network:

The Edronax Case: In 1997 the antidepressant Edronax, which contains the ingredient Reboxetine and was manufactured by the pharmaceutical company Pfizer, was licensed in Germany and other EU countries, although an attempt to have the drug licensed in the United States had failed. In 2010 the *British Medical Journal* revealed (as was confirmed by later studies carried out by the Institute for Quality and Efficiency in Health Care (IQWiG)) that less than two thirds of the studies actually carried out, specifically those with positive results, had been duly published by Pfizer, while no mention was made of those studies that showed that in comparison with placebos the drug was not only ineffective but also had harmful side effects.[2]

The BASF Versus Dong Case: Boots Pharmaceuticals (now the Knoll Pharmaceutical Company), a subsidiary of BASF, commissioned the research scientist Prof Betty Dong of the University of California, San Francisco, to investigate the effectiveness of Synthroid, the drug most

1 The poet Diagoras of Melos poses this provocative question when a priest shows him the votive pictures of people who have been saved (by prayer) from shipwreck as a proof of the existence of God. Diagoras was subsequently sentenced to death. From Cicero's *De Natura Deorum*.

2 Eyding et al., 'Reboxetine'.

frequently prescribed for thyroid in the USA, in return for an advance payment for the research in the amount of a quarter of a million dollars. In return, Dong had to sign a contract stating that she would not publish any negative study results without Knoll's agreement. In fact, Synthroid was found not to have any advantages in terms of its effectiveness by comparison with comparable and cheaper generic products. On the basis of the contractual clause, and by making defamatory statements concerning Dong and her scientific methods, Boots then prevented publication for seven years. As a result, by claiming that Synthroid was a superior product, the Group was able to further expand its market share. When the *Wall Street Journal* made the case public in 1996, BASF had to face class action lawsuits from approximately 5 million claimants for inadmissible suppression of the study, unfair competition practices and violation of consumer protection regulations. The company ultimately agreed to a settlement.[3]

The Hormone Replacement Therapies Case: Alongside many other pharmaceutical companies which had been in competition with each other from as far back as the 1940s over the prevention of symptoms of menopause by hormone replacement therapies, Wyeth (now Pfizer) organised marketing campaigns well into the 1990s. Without any basis in terms of the results of solid scientific studies, Wyeth promoted the preventive effect of the treatments. Only when an external randomised study was carried out in 1998, with further follow up studies and a Women's Health Initiative in 2002, was the preventive effect refuted and evidence produced concerning the health risks to women who had used these treatments, and who had had strokes or had developed breast cancer, thrombosis, dementia and incontinence more frequently after receiving the treatment. Media, such as the *Public Library of Science* and *The New York Times* obtained court decisions forcing the disclosure of the marketing documents by the manufacturer, Wyeth, in parallel with the compensation claims filed by the women whose health had been damaged. In the course of all this it emerged that the majority of the scientific articles on which the marketing campaign was based had been written in cooperation with communications agencies and ghost writers.[4]

There is a long list of such scandals involving the big pharmaceutical companies. Over and over again, scientific findings concerning the harmful effects of medicinal products for patients' health, or the total absence of any effects whatsoever for health, are not reaching the public, or only on a selective basis. These manipulations take many different

[3] Cf. United States Court of Appeals, 7th Cir. (2008) *BASF AG* v. *Great American Assurance Co.*, 522 F.3d 813, 816. See Krimsky, *Science in the Public Interest.*

[4] Fugh-Berman, 'The Haunting of Medical Journals'.

forms, including selective publication,[5] censorship clauses in research contracts, the use of ghost writers, the application of pressure on researchers to prevent studies from being carried out[6] and even the dismissal of researchers by financially dependent research institutions.[7] Underlying these cases is a conflict of incompatible rationalities[8] that ultimately leads to a publication bias.[9] This term is used to describe the statistical distortion of data when research data are suppressed or manipulated in scientific publications.

Publication bias is a worldwide problem that stems from the massive conflicts of interest that exist between research institutions, the pharmaceutical industry, the healthcare system, the publishing world, investors and political regulation bodies. For example, a study that compared protocols and subsequently published articles in 102 studies of medicinal products showed that in 62 per cent of cases the published article seriously deviated from the study protocol.[10] In a steadily increasing number of cases, negative (i.e., unwelcome) study results that will not be effective in terms of the marketing of the substances concerned are withheld or manipulated, and only the positive results are published in the specialist journals. Thus, only a portion of the clinical studies carried out reach the public domain.

It is not sufficient to describe publication bias as a consequence of individual corruption, which can be controlled by the regulatory bodies of national governments. In light of the worldwide activities of the big pharmaceutical companies and the globalisation of academic research, this is a conflict with transnational dimensions.[11] At the same time it points to a structural conflict within society, which political control will

[5] Cf. also the criticisms made in the case of the Vioxx study (involving Merck as manufacturer), in which the myocardial infarction risk was concealed (Bombardier et al., 'Comparison', pp. 1520–8) and in the case of the study on the licensed swine flu drug Tamiflu, manufactured by Roche (Jefferson et al., 'Neuraminidase Inhibitors').

[6] See the case of the so-called MIDAS study of the efficacy of calcium blockers (involving Sandoz, subsequently Novartis as manufacturer), in which the researchers successfully defended themselves. Applegate et al., 'Midas', pp. 297–8.

[7] For example, the dismissal of the research scientist Nancy Olivieri from the University of Toronto when she wanted to issue warnings about negative study results; her employer was receiving research grants from Apotex, the manufacturer of the drug under investigation. See Viens and Savulescu, 'Olivieri Symposium', pp. 1–7.

[8] For conflicts of incompatible rationalities in modern societies, see Weber, *Gesammelte Aufsätze*, pp. 605ff.; Luhmann, *Theory of Society*, p. 18.

[9] See the early use of this term by Smith, 'Publication bias', pp. 22–4.

[10] Chan et al., 'Empirical Evidence for Selective Reporting of Outcomes', pp. 2457–65.

[11] Petryna, *When Experiments Travel.*

only be able to correct in isolated cases, without effectively getting to grips with the problem. Underlying the circumstances of the individual cases is a problem of constitutional rights – the conflict between different social rationalities. The hazards of constitutional autonomies provoke political regulations, judicial considerations, but more crucially and fundamentally, social self-regulations. Therefore, we analyse the effects of these social constitutional rights and their repercussion on politics and law.

Third party effect of constitutional rights: a critique and some alternatives

Can constitutional rights be used as conflict of laws rules to overcome this multidimensional conflict that is being played out both in a national and a transnational context? Obviously there is a massive clash between the interest of transnational pharmaceutical groups in the successful marketing of their products and the interests of the research community in publishing their results without hindrance, as well as the interest of the patients in having effective health protection. Of legal relevance here is the third party effect of constitutional rights, according to which actors can assert their constitutional rights (academic freedom and the right to health being the relevant rights here) not only vis-à-vis governmental bodies but also vis-à-vis private actors.[12] The term 'third party effect' implies a transfer of constitutional rights in public law to relationships under private law. A central concern in this transfer is that the principles of private law are not violated in the process. For this reason a direct third party effect is usually rejected, and only an indirect third party effect is accepted, whereby the value system of constitutional rights is transformed by the general clauses of private law, and addressed to the judiciary. Parallel to this, the doctrine of protective duties establishes a responsibility of the legislator in regard to constitutional rights in private relationships. In essence, all third party effect concepts envisage a balancing of the private law subjects' opposing rights taking place on the basis of the individual case.

[12] For the current discussion in Germany, Rüfner, 'Grundrechtsadressaten', paras. 83–125; in a historical perspective, Stolleis, *Geschichte des öffentlichen Rechts*, pp. 216ff. Concerning the legal position in Europe, Clapham, *Human Rights Obligations*. For international law, Gardbaum, 'The "Horizontal Effect"', pp. 387–459; Ruggie, 'Protect, Respect and Remedy', pp. 6–13.

By comparison with the longstanding tradition of constitutional rights, which are based exclusively on the relationship between the individual and the state, the third party effect represents a significant change. It responds to the emergence of intermediary social forces with the transfer of public law norms into private law relationships. Yet it is precisely in the image of a transfer that the problem lies. The differences between the sender's context and the recipient's context are so great as to make any transfer of norms in the strict sense impossible. Instead, what is needed is a separate reconstruction of constitutional rights that is dependent on the recipient's context. The transfer metaphor may still be convincing as a kind of transitional explanation, whereby constitutional rights asserted against the state are 'transferred' to private law and acquire 'third party effect' vis-à-vis social actors. In the long term, however, constitutional rights within society can only be understood on the basis of their different origin of intra-societal conflicts. Intra-societal conflicts are fundamentally different from state-society conflicts. They differ in the circumstances of the constitutional right violation and in their appropriate sanctions, so that the simple term 'third party effect' of constitutional rights originally asserted against the state is misleading.

The challenge consists in releasing the third party effects in private law from their clandestine attachment to the state, and developing their standards from the outset on the basis of intra-societal conflicts. In the following, therefore, *publication bias* is taken as a basis for a critical examination of the four central aspects of third party effect theory and for the development of alternatives. We will develop four theses:

(1) The third party effect has so far been configured in an individualist perspective only, as balancing individual constitutional rights of private actors against each other. However, in order to deal with massive structural conflicts within society, constitutional rights in private relations have to be reformulated in their collective-institutional dimension.

(2) Instead of being limited to the protection against state-equivalent power in society, the third party effect must be widened and directed against all communication media with expansive tendencies.

(3) Contextualising constitutional rights ought not to be limited to adapting these rights to the particularities of private law only. It must go further than this and take into account the particular normative nature of the autonomous social institutions that are at risk.

(4) Instead of imposing duties to protect exclusively on state actors, third party effects must actually address the private actors who violate constitutional rights themselves and at the same time activate counter-forces within society.

Constitutional rights as collective institutions

An initial critique is directed against the prevailing understanding of the third party effect as a balancing of individual constitutional rights.[13] If the third party effect is seen as a transfer of public constitutional rights into private relationships, this ignores the fact that a mere transfer will alter the structure of the rights and reduce legal protection. The question of the possible unlawfulness of any interference is not examined; instead, legal subjects under private law are classified as 'violators' and 'violated' and their equally justified constitutional right positions are brought into 'practical concordance' in the individual case.[14] This does not provide more than a purely formal additional value by comparison with the protection of subjective rights in tort law. On the contrary, the legal protection is reduced, since violations of constitutional rights are much more difficult to establish, the balancing dimensions multiply, and the political leeway for balancing expands.[15] And making the decision concerning violations of constitutional rights dependent on the circumstances of the individual case makes it impossible to formulate general norms for such far-reaching issues. This amounts to a level of casuistry that is conceptually uncontrollable.

However, the most important objection to such an exclusive focusing on individual rights is that we fail to address the central problem of violations of constitutional rights within society. While it has long been recognised in public law that constitutional rights serve to protect both individual rights and social institutions,[16] the third party effect in private law has so far generally only focused on individual protection and has

[13] Ladeur, *Kritik der Abwägung*; Fischer-Lescano, 'Kritik der praktischen Konkordanz', pp. 166–77. A critique of the legal situation in the United States, Mathews and Stone Sweet, 'All Things in Proportion?', p. 116.

[14] The principle is defined by Hesse, *Grundzüge des Verfassungsrechts*, MN. 72; Alexy, 'Verfassungsrecht und einfaches Recht', pp. 7ff. Early on, BVerfG, BVerfGE 83, 130 – Mutzenbacher.

[15] For a critical view on state duties of care in the 'risk society' see Christensen and Fischer-Lescano, *Das Ganze des Rechts*, pp. 311ff.

[16] In general Dreier, *Dimensionen der Grundrechte*, pp. 27ff.

neglected the protection of institutions. The German Federal Constitutional Court (BVerfG) regards the conflict here as only between individual subjective rights of 'equal-ranking holders of constitutional rights', between 'conflicting constitutional right positions' 'in their interdependency'.[17] In so doing, the court ignores the fact that here the collective-institutional dimension of constitutional rights becomes virulent.

In the conflict between collective institutions, however, lies the really controversial problem of the third party effect. The term 'collective-institutional' distances itself from Carl Schmitt's institutionalism and refers explicitly to Helmut Ridder's theory of 'non personal constitutional rights', according to which 'constitutional rights are aimed at the specific freedom of a social field through the organisation of that field' – freedom of science or freedom of art, for example.[18] It should in particular be emphasised that in contrast to politically conservative preconceptions, 'institution' is understood not as a legal guarantee for the permanent existence of social structures against tendencies of political change – in Carl Schmitt's definition: 'what is present, formally and organisationally exists and is at hand'[19] – but as a socio-legal normativisation process which is subject to constant change.

Admittedly it is entirely possible, in the case of publication bias, for scientists to assert individual defence claims against the censorship imposed by the big pharmaceutical companies, or to plead the nullity of contracts that prevent publication, or for patients to sue for damages. But all private litigation by individual actors fails to take account of the collective-institutional dimension, and therefore also the really difficult conflicts within society. For the manipulations of the big pharmaceutical companies do not merely violate individual rights of scientists and patients, but also – and in a more profound way – the integrity of social institutions, scientific research and the provision of healthcare.[20]

17 BVerfGE 89, 214 – Bürgschaft.

18 Ridder, *Die soziale Ordnung des Grundgesetzes*, pp. 90–1 (translation by the authors); Ridder, *Die Freiheit der Kunst*. Definition of the term by Steinhauer, 'Das Grundrecht der Kunstfreiheit', pp. 247–82, who for reasons of clarity introduced the term 'collective-institutional' and used it to describe Ridder's concept in contradistinction to Carl Schmitt's 'institutional' constitutional rights theory.

19 Schmitt, 'Freiheitsrechte und institutionelle Garantien', p. 155 (translation by the authors).

20 The fact that academic freedom is put at risk not only through governmental interference is emphasised by Augsberg, 'Dimensionen der Wissenschaftsfreiheit', p. 74. The same is true for the global health system, Krajewska, 'Global Health Law'.

It needs to be stressed that the collective-institutional dimension plays a part not only for the victims of the rights violations, but also on both sides of the horizontal constitutional rights relationship. If the victim side includes institutions as well as individuals, then on the perpetrators' side it is not only people, but also anonymous social processes that in some cases must be held responsible for the violation of constitutional rights. This two-sided aspect of the collective-institutional relationship is often overlooked. However, the discussion in criminal law, concerning the so-called macro-criminality and the criminality of formal organisations, which has as its background the sociological debate on 'structural violence',[21] has developed such a collective-institutional perspective for the perpetrators' side also.

In such cases, violations of constitutional rights are ultimately attributable to non-personal social processes, which use human actors as their agents.[22] Structural violence assumes an 'anonymous matrix', that is not only 'collective actors' which tend to be more visible (states, political parties, commercial companies, groups of companies, associations), but as well (with an equal if not greater intensity) anonymous communicative processes (institutions, functional systems, networks), which are difficult to address because they are definitely not personified as collective actors.[23] The hazards that emanate from the digital processes of the Internet are a particularly clear example.[24] At the centre of the conflict is the clash between irreconcilable rationalities: action that is economically rational has a structurally corrupting effect on the particular rationalities of scientific activities and of the healthcare system. A particular feature of the clash is its asymmetry. Constitutional rights have to be protected in such asymmetrical situations, in which the expanding economic dynamic weakens the fragile internal functioning mechanisms of scientific research and healthcare.

Constitutional rights as a collective institution means, therefore, a two-sided relationship in which guarantees of autonomy are given in respect of social processes to prevent them from being overwhelmed by the

[21] *Locus classicus* on structural violence, Galtung, 'Institutionalized Conflict Resolution', pp. 348–97; for macro-criminality, Jäger, *Makrokriminalität*.

[22] For clarity it should be stressed that this does not mean that individual responsibility is eclipsed by collective responsibility, but rather that both exist side by side at all times, although they are subject to different preconditions.

[23] More details in Teubner, 'The Anonymous Matrix', pp. 327–46. For the transnational arena, Viellechner, *Transnationalisierung*, pp. 217ff.

[24] Cf. Han, 'Im digitalen Panoptikum', p. 106.

totalising tendencies of other social processes.[25] In this collective-institutional dimension, constitutional rights function as conflict of laws rules that operate within the conflict between the opposing rationalities of different parts of society. They seek to protect the integrity of art, of the family, and of religion in the face of the totalising tendencies at work in society, that is technology, the media, and industry. It is obvious that we will not advance any further in this context if we try to balance individual constitutional rights against each other.

Instead, the horizontal protection of constitutional rights must be consistently transmuted into organisation and process. Formulations aimed at providing institutional protection for areas of social autonomy have been implemented for some time in public law, particularly in media law.[26] In the field of the mass media, freedom of opinion cannot be effectively protected by means of subjective rights, but only through organisation and process.[27] This insight needs to be applied more generally and implemented and reproduced, particularly in regard to the horizontal effect of constitutional rights in different social areas.

The ultimate deciding point is the contextual adequacy of any such collective-institutional protection of constitutional rights. Organisation and process must be selected in such a way as to be oriented to the specific contexts on both sides of the violation – the violators as much as the violated.[28] In the case of publication bias, the question by which we should be guided is therefore: under what conditions is the economic exploitation of research results intrusive in such a way that it violates the core area of the integrity of research, on the one hand, and the provision of healthcare on the other? The search for criteria must then proceed in two different directions: (1) What constitutes the specific risk potential of processes that violate constitutional rights, when economically motivated pressure is applied with respect to the publication of research results?

[25] This formulation goes beyond Luhmann's concept of constitutional rights in so far as it deals not only with the totalising tendencies of politics, but also those of other systems with expansionary tendencies, Luhmann, *Grundrechte als Institution*. In a recent article Horatia Muir Watt re-interprets human rights as conflict of law rules. Such an 'enriched conflict of laws theory has the potential to serve at the problematic heart of global law and its relationship to global justice, by contributing principles with which to govern non-state authority; infuse hybrid normative interactions with ideas of tolerance and mutual accommodation.' Muir Watt, 'Conflict of Laws Unbounded: The Case of Legal-Pluralist Revival'.

[26] BVerfGE 57, 295, 320 – 3. Rundfunkentscheidung.

[27] Vesting, 'Die Tagesschau-App', pp. 1ff.

[28] For details, Teubner, 'Constitutional Fragments', pp. 142ff.

(2) How, in this connection, are we to define the core area of scientific research and the healthcare system that is being violated by the manipulation of results? Only when these two questions have been answered with sufficient accuracy can we determine how organisation and process have to be structured so as to be capable of restoring the violated integrity of scientific research and the healthcare system.

Expansionary tendencies of the communication media

A second weak point of traditional third party effect doctrines is that they concentrate exclusively on protection from social power.[29] This is made particularly clear by the state action doctrine of American constitutional rights theory.[30] A third party effect of constitutional rights is deemed to exist, analogously to the state constitutional rights effect, if a socio-economic power which is equivalent to state power emanates from private actors.[31] But even the direct and indirect third party effect theory links up with structural imbalances and hazards, and only takes social power phenomena into consideration.

Indisputably, legal protection in the face of social power is an important area of application of the third party effect, but here again the weakness of the transfer principle is noticeable. For only if the issue were to relate to the transfer of state-directed constitutional rights to intra-societal conflicts would it be plausible to restrict protection of constitutional rights to cases in which private power of an intensity comparable to state power has arisen in society. For this reason the third party effect has also been uncommonly successful in labour law, since private ownership is transformed here into organisational power of the private government, which in terms of its impact is in no way inferior to the exercise of state power.[32]

Yet if we focus exclusively on social power we fail to see other, subtler causes of collective-institutional constitutional rights violations.

[29] Nolan, 'With Power Comes Responsibility: Human Rights and Corporate Responsibilities', pp. 582–3. For the German discussion Schwabe, *Die sogenannte Drittwirkung*, pp. 12ff.

[30] Cf. US Supreme Court (1883), Civil Rights Cases, 109 US 3. For a critique, Gardbaum, 'The "Horizontal Effect"', pp. 387–459.

[31] Clapham (fn. 12). A thorough critique of this exclusive focus on power is formulated by Kanalan, 'Horizontal Effect of Human Rights in the Era of Transnational Constellations', pp. 31ff.

[32] Gamillscheg, 'Die Grundrechte im Arbeitsrecht', pp. 385–445.

Although it may be appropriate for constitutional rights to be aimed against power phenomena in the sphere of the state, it is not appropriate to limit constitutional rights to the communication medium of power if social constitutional rights violations occur. In principle, constitutional rights are put at risk from all independent communicative media as soon as autonomous subsystems develop expansionary dynamics of their own. In today's world, that means primarily the expansionary tendencies of the economy, technology, medicine and (of particular relevance at the present time) the information media. Social power is thus only a partial phenomenon of the social risks to which constitutional rights are exposed. The main differences between social and political constitutional rights are always the result of the respective internal reproduction conditions of the affected sphere of society. In politics, constitutional rights are primarily directed against the dangers of power. In other social systems, constitutional rights are directed against risks emanating from the specific communication media for the social system in question, that is from payment operations in the economy, from cognitive-technical operations in science and technology and from information flows in the media system.[33] Often, these risks appear as phenomena of social power which necessitates the protection of constitutional rights against them. But this protection is needed whenever these operations violate constitutional rights, even in cases where no social power is involved.

In the case of publication bias, power certainly plays an important role. In particular, the censorship contracts forced on scientists by the pharmaceutical industry indicate an asymmetric power distribution in the contractual relationships. Nevertheless, we ought not to focus solely on the power phenomenon. In addition, we must also take action against the subtler ways in which the pharmaceutical groups exert influence, which – without any manifest exercise of power – 'substitute extra-scientific values and standards for intra-scientific relevance'.[34] In particular, we must take into consideration the corruptive influence of payment flows, above all when these are not transformed into organisational or contractual power. In these situations, the massive influence exercised by the pharmaceutical companies is not 'prohibitive or repressive, but seductive. [. . .] It leads its victims astray rather than telling them what

[33] As emphasised by Wheatley, 'Deliberating About Cosmopolitan Ideas'; Verschraegen, 'Differentiation and Inklusion', pp. 61–80.

[34] Stichweh, *Wissenschaft, Universität, Profession*, p. 28.

they must not do'.[35] Its motivating power is based not on the power of negative sanctions, but on the vast financing requirements of scientific research, towards which the seductive techniques of the pharmaceutical companies are directed with pinpoint accuracy. 'Because research is so intensive in terms of staff and resources, the financing of scientific activity is the "nerve centre" of its freedom.'[36] This represents another reason why, if constitutional rights are merely structured as defensive rights against power, they are only able to achieve a limited amount against the massive influences exerted by the medium of money. The establishment of effective protection from these seductive techniques thus becomes the challenge that has to be addressed by the third party effect concept.[37]

Of course, not every economic influence, which is brought to bear on scientific research, is necessarily a violation of constitutional rights. The contact between science and industry takes many different forms, including the economic exploitation of scientific results, influence over the choice of research topics as a result of companies sitting on university supervisory committees, the financing of profitable projects, the practice of industrial research, applied research generally and the close cooperation between industry and science in Silicon Valley contexts.[38] All of these may give rise to political regulations, but as long as the core autonomy of science is not affected they do not constitute a violation of constitutional rights.

However, when the external influences systematically manipulate the scientific code itself, that is seek to determine from outside what is true and what is false – as in the case of the politically inspired theories of Trofim Lysenko in the Soviet Union – then the core area of the scientific research system is violated.[39] When economic rational choice usurps the role of scientific rationality, when it replaces the scientific code with the economic code, the violation of academic freedom is obvious. But this is

[35] The formulations that were coined for digital manipulation apply equally to manipulation in the context of publication bias, Han, 'Im digitalen Panoptikum'. Whether this should be referred to in terms of 'power technique', as currently often occurs under the influence of Foucault, is doubtful because in this case the medium of communication is not power but money, and constitutional rights risks arise before the translation of money into power.

[36] Schmidt-Aßmann, 'Wissenschaftsplanung im Wandel', p. 657.

[37] See section 'Contextualisation' for further detail on this point.

[38] For trends towards commercialisation of science, Bumke, 'Universitäten im Wettbewerb', pp. 407–61.

[39] See Medwedjew, *Der Fall Lyssenko*.

precisely what does not normally happen in the context of publication bias. The pharmaceutical industry (probably wisely) is wary of directly interfering in research processes and telling scientists what results they are to produce.[40] Any such crude external interference in the binary code of scientific research or its programmes would – as the Lysenko disaster demonstrated – be regarded as risible in light of the established practice of scientific research. The manipulation in question here is much subtler, and therefore more dangerous, because the way in which it becomes inscribed into the research process itself and gives rise to publication bias is almost imperceptible. Evidence is therefore also extremely difficult to obtain. Only time-consuming empirical and statistical research (like those cases described at the beginning of this paper) is able to finally prove the systematic falsification of the publication process.

This makes it even more difficult to determine precisely how scientific autonomy is being put at risk in such situations. Our thesis is that the reason why the manipulations which give rise to publication bias do not encroach on the core area of science is not that they directly violate the 'truth code' of science or its programmes, methods and theories. On the contrary, they interfere with the evolution of science in that they systematically falsify the fragile selection mechanism. The precarious interconnections between variation, selection and retention of scientific evolution are exposed to the economically motivated manipulations of the publication mechanism. This has dramatic consequences as far as the differentiation of the scientific system is concerned. At the same time, in the interplay of social autonomous areas, the economic infiltration of science violates the integrity of the healthcare system.

Violation of the publication mechanism

With publication, the evolution of the science system has developed a selection mechanism[41] that selects system-relevant results from among the variations of ongoing research activity. Initial publication in relevant specialist journals has the function of filtering out, from among the many different variations of the internal research process, the results that

40 Admittedly this does not always apply. In many cases industry (which depends upon market-capable innovations) attempts to directly control the actual processes of scientific output and even to cause scientists to openly falsify the allocation of the values of the science code.

41 See Luhmann, *Wissenschaft*, pp. 576ff.; Stichweh, 'Wissenschaftssystem', pp. 213–28.

will determine the direction of further development. By making new knowledge visible, publication makes a selection from among the variations of the scientific process, which are running via the binary code and the programmes, and makes it possible for research results to be stabilised as the 'status of knowledge' in educational literature and manuals; this stabilisation stimulates new variations in its turn.[42] The practice of publication establishes scientific objectivity and impartiality because it makes it possible for scientific findings to be verified according to the criteria of integratability into other areas of research and openness to criticism. Thus the social institution of the functioning practice of publication is just as much part of the protection of scientific freedom as is the principle of freedom of publication itself. Here we can see the interplay between the individual and the collective-institutional levels of constitutional rights. Constitutional rights relate not only to individuals, but also to 'collective institutions ... which cannot be seen as a counterpart to the subject, because they are involved in the (re)production of the subject, without being a macro-subject'.[43]Individual constitutional rights are not limited by collective institutions, but function as the space in which collective institutions are realised.[44] Conversely, enforceable individual constitutional rights have an advocatory function in regard to the protection and further development of collective institutions.

Economically motivated manipulation impairs this mechanism both directly and indirectly. In the direct sense, the contractual rights of disposal and exploitation and censorship clauses imposed by the pharmaceutical networks may not intervene in the 'production' of scientific results, but they certainly intervene in their 'presentation'.[45] Negative studies are withheld and study results are manipulated so that the population of publication records is increased in the direction of profitable results, i.e. the frequency distribution of positive and negative research results is significantly shifted in favour of the positive results.

By contrast, indirect impairment occurs if financing pressure is brought to bear on the scientific world's internal interest in its research findings. In that case, the publication of positive study results is more

[42] Concerning the complex relationship between variation, selection, and stabilisation in the development of science, Luhmann, *Wissenschaft*, p. 583, pp. 587–8.

[43] Steinhauer, 'Das Grundrecht der Kunstfreiheit', p. 4.

[44] For the institutional dimension of academic freedom, for example BVerfG, BVerfGE 35, 79, 112; Augsberg, 'Dimensionen der Wissenschaftsfreiheit', pp. 77–80.

[45] See Nowotny, 'Public Science', pp. 1–28; Lexchin et al., 'Pharmaceutical Industry Sponsorship', pp. 1167–77.

lucrative and more interesting for the researchers than the publication of negative study results.[46] 'Good scientific practice' as an internal criterion for behaviour among scientists, which would have regarded any such selective publication as scientific misconduct, becomes less relevant.[47] An imperceptible change thus takes place in the way in which the scientific world itself understands what the purpose of publication is. Symptomatic of this development is the increasing and barely transparent use of so-called communications agencies and ghost writers. Prominent researchers seeking to enhance their reputations are falsely named as the authors of studies that have actually been written by anonymous writers, consultancy companies or employees of the big pharmaceutical companies.[48]

Some publishing houses also encourage such manipulations by adapting their publication methods to the expectations of the big pharmaceutical companies and the financial pressures imposed by them and by accepting mainly positive results.[49] Not infrequently, agreements are reached between widely circulated medical publishing houses and the big pharmaceutical companies, who co-finance the publishing houses through drugs advertising. Agreements are reached in regard to both the orientation of the specialist journal and the publication criteria.[50] In addition there is the problem of finding independent experts to carry out peer reviews in the pharmaceutical sphere, to ensure that conflicts of interest, which may influence the results, can be avoided.

If economic interests influence the practice of scientific publication in this way, the internal selection criteria by which scientists operate will be replaced by criteria that have nothing to do with science. Peer review processes will be pointless, because negative data do not appear. The possibility of integration into subsequent and parallel research is put at risk, or worse still, the falsification is incorporated into subsequent research.[51] For if false data are used as a basis for follow-up research,

46 Easterbrook et al., 'Publication Bias', pp. 867–72; Dickersin et al., 'Factors Influencing Publication of Research Results', pp. 374–8.

47 Cf. Fanelli, 'Do Pressures to Publish Increase Scientists' Bias?', pp. 1–7. For a *time-lag bias*, Stern and Simes, 'Evidence of Delayed Publication', pp. 640–5. Concerning the distorting effect of multiple publication, Tramèr et al., 'Covert Duplicate Publication', pp. 635–40.

48 The PLoS Medicine Editors et al., 'Ghostwriting Revisited'.

49 See Franzen, *Breaking News*, pp. 73ff., pp. 88ff.

50 Cf. the study by Becker and Dörter, 'Journal's Source of Revenue', p. 5448. For the independence initiative by the International Society of Drug Bulletins and WHO, Schaaber et al., 'Unabhängige Arzneimittelzeitschriften', pp. 237ff., pp. 244ff.

51 See Ahmed et al., 'Assessment of Publication Bias'.

this will ultimately affect the way in which the values of the 'truth code' of science itself are allocated. The repercussions of publication bias for research practice tend to loosen the connection between research and publication. The core of scientific self-reproduction is put at risk.

Violation of the healthcare system

At the same time, the manipulations which give rise to publication bias violate the right to health, in both a collective-institutional sense and an individual sense. The collective institutions of politics and of the health system are dependent (as are doctors administering treatment) on full disclosure of all studies carried out in regard to a medicinal product. If findings relating to negative consequences for health are withheld or manipulated, the effects of substances cannot be objectively recorded because of the selective nature of the data in specialist journals. This leads to seriously wrong decisions being taken, because the positive effects are overestimated, in the context of both drug licensing and patient treatment.[52] Since according to §§ 21ff. of the German Medicinal Products Act (AMG) clinical studies in Germany serve as a basis for drug licensing and the medicinal products, regulatory authorities no longer investigate such products independently; this manipulation directly results in the efficacy and usefulness of drugs being incorrectly evaluated, as the Edronax case demonstrates.[53]

The risks to patients and subject groups are obvious. As a result of the distortion of studies, patients are exposed to useless or even harmful treatments. Drugs, which are actually effective remain hidden from view and are withheld from patients. As a result of the concealment of studies that have already been carried out, test subjects unnecessarily undergo new studies.[54]

Contextualisation

The third weak point of the traditional third party effect theory is also connected with the misapplied transfer principle. Normally the third party effect is understood simply as the transfer of constitutional rights

[52] Tonks, 'A Clinical Trials Register for Europe', pp. 1314–5.

[53] An analysis of defective conclusions in Sutton et al., 'Effect of Publication Bias', pp. 1574–7.

[54] Horton, 'Medical Editors Trial Amnesty', p. 756.

which have been shaped by public law to relationships that exist in private law, due care being exercised to ensure that the basic principles of private law are not violated. Accordingly, the theory of the indirect third party effect regards the adaptation to private law as best guaranteed if the constitutional rights are indirectly incorporated into private law through the general clauses. The theory of the duty of protection requires the involvement of legislation, which on the basis of the same considerations ought only to formulate standards that are adequate under private law.

This is correct in so far as it is necessary to ensure that social constitutional rights are adequate to their context. But the new context is definitely too narrowly understood if it is merely defined as the world of private law. The claim, in the context of the transfer of constitutional rights, 'of holding fast to the fundamental independence and autonomy of civil law vis-à-vis the system of constitutional rights under constitutional law'[55] only describes a first step in the process of contextualisation. The second step places us before a much more difficult challenge: state-directed constitutional rights are to be modified not only according to the context of private law, but also according to the different contexts of society. They have to be newly calibrated in order to ensure the protection of the particular rationality and normativity of each different area of society in which constitutional rights are at risk.[56]

This is where the transfer principle comes up against its limits, in so far as it has not already done so. While in the individual case it may be possible for constitutional rights which have been shaped according to public law to be transferred into private law relationships, any institutional transfer of constitutional rights, that is a transfer of previously defined organisation and already established processes, is bound to fail because of the large number of particular social normativities and the specific nature thereof.[57] Adequate protection of constitutional rights is

55 Dürig, 'Grundrechte und Zivilrechtsprechung', pp. 158–9.

56 Concerning the reformulation of constitutional rights in the business context, the classic study by Selznick, *Law, Society and Industrial Justice*, pp. 75ff., pp. 259ff.; more recently Schierbeck, 'Human Rights Issues in Corporate Operations', p. 168. According to Vesting and Kanalan the horizontal effect requires constitutional rights to be adapted to the context of sectorial constitutions and not to the standards of the political constitution, Vesting, *Computernetzwerke*, § 3, II 3; Kanalan, 'Horizontal Effect of Human Rights in the Era of Transnational Constellations', pp. 46ff.

57 Luhmann, *Grundrechte als Institution*, p. 188: The special nature of social spheres deserves protection against the levelling effect of politicisation.

not to be obtained by means of a standardised conception of the protection of constitutional rights to be applied to all areas of society, it has to be ensured 'on site' by careful and sensitive contextualisation.

The question of what organisation and what processes serve to protect the constitutional rights of the collective institutions of scientific research and healthcare against the harm that can be done by the industry must be answered primarily on the basis of the normative self-understanding of the social practices that are at risk.[58] In their codes and programmes, science and healthcare develop normative orientations, which are not the same as the commonly held opinions of individuals, instead having a collective-institutional character.[59] Such collective-institutional norms, which are rooted in structures that have evolved historically, are critically discussed in the reflective discourses of science and healthcare before being examined by the law according to its own criteria and becoming established as legal norms.[60] A good example is the trial registration as third party effect of academic freedom and the right to health through organisation and process.[61] Publicly accessible registers of studies and results are set up on a binding basis, which fully record studies from their inception in order to ensure transparency and inspection throughout the entire research process.[62] This protection of constitutional rights becomes effective only through the cooperation of the specialist journals,

[58] This corresponds to the practice of the BVerfG, in the context of the legal description of the concept of science, art and other social spheres, of relying on their own self-understanding, BVerfGE 111, 333, 354; decision of 20 July 2010, case no. 1 BvR 748/06, printed in: *JZ*, 66 (2011), pp. 308–13. Comprehensively on this subject, Augsberg, 'Dimensionen der Wissenschaftsfreiheit', pp. 74–5, p. 84.

[59] Vesting, *Rechtstheorie*, pp. 95ff. speaks in this context of 'social conventions and implicit knowledge'. For science, Augsberg, ibid., for the health sector, Krajewska, 'Global Health Law'

[60] Here we refer to Wiethölter's concept of proceduralisation as liberation of social normativity, Wiethölter, 'Justifications', pp. 71ff., p. 75.

[61] The United States has provided a model in the form of the 'FDA Amendments Act' of 2007, Food and Drug Administration: FDA Amendments Act (FDAAA) of 2007, public law no. 110–85 § 801 (www.gpo.gov/fdsys/pkg/PLAW-110publ85/pdf/PLAW-110publ85.pdf). For the development of the legal situation in Europe, Quack and Wackerbeck, 'Die Verpflichtung zur Registrierung', pp. 6–12. Because of societal pressure the European legislator finally has been taking action. See Regulation (EU) No 536/2014 of 16 April 2014 on clinical trials on medicinal products for human use and repealing Directive 2001/20/EC, OJ L 158/1 of 27 May 2014.

[62] Initial attempts are offered by the US governmental study register ClinicalTrials.gov or the German Clinical Trials Register at the University Medical Center of Freiburg (www.germanctr.de). At the European level also the EudraCT database (which is limited to access by the authorities of the Member States) and public databases such as Eudra

which make registration of all studies carried out a precondition for publication.[63] Results for drugs, which are intended for distribution on the market, may only be published if the clinical studies on which they are based have been entered in the Clinical Trial Register and if all results have been included, both positive and negative.

Trial registration is particularly appropriate for dealing with the conflict between economic rational action and the rationality of scientific research. For in the processes and organisation of the protection of constitutional rights, the duty of registration applies precisely from the point at which (as has been described earlier) manipulation falsifies the process of the evolution of scientific knowledge. Unlike other possible sanctions, the duty of registration is aimed precisely at the critical selection mechanism upon which the interests of industry, science and healthcare come into conflict. Trial registration does not counteract repressive or prohibitive power techniques applied by the big pharmaceutical companies, operating instead as a corrective against their 'seductive' manipulation techniques.[64] It ensures transparency, but – even more decisively – it stabilises and protects the very act of publication, in that publication is no longer restricted to results, but is expanded to include the entire research project. And it does this before any results are known. It thus forces the parties to define their publication conduct under a veil of ignorance. Even when there is still uncertainty as to the results, research projects have to be made accessible to the medical public. The contingent nature of the research project in question is thereby made public. Publication practice faces a systematic pressure in regard to the frequency distribution of positive and negative results.

The duty of registration therefore comes into play precisely in regard to the selection mechanism of the evolution of scientific knowledge, a mechanism which (unlike individual court actions) does not operate solely in the individual case, but exerts a continuing influence on the

Pharm (www.eudrapharm.eu/eudrapharm/clinicaltrials.do) and the Clinical Trial Register (www.clinicaltrialsregister.eu) are becoming established.

63 De Angelis and Drazen, 'International Committee of Medical Journal Editors', pp. 1250–1. There are also a few online journals that primarily publish negative results, for example the Journal of Negative Results in Biomedicine (www.jnrbm.com/). See Pfeffer and Olsen, 'Journal of Negative Results', p. 2.

64 Han makes reference to this decisive difference, see 'Im digitalen Panoptikum' The protection of constitutional rights against the 'anonymous matrix' must therefore be structured differently from the protection of constitutional rights against state power, see Teubner 'The Anonymous Matrix', pp. 40ff.

joint development of industry, scientific knowledge and medical practice. The effect of the duty of registration is to strengthen the internal scientific selection criterion of novelty, without consideration of positive or negative results, and to weaken the economic selection criteria that give rise to publication bias. At the same time, it strengthens the selection criteria for medical practice, for which knowledge concerning harmful side effects or indeed the lack of efficacy of a drug is just as important as information about positive curative effects. This tends to restore the connection between research and publication, which forms the basis of the self-production of scientific knowledge, and which the seductive manipulation techniques of the pharmaceutical companies seek to sabotage.

Beyond the state's duties of protection: alternatives to state regulation of publication practice

The currently generally accepted concept of the duty of protection, as it has been developed by the third party effect doctrine, also has to accept the criticism that it is fixated on the state in a way that is bound to be misleading: although it is private actors that are violating constitutional rights, the concept primarily includes the state in the sphere of the duty to protect, and not the private actors themselves. This is particularly problematic in the sphere of scientific knowledge, since the self-administrative autonomy of the scientific community resists governmental duties to protect to some extent. By contrast, trial registration comes into play in the context of the social processes themselves, in order to protect science from being abused by industry. The characteristic feature of the process is that it takes up the particular dynamic of the conflict and protects the integrity of science from the inside, by motivating large numbers of constitutional rights actors to become involved in the process on the basis of their respective functional rationalities. In so doing it mobilises opposing forces to combat the expansionary tendencies of the pharmaceutical networks. As far as science is concerned, it functions almost as an immune system, which identifies and combats elements that are foreign to science.[65]

There is certainly a political element here, but it does not operate as external state control; on the contrary, it alters the self-reproduction of

[65] 'Social systems need contradiction for their immune system, for the continuation of their self-reproduction under difficult circumstances.' Luhmann, *Social Systems*, p. 385; Luhmann, *Wissenschaft*, p. 623.

academic activity. State concepts of the duty to protect, which in the name of academic freedom impose duties of publication developed by legislative bodies, reduce the potential of autonomous scientific processes. External standard setting underestimates the scientific community's need for autonomy and fails to take account of its evolutionary mechanisms. Of necessity it is bound to fail to fulfil social needs because it regards the actors involved as mere objects to be regulated. These actors however, are responsible (co)authors in the protection of the autonomy of 'their' respective social areas.[66] As an alternative to comprehensive organisational responsibility of the state, therefore, a procedurally based reconnection of constitutional rights to society is proposed. The setting of standards relating to constitutional rights is not an exclusive task of state policy, but primarily a function of societal self-organisation. The ultimately decisive reason for adopting this approach is 'that no superior information exists outside of an emergent systematisation context regarding the possibilities of and the requirement for systematisation in this connection'.[67] The role of the state should then be limited to generally indirect forms of control through organisation and process.

Trial registration is thus a means of dealing with conflicts of interest, which takes account of the needs of science because it protects academic freedom through a process of scientific self-regulation. It represents an alternative to the previously proposed scientific third party effect mechanism of a 'plurality of sources of finance', an alternative that takes into account the particular nature of the conflict situation.[68] Trial registration has one outstanding feature: because it is the publishing houses that organise trial registration, they encourage the tendency to develop a specific (self-)control network as a power that can stand up to the pharmaceutical networks. In so doing, it addresses the difficult and frequently discussed problem of how networks can be regulated when their decentralised structure means that they do not have any addressee.

This network of the realisation of constitutional rights consists of various social actors who, each having their own motives, are able to effect the protection contained within the register mechanism. The central role will be played by the specialist journals, if they make

[66] Gerstenberg, 'Private Law, Constitutionalism and the Limits of Judicial Role', pp. 687–703; Karavas, Digitale Grundrechte, pp. 87ff., p. 99.

[67] Stichweh, 'Wissenschaftssystem', p. 84.

[68] Concerning the pluralism of sources of finance, Graber, Zwischen Geist und Geld, pp. 227ff.

registration a precondition for publication. In addition they can accord a special weight to negative studies in the context of publication, either by publishing negative studies separately or by establishing a duty to take them into consideration in the peer review. The specialist journals are self-motivated, since they aim to maintain their function as a neutral medium of scientific knowledge in contradistinction to mass media, and to avoid being used as a mere tool for advertising.[69]

Universities, research funding institutions, scientific councils and medical associations can make a decisive contribution to the success of *trial registration*.[70] By institutionalising their own registers, internal registration obligations, ethics commissions and ombudsman proceedings, they reinforce the duty of registration which has been created by the publishing houses.[71] Within the scientific sphere, the duty of registration raises the standard of care, because it requires the details of studies to be disclosed. Doctors will have a personal responsibility to inform themselves using study results published in the registers and to correlate this information with the specialist journals. In addition, global control mechanisms will also be able to prevent any attempts at circumventing *trial registration*. Possible ways of achieving this do exist if transnational actors such as NGOs, the media and public interest litigation with their 'scandalisation' strategies become involved with trial registration. In 2007 the World Health Organization set up the registration network International Clinical Trials Registry Platform (ICTRP) in order to coordinate private and public activities relating to the registration of clinical studies on a worldwide scale.[72] Private and public registers that have to fulfil certain quality standards feed their data into the meta-register on a regular basis. The aim is to ensure the quality of the register entries. The meta-register serves as a seal of quality, in particular for smaller, private registers, and removes the burden of the concept (which would be difficult to implement) of a standard international public register.

[69] Cf. Dirnagl and Lauritzen, 'Fighting Publication Bias', pp. 1263–4; Franzen, *Breaking News*, pp. 246ff.

[70] Thus the World Medical Association Declaration of Helsinki, following the extensions of 2000 and 2008, establishes the duty 'to register each clinical study ... in a publicly accessible database before recruitment of the first subject' (Art. 35) and to publish negative studies (Art. 36), available at: www.wma.net/en/30publications/10policies/b3/index.html.

[71] Such as the Ethical Commission of the Freiburg Medical Faculty (www.uniklinik-freiburg.de/ethikkommission/live/antragstellung/gemaessMPG.html#Publikationsvorhaben).

[72] WHO, 'ICTRP'.

Conclusion: constitutional rights as conflict of laws regulations

From this perspective, state-directed constitutional rights are now only a specific normative means of safeguarding the relationship between the citizen and the state, and cannot lay any claim to forming a comprehensive value system for society or even a 'common frame of reference'. The dogma-based system of state-directed constitutional rights is faced with the many and varied conflicts of constitutional rights that arise within society, which do not require any external justification from the spheres of protection and valuation.[73] Specific clashes between constitutional rights give rise to idiosyncratic conflict rules, which do not include any priority rules or burdens of justification, but which are characterised by the specific need for autonomy of the social areas affected.

Like the 'hard won' defensive function of state-directed constitutional rights in the relationship between the citizen and the state, the process that has been sketched out here, that of the self-constitution of academic freedom in this conflict, is a long-term process of the drawing of boundaries. Just as state-directed constitutional rights have historically been won from the conflicts that have arisen between the state and its citizens, academic freedom is constituted in the conflict with other social rationalities, in particular the rationality of economic action. The clash becomes a productive process, since it challenges science to define itself in the conflict.[74] It is not sufficient to simply see the horizontal effect of constitutional rights as a transfer of positivised (state-directed) constitutional rights. Certainly, the historical experience of state-directed constitutional rights is an element to be taken into consideration, and the protection level of the horizontal effect must be measured against this. Governmental obligations of protection are therefore not superfluous, but form another possibility for dealing with conflicts, occupying a legitimate position alongside the potential solutions of the global regime conflict involving industry, scientific research and the healthcare system.[75]

Within this relationship of tension, science has an opportunity to reformulate the limits of its autonomy under the pressure exerted by society's conflicting rationalities. As far as the emergence of transnational constitutional rights is concerned, what Niklas Luhmann has already

[73] Luhmann, *Grundrechte als Institution*, p. 36.

[74] For an analysis concerning the autonomy of science, see Augsberg, 'Dimensionen der Wissenschaftsfreiheit', pp. 74ff.

[75] For the regime term, see Fischer-Lescano and Teubner, 'Regime-Collisions', pp. 999–1045.

confirmed in regard to the 'most primal' development of the paradox of human rights also applies.[76] It is in the direct experience of their violation, in cases of acute disappointment, that constitutional rights acquire their shape and form. It is only when the selection mechanism of publication is violated that its significance for the way science operates and performs is defined. This is the origin of social conflict solutions as experiments in the creation of law.

Constitutional rights as collective institutions as a formula emphasises the dual character of constitutional rights as social process and legal standardisation at one and the same time. The provision of legal security must not be allowed to put the social dynamic of the protection of constitutional rights at risk. It is only at that point that constitutional rights, in their collective-institutional dimension, are able to function as conflict of laws rules and fulfil their function of supporting social differentiation. It is precisely for this reason, however, that they elude any standardised objectivisation by means of legal form. Instead of defining common constitutional rights standards that apply to both state and society, the law must constantly react to 'social normativity consolidation' in a context-sensitive manner.[77] The law can act as an anchor for the creative development of the dynamics of social areas, but must not prescribe their content.[78] Understood in this way, legal obligations of protection vis-à-vis the self-regulation mechanisms of society are directed not towards content but towards procedures. The task of the law would be to set up areas of protection in which social defence mechanisms (specifically, in our case, trial registration) are able to develop.[79] Through mobilisation and simultaneous pluralisation of dissenting voices, the process ensures that research results that run counter to economic interests cannot be manipulated. It institutionalises a social mechanism which provides a much more appropriate solution to the

[76] Luhmann, 'Paradox der Menschenrechte', p. 222.

[77] Selznick, *Law, Society and Industrial Justice*, pp. 32ff.; Luhmann, *Grundrechte als Institution*, p. 192. This is the methodological point of Muir Watt, 'Conflict of Laws Unbounded: The Case of Legal-Pluralist Revival' when she defines human rights as conflict of laws rules.

[78] Concerning the structural primacy of learning adaptation in world society and a shift in the law towards the licensing of cognitive expectations, Luhmann, 'The World Society', pp. 175–90.

[79] Concerning such an impartially 'partisan' law, which is in favour of social autonomy but which exercises this 'partisanship' on an impartial basis, Wiethölter, 'Justifications'. Concerning the function of the law as an anchor, also Christensen and Fischer-Lescano, *Das Ganze des Rechts*, p. 316.

roblem of publication bias than any state regulation could achieve. Because trial registration shifts the focus on to an enabling law, it has the potential to strengthen the scientific world against the expansionary tendencies of the financial world.

Bibliography

Ahmed, I., A. Sutton and R. Riley, 'Assessment of Publication Bias, Selection Bias, and Unavailable Data in Meta-analyses Using Individual Participant Data: A Database Survey', *British Medical Journal*, 344 (2012), d7762.

Alexy, R., 'Verfassungsrecht und einfaches Recht – Verfassungsgerichtsbarkeit und Fachgerichtsbarkeit', *Veröffentlichungen der Vereinigung der Deutschen Staatsrechtslehrer*, 61 (2002), pp. 7–33.

Applegate, W. B., C. D. Furberg and R. P. Byungton, 'The Multicenter Isradipine Diuretic Athersclerosis Study (Midas)', *Journal of the American Medical Association*, 277 (1996), pp. 297–8.

Augsberg, I., 'Subjektive und objektive Dimensionen der Wissenschaftsfreiheit' in F. Voigt (ed.), *Freiheit der Wissenschaft. Beiträge zu ihrer Bedeutung, Normativität und Funktion* (Berlin: De Gruyter, 2012), pp. 65–89.

Becker, A., and F. Dörter, 'The Association between a Journal's Source of Revenue and the Drug Recommendations Made in the Articles it Publishes', *Canadian Medical Association Journal*, 183 (2011), pp. 544–8.

Bombardier, C., L. Laine and A. Reicin, 'Comparison of Upper Gastrointestinal Toxicity of Rofecoxib and Naproxen in Patients with Rheumatoid Arthritis. VIGOR Study Group', *The New England Journal of Medicine*, 343 (2000), pp. 1520–8.

Bumke, C., 'Universitäten im Wettbewerb', *Veröffentlichungen der Vereinigung der Deutschen Staatsrechtslehrer*, 69 (2009), pp. 407–61.

Chan, A.-W., A. Hróbjartsson and M. T. Haahr, 'Empirical Evidence for Selective Reporting of Outcomes in Randomized Trials: Comparison of Protocols to Published Articles', *Journal of the American Medical Association*, 291 (2004), pp. 2457–65.

Christensen, R., and A. Fischer-Lescano, *Das Ganze des Rechts. Vom hierarchischen zum reflexiven Verständnis deutscher und europäischer Grundrechte* (Berlin: Duncker & Humblot, 2007).

Cicero, M. T., *De Natura Deorum* (London: Methuen, 1896).

Clapham, A., *Human Rights Obligations of Non-State Actors* (Oxford University Press, 2006).

Conrad, D., *Freiheitsrechte und Arbeitsverfassung* (Berlin: Duncker & Humblot, 1965).

De Angelis, C., and J. M. Drazen, 'Clinical Trial Registration: A Statement from the International Committee of Medical Journal Editors', *The New England Journal of Medicine*, 351 (2004), pp. 1250–1.

Dickersin, K., Y.-I. Min and C. L. Meinert, 'Factors Influencing Publication of Research Results. Follow-up of Applications Submitted to two Institutional Review Boards', *Journal of the American Medical Association*, 267 (1992), pp. 374–8.

Dirnagl, U., and M. Lauritzen, 'Fighting Publication Bias: Introducing the Negative Results Sections', *Journal of Cerebral Blood Flow and Metabolism*, 30 (2010), pp. 1263–4.

Dreier, H., *Dimensionen der Grundrechte. Von der Wertordnungsjudikatur zu den objektiv-rechtlichen Grundrechtsgehalten* (Hannover: Hennies and Zinkhusen, 1993).

Dürig, G., 'Grundrechte und Zivilrechtsprechung' in T. Maunz (ed.), *Vom Bonner Grundgesetz zur gesamtdeutschen Verfassung: Festschrift Hans Nawiasky* (München: Isar, 1956), pp. 157–210.

Easterbrook, P. J., J. A. Berlin, R. Gopalan and D. Matthews, 'Publication Bias in Clinical Research', *The Lancet*, 337 (1991), pp. 867–72.

Eyding, D., M. Lelgemann and U. Grouven, 'Reboxetine for a Cute Treatment of Major Depression: Sytematic Review and Meta-Analysis of Published and Unpublished Placebo and Selective Serotonin Reuptake Inhibitor Controlled Trials', *British Medical Journal*, 341 (2010), c4737.

Fanelli, D., 'Do Pressures to Publish Increase Scientists' Bias? An Empirical Support from US States Data', *PLoS ONE*, 5 (2010), pp. 1–7.

Fischer-Lescano, A., 'Kritik der praktischen Konkordanz', *Kritische Justiz*, 2 (2008), pp. 166–77.

Fischer-Lescano, A., and G. Teubner, 'Regime-Collisions: The Vain Search for Legal Unity in the Fragmentation of Global Law', *Michigan Journal of International Law*, 25 (2004), pp. 999–1045.

Franzen, M., *Breaking News: Wissenschaftliche Zeitschriften im Kampf um Aufmerksamkeit* (Baden-Baden: Nomos, 2011).

Fugh-Berman, A. J., 'The Haunting of Medical Journals: How Ghostwriting Sold "HRT"', *PLoS Medicine*, 7 (2010), e1000335.

Galtung, J., 'Institutionalized Conflict Resolution: A Theoretical Paradigm', *Journal of Peace Research*, 2 (1965), pp. 348–97.

Gamillscheg, F., 'Die Grundrechte im Arbeitsrecht', *Archiv für die civilistische Praxis*, 164 (1964), pp. 385–445.

Gardbaum, S., 'The "Horizontal Effect" of Constitutional Rights', *Michigan Law Review*, 102 (2003), pp. 387–459.

Gerstenberg, O., 'Private Law, Constitutionalism and the Limits of Judicial Role' in C. Scott (ed.), *Torture as Tort: Comparative Perspectives on the Development of Transnational Human Rights Litigation* (Oxford: Hart Publishing, 2001), pp. 687–703.

Graber, C., *Zwischen Geist und Geld: Interferenzen von Kunst und Wirtschaft aus rechtlicher Sicht* (Baden-Baden: Nomos, 1994).

Han, B.-C., 'Im digitalen Panoptikum: Wir fühlen uns frei. Aber wir sind es nicht', *Der Spiegel*, (2014)2, p. 106.

Hesse, K., *Grundzüge des Verfassungsrechts der Bundesrepublik Deutschland*, 4th edn. (Heidelberg: C.F. Müller, 1999).

Horton, R., 'Medical Editors Trial Amnesty', *The Lancet*, 350 (1997), pp. 756ff.

Jäger, H., *Makrokriminalität: Studien zur Kriminologie kollektiver Gewalt* (Frankfurt: Suhrkamp, 1989).

Jefferson, T., M. Jones, P. Doshi, C.B. Del Mar, C.J. Heneghan, R. Hama and M.J. Thompson, 'Neuraminidase Inhibitors for Preventing and Treating Influenza in Healthy Adults and Children', *Cochrane Database of Systematic Reviews*, (2012), Art. No.: CD008965.

Kanalan, I., 'Horizontal Effect of Human Rights in the Era of Transnational Constellations: On the Accountability of Private Actors for Human Rights Violations', http://ssrn.com/abstract=2539110 (2014).

Karavas, V., *Digitale Grundrechte: Zur Drittwirkung der Grundrechte im Internet* (Baden-Baden: Nomos, 2006).

Krajewska, A., 'In Search of the Holy Grail of Transparent and Coherent Global Health Law', 2013, available at: http://campus.hec.fr/global-transparency/wp-content/uploads/2013/10/Krajewska-Transparency-and-global-health.pdf.

Krimsky, S., *Science in the Public Interest: Has the Lure of Profits Corrupted Biomedical Research?* (New York: Rowman & Littlefield Publishers, 2003).

Ladeur, K. H., *Kritik der Abwägung in der Grundrechtsdogmatik* (Tübingen: Mohr Siebeck, 2004).

Das Medienrecht und die Ökonomie der Aufmerksamkeit. In Sachen Dieter Bohlen, Maxim Biller, Caroline von Monaco u.a. (Köln: Halem, 2007).

Lexchin, J., L. Bero, B. Djulbegovic and O. Clark, 'Pharmaceutical Industry Sponsorship and Research Outcome and Quality: Systematic Review', *British Medical Journal*, 326 (2003), pp. 1167–77.

Luhmann, N., *Grundrechte als Institution: Ein Beitrag zur politischen Soziologie* (Berlin: Duncker & Humblot, 1965).

Die Wissenschaft der Gesellschaft (Frankfurt: Suhrkamp, 1990).

'The World Society as a Social System' in N. Luhmann (ed.), *Essays on Self-Reference* (New York: Columbia University Press, 1990), pp. 175–90.

'Das Paradox der Menschenrechte und drei Formen seiner Entfaltung' in N. Luhmann (ed.), *Soziologische Aufklärung 6: Die Soziologie und der Mensch* (Opladen: Westdeutscher Verlag, 1995), pp. 229–36.

Social Systems, 2 vol. (Stanford University Press, 1995).

Theory of Society (Stanford University Press, 2013).

Mathews J., and A. Stone Sweet, 'All Things in Proportion? American Rights Review and the Problem of Balancing', *Emory Law Journal*, 4 (2011), pp. 102–79.

Medwedjew, S. A., *Der Fall Lyssenko. Eine Wissenschaft kapituliert* (Hamburg: Hoffmann & Campe, 1971).

Muir Watt, H., 'Conflict of Laws Unbounded: The Case of Legal-Pluralist Revival', *Transnational Legal Theory*, 7 (2016 forthcoming).

Nowotny, H., 'The Changing Nature of Public Science' in H. Nowotny (ed.), *The Public Nature of Science under Assault. Politics, Markets, Science and the Law* (Berlin and Heidelberg: Springer, 2005), pp. 1–28.

Nolan, J., 'With Power Comes Responsibility: Human Rights and Corporate Responsibilities', *University of New South Wales Law Journal*, 28 (2005), p. 581ff.

Nowrot, K., 'Den "Kinderschuhen" entwachsen: Die (Wieder-) Entdeckung der rechtssoziologischen Perspektive in der Dogmatik der Völkerrechtssubjektivität', *Zeitschrift für Rechtssoziologie*, 28 (2007), pp. 21–48.

Petryna, A., *When Experiments Travel: Clinical Trials and the Global Search for Human Subjects* (Princeton University Press, 2009).

Pfeffer, C., and B. R. Olsen, 'Editorial: Journal of Negative Results in Biomedicine', *Journal of Negative Results in BioMedicine*, 1 (2002), p. 2.

Public Library of Science, Medicine Editors, 'Ghostwriting Revisited: New Perspectives but Few Solutions in Sight', *PLoS Medicine*, 8 (2011), e1001084.

Quack, C., and A. Wackerbeck, 'Die Verpflichtung zur Registrierung und Veröffentlichung klinischer Studien: Darstellung der europäischen Rechtslage im Vergleich zur US-Regelung nach dem FDA Amendment Act', *Gesundheits-Recht*, 1 (2010), pp. 6–12.

Ridder, H., *Die Freiheit der Kunst nach dem Grundgesetz* (Berlin: Vahlen, 1963).

Die soziale Ordnung des Grundgesetzes (Opladen: Westdeutscher Verlag, 1975).

Rüfner, W., 'Grundrechtsadressaten' in J. Isensee and P. Kirchhof (eds.), *Handbuch des Staatsrechts der Bundesrepublik Deutschland* (Heidelberg: C.F. Müller, 2011), pp. 83-125.

Ruggie, J., 'Protect, Respect and Remedy: A Framework for Business and Human Rights, Report of the Special Representative of the Secretary-General on Human Rightsand Transnational Corporations and Other Business Enterprises', UN Doc. A/HRC/8/5 (7 April 2008).

Schaaber, J., M. Kochen, B. Müller-Oerlinghausen and W. Niebling, 'Warum unabhängige Arzneimittelzeitschriften und Fortbildungsveranstaltungen wichtig sind' in K. Lieb, D. Klemperer, W.-D. Ludwig and M. Kochen (eds.), *Interessenskonflikte in der Medizin – Hintergründe und Lösungsmöglichkeiten* (Berlin, Heidelberg: Springer, 2011), pp. 238–50.

Schierbeck, J., 'Operational Measures for Identifying and Implementing Human Rights Issues in Corporate Operations' in A. Eide, O. Bergesen and P. Goyer (eds.), *Human Rights and the Oil Industry* (Antwerpen: Intersentia, 2000), pp. 161–77.

chmidt-Aßmann, E., 'Wissenschaftsplanung im Wandel' in W. Erbguth, J. Oebbecke and H.-W. Rengeling (eds.), *Planung. Festschrift für Werner Hoppe zum 70. Geburtstag* (München: C.H. Beck, 2000), pp. 649–65.

chmitt, C., 'Freiheitsrechte und institutionelle Garantien der Reichsverfassung (1931)' in C. Schmitt (ed.), *Verfassungsrechtliche Aufsätze aus den Jahren 1924–1954* (Berlin: Duncker & Humblot, 1985), pp. 140–78.

chott, G., H. Pachl and U. Limbach, 'Finanzierung von Arzneimittelstudien durch pharmazeutische Unternehmen und die Folgen; Teil 1: qualitative systematische Literaturübersicht zum Einfluss auf Studienergebnisse, -protokoll und -qualität', *Deutsches Ärzteblatt international*, 107 (2010), pp. 279–85.

'Finanzierung von Arzneimittelstudien durch pharmazeutische Unternehmen und die Folgen; Teil 2: qualitative systematische Literaturübersicht zum Einfluss auf Autorenschaft, Zugang zu Studiendaten sowie -registrierung und Publikation', *Deutsches Ärzteblatt international*, 107 (2010), pp. 295–301.

Schwabe, J., *Die sogenannte Drittwirkung der Grundrechte. Zur Einwirkung der Grundrechte auf den Privatrechtsverkehr* (München: Goldmann, 1971).

Selznick, P., *Law, Society and Industrial Justice* (New York: Russell Sage, 1969).

Smith, M. L., 'Publication Bias and Meta-analysis', *Evaluation in Education*, 4 (1980), pp. 22–4.

Steinhauer, F., 'Das Grundrecht der Kunstfreiheit: Kommentar zu einem Grundlagentext von Helmut Ridder' in T. Vesting, S. Korioth and I. Augsberg (eds.), *Grundrechte als Phänomene kollektiver Ordnung. Zur Wiedergewinnung des Gesellschaftlichen in der Grundrechtstheorie und Grundrechtsdogmatik* (Tübingen: Mohr Siebeck, 2014), pp. 247–82.

Stern, J., and R. J. Simes, 'Publication Bias: Evidence of Delayed Publication in a Cohort Study of Clinical Research Projects', *British Medical Journal*, 315 (1997), pp. 640–5.

Stichweh, R., *Wissenschaft, Universität, Professionen* (Frankfurt: Suhrkamp, 1994).

'Einheit und Differenz im Wissenschaftssystem der Moderne' in J. Halfmann and J. Rohbeck (eds.), *Zwei Kulturen der Wissenschaft - Revisited* (Weilerswist: Velbrück, 2007), pp. 213–28.

Stolleis, M., *Geschichte des öffentlichen Rechts in Deutschland* IV (München: C.H. Beck, 2012).

Sutton, A., S. J. Duval and R. L. Tweedie, 'Empirical Assessment of Effect of Publication Bias on Meta-Analysis', *British Medical Journal*, 320 (2000), pp. 1574–7.

Teubner, G., 'The Anonymous Matrix: Human Rights Violations by "Private" Transnational Actors', *Modern Law Review*, 69 (2006), pp. 327–46.

Constitutional Fragments: Societal Constitutionalism and Globalization (Oxford University Press, 2012).

Tonks, A., 'A Clinical Trials Register for Europe', *British Medical Journal*, 325 (2002), pp. 1314–5.

Tramèr, M. R., D. J. Reynolds, A. Moore and H. McQuay, 'Impact of Covert Duplicate Publication on Meta-Analysis: a Case Study', *British Medical Journal*, 315 (1997), pp. 635–40.

Verschraegen, G., 'Differentiation and Inclusion: A Neglected Sociological Approach to Fundamental Rights' in M. R. Madsen and G. Verschraegen (eds.), *Making Human Rights Intelligible: Towards a Sociology of Human Rights* (Oxford: Hart, 2013), pp. 61–80.

Vesting, T., *Rechtstheorie: Ein Studienbuch* (München: Beck, 2007).

'Die Tagesschau-App und die Notwendigkeit der Schaffung eines "Intermedienkollisionsrechts"' in I. Spiecker (ed.), *Karlsruher Dialog zum Informationsrecht* (Karlsruhe: KIT Scientific Publishing, 2013), vol. IV, pp. 1–23.

Die Medien des Rechts: Computernetzwerke (Weilerswist: Velbrück, 2015).

Viellechner, L., *Transnationalisierung des Rechts* (Weilerswist: Velbrück, 2013).

Viens A. M., and J. Savulescu, 'Introduction to the Olivieri Symposium', *Journal of Medical Ethics*, 30 (2004), pp. 1–7.

Weber, M., *Gesammelte Aufsätze zur Wissenschaftslehre*, 3rd edn. (Tübingen: Mohr Siebeck, 1968).

Wheatley, S., 'Deliberating about Cosmopolitan Ideas: Does a Democratic Conception of Human Rights Make Sense?' in O. d. Frouville (ed.), *Le Cosmopolitisme Juridique* (Paris: Pedone, 2015), available at: SSRN: http://ssrn.com/abstract=2485068.

Wiethölter, R., 'Justifications of a Law of Society' in O. Perez and G. Teubner (eds.), *Paradoxes and Inconsistencies in the Law* (Oxford: Hart, 2005), pp. 65–77.

World Health Organization, 'International Clinical Trials Registry Platform (ICTRP)', 2012, available at: www.who.int/ictrp/en.

Zöllner, W., 'Regelungsspielräume im Schuldvertragsrecht: Bemerkungen zur Grundrechtsanwendung im Privatrecht und zu den sogenannten Ungleichgewichtslagen', *Archiv für die civilistische Praxis*, 196 (1996), pp. 1–36.

6

(Dis)Solving constitutional problems

Transconstitutionalism beyond collisions[1]

MARCELO NEVES[2]

Introduction

This article discusses a theoretical model that emphasises the collisions between legal and constitutional regimes in the light of the theory of transconstitutionalism. To begin, I distance my view from the currently widespread idea that there has been an emergence of a multitude of new constitutions, something that was followed by an inflationary use of the very term 'constitution' – the current constitutional catharsis. In a second step, the paper develops a critical approach to the fragmentation model of legal and constitutional regimes in order to call attention to the need for weaving these fragments into the perspective of a transversal rationality: emphasis is not on the entangled systems, regimes or orders, but on the entanglements themselves. Among several transconstitutional cases I have studied, I choose to discuss one concerning the 'infanticide' of newborn children with disabilities carried out by Suruwahá and other indigenous groups. The intention is to approach the transconstitutional paradox in regard to a hard collision between normative orders in a way that goes beyond Western and simplistic cosmopolitan global constitutionalism models and soft collision analyses, which are privileged in the so-called 'Global North'. The focus is on the collision between a state constitutional right (international rights declared by ILO Convention No. 169 are mentioned only secondarily) and the normative orders of

[1] This article is based on my book *Transconstitucionalismo* (São Paulo: WMF Martins Fontes, 2009) [English trans.: Transconstitutionalism (Oxford: Hart, 2013)].

[2] I wish to express my thanks to Andreas Fischer-Lescano, Hannah Franzki, Carina Calabria and Pedro Henrique Ribeiro for the considerate comments and critical remarks that aided me in reviewing this material and drawing up this version. I reaffirm my responsibility over any possible inaccuracy or mistakes that may have remained in this chapter.

indigenous people in Latin America. At the legal-constitutional level, this collision expresses a societal collision between two very different self-understandings of human life: it is thus not properly a discussion between life and life form. Finally, I point to a path that goes beyond recognising that every observer has a blind spot in order to gain a perspective of alterity, in which a blind spot can be seen by another in a transversal connection of double contingency.

From constitutional inflation to transconstitutionalism

Towards the end of the last century, constitutional law scholars from different theoretical traditions and a wide array of countries, but all strongly linked to the study of state constitutions, began to concern themselves with the new challenges of cross-border constitutional law relevant to other legal orders, including non-state orders. In the United States, for example, Bruce Ackerman acknowledged that 'American practice and theory have moved in the direction of emphatic provincialism', and stressed that 'we should resist the temptations of a provincial particularism'.[3] Later, in a paper delivered to the Hague Institute for the Internationalisation of Law, Mark Tushnet spoke of 'the inevitable globalisation of constitutional law',[4] clarifying that he was concerned with domestic constitutional law and not with the 'separate question of ... whether there is something fairly called a constitution of the international order or a global constitution'.[5] On the other side of the Atlantic, J. J. Gomes Canotilho, basing his argument on Lucas Pires's, referred to 'interconstitutionality', albeit restricted to the relationship between the legal order of the European Union and the constitutional orders of EU Member States.[6] Meanwhile, in Germany, Ingolf Pernice has also developed a model of 'multilevel constitutionalism', mainly taking into account the European experience.[7]

Outside the circle of constitutional lawyers working in the tradition of national law, it has become commonplace to use the term 'constitution' in other disciplines to refer to widely differing situations: the Constitution of

3 Ackerman, 'The Rise of World Constitutionalism', pp. 773, 794.

4 Tushnet, 'The Inevitable Globalization of Constitutional Law'.

5 Ibid., p. 2, note 7.

6 Canotilho, 'Brancosos' e interconstitucionalidade, pp. 265ff.; Pires, Introdução ao direito constitucional europeu, pp. 101ff.

7 Pernice, 'Multilevel Constitutionalism and the Treaty of Amsterdam'; 'Multilevel Constitutionalism in the European Union'.

Europe,[8] the Constitution of the International Community,[9] 'global civil constitutions',[10] and so on. This inflation in the use of the term has led to considerable vagueness, and 'constitution' has begun to lose much of its historical, normative, and functional meaning. In this context, 'the importance of being called a Constitution'[11] has taken the spotlight, resulting in the persistence of the mistake of nominalism to which Ackerman refers in his analysis of comparative constitutional law: 'Important differences are frequently obliterated by loose talk invoking a common label'.[12]

Thus, the concept of constitution discussed here is not a historical-universal one,[13] according to which the formula 'no state without a constitution' is valid.[14] Writing from the perspective of a history of the constitution, Reinhart Koselleck extends the concept to include 'all legally regulated institutions and their forms of organisation, without which a social community of action is not politically capable of acting'. And he clarifies this as follows:

> My proposal that the history of the constitution should encompass all domains characterised by repeatability by virtue of legal rules is therefore designed to bridge the gap between pre-modern histories of law and modern histories of the constitution so as to include not just interstate but also post-state and to some extent supra-state phenomena of our times.[15]

Chris Thornhill also proposes a historical-universal concept of constitution 'in terms that can be applied to many societies in different historical periods', although limiting his view of constitution to 'the fact that it refers primarily to the function of states [in general, not the modern states], and it establishes a legal form relating to the use of power by states, or at least by actors bearing and utilizing public authority'.[16] Nevertheless, the extreme proposal of a historical-universal

[8] Weiler, *The Constitution of Europe.*

[9] See, e.g., Fassbender, 'The United Nations Charter as Constitution of the International Community'; Tomuschat, 'Die internationale Gemeinschaft', p. 7.

[10] Teubner, '*Globale Zivilverfassungen*' [English trans.: 'Societal Constitutionalism'].

[11] Maduro, A Constituição Plural, pp. 335ff.

[12] Ackerman, 'The Rise of World Constitutionalism', p. 794.

[13] Canotilho, Direito constitucional, p. 59.

[14] Biaggini, 'Die Idee der Verfassung', p. 447.

[15] Koselleck, 'Begriffsgeschichtliche Probleme der Verfassungsgeschichtsbeschreibung', pp. 370–1. One might say that Koselleck also falls into anachronism by extending the concept of constitution to embrace historically very different institutions and experiences.

[16] Thornhill, *A Sociology of Constitutions*, p. 11. Unlike what Thornhill (ibid., pp. 9–10) suggests, I think that this discussion must not be confused with the issue whether there is 'formally written constitutions'.

concept is offered by Gunther Teubner, who states: 'not just ubi societas, ibi ius, as Grotius once said, but ubi societas, ibi constitutio'.[17]

Normally, the historical-universal concept of a constitution presents itself at the empirical level (i.e., in social-cognitive, not in legal-normative terms), showing that every society or state has basic structural power relations that also determine juridical forms. According to this conception, which is to be found in authors as disparate as Friedrich Engels, Ferdinand Lassalle and Max Weber,[18] the presence of a constitution cannot be excluded from any social order, including archaic societies, since basic structures of 'diffuse power'[19] exist there too. But the historical-universal conception also presents itself in the idea of a constitution in the material sense as a set of supreme positive legal norms,[20] since a supreme normative nucleus can be detected in any legal order. Such a concept could exclude primitive legal orders, insofar as they lack the secondary rules of organisation, especially the ultimate rule of recognition, considered as a constitution in the material sense; nevertheless, for each and every state there must be a constitution (ultimate rules of recognition).[21] Lastly, the culturalist conception may also be historical-universal, when it defines a state constitution either as the 'dialectics' of political normality and juridical normativity[22] or as a 'process of integration',[23] since 'dialectics' and 'processes' of this kind can be found in any type of state including pre-modern, absolutist and authoritarian states. It is very hard to analyse the specificity of the meaning and function of a constitution as one of the few 'achievements of modern civilisation' that are 'the result of intentional planning',[24] when the analytical tools to be used are these historical-universal concepts.[25]

[17] Teubner, *Verfassungsfragmente*, p. 63 [English trans.: *Constitutional Fragments*, p. 35 – only here the reference to Grotius appears].

[18] Engels, 'Die Lage Englands. II. Die englische Konstitution', especially 572ff; Lassalle, 'Über Verfassungswesen', p. 130; Weber, 'Über Verfassungswesen', p. 27.

[19] Burdeau, *Traité de Science Politique*, vol. I, pp. 249–51.

[20] Kelsen, *Reine Rechtslehre*, pp. 228–30; *General Theory of Law and State*, pp. 124–5; *Allgemeine Staatslehre*, pp. 251–3.

[21] Cf. Hart, *The Concept of Law*, pp. 91–123, especially p. 107. Hart also speaks of 'constitutional matters' in respect of the secondary rules for alteration (ibid., p. 60).

[22] Heller, *Staatslehre*, pp. 249ff.

[23] Smend, 'Verfassung und Verfassungsrecht (1928)', especially pp. 136ff. and pp. 189–91.

[24] Luhmann, 'Verfassung als evolutionäre Errungenschaft', p. 176.

[25] Cf. ibid., p. 212. Unlike what Thornhill (*A Sociology of Constitutions*, p. 19) asserts, Luhmann has not 'accepted latitude in the definition of constitution'; rather, he has proposed a very

I aim to avoid the tendency to invoke the creation of a new constitution whenever a legal order, institution or organisation emerges in contemporary society. I start from the firm idea that the meaning of 'constitution' in the strictly modern sense is linked to the constitutionalism that resulted from the liberal revolutions of the eighteenth century in France and the United States, as well as from British political and legal history, albeit atypically so in the latter case. From this conceptual starting point, I set out to identify the problems that presented themselves as a condition for the historical possibility of the emergence of the constitutional state. Having determined such problems, it is relevant to ask what functional and normative answers the constitutions of modern states were intended to embody. It is precisely this relationship between problems and solutions that enable the concept of constitution arising from constitutionalism to be established.

Two problems were of vital importance to the appearance of constitutions in the modern sense. On the one hand, the emergence of demands for fundamental or human rights in a society of increasing systemic complexity and social heterogeneity. On the other, and associated with this, the organisational question about the limitation and internal and external control of power (including participation by the governed in procedures, especially those involved in determining the composition of government bodies). Related hereto was the question of the growing specialisation of functions, a condition for greater efficiency of state power. As world society has become more integrated, these problems have recently become untreatable by any single national legal order within its territory alone. Problems of human or fundamental rights and power limitation or control are increasingly becoming relevant to more than one legal order at the same time; many of these are non-state orders but they, too, are called upon to offer solutions to such problems. This entails permanent interweaving relationships among legal orders revolving around shared constitutional problems. Thus, constitutional law emancipates itself from the state, in which its foundations were originally located, not exactly because a multitude of new constitutions have appeared, but rather because other legal orders are directly involved in resolving basic constitutional problems, frequently prevailing

strict concept of constitution: 'My theses will be that the concept of constitution – contrary to the first impression – responds to a differentiation between law and politics, even more: to a separation of these both functional system and to the need arising therefrom for linkage' (Luhmann, 'Verfassung als evolutionäre Errungenschaft', pp. 179–80).

over the orientation of the legal orders of the respective nation states. Furthermore, permanent direct relations are formed between states to deal with the constitutional problems they have in common. The exception has become the rule in both cases.

To address this situation I propose the concept of transconstitutionalism. On the one hand, transconstitutionalism should not be confused with mere trans-juridicism, such as, for example, in relations between legal orders in mediaeval pluralism, especially between canon law (including Roman law), urban law, royal law, and feudal law,[26] since mediaeval experience did not involve constitutional problems in the modern sense. Thus it was not a matter of fundamental rights or of the legal limitation and control of power, much less of various claims for the self-referentiality of the foundations of law (ultimately the law had sacred foundations[27]).

On the other hand, what I am proposing to discuss is not international, transnational, supranational, national, or local constitutionalism. The concept of transconstitutionalism points precisely to the development of legal problems that cut across the various types of legal order. A transconstitutional problem entails an issue that may involve national, international, supranational, and transnational courts or arbitration tribunals, as well as native local legal institutions, in the search for a solution. In discussing transconstitutionalism I refer to Wolfgang Welsch's concept of 'transversal reason',[28] although I keep my distance somewhat from this ambitious view, to analyse the limits and possibilities of the existence of 'transversal rationalities' (or 'bridges of transition'), both between the legal system and other social systems (transversal constitutions) and among legal orders within the law as a functional system of world society.[29]

Moreover, while discussing transconstitutionalism I do not consider it merely as a functional requirement and normative claim for transversal rationality among legal orders; I also take into consideration the negative aspects of transconstitutional entanglements, such as cases where the problem involves situations of anti-constitutional orders or practices, that is, those which counteract the protection of human and fundamental rights or which counteract the control and limitation of power. Similarly,

[26] Cf. Berman, *Law and Revolution*, figure 2, pp. 522–6.

[27] See Neves, *Transconstitucionalismo*, pp. 8–10 and p. 16, note 63 [English trans.: *Transconstitutionalism*, pp. 9–11 and p. 14, note 63].

[28] Welsch, *Vernunft*; *Unsere postmoderne Moderne*, pp. 295–318.

[29] Cf. Neves, *Transconstitucionalismo*, pp. 38ff. [English trans.: *Transconstitutionalism*, pp. 28ff.].

address the question of anti-constitutional practices found within the orders of typically constitutional states.[30] Therefore, it is worth distinguishing transconstitutionalism (genus), which includes relations between constitutional and anti-constitutional orders, from interconstitutionalism (species), which comprises only relations between legal orders to fulfil constitutionalist requirements.

Transconstitutionalism does not take any single legal order or type of order as a starting point or ultima ratio. It rejects nation-statism, internationalism, supranationalism, transnationalism, and localism as privileged spaces for solving constitutional problems. Instead, it points to the need to build 'bridges of transition', promote both 'constitutional conversations' or 'dialogue' and 'constitutional collisions'[31] as well as strengthen constitutional entanglements among the various legal orders, be they national, international, transnational, supranational, or local. The transconstitutional model avoids the dilemma of 'monism versus pluralism'. From the standpoint of transconstitutionalism, a plurality of legal orders entails a complementary relationship between identity and alterity. The orders involved in solving a specific constitutional problem continuously reconstruct their identity at the level of their self-referential foundations by means of transconstitutional entanglement with another order or with other orders: identity is rearticulated on the basis of alterity. Thus rather than seeking a 'Herculean Constitution', transconstitutionalism points to the need to tackle the many-headed Hydra of constitutional problems by articulating reciprocal observations among the various legal orders of world society.

At this point, one may ask if transconstitutionalism entails an empirical and functional or a normative approach. Although the normative dimension is not totally disconnected from the functional dimension, it is necessary to distinguish between the plane of functional requirements (relations between problems and solutions) and that of normative claims, which has to do with expectations that are counterfactually stabilised in the sphere of world society.[32] From this, elementary normative structures

[30] See, e.g., Scheppele, 'The Migration of Anti-constitutional Ideas'; Roach, 'The Post-9/11 Migration of Britain's Terrorism Act 2000'; Gross, '"Control Systems" and the Migration of Anomalies'.

[31] On my use of 'conversation' and 'dialogue' see later, especially footnote 53. Here, these terms do not have any ideal-normative sense.

[32] On the distinction between normative expectations (resistant to the reality that disappoints them) and cognitive expectations (willing to learn and change in response to the disappointments of reality), see Luhmann, *Rechtssoziologie*, pp. 40–53 [English trans.:

related to the highly complex multicentric society derive.[33] Indeed, the normative aspect of transconstitutionalism cannot be entirely separated from its empirical dimension, for it emerges under the factual conditions of law and politics in world society, giving these a counterfactual shape (normative expectations). Transconstitutionalism presents itself as a basic normative counterpoint to both the expansionary primacy of the cognitive structures of world society (linked to the economy, technology, and science) and the semantics of the control of information (and knowledge) by the mass media.

From legal and constitutional fragmentation to transconstitutionalism

The transconstitutional model does not share without reservations the widely held idea of the fragmentation of law, which has been given precise systemic-theoretical outlines in the work of Gunther Teubner and Andreas Fischer-Lescano.[34] Considering that systems theory adopts

A Sociological Theory of Law, pp. 31–40]; *Soziale Systeme*, pp. 436–43 [English trans.: Social Systems, pp. 319–25].

33 On the distance he takes from normative theories of society, Luhmann explains: 'This sceptical abstinence vis-à-vis norm-centred theory does not, of course, imply that one can imagine a possible societal life without norms. Binding oneself to norms or values is a pervasive aspect of social life' (*Soziale Systeme*, p. 444; English trans.: Social Systems, pp. 325–6). It has not to do with distinction between the 'being' and 'ought' in the sense that traces back to the enlightenment: 'Although counterfactually oriented, the meaning of the ought is no less factual than the meaning of being. All expectation is factual, its fulfilment as much as its non-fulfilment. The factual includes the normative. *The usual contrast between the factual and normative should therefore be abolished.* . . . The normative finds its adequate contrast not in the factual but in the cognitive: one can meaningfully choose only between these two positions. Furthermore, it is important not immediately to inflate this differentiation between cognitive and normative expectations into the ancient factual/logical contrast between being and ought, but first to recognise the function of the differentiation itself. It suggests two different, but still functionally equivalent, strategies of life after disappointments. One can learn or not learn. Both possibilities can help to overcome situations of disappointment and thus far, although in opposite ways, *both fulfil the same function*. It is on the fact that not only "similar" but directly opposed behaviour fulfils the same function that success is founded. This eases finding a solution for each case of disappointment. One can decide to maintain or give up an expectation in relation to its significance and chances of being realised' (Luhmann, *Rechtssoziologie*, pp. 43–4; English trans.: A Sociological Theory of Law, pp. 33–4, my emphasis).

34 See Teubner, *Verfassungsfragmente* [English trans.: Constitutional Fragments]; 'Die Anonyme Matrix', pp. 175ff. [English trans.: 'The Anonymous Matrix', pp. 338ff.]; Fischer-Lescano and Teubner, Regime-Kollisionen; 'Fragmentierung des Weltrechts'; Fischer-Lescano, Globalverfassung, pp. 187ff.

concepts originating in biology such as differentiation, evolution, coevolution, autopoiesis and structural coupling, among others, not as analogies but as generalisations,[35] it seems to me that the social-theoretical or sociological-juridical notion of fragmentation should be understood in connection with its roots in the biological conception of fragmentation as a reproductive process. If we understand it in this way, we run into problems that have not been addressed satisfactorily by social or legal theories of the fragmentation of society or law. Here it is interesting to bring in the Red Queen hypothesis, based on the Red Queen's telling Alice in Lewis Carroll's Through the Looking-Glass that 'it takes all the running you can do, to keep in the same place'.[36] The Red Queen hypothesis, presented firstly by Leigh Van Valen,[37] points, especially in the variant developed by William D. Hamilton,[38] to the role of sexual reproduction in promoting genetic variability and an enhanced capacity for selection in response to environmental elements and factors, especially parasites.[39] Fragmentation, in contrast, is a typical form of asexual reproduction, as occurs with starfish, for example, and entails limited genetic variation, as well as weak capacity for selection and response to the adversities of the environment, which means few evolutionary alternatives. One of the advantages enjoyed by sexual over asexual species is 'abundant polymorphism',[40] so that sexual species are more fit to respond to the environmental adversities.[41] Despite divergences,

[35] See Teubner, *Recht als autopoietisches System*, especially pp. 66ff. [English trans.: Law as an Autopoietic System, pp. 51ff.].

[36] 'Now, here, it takes all the running you can do, to keep in the same place. If you want to get somewhere else, you must run at least twice as fast as that' (Carroll, 'Through the Looking-Glass and What Alice Found There', p. 166).

[37] Van Valen, 'Molecular Evolution as Predicted by Natural Selection', pp. 90ff.

[38] See, e.g., Hamilton, 'Sex Versus Non-sex Versus Parasite'; Hamilton, Henderson and Moran, 'Fluctuation of Environment and Coevolved Antagonist Polymorphism as Factors in the Maintenance of Sex'; Hamilton, Axelrod and Tanese, 'Sexual Reproduction as an Adaptation to Resist Parasites'.

[39] In this regard, see the panoramic exposition offered by Ridley, The Red Queen. With some restrictions, see Neiman and Koskella, 'Sex and Red Queen'.

[40] Ridley The Red Queen, p. 84; see Hamilton, 'Sex Versus Non-sex Versus Parasite', especially p. 283; Hamilton, Henderson and Moran, 'Fluctuation of Environment and Coevolved Antagonist Polymorphism as Factors in the Maintenance of Sex', especially p. 66, who emphasised, however, that they intended to go beyond the question of polymorphism to concentrate its focus on the problem of sex (p. 65). The issue of the importance of polymorphism is traced back to Haldane ('Disease and Evolution'), who also pointed out 'the danger of homogeneity' (p. 329 or p. 6 in the original).

[41] In Ridley's metaphorical language, 'Sexual species can call on a sort of library of locks that is unavailable to asexual species' (Ridley, The Red Queen, p. 72). According to Hamilton,

precursory elements of the Red Queen hypothesis can be identified in the work of Charles Darwin, who, while considering that asexual species are not totally incompatible with evolution,[42] emphasised that even in sexual reproduction self-fertilisation involves very limited or implausible evolutionary capacity, asserting 'that it is a general law of nature that no organic being fertilises itself for a perpetuity of generations, but that a cross with another individual is occasionally – perhaps at long intervals of time – indispensable'. Furthermore, he pointed out the disadvantage of close interbreeding:

> I have collected so large a body of facts, and made so many experiments, showing ... that with animals and plants a cross between different varieties, or between individuals of the same variety but of another strain, gives vigour and fertility to the offspring; and on the other hand, that close interbreeding diminishes vigour and fertility.[43]

This means sexuality between genetically diverse organic beings is important to the evolution of species.

I am aware of the danger of a conservative reading of the Red Queen hypothesis if it is transported from a biological context into the field of social science in the terms of the socio-biology, as well as mindful of the fact that the systems theory developed by Luhmann maintains the thesis of 'emergence from above' in regard to the relation between biology, psychological and social systems, according, indeed, to the fathers of the sociology, but radicalising it.[44] A socially adequate re-reading is in place here. It seems opportune to remark that mere fragmentation is incompatible with adequate transformations of social systems in response to their

Axelrod and Tanese, 'success of sex increases with the number of loci involved in defence against parasites' ('Sexual Reproduction as an Adaptation to Resist Parasites', p. 3568). They state: 'The essence of sex in our theory is that it stores genes that are currently bad but have promise for reuse. It continually tries them in combination, waiting for the time when the focus of disadvantage has moved elsewhere. When this has happened, the genotypes carrying such genes spread by successful reproduction, becoming simultaneously stores for other bad genes and thus onward in continuous succession' (ibid., p. 3569).

42 Darwin, The Origin of Species, p. 24.

43 Ibid., p. 95. See Meirmans, 'The Evolution of the Problem of Sex', pp. 22ff.

44 Luhmann, *Soziale Systeme*, pp. 43–4 [English trans.: Social Systems, pp. 22–3]; Teubner, *Recht als autopoietisches System*, pp. 40–1 [English trans.: Law as an Autopoietic System, pp. 29–30]. Even so, Luhmann and Teubner invoke the concepts of the biological theory set up by Maturana and Varela, who argue in favour of the 'emergence from below', considering the living beings as components of the social systems (Maturana and Varela, Autopoiesis and Cognition, pp. 107–11; Der Baum der Erkenntnis, pp. 196ff.).

increasingly complex environment. Problems are renewed and social systems or legal orders must constantly not only construct structural couplings with their environment, but also build new 'transition bridges' with other legal order and social systems, in order to properly face the ongoing fluctuation of factors from the environment. Simple fragmentation cannot offer a solution to the new problems that emerge in processes of continuous social change. Without the development of 'polymorphism' through flexible 'transition bridges', the reproduction of legal systems or orders would be paralysed. These would be forced to 'die' by crystallisation, falling into hyper-integration through excessive redundancy.[45] In other words, the building of sluices, especially concerning law, depends, paradoxically, on transversal connections between social systems and legal orders. For this reason, the functional orientation of the relationship between problem and solution must take into account the way in which fragments are woven into a differentiated communication order. A certain amount of internal disintegration is therefore required, and this cannot be dissociated from increased flexibility or variety in relation to the outside, relying on inter-crossings able to promote the continuous renewal of identity in view of alterity. In sum, this means problems of collision are not addressed or resolved at each step on the level of mere fragmentation or simple fragments, but via bridges built transversally between the constituent units of a differentiated communication order under constant renewal.

From the standpoint of the legal system, this situation is even more patent if we bear in mind that the various legal orders belonging to the world legal system use the same binary code of communication (lawful/unlawful), but have utterly different structures and levels of autonomy. It is worth pointing out another problem with the conception of legal pluralism in world society. The heterarchical model of the mainstream of systems theory is grounded in quasi-aprioristic concepts of autonomy or autopoiesis for fragmented regimes that are supposed to be constitutional, in a fully realised dynamic of functional differentiation.[46]

[45] I am using a metaphor suggested by Atlan (Entre le cristal et la fumée, p. 281), by distinguishing, ultimately, between 'death by rigidity, that of the crystal, the mineral, and the death by decomposition, that of the smoke', i.e., between excess of redundancy and excess of variety.

[46] 'Globalisation means that functional differentiation, first realised historically within the nation states of Europe and North America, now encompasses the whole world' (Teubner, *Verfassungsfragmente*, p. 72 [English trans.: Constitutional Fragments, p. 42]; see also ibid., pp. 119–20 [English Trans. pp. 74–5], regarding the relation between constitution and autonomy of the legal system in terms of global constitutional pluralism).

However, it can be seen empirically that several legal forms and orders in the world legal system do not have a minimum of autonomy, let alone constitutional autonomy, not only because they are instruments (law as means) of politics (totalitarianism and authoritarianism) or the economy (forms of law oriented almost exclusively to market efficiency), but also because they lack even so-called secondary rules of organisation, such as rights for indigenous and tribal people. Yet they are all exposed to the same constitutional problems. When the dominant model of constitutional pluralism faces the problem of tribal legal orders, it limits itself to consider, especially from the perspective of intellectual property rights, how these orders will be made compatible with the model of patent rights.[47] One should take seriously Niklas Luhmann's ironic (some would say cynical) remark that the model of differentiation of law may be nothing but a 'European anomaly'.[48] This is the paradox of world society: the functional differentiation and autonomy of systems radiated out from the centre as a functional requirement and, to some extent, as a normative claim, and was practically imposed on the periphery (selectively of course), which was and still is unable to correspond or unwilling to adapt to the differentiation model. This is due to the immense asymmetry of world society, which cannot be considered from a simplified evolutionary perspective.

In connection with this point, I would like to stress here that the dominant model of constitutional pluralism is based on the assumption of linear evolution in world society, which considers only the development of law in central modernity as a passage from liberal law (formal rationality) via social-state law (material rationality) to the achievement of reflexive law in the aftermath of the crisis in social-state law.[49] As in the case of autonomy mentioned earlier, the dominant constitutional pluralism ignores the fact that no liberal states, let alone social states,

[47] Cf. Teubner and Fischer-Lescano, 'Cannibalizing Epistemes'; Teubner, *Verfassungsfragmente*, pp. 242ff. [English trans.: Constitutional Fragments, pp. 162ff.]. Indeed, in this passage Teubner is discussing 'intercultural collisions'. However, he focuses on 'biopiracy' and 'land-grabbing', which in my view are conflicts of interest in the field of property rights based on the current economic system of the world society (capitalism?!), rather than intercultural collisions, not depending on the occurrence of such collisions.

[48] Luhmann, *Das Recht der Gesellschaft*, p. 586 [English trans.: Law as a Social System, p. 490].

[49] Teubner, *Verfassungsfragmente*, pp. 33ff. and pp. 45ff., especially pp. 62–3 [English trans.: Constitutional Fragments, pp. 15ff., pp. 24ff., especially p. 35]. See also as a first presentation of this model: Teubner, 'Reflexives Recht', pp. 24–9.

have been built in most of the geographic and demographic contexts of communication in modern society. We cannot speak of a crisis of the social or welfare state in these contexts. In many regions of the globe, social movements are demanding the presence of a minimal social state, without which it is meaningless to speak of post-modern legal pluralism, except as a post-colonial romanticising of extreme poverty. This is the paradox and also the mistake deriving from legal pluralism in world society: how can we speak of insertion into transactional networks without considering the glaring asymmetries, and not just the new 'avalanche of exclusion' due to the dismantling (breakdown) of the social state,[50] but also the persistence of devastating exclusion in the peripheral areas of world society? Moreover, how can we include in the linear evolution of liberal (formal) law, social-state (material) law and reflexive law the tribal forms of undifferentiated legal orders, which rather than being involved in the difference inclusion/exclusion, involve the problem of isolation/non-isolation?

Transconstitutionalism takes these asymmetries seriously in affirming 'transition bridges' that are both contentious and cooperative. In this regard, I have spoken on 'dialogue', a term that can lead the reader to misunderstandings. Of course, it does not mean constitutional 'dialogues' oriented to an understanding between courts or instances of different legal orders. Transconstitutional problems necessarily have a contentious dimension. And even when what is at stake is 'dialogue', this 'dialogue' should be understood not in terms of conciliation or consensus, but rather as referring to forms of communication designed to absorb dissent, assuming double contingency.[51] It should be noted that double contingency refers not only to the relationships between alter and ego as persons in interaction, but also to systems (and not only organisational systems), inasmuch as systems observe each other, as Luhmann stresses in going beyond the double contingency model proposed by action theory.[52] Between different legal orders, especially on the plane of constitutional problems, 'dialogue' should point to transversal communication, grounded in double contingency. 'Dialogue' here could have an analogous meaning to that formulated by Paul Feyerabend,[53] referring to

[50] Luhmann, *Die Politik der Gesellschaft*, pp. 427–8.

[51] Neves, *Transconstitucionalismo*, pp. 270ff. [English trans.: Transconstitutionalism, pp. 169ff.].

[52] Luhmann, *Soziale Systeme*, pp. 152, 155 [English trans.: Social Systems, pp. 106, 108].

[53] 'It can show the effect of arguments on outsiders or on experts from a different school', as well as 'demonstrate the chimerical nature of what we believe to be the most solid parts of our lives' (Feyerabend, Three Dialogues on Knowledge, pp. 164–5).

forms of communication oriented to influencing and modifying each other, showing the limits of the concerned perspectives, without something like consensus being expected to result from this.[54] But even in this non-consensual sense the possibility of 'dialogue' is merely a limited dimension of transconstitutionalism between legal orders. Reciprocal learning through conflict and contention in 'transition bridges' may be far more important. And this implies the paradox deriving from the need for us all to be permanently surprised by each other and ourselves.

On this point I shall limit my remarks to just one case discussed in my book Transconstitutionalism, in which the transconstitutional paradox is very striking indeed.

An emblematic case: transconstitutionalism between the normative order of an indigenous community and the constitutional law of the Brazilian state

Transconstitutionalism encompasses problematic relations between state legal orders and extra-state orders of native groups, whose anthropological and cultural assumptions are not compatible with the model of state constitutionalism.[55] In this case, it is evidently a matter of 'archaic' orders that do not have principles or secondary rules of organisation and therefore do not fit into the reflexive model of constitutionalism. Strictly speaking, they do not admit juridical-constitutional problems of human rights and legal constraints on power. When normative orders of this kind collide with institutions of a state's constitutional legal order, a 'unilateral transconstitutionalism' of tolerance and, to some extent, learning is required from the involved state. This form of transconstitutionalism is indispensable because, although the legal orders in question are very far from complying (in many of their norms and practices) with the

[54] Therefore, transconstitutionalism has not to do with the idea that a normative order can only be conceptualised as law if it is recognised by a correlated legal order, as Michaelis ('Was ist nichtstaatliches Recht?', p. 55) maintains: 'Indeed, for my concept of law the recognition by the state definitely plays a role. However, I generalise this necessity of recognition and apply it just also to the recognition of the state by other orders'. In the transconstitutional perspective, I have proposed that the double contingency implies complex entanglements of trust and distrust, esteem and disesteem, conflicts and dialogs, recognition and non-recognition between the normative orders compulsorily involved in the same constitutional question.

[55] I mean problematic relations for both normative orders, insofar as they irritate each other in the limits of their respective identities.

model of human rights and legal constraints on power that prevails in the legal system of world society, the mere unilateral granting of 'human rights' to members of the respective indigenous community runs counter to transconstitutionalism. Measures in this direction tend to have destructive effects on bodies and minds, and are contrary to the very concept of human rights.[56] In this context there is a paradoxical aspect to transconstitutionalism, insofar as it is involved in constitutional 'conversations' with normative orders that lie outside constitutionalism itself.[57] This situation, however, results from the necessity, intrinsic to transconstitutionalism, of developing alternative institutes that make possible a constructive 'dialogue' with these orders of people who are anthropologically/culturally 'different' and have lived for millennia in the territory of the respective state. Thus, transconstitutionalism, albeit limited, does not lose its significance for the development of the normative dimension of contemporary world society.

Latin American experience is rich in juridical-constitutional problems deriving from entanglements between native normative orders and state constitutional orders, especially with regard to fundamental rights.

One of the most delicate recent cases involved relations between the Brazilian state legal order and the normative order of the Suruwahá people who live in Tapauá, a municipality located in Amazonas State, and remained voluntarily isolated until the end of the 1970s.[58] Under Suruwahá customary law, children born unhealthy or disabled must be killed. Another case involved the Yawanawá, living in Acre on the border between Brazil and Peru, among whom a customary normative order required the killing of one newborn twin. In this context, it also became public that practises of this kind were common amongst the Yanomami and other indigenous groups. This situation led to controversy, since it involved a practically irresolvable conflict between the right to cultural

56 'The human rights question in the strictest sense must today be seen as endangerment of individuals' integrity of body and mind by a multiplicity of anonymous and today globalised communicative processes' (Teubner, 'Die Anonyme Matrix', p. 180; English trans.: 'The Anonymous Matrix', p. 341).

57 In other perspective, Merry ('Transnational Human Rights and Local Activism', p. 49) points out a similar paradox: 'This is the paradox of making human rights in the vernacular: To be accepted, they have to be tailored to the local context and resonant with the local cultural framework. However, to be part of the human rights system, they must emphasise individualism, autonomy, choice, bodily integrity and equality – ideas embedded in the legal documents that constitute human rights law'. See notes 68 and 76.

58 Segato, 'Que cada pueblo teja los hilos de su historia', p. 363.

autonomy and the right to life. The problem had already come to light in 2002, when a Yawanawá woman attending a human rights workshop at FUNAI, the Brazilian National Indian Foundation, described her community's practise of killing one sibling when twins were born and said she was a victim of this customary law, being a mother of twins.[59] In this context, the problem was also presented as a conflict between the right to cultural autonomy and women's rights. However, it became a subject of widespread public debate in connection with the child's right to life, due in no small part to coverage in the media of a case involving a Suruwahá infant with a severe growth hormone deficiency problem who was condemned to death by the tribe but removed by missionaries.[60]

The impact of this case on public opinion led Brazilian Congressman Henrique Afonso, representing the state of Acre, to draft a bill that would have criminalised this practice in indigenous communities (Projeto de Lei 1057/2007). The initial statement of the bill's purpose (*ementa*) read as follows: 'Act establishing ways to combat harmful traditional practises and protect the fundamental rights of indigenous children and children belonging to other societies said to be non-traditional'.[61] As a basis for specific measures to combat such practises, including the criminalisation of any people who know of them through contact with the indigenous community but fail to notify the relevant authorities and of authorities who fail to take appropriate action (Articles 3, 4 and 5), Article 2.I-VIII listed the following reasons given for 'neonatal homicide': 'cases where one of the parents is absent'; 'cases of multiple gestation'; 'newborns with physical and/or mental illnesses'; 'when there is gender preference'; 'when there is a short interval between a previous pregnancy and the birth in question'; 'cases where the number of children appropriate for the group is exceeded'; 'newborns with some blemish or birthmark that distinguishes them from the rest'; 'when they are considered unlucky for the family or group'. The original bill also proposed to define types of 'child homicide in cases when the group believes a child is undernourished because of a curse or involving any other belief that leads to intentional death from malnutrition' (Article 2.IX). These hypotheses specified in the bill as well as others referring to sexual abuse, mistreatment and other physical and mental aggression against children based on traditional customs (Article 2.X-XII), correspond to practises observed to

[59] Ibid., pp. 357–8. [60] Cf. ibid., p. 363.

[61] Available at www.camara.gov.br/proposicoesWeb/fichadetramitacao?idProposicao=351362.

take place amongst the indigenous communities located in the territory of the Brazilian state. The Human Rights Committee of the Chamber of Deputies, Brazil's lower house, held a public hearing to discuss the bill.[62] While the measure was not taken further, the context in which it was drafted and the discussion to which it led constituted a unique instance of transconstitutional 'dialogue' between the state legal order and the local normative orders of indigenous communities.

The bill's drafters and advocates took as their basic starting point the idea of the absolute primacy of the individual's fundamental right to life in accordance with Western, Christian morality. Secondarily, the mother's fundamental right to motherhood also contributed to the proposition behind the bill. This unilateral advocacy of individual rights to the detriment of the cultural autonomy of indigenous communities did not seem adequate to those who took part in the debate from a broader anthropological perspective. Straightforward criminalisation of indigenous practises in the name of protecting the right to life, moreover, can be seen as tantamount to cultural genocide and destruction of the community via the destruction of its most deeply held beliefs.

Rita Laura Segato is one of the anthropologists who participated in the intense debate that included a public hearing held on 5 September 2007 in the Chamber of Deputies.[63] Her remarks shed some light on likely implications of this collision and pointed to the need for a transversal communication between normative orders in terms that can be considered appropriate to a constructive model of transconstitutionalism. In the context of the debate, Segato acknowledged that she was faced with

62 Convened by the Human Rights Committee of the Chamber of Deputies in August 2007, the hearing took place on 5 September 2007 (cf. Segato, 'Que cada pueblo teja los hilos de su historia', p. 357 and p. 369). Major alterations to this bill later reduced it to generic declarations and promises of support for the respective communities, in the following terms:

'Art 54-A. Respect and support for traditional indigenous practices are reaffirmed whenever such practices are in conformity with the fundamental rights established in the Federal Constitution and with the international treaties and conventions on human rights to which the Federative Republic of Brazil is a party.

Sole paragraph. The agencies responsible for indigenous peoples policy shall offer suitable opportunities for indigenous peoples to acquire knowledge about society as a whole when the following practices are identified by anthropological studies:

I – infanticide
II – indecent assault or rape
III – abuse
IV – physical and mental violence against children and their parents'.

63 See Segato, 'Que cada pueblo teja los hilos de su historia', pp. 370ff.

'the ungrateful task of arguing against this bill, but at the same time I would wager strongly on a change in customs'.[64] Her contribution included a report on empirical research showing that there were sixteen births, twenty-three suicides and two homicides of newborns (referred to as 'infanticide' by the anthropologists but not in the same technical sense as the legal definition used in the Brazilian Penal Code), and one death from disease among 143 Suruwahá between 2003 and 2005. Thus while 7.6 per cent of all Suruwahá deaths in the period were due to 'infanticide', 57.6 per cent were due to suicide.

This situation points to an understanding of life that differs starkly from the Christian one dominant in the West. The view traditionally held by indigenous peoples is that a good life is a life without excessive suffering for both the individual and the community. In other words, it makes sense to live only if life is placid and enjoyable. Thus, infant homicide is justified in certain cases.[65] According to this view, the meaning of life and death for the Suruwahá deserves as much respect as the meaning attributed by Christianity: 'We also found a complex, sophisticated vision of great philosophical dignity that owes nothing to Christianity'.[66]

The argument is reinforced by reference to Yanomami practise giving women absolute autonomy to decide whether their children should live. The mother withdraws into the forest to give birth, so that delivery occurs outside the context of social life, leaving the choice to the mother:

> If she does not touch the newborn child or welcome it into her arms, but leaves it on the ground where it fell, that means it has not been accepted into the world of culture and social relations. It is therefore not human. Thus it is cannot be said that a homicide has occurred from the viewpoint of this indigenous group, since one who remains on the ground is not a human life.[67]

This very different idea of human life genuinely entails a delicate problem involving the paradox between 'local' and 'universal' claims, which I also consider incompatible with the mere imposition of external conceptions of life and death by means of what in another context I have paradoxically called 'human rights imperialism'.[68] This is valid not only from an

[64] Ibid., p. 358. [65] Ibid., pp. 364–5 [66] Ibid., p. 364. [67] Ibid., p. 365.

[68] Neves, 'A força simbólica dos direitos humanos', p. 23 and p. 27 [English trans.: 2007, p. 432 and p. 436]. In another context and from a different theoretical standpoint, Merry ('Transnational Human Rights and Local Activism', pp. 48–9) similarly acknowledges this paradox: 'The larger structure of economic and political power that surrounds human rights activism means that translation is largely a top-down process from the

nthropological/cultural or anthropological/legal standpoint, but also rom the perspective of transconstitutionalism.

In this context, it is fundamental to consider the collision between two istinct perspectives on rights while endeavouring to avoid 'injustice' by mposing one, the order of the strongest, on the other, the order of the veakest. On one side is the right to collective autonomy, on the other the ight to individual autonomy. Simply submitting the former, considered he expression of an ethical way of life, to the latter, considered the xpression of universal morality as the basis for human rights,[69] does ot seem to be the most appropriate solution in a model of transcontitutionalism, for such a solution would lead to the hierarchical destrucion of several indigenous life forms by the state to the detriment of eterarchical collisions managing. On the contrary, in this context of adical collision between the state legal order and indigenous normative rders, it is necessary to consider and weigh the relative importance of the individual subject's right to life and the collective subject's right to ife', as Segato argues.[70] The 'ultra-criminalisation' of homicide practised gainst newborn children within indigenous communities proposed by

transnational to the local and the powerful to less powerful'. However, Merry (ibid., p. 49) seems to be impressed with the possibility of homogenising human rights in an 'emancipating' prospective as an 'important part of expansion of a modernist view of the individual and society embedded in the Global North, which promotes it along with democracy, the rule of law, capitalism and free market'. Although expressing doubts on the success of this 'emancipatory' project, she argues for promoting and expanding it: 'As translators vernacularize these transnational institutions and ideas, they promote this modernist view, with its emancipatory and homogenising effects. Whether or not they achieve an expanded human rights subjectivity is far more uncertain'. See note 57 and note 76.

69 Günther, while arguing that '[t]he appropriate application of legitimate norms may not harm forms of life without reason' (my emphasis), actually appears to be in favour of this approach insofar as he claims that 'conflicts between principles of justice and orientations of the good life at the post-conventional level can only be resolved universally, that is, in favour of justice' (*Der Sinn für Angemessenheit*, p. 196; English trans.: The Sense of Appropriateness, p. 153). It should be noted, however, that in the terms of Habermas's theory of communicative action and discourse, which Günther espouses, the collision in this case would be between post-conventional and pre-conventional morality. On the levels of development of moral consciousness in Habermas's theory of social evolution, see Neves, Entre Têmis e Leviatã, pp. 25ff.

70 Segato, 'Que cada pueblo teja los hilos de su historia', p. 367. At the public hearing mentioned earlier, Segato explained what she understood by 'the expression "right to life"' in this context: 'This expression can indicate two different types of right to life: the individual's right to life, i.e., protection for the individual subject of rights; and the right of life of collective subjects, i.e., to protection for the life of peoples in their condition as peoples' (ibid., p. 372).

the aforementioned bill (Projeto de Lei 1057/2007) could lead to 'ethnocide by eliminating cultural values indispensable to the biological and cultural life of a people'.[71] Such a legal solution, moreover, would have implications that it would be hard to make compatible with the constitutional order of the Brazilian state.[72] Under such circumstances, a search for a different route would appear necessary.

The proposal that appears best suited to transconstitutionalism resides in guaranteeing 'ethnic jurisdiction or an ethnic forum', so that each indigenous community can 'settle its disputes and work out a solution to internal dissent in its own way'.[73] This does not simply mean tolerance by the most powerful, or even tolerating the intolerant,[74] but rather the ability to acknowledge the autonomy of others, that is, of the sphere of communication, of the different language game or the different life form of indigenous people, without submitting them to the models of state constitutionalism. It is even less appropriate to speak of 'decent' and 'indecent' societies, or societies that are worthy or unworthy of 'dialogue' with the 'liberal' societies of the constitutional democratic state,[75] as if we were not all in the same world society with collisions and conflicts between domains of communication and language games. Nevertheless, it is necessary to bear in mind that, not just from an anthropological standpoint but also from that of transconstitutionalism, faced with dissent and disputes within indigenous communities, not least with regard to the practice of killing infants,

> the role of the state, in the person of its agents, must be to be available to supervise, mediate or intervene with the sole aim of ensuring that the internal process of deliberation can take place freely, without abuse by the most powerful individuals in that society.[76]

[71] Botero, Entre el Juez Salomón y el Dios Sira, p. 156, also cited by Segato, 'Que cada pueblo teja los hilos de su historia', p. 367.

[72] Specifically Article 231 of the Brazilian Federal Constitution: 'Recognition is hereby granted to the social organisation of the Indians, their customs, languages, beliefs and traditions, and their original rights to the lands which they have traditionally occupied. The federal government shall demarcate those lands, and shall protect and ensure respect for all of their possessions'.

[73] Segato, 'Que cada pueblo teja los hilos de su historia', p. 375 and p. 377.

[74] Rawls, A Theory of Justice, pp. 216–21.

[75] Rawls, The Law of Peoples, pp. 4–5 and pp. 59ff.

[76] Segato, 'Que cada pueblo teja los hilos de su historia', p. 375. On this point, Segato adds: 'Nor it is appropriate to demand the withdrawal of the state, because as evidenced by the many demands for public policy in this matter raised by indigenous peoples on the basis of the 1988 Constitution, after the intense and pernicious disorder created by contact, the

In this regard the transconstitutional stance aims to place a legal limit on abusive power inside the community. This is because if there is manipulation of community decisions by the most powerful, without legitimacy in the respective normative order, the result is the disappearance of the ethnic autonomy that is the starting point for a constitutional 'dialogue'. Hence, it can be seen that no form of presentation of autonomy for social spheres, including those constructed by indigenous communities that are not functionally differentiated, is absolute: all are relative in the context of today's world society.

This delicate problem involving the collision of very different normative orders with extremely diverse self-understandings (one of the modern state, the other of tribal peoples) is not confined to the dilemma between ethical relativism (oriented to particular cultures) and moral universalism (oriented to human rights). It also points to the possibility of coexistence between legal orders based on distinct historical experiences,[77] requiring moderation, especially on the part of the constitutional state, with regard to their claim to concretise their specific norms when these collide with the norms of indigenous communities with essentially different cultural foundations. Discretion and self-restraint seem in this case to be the right way to go about engaging in constructive 'conversations' capable of stimulating internal self-transformation by indigenous communities so that they have less conflicting relationships with the state order. An attempt to pursue internal models of optimisation in accordance with the theory of principles could be disastrous under these circumstances. Instead, when dealing with the 'other', with the different order of indigenous peoples, it is advisable to adopt a transconstitutional

state can no longer simply abstain. It must remain permanently available to offer guarantees and protection when called upon to do so by members of the communities, provided that such intervention involves a dialogue between representatives of the state and representatives of the community in question. Its role in this case can be none other than to promote and facilitate dialogue between the powers of the village and its weakest members' (ibid., pp. 375–6). Nevertheless, concerning these kinds of 'soft mediation', 'supervision' or 'intervention', one must be aware of the paradox put by Merry ('Transnational Human Rights and Local Activism', p. 48) in the light of empirical materials related to 'women's human rights': 'translators are restricted by the discursive fields within which they work. All the translators used human rights discourse, with its reference to international standards and its focus on individual injury and cultural oppression than rather structural violence'. See notes 57 and 68.

77 Cf. Segato, 'Que cada pueblo teja los hilos de su historia', pp. 375–7; see also Segato, 'Antropologia e direitos humanos', for a broader treatment. On the intrinsic relationship between universalism and difference, see Neves, 'Justicia y Diferencia en una Sociedad Global Compleja'.

stance of self-containment with regard to the fundamental rights whose optimisation could lead to disintegration of life forms, with destructive consequences for the minds and bodies of the members of the communities involved.[78]

Nevertheless, this problem is not limited to the relation between the customary orders of indigenous communities and legal state order, but involves also the international legal order. In this context it is relevant to note ILO Convention No. 169 concerning Indigenous and Tribal Peoples in Independent Countries,[79] which states in Article 8, paragraph 2: 'These peoples shall have the right to retain their own customs and institutions, where these are not incompatible with fundamental rights defined by the national legal system and with internationally recognised human rights'. This provision further complicates the collision between native local orders and the order of state fundamental rights and international human rights. A literal reading of the provision, applied to absolute protection of the lives of newborns, would tend to lead to cultural genocide against the respective indigenous communities. In such cases, it is necessary but not sufficient to engage in an adequately complex re-reading of both state fundamental rights norms and international human rights norms. A superficial universalism of human rights, based in linear fashion on a certain Western ontological conception of such rights, is incompatible with a constitutional 'dialogue' with indigenous orders that do not correspond to this model. On the contrary, a refusal to engage in a transversal communication with indigenous orders on this issue is itself a violation of human rights, since it would entail the 'ultra-criminalisation' of the entire community of perpetrators of the acts concerned, indiscriminately affecting their bodies and minds by means of destructive interference. In such cases, what is required in the name of positive transconstitutionalism is the readiness of state and international orders to assume that they are not the privileged loci of the constitutional problem, rather being in competition with other loci (transnational, supranational, local orders etc.), and, therefore, to experience the surprise of reciprocal learning from the experience of the other, here the indigenous community in its self-understanding.

[78] See note 57.

[79] On this Convention, see the brief exposition by Wolfrum, 'The Protection of Indigenous Peoples in International Law'.

Final comment

Transconstitutionalism between normative orders, be they of the same or of different kinds, may not only occur in the form discussed in the previous section, going far beyond cases of this type. As I have presented it in my work on this subject in the light of several cases, it is possible to envisage the entanglement of constitutional problems between state legal orders, between international orders, between transnational orders, between local orders, between international and state legal orders, international and supranational orders, transnational and state legal orders, international and transnational orders, transnational and local orders, transnational and supranational orders, supranational and local orders and prospectively between supranational orders in the strict sense. For the purpose of the present chapter, I have chosen an example that serves to put in check some Western minded or Eurocentric conceptions of legal and constitutional collision, which go – according to an ironic expression of Luhmann – from the 'European anomaly'[80] of the autonomy of law to explain the much more complex legal problems of world society.

What transconstitutionalism evidences above all is the profound change that has taken place under the conditions prevailing in today's world society, whereby provincial or parochial constitutionalism is being transcended. This change should be taken seriously. The state has ceased to be a privileged locus for solving constitutional problems. Albeit fundamental and indispensable, it is only one of several loci for cooperation and competition in pursuit of solutions to such problems. The increasing system integration of world society has led to the de-territorialisation of juridical-constitutional problem cases, which, as it were, have emancipated themselves from the state. This situation, however, should not lead to new illusions, such as a search for definitive 'inviolate levels': internationalism as ultima ratio, in a new absolute hierarchisation; supranationalism as a legal panacea; transnationalism as fragmentation to cast off the shackles of the state; localism as the expression of a definitively inviolate ethicality.[81]

80 Luhmann, *Das Recht der Gesellschaft*, p. 586 [English trans.: Law as a Social System, p. 490].

81 In the dynamic transconstitutional game the 'inviolate level' may be involved (tangled) with other levels, forming a 'super-tangled level', in the term of Hofstadter, *Gödel, Escher, Bach*, pp. 686ff.

Against these tendencies, transconstitutionalism entails the recognition that the various legal orders entangled in the search for a solution to a constitutional problem case that is concomitantly relevant to all of them – involving fundamental or human rights and the legitimate organisation of power – must pursue transversal forms of articulation in order to develop such a solution, each observing the others in an effort to understand its own limits and possibilities for contributing to the solution. Its identity is thereby reconstructed as long as it takes alterity seriously, always observing the other. In my view this is productive and enriching for identity itself, since every observer has a 'blind spot' and hence limited vision due to being in a certain position or observing from a certain vantage point.[82] However, while it is true, considering the diversity of vantage points from which alter and ego observe, that 'I see what you do not see',[83] it should be added that what is unseen by one observer owing to this 'blind spot' can be seen by another. In this sense, it can be asserted that transconstitutionalism entails the recognition of the limits to observation of any given order and acknowledges the alternative: the other can see your blind spot.

Bibliography

Ackerman, B., 'The Rise of World Constitutionalism', *Virginia Law Review*, 83 (1997), pp. 771–97.

Atlan, H., *Entre le cristal et la fumée: essai sur l'organisation du vivant* (Paris: Seuil, 1979).

Berman, H. J., *Law and Revolution: The Formation of the Western Legal Tradition* (Cambridge, MA and London: Harvard University Press, 1983).

Biaggini, G., Die Idee der Verfassung – Neuausrichtung im Zeitalter der Globalisierung?', *Zeitschrift für Schweizerisches Recht*, 119 (2000), pp. 445–76.

Botero, E. S., *Entre el Juez Salomón y el Dios Sira. Decisiones interculturales e interés superior del niño* (Bogotá: University of Amsterdam and Unicef, 2006).

Burdeau, G., *Traité de Science Politique*, 2nd edn (Paris: Librairie Générale de Droit et de Jurisprudence, 1968), vol. I.

Canotilho, J. J. G., *Direito constitucional.* 5th edn (Coimbra: Almedina, 1991).

'Brancosos' e interconstitucionalidade: Itinerários dos discursos sobre a historicidade constitucional (Coimbra: Almedina, 2006).

[82] Von Foerster, 'On Constructing Reality', pp. 288–9

[83] Luhmann, 'Ich sehe was, was Du nicht siehst'.

alliess, G.-P., 'Reflexive Transnational Law: The Privatisation of Civil Law and the Civilisation of Private Law', *Zeitschrift für Rechtssoziologie*, 23 (2002), pp. 185–216.

alliess. G.-P., and A. Maurer, 'Transnationales Recht – Eine Einleitung' in G.-P. Calliess (ed.), *Transnationales Recht* (Tübingen: Mohr Siebeck, 2014), pp. 1–36.

alliess, G.-P., and P. Zumbansen, *Rough Consensus and Running Code: A Theory of Transnational Private Law* (Oxford: Hart, 2010).

arroll, L., 'Through the Looking-Glass and What Alice Found There [1872]'. *The Complete Works of Lewis Carroll* (London: The Nonesuch Press and New York: Random House, 1939), pp. 133–272.

arwin, C., *The Origins of Species*. Introduction by L. H. Matthews (London: J. M. Dent & Sons Ltd, 1971) [6th edn, 1872].

ngels, F., 'Die Lage Englands. II. Die englische Konstitution' in K. Marx and F. Engels (eds), *Werke*. 15th edn (Berlin: Dietz Verlag, 1988), Vol. I, pp. 569–92 [first published in *Vorwärts!*, No 75, 18 September 1844].

assbender, B., 'The United Nations Charter as Constitution of the International Community', *Columbia Journal of Transnational Law*, 36 (1998), pp. 529–619.

eyerabend, P. K., *Three Dialogues on Knowledge* (Oxford: Basil Blackwell, 1991).

ischer-Lescano, A., *Globalverfassung: Die Geltungsbegründung der Menschenrechte* (Weilerswist: Velbrück, 2005).

ischer-Lescano, A., and G. Teubner, *Regime-Kollisionen: Zur Fragmentierung des globalen Rechts* (Frankfurt am Main: Suhrkamp, 2006).

'Fragmentierung des Weltrechts: Vernetzung globaler Regimes statt etatischer Rechtseinheit' in M. Albert and Rudolf Stichweh (eds.), *Weltstaat und Weltstaatlichkeit: Beobachtungen globaler politischer Strukturbildung* (Wiesbaden: VS Verlag, 2007), pp. 37–61.

riedman, L. M., 'Frontiers: National and Transnational Order' in K.-H. Ladeur (ed.), *Public Governance in the Age of Globalization* (Aldershot: Ashgate, 2004), pp. 25–50.

ross, O., '"Control Systems" and the Migration of Anomalies' in S. Choudhry (ed.), *The Migration of Constitutional Ideas* (Cambridge: Cambridge University Press, 2006), pp. 403–30.

ünther, K., *Der Sinn für Angemessenheit: Anwendungsdiskurse in Moral und Recht* (Frankfurt am Main: Suhrkamp, 1988) [English trans.: *The Sense of Appropriateness: Application Discourses in Morality and Law* (Albany: State University of New York Press, 1993)].

Haldane, J. B. S., 'Disease and Evolution' in K. R. Dronamraju (ed.), *Selected Genetic Papers of J. B. S. Haldane* (New York and London: Garland, 1990), pp. 325–34 [first published in *La Ricerca Scientifica, Supplemento*, 19 (1949), pp. 2–11].

Hamilton, W. D., 'Sex versus Non-Sex versus Parasite', *Oikos*, 35 (1980), pp. 282–90.

Hamilton, W. D., R. Axelrod and R. Tanese, 'Sexual Reproduction as an Adaptation to Resist Parasites (A Review)', *Proceedings of the National Academy of Sciences of the United States of America*, 87 (1990), pp. 3566–73.

Hamilton, W. D., P. A. Henderson and N. A. Moran, 'Fluctuation of Environment and Coevolved Antagonist Polymorphism as Factors in the Maintenance of Sex' in R. D. Alexander and D. W. Tinkle (eds.), *Natural Selection and Social Behavior: Recent Research and New Theory* (New York: Chiron Press, 1981), pp. 363–81.

Hart, H. L. A., *The Concept of Law*, 2nd edn (Oxford: Clarendon Press, 1994).

Heller, H., *Staatslehre* (Leiden: A. W. Sijthoff, 1934).

Hofstadter, D., *Gödel, Escher, Bach: An Eternal Golden Braid* (Hassocks: The Harvester Press, 1979).

Jessup, P. C., *Transnational Law* (New Haven: Yale University Press, 1956).

Kelsen, H., *Allgemeine Staatslehre* (Bad Homburg v. d. Höhe, Berlin and Zurich: Gehlen, 1925).

General Theory of Law and State, English trans. by A. Wedberg (Cambridge, MA: Harvard University Press, 1946).

Kelsen, H., *Reine Rechtslehre*, 2nd edn (Vienna: Franz Deuticke, 1960).

Koselleck, R., 'Begriffsgeschichtliche Probleme der Verfassungsgeschichtsschreibung' in R. Koselleck (ed.), *Begriffsgeschichten: Studien zur Semantik und Pragmatik der politischen und sozialen Sprache* (Frankfurt am Main: Suhrkamp, 2006), pp. 365–401.

Lassalle, F., 'Über Verfassungswesen' [1962] in H. J. Friederici (ed.), *Reden und Schriften* (Cologne: Röderberg, 1987), pp. 120–47.

Luhmann, N., *Rechtssoziologie* 3rd edn (Opladen: Westdeutscher Verlag, 1987) [English trans.: *A Sociological Theory of Law*, 2nd edn (Abingdon, UK and New York: Routledge, 2014)].

Soziale Systeme: Grundriß einer allgemeinen Theorie (Frankfurt am Main: Suhrkamp, 1984) [English trans.: *Social Systems* (Stanford University Press, 1995)].

'Verfassung als evolutionäre Errungenschaft', *Rechtshistorisches Journal*, 9 (1990), pp. 176–220.

'Ich sehe was, was Du nicht siehst' in N. Luhmann (ed.), *Soziologische Aufklärung 5: Konstruktivistische Perspektiven* (Opladen: Westdeutscher Verlag, 1990), pp. 228–34.

Das Recht der Gesellschaft (Frankfurt am Main: Suhrkamp, 1993) [English trans.: *Law as a Social System* (Oxford University Press, 2004)].

Die Politik der Gesellschaft (Frankfurt am Main: Suhrkamp, 2000).

Maduro, M. P., *A Constituição Plural: Constitucionalismo e União Européia* (Cascais: Principia, 2006).

Maturana, H. R., and F. J. Varela, *Autopoiesis and Cognition: The Realization of the Living* (Dordrecht: D. Reidel Publishing Company, 1980).

Der Baum der Erkenntnis: Die biologischen Wurzeln des menschlichen Erkennens, German trans. by Kurt Ludewig, 3rd edn (Bern, Munich and Vienna: Scherz, 1987).

Meirmans, S., 'The Evolution of the Problem of Sex' in I. Schön, K. Martens and P. van Dijk (eds.), *Lost Sex: The Evolutionary Biology of Parthenogenesis* (Dordrecht, Heidelberg, London and New York: Springer, 2009), pp. 21–46.

Merry, S. E., 'Transnational Human Rights and Local Activism: Mapping the Middle', *American Anthropologist*, 108 (2006), pp. 38–51.

Michaelis, R., 'Was ist nichtstaatliches Recht? – Eine Einführung' in G.-P. Calliess (ed.), *Transnationales Recht* (Tübingen: Mohr Siebeck, 2014), pp. 39–56.

Neiman, M., and B. Koskella, (2009), 'Sex and Red Queen' in I. Schön, K. Martens and P. van Dijk (eds.), *Lost Sex: The Evolutionary Biology of Parthenogenesis* (Dordrecht, Heidelberg, London and New York: Springer, 2009), pp. 133–59.

Neves, M., 'Justicia y Diferencia en una Sociedad Global Compleja', *Doxa – Cuadernos de Filosofía del Derecho*, 24 (2001), pp. 349–77.

'A força simbólica dos direitos humanos', *Revista Eletrônica de Direito do Estado*, 4 (2005), pp. 1–35 [English trans.: 'The Symbolic Force of Human Rights', *Philosophy & Social Criticism*, 33 (2007), pp. 411–44].

Entre Têmis e Leviatã: uma relação difícil – o Estado democrático de direito a partir e além de Luhmann e Habermas (São Paulo: Martins Fontes, 2006).

Transconstitucionalismo (São Paulo: WMF Martins Fontes, 2009) [English trans.: Transconstitutionalism (Oxford: Hart, 2013)].

Pernice, I., 'Multilevel Constitutionalism and Treaty of Amsterdam: European Constitution-Making Revisited?', *Common Market Law Review*, 36 (1999), pp. 703–50.

'Multilevel Constitutionalism in the European Union', *European Law Review*, 27 (2002), pp. 511–29.

Pires, F. L., *Introdução ao direito constitucional europeu (seu sentido, problemas e limites)* (Coimbra: Almedina, 1997).

Rawls, J., *A Theory of Justice* (Oxford University Press, 1990 [orig. 1972]).

The Law of Peoples, with 'The Idea of Public Reason Revisited' (Cambridge, MA and London: Harvard University Press, 1999).

Ridley, M., *The Red Queen: Sex and Evolution of Human Nature* (New York: Harper Collins, 2003).

Roach, K., 'The Post-9/11 Migration of Britain's Terrorism Act 2000' in S. Choudhry (ed.), *The Migration of Constitutional Ideas* (Cambridge University Press, 2006), pp. 373–402.

Scheppele, K. L., 'The Migration of Anti-constitutional Ideas: the Post-9/11 Globalization of Public Law and the International State of Emergency' in S. Choudhry (ed.), *The Migration of Constitutional Ideas* (Cambridge University Press), pp. 347–73.

Segato, R. L., 'Antropologia e direitos humanos: alteridade e ética no movimento de expansão dos direitos universais', *Mana: Estudos de antropologia social*, 12 (2006), pp. 207–36.

'Que cada pueblo teja los hilos de su historia. El pluralismo jurídico en diálogo didáctico con legisladores' in N. Chenaut, M. Gómez, H. Ortiz and M. T. Sierra (eds.), *Justicia y diversidad en América Latina. Pueblos indígenas ante la globalización* (Mexico: CIESAS and Quito: FLACSO, 2011), pp. 357–81.

Smend, R., 'Verfassung und Verfassungsrecht' in R. Smend, (ed.) *Staatsrechtliche Abhandlungen und andere Aufsätze*, 2nd edn (Berlin: Duncker & Humblot, 1968 [orig. 1928]), pp. 119–276.

Teubner, G., (1982). 'Reflexives Recht: Entwicklungsmodelle des Rechts in vergleichender Perspektive', *Archiv für Rechts- und Sozialphilosophie*, 68 (1982), pp. 13–59.

Recht als autopoietisches System (Frankfurt am Main: Suhrkamp, 1989) [English trans.: *Law as an Autopoietic System* (Oxford and Cambridge, MA: Blackwell, 1993)].

'Globale Zivilverfassungen: Alternativen zur staatszentrierten Verfassungstheorie', *Zeitschrift für ausländisches öffentliches Recht und Völkerrecht*, 63 (2003), pp. 1–28 [English trans.: 'Societal Constitutionalism: Alternatives to State-Centred Constitutional Theory?', in C. Joerges, I.-J. Sand and G. Teubner (eds.), *Transnational Governance and Constitutionalism* (Oxford: Hart, 2004), pp. 3–28].

'Die Anonyme Matrix: Zu Menschenrechtsverletzungen durch "private" transnationale Akteure', *Der Staat*, 45 (2006), pp. 161–87 [English trans.: 'The Anonymous Matrix: Human Rights Violations by "Private" Transnational Actors', *Modern Law Review*, 69 (2006), pp. 327–46].

Verfassungsfragmente: gesellschaftlicher Konstitutionalismus in der Globalisierung (Berlin: Suhrkamp, 2012) [English trans.: Constitutional Fragments: Societal Constitutionalism and Globalisation (Oxford University Press, 2012)].

Teubner, G., and A. Fischer-Lescano, 'Cannibalizing Epistemes: Will Modern Law Protect Traditional Cultural Expressions?' in C. B. Graber and M. Burri-Nenova (eds.), *Traditional Cultural Expressions in a Digital Environment* (Cheltenham: Edward Elgar, 2008), pp. 17–45.

Thornhill, C., *A Sociology of Constitutions. Constitutions and State Legitimacy in Historical-Sociological Perspective* (Cambridge University Press, 2011).

Tomuschat, C., 'Die internationale Gemeinschaft', *Archiv des Völkerrechts*, 33 (1995), pp. 1–20.

Tushnet, M., 'The Inevitable Globalization of Constitutional Law', paper presented at the seminar 'The Changing Role of Highest Courts in an Internationalizing World', sponsored by the Hague Institute for the Internationalisation of Law, 23–24 October 2008 (available at SSRN: http://ssrn.com/abstract=1317766).

Van Valen, L., 'Molecular Evolution as Predicted by Natural Selection', *Journal of Molecular Evolution*, 3 (1974), pp. 89–901.

Viellechner, L. 'Was heißt Transnationalität im Recht?' in G.-P. Calliess (ed.), *Transnationales Recht* (Tübingen: Mohr Siebeck, 2014), pp. 57–76.

Von Foerster, H., 'On Constructing Reality' in H. von Foerster (ed.), *Observing Systems* (Seaside: Intersystems Publications, 1981), pp. 288–309.

Weber, M., *Wirtschaft und Gesellschaft: Grundriß der verstehenden Soziologie*, J. Winckelmann (ed.), 5th edn (Tübingen: Mohr, 1985) [1st edn 1922].

Weiler, J., *The Constitution of Europe: 'Do the New Clothes Have an Emperor?' and Other Essays on European Integration* (Cambridge University Press, 1999).

Welsch, W., *Vernunft: Die zeitgenössische Vernunftkritik und das Konzept der transversalen Vernunft*, 2nd edn (Frankfurt am Main: Suhrkamp, 1996).

Unsere postmoderne Moderne, 6th edn (Berlin: Akademie Verlag, 2002).

Wolfrum, R., 'The Protection of Indigenous Peoples in International Law', *Zeitschrift für ausländisches öffentliches Recht und Völkerrecht*, 59 (1999), pp. 369–82.

Zumbansen, P., 'Transnational Law' in J. Smits (ed.), *Encyclopaedia of Comparative Law* (London: Edward Elgar, 2006), pp. 738–54.

7

Governance polycentrism or regulated self-regulation

Rule systems for human rights impacts of economic activity where national, private, and international regimes collide

LARRY CATÁ BACKER

It has become something of a commonplace to understand that at just the moment when a half millennium of effort devoted to the construction of an impermeable and eternal political system of states – omnipotent internally within their territorial borders and incarnate beings interacting as aggregate persons among a species of similarly constituted beings within a societally ordered community of states[1] – produced instead the framework of its own eclipse, but not its obliteration.[2] That political moment, when the structures of economic globalization acquired enough of a momentum to produce a reality of economic and social interactions beyond the ability of any single political system to control, produced a space (we argue whether it is political, social, economic, religious, cultural, moral, or mixed) from out of which other governance systems have emerged and operate, to the chagrin and despite the opposition of the law-state system and its acolytes.[3] The State and its detritus remains an obsession, especially among lawyers and theorists of governance, even those driven by the dictates of emerging functional realities of practice to reconsider the state system within a larger governance context.[4] Loyalty, here, might well be a necessity of the construct of the lawyer, the judge, and legal academic, to the system of which they form an integral part, the passing of which might well reduce their privileged role as seneschals of the law-state system.[5]

Yet even for those who do not dismiss the reality and power of societally constituted regimes, the institutional premises of the old order

[1] Anghie, *Imperialism, Sovereignty*. [2] Zürn, "Sovereignty and Law," pp. 39–71.
[3] Falk, *Predatory Globalization*; Sachs, "Beyond the Liability Wall," p. 843.
[4] Weissbrodt, "Keynote Address," pp. 384–90.
[5] See, e.g., Backer, "Retaining Judicial Authority."

urvive in large measure and a certain nostalgia for reproducing the ncient regime of an orderly and vertically integrated universe constiuted under rules produced by *Natura* or some variant of an Enlightennent deity. It is possible that even the vanguard of the societal onstitution movement distrust a heterodox governance system without rder or hierarchy.[6] It is also possible that some find it comforting to ranspose the premises and habits of law and law-state systems (includng its elaborate systems of justifications and legitimacy) onto emerging overnance regimes, if only because familiarity makes analysis easier. More pointedly, such transposition might permit an easier disciplining of merging regimes within the premises of the old.[7]

It is in this context that it is useful to speak to the issue of "regime ollisions."[8] The concept can be used to describe the fact that fragmentaion into an increasing number of international regimes with overlapping reas of competence can lead to contradictory decisions or mutual bstruction. For some, given that such regimes are driven by radically lifferent rationalities, this poses more than a technical problem. The roblem is the same of that which confronted the political bodies when hey sought to craft public international law as an ordering system mong otherwise autonomous actors with distinct character and mbition. They argue, for example, that in the absence of a hierarchy of norms, only heterarchic "collision rules" can coordinate parallel action nd manage collisions by allocating competences, taking into account the lifferent regime rationales.

I have suggested otherwise, positing that it is necessary to move away from state-focused legal paradigms, redolent with hierarchy and order, and to embrace ἄναρχος (anarxos), an aggregation of systems without rulers, but with an order quite distinct from the late feudalism of the law-state system embedded within it.[9] I have previously written[10] that what I call global law, the law of non-state governance systems, can be understood as the systematization of anarchy, as the management of a loosely intertwined universe of autonomous governance frameworks operating dynamically across borders and grounded in functional

[6] But see Calliess and Zumbansen, *Rough Consensus and Running Code.*

[7] Consider in this light, Alston, "The 'Not-a-Cat' Syndrome," p. 17; Johns, "The Invisibility of the Transnational Corporation"; Ward, "Securing Transnational Corporate," pp. 461–2.

[8] See, e.g., Teubner, *Constitutional Fragments.*

[9] Backer, "Transnational Constitutions," p. 879.

[10] Backer, "The Structural Characteristics of Global Law."

differentiation among governance communities. Considered in this context, the structure of global law can be understood as an amalgamation of four fundamental characteristics that together define a new order in form that is, in some respects, the antithesis of the orderliness and unity of the law-state system it will displace (though not erase). These four fundamental characteristics – fracture, fluidity, permeability, and polycentricity – comprise the fundamental structure of the disordered orderliness of global governance, which now includes but is not limited by law. These also serve as the structural foundations of its constitutional element, its substantive element, and its process element. Rather than order grounded in public international law, now transformed to serve a wider assemblage of governance actors, disorder premised on a polycentric ecosystem of competing and cooperating systems in constant, sometimes friction producing, interaction, defines the stability of governance systems in globalization. As a consequence, the problem of societally constituted organisms in a world once populated entirely by states and their creatures operating through the rigidly organized hierarchies of law, may well be the intrusion of law where it is neither necessary nor natural.

The purpose of this essay, then, is to consider the issue of collision within one of its most interesting nexus points: in the elaboration of governance frameworks touching on the human rights impacts of economic activity by states, enterprises, and individuals. That elaboration produces collisions between the state and international, public, and private organizations (enterprises and civil society actors), each with their distinct governance regimes. The thesis of this essay is as follows: the development of governance regimes for the human rights impacts of economic activity suggests the way in which non-legal approaches play a crucial role in the creation of structures within which the collisions of polycentric governance, its necessary character as ἄναρχος, can be managed (but not ordered), and consequently the way in which law (and its principles of hierarchy and unitary systemicity) plays a less hegemonic role, that is, the way in which law has less to contribute toward the governance problem thus posed.

The thesis is explored by considering the way in which the management of anarchy and the collision of governance regimes are being attempted through the operationalization of the United Nations Guiding Principles for Business and Human Rights (UNGP),[11] and the three

[11] Special Representative of the Secretary-General, "Guiding Principles on Business and Human Rights," endorsed by the UN Human Rights Council in 2011. UN Doc. A/HRC/RES/17/4 (July 6, 2011) [hereafter UNGP].

pillar framework from which it arose (state duty to protect, corporate responsibility to respect, and effective remedies for adverse effects of human rights),[12] and its incorporation into the Organization for Economic Cooperation and Development (OECD) Guidelines for Multinational Enterprises.[13] The focus of that effort has been the management of the behavior of enterprises in accordance with international human rights norms. The operationalization of that framework touches on collisions between the governance aspirations of public international organizations, the prerogatives of states, governance structures of the largest global economic enterprises, and the emergence of global civil society, media and other stakeholder communities that have morphed into members of the *demoi* of shifting governance communities. But rather than order and the privileging of international law, fracture and polycentric co-existence appear to be emerging as the stable state.

Section I ("The guiding principles for business and human rights as framework for inter-systemic collisions") considers the structures and premises of the emerging governance framework built into the UNGP and its points of collision with law-based systems. Section II ("From out of disorder . . .) then considers the ramifications of collision and the possibilities for systemic equilibrium by reference to three questions suggested by the thesis: (1) What may be the role of law for the solution of collision problems, and how does that role relate to non-legal regimes?; (2) What may be the role of non-legal approaches to a solution, and how do they relate to law?; and (3) What might concrete solutions look like? Law remains an important element, but no longer the sole ordering principle of a unified system within which rule collisions may be resolved. Non-legal systems built around societally constituted governance organisms, autonomous from each other and from the law system with which they collide, may better serve as the framework for mediating collisions among these constellations of governance orders. The most useful means for providing these collision management structures may be sought within public international organizations that provide an arena within which such collisions may be made predictable and their results more certain. The answers may not be positive for those who still cling to the ideals of the primacy of law. First, law both supports and impedes

[12] UN Human Rights Council, Forum on Business and Human Rights, A/HRC/FBHR/2013/2, para. 10.

[13] OECD, Guidelines for Multinational Enterprises (2011).

solution to collision problems precisely because, by its nature, it invariably seeks to privilege itself over non-law regimes. Second, the societally constituted autonomous regulatory regimes that can produce increasingly dense networks of jurisprudence with the functional effect of customary law but in the absence of the state is threatened by law, which seeks to subsume societally constituted systems, and the social norms that animate it, within the domestic legal orders of states. Third, the concrete solution may well look like the UNGP–OECD Guidelines framework itself.

I. The guiding principles for business and human rights as framework for inter-systemic collisions

The UNGP framework sought to capture the essence of the emerging diffusions of governance among an emerging constellation of distinct political organizations only one group of which are nation-states.[14] It identified at least three principal self-constituted governance group "types": states, economic enterprises, and international organizations. It then sought to establish a framework within which these three groups might harmonize their interactions – that is, minimize the friction of their collisions – in the service of a singular objective, the safeguarding of the human rights of individuals and communities against deprivations proceeding from economic activity.[15] This it sought to accomplish in three ways. First it sought to weave together the domestic legal order regimes of states, the societally constituted governance orders of enterprises, and the autonomous multilateral law-norm regimens of international organizations. Second, it sought to intermesh this framework into the internal governance orders of these three groups of regimes. Third, it sought to describe a governance space within which remedial projects might be undertaken in the service of the objective. To that end, it structured itself with direct reference to the government obligations of two of the three great governance great actors – states and multinational enterprises.[16] On that foundation, the UNGP then knit together the respective duties and responsibilities of states and enterprises through the mediating (and legitimating) offices of public (and private) international organizations, which were to be expressed (and applied) through

[14] Ruggie, *Just Business*. [15] UNGP, General Principles.
[16] UNGP, General Principles.

aw (the state), behavior controlling norms (enterprises), and the remedial structures offered through both.[17]

With respect to states, the UNGP speaks to the human rights law obligations of states, that is, of their duty to protect human rights.[18] Thus, tates must protect against human rights *abuses* within their territories and against those actors within their jurisdiction.[19] States should transpose these obligations onto their domestic legal orders for transparent application to enterprises under their control.[20] But the extent of that obligation is ambiguous. It speaks to the human rights *law* obligations of states as setting the borders of a state's duty, but does not specify whether hat border is set by the international organizations from which these proceed, or the more conventional notion of only that portion of international law that has been embraced within the domestic legal order of a particular state.[21] It appears to seek to minimize the problems of the vagaries of a state-based embrace of international law by also suggesting a role for regulation through *policy* as well as law.[22] Policy oriented approaches by states recognize its role both as a regulator and a participant in markets over which it has varying degrees of control. Policy, then, is understood as a means of extending beyond the constraints of law in the face of its irrelevance in areas where state may engage in activity but within which the traditional mechanics of law prove inadequate. These include the troublesome area of state owned enterprises,[23] privatization activities,[24] and especially where states engage as participants in markets for economic activity.[25]

Likewise the UNGP state duty to protect appears to nod approvingly toward the extraterritorial application of international human rights law,[26] especially in so-called conflict or weak governance zones where extraterritoriality is meant to substitute foreign governance apparatus for its domestic absence, at least in part.[27] Yet the door opening for

[17] UNGP General Principles (c). [18] UNGP paras. 1–10. [19] UNGP para. 1.

[20] UNGP para. 2. [21] UNGP para. 1 Commentary.

[22] UNGP Principle, para. 3, which speaks both to the transposition of international legal obligations into domestic legal orders (and their enforcement) and to the obligation of states to develop guidance measures for enterprises (ibid., para. 3(c)) and soft law provisions that serve to "encourage, and where appropriate, require, business enterprises to communicate how they address their human rights impacts" (ibid., para. 3(d)). This last of course is meant to harmonize national with global efforts of transparency and markets driven conduct regulation. See, e.g., Backer, "From Moral Obligation to International Law," pp. 591–653.

[23] UNGP para. 4. [24] UNGP para. 5. [25] UNGP para. 6.

[26] UNGP para. 2 Commentary. [27] UNGP para. 7.

extraterritorial application also provides a gateway for the internationalization of both law-norm making and the elaboration of remedial architectures, and notably among them the integration of state legal architectures with the governance mechanisms of public international bodies, and principally among them "multilateral soft-law instruments such as the Guidelines for Multinational Enterprises of the Organisation for Economic Co-operation and Development."[28] That integration effort is also suggested through policy based obligations that may be understood as a consequence of the state duty arising from its insertions within the web of international law. Thus states "should maintain adequate domestic policy space to meet their human rights obligations when pursuing business-related policy objectives with other States or business enterprise."[29] Likewise, these suggestions (for states *should* but are not *obliged* under the UNGP) extend to state participation in multilateral organizations.[30] This last opening reinforces both the autonomy of public international actors and the role of states within them, producing a circularity in which the international obligations of states are reinforced by privileging the international sources of state domestic duty in organizing and applying domestic legal (and now policy) order.[31]

In contrast to the language of law, of policy, and of the intermeshing and consolidation of state legal duty within the greater contours of international law, the UNGP quite radically uses the *language of responsibility*, and of the binding character of societally constituted governance regimes in the context of the behavior constraints of multinational enterprises.[32] Business enterprises, the UNGP declare,[33] should respect human rights.[34] This responsibility to respect human rights derives not from law but from the societally constituted governance constraints of multinational enterprises themselves.

[28] Ibid. [29] UNGP para. 9. [30] UNGP para. 10.

[31] Thus, when acting as members of multilateral institutions that deal with business related issues, states should "(c) draw on these Guiding Principles to promote shared understanding and advance international cooperation in the management of business and human rights obligations" UNGP para. 10.

[32] UNGP paras. 11–24.

[33] "Nothing in these Guiding Principles should be read as creating new international law obligations, or as limiting or undermining any legal obligations a State may have undertaken or be subject to under international law with regard to human rights" UNGP General Principles. However, that limitation on the *law-based* project of the UNGP is directed only to states.

[34] UNGP para. 11.

> The responsibility to respect human rights is a global standard of expected conduct for all business enterprises wherever they operate. It exists independently of States' abilities and/or willingness to fulfill their own human rights obligations, and does not diminish those obligations. And it exists over and above compliance with national laws and regulations protecting human rights.[35]

It arises within those governance spaces beyond the state but connected to the equally autonomous public international governance orders, which reflect and produce the normative content of global non-state governance. Thus, the UNGPs define the human rights responsibilities of enterprises with reference to international law and norms, a task that was impossible under the international law framework applicable to states, and indeed one that includes norms that would not bind states as law.[36]

This responsibility to respect exists not just autonomously of states, but also potentially adverse to the legal structures of state-based governance, the harmonization of which is an object of the UNGP themselves, as between the autonomous governance frameworks of states and societally constituted enterprises, but also with respect to the relationship of both to the objects of these governance efforts – those adversely impacted by the activities of states and enterprises whose remedial rights are meant to serve as a focal point of convergence.[37] And thus the UNGP devote attention to its principal function – as a collision mediating apparatus.[38] It sets out a mechanism for both acknowledging conflict and resolving them among different political organizations – in this case states and enterprises. That mechanism relies principally on a premise that may be hard for either to accept – the privileged status of international law and norms as the basis of the constitutional constraints of both states and enterprise organizations.[39] The UNGP thus posit that enterprises are

35 UNGP para. 11 Commentary. 36 UNGP para.12.

37 Ibid., "Business enterprises should not undermine States' abilities to meet their own human rights obligations, including by actions that might weaken the integrity of judicial processes."

38 The Working Group framed the objective in collision reduction terms: "The Guiding Principles reflect the differentiated, but complementary roles of States and businesses with regard to human rights. By outlining more clearly the role of each, the Guiding Principles provide a framework that attributes the respective duties or responsibilities to States and businesses to help them address their adverse human rights impacts in specific instances." UN Human Rights Council, Forum on Business and Human Rights, A/HRC/FBHR/2013/2, para. 25.

39 Cf. Peters, "Compensatory Constitutionalism."

bound to comply with law but understood in two senses – the domestic legal order of states in which they operate or within which they might owe some duty, and internationally recognized human rights now transposed into their own societally constituted governance apparatus.[40] Where these conflict, enterprises (but not, it appears, states) must "seek ways to honor the principles of internationally recognized human rights."[41] But where enterprises may not avoid conflict they are bound to "treat the risk of causing or contributing to gross human rights abuses as a legal compliance issue wherever they operate."[42] In this later case, the object is to avoid complicity in the breach, effectively, by states of their paramount duty to protect human rights.[43]

The character of the human rights responsibility of business enterprises is centered on avoiding causing or contributing to adverse human rights impacts,[44] and preventing or mitigating such adverse impacts.[45] In keeping with the foundational premise that the UNGPs deal with enterprises beyond the constraints or organizing principles of aggregated economic activity in national law, it rejects any limitation of law in the application to the activities of the global operations of business enterprises however organized. Though states deal with economic enterprises as creatures subject to their law in those circumstances when their power may extend to them and to the extent that the domestic legal orders of states do not otherwise protect enterprises from liability, especially with respect to the partitioning of their assets,[46] the UNGP recognize societal reconstitution beyond these legal constraints.[47] And the expression of that responsibility is understood by its societally constituting gestures – a policy commitment to acknowledge and meet its responsibilities expressed through its constituting documents,[48] a human rights due diligence process to implement this societally constituted obligation,[49] and a process of remediation through which the enterprise expresses its

[40] UNGP para. 23(a). [41] UNGP para. 23(b). [42] UNGP para. 23 (c).
[43] UNGP para. 23 Commentary. [44] UNGP para. 13(a). [45] UNGP para. 13(b).
[46] Discussed in Backer, "The Autonomous Global Corporation." [47] UNGP para. 14.
[48] UNGP paras. 15(a), 16.
[49] UNGP paras.15(b), 17–21. Human rights due diligence includes both a transparency and a risk assessment/mitigation aspect. Enterprises must implement systems that identify and assess actual or potential adverse human rights risks (UNGP para. 18), integrate the findings from impact assessments across relevant internal functions and processes (UNGP para. 19), track the effectiveness of their responses (UNGP para. 20), and account for their human rights due diligence operations transparently with outside stakeholders through programs of disclosure (UNGP para. 21).

power to bind.[50] There is collision conflict reduction with respect to the remedial obligation as well.[51]

The joint obligation of states and enterprises to provide mechanisms for appropriate remediation provides a point of convergence of the respective obligations of both operationalized through states but grounded in international public law and *norms*.[52] The UNGP seems to circle back to the state as a primary actor, and law as the primary legitimating structure, of remedying human rights wrongs, a perspective that civil society actors have sought to advance.[53] The central premise of the remedial mechanisms of the UNGP framework is the state duty to protect human rights (internationally defined and transposed into domestic legal orders) on a territorially based jurisdiction-by-jurisdiction basis.[54] Though the state serves as the nexus point for remedy, it is understood to serve in that capacity sometimes more as a gateway (though quite a narrow one) to rather than as the resting place for remedial mechanisms, founded on state based remedies but integrated with operational level grievance mechanisms and those of supra national human rights mechanisms.[55] Thus UNGP Principle 25 speaks to the administration of state-based grievance mechanisms through a variety of bodies, some of which are non-judicial, and at least one of which transposes remedy from the state to a state administered international apparatus.[56] The operational principles of remedial mechanisms draw much from the emerging set of international norms on the operation of a legitimate result producing judicial enterprise. These include reducing barriers to relief,[57] avoiding limiting state-based relief structures to the judiciary and the courts,[58] and the provision of a space

[50] UNGP paras. 15(c), 22.

[51] UNGP para. 24 provides a rule of precedence where the local legal framework is absent or ambiguous.

[52] UNGP paras. 25–31.

[53] See, e.g., Skinner, McCorquodale, and De Schutter, "The Third Pillar."

[54] UINGP para. 25.

[55] UNGP para. 25 Commentary.

[56] "Examples include the courts (for both criminal and civil actions), labour tribunals, national human rights institutions, National Contact Points under the Guidelines for Multinational Enterprises of the Organisation for Economic Co-operation and Development, many ombudsperson offices, and Government-run complaints offices" UNGP para. 25 Commentary.

[57] UNGP para 26.

[58] UNGP para. 27. Here the UNGP make a case for the expansion of the remedial apparatus beyond the courts to a variety of new actors, some of which may be quite problematic under the constitutional constraints and traditions of some states.

for non-state-based grievance mechanisms.[59] Surprisingly, for all of the language about the autonomy of enterprise societally constituted governance systems, these autonomous characteristics do not appear to extend to the remedial function, one that appears firmly embedded within national legal structures under the UNGP. Thus, for example, non-state grievance remedial structures are understood as subordinate adjuncts to the principal roles that are played by state based mechanisms for remedies.[60] Likewise the UNGP warn that non-state grievance mechanisms "should not be used to undermine the role of legitimate trade unions in addressing labour-related disputes, nor to preclude access to judicial or other non-judicial grievance mechanisms."[61] Indeed, an alternative not embraced might have grounded the remedial duty as centered on the individuals who suffer human rights wrongs, internationalizing constitutional principle of human dignity, the consequences of which include the obligation for states and other actors to remedy wrongs.[62]

At the same time, the door is left open to multilateral non-state-based remedial mechanisms. These suggest, though more subtly perhaps, that the grievance mechanisms of non-state organizations, both public and private, might also serve the same function as those of states, and might, indeed, substitute for those of the state.[63] These are embedded in the societal constitutions of non-state actors:

> commitments undertaken by industry bodies, multi-stakeholder and other collaborative initiatives, through codes of conduct, performance standards, global framework agreements between trade unions and transnational corporations, and similar undertakings.[64]

But for these, the UNGP are careful to transpose a number of principles for legitimate and effective operation – these are more likely to affect the constitution of a remedial mechanism within enterprise and non-state organization than those of states.[65]

The broad hints for coordination set out in the UNGP have had some success in enlisting a number of states and non-state organizations to

[59] UNGP paras. 28–29. [60] UNGP para. 28 Commentary.
[61] UNGP para. 29 Commentary.
[62] Cf. Bailey and Mattei, "Social Movements as Constituent Power." [63] UNGP para. 30.
[64] UNGP para. 30 Commentary.
[65] UNCP para. 31 (including principles of accountability, accessibility, predictability, fairness, transparency, rights compatibility, and self-referencing character grounded in communication among organizational stakeholders).

mbrace them as a means of collision conflict reduction.[66] Among the nost interesting might be the embrace of the UNGP by the OECD hrough its Guidelines for Multinational Enterprises (2011). The focus f that interest centers on three aspects of the Guidelines. The first is that he Guidelines incorporated the UNGP within its substantive provisions s a mechanism for binding enterprises to a set of internationalized social norms[67] to be enforced through the Guidelines' societally constituted governance organs.[68] The second is that the Guidelines provide – in a potentially path breaking way – for the development of a remedial nechanism that is centered in a public international organization but grounded in the autonomous international standards that describe the onstitutional constraints of societal constitutions with respect to human ights responsibilities specified in the UNGP.[69] The third is that the nechanics of this transposition of internationalized standards onto utonomous systems of non-state governance implemented through a quasi-judicial complaints system independent of states are administered hrough states as part of their obligations as states adhering conventionally to their obligations under the OECD framework.[70]

Chapter IV of the Guidelines now incorporates the UNGP within its substantive framework. It recognizes the autonomous obligations of enterprises beyond that imposed by the domestic legal orders of the states in which they operate,[71] as well as the relationship between those standards and the elaboration of international pronouncements (law,

66 UN Human Rights Council, Forum on Business and Human Rights, A/HRC/FBHR/2013/2, para. 28. See also ibid., Annex, "Other inter governmental mechanisms, tools and guidance."

67 "The Guidelines' recommendations express the shared values of the governments of countries from which a large share of international direct investment originates and which are home to many of the largest multinational enterprises" OECD Guidelines, Forward.

68 "The Guidelines occupy a central role in the current landscape of RBC [responsible business conduct] tools: they are endowed with a unique implementation mechanism and include a human rights chapter that is drawn from the UN Guiding Principles" OECD, Annual Report 2013, Executive Summary, p. 10.

69 OECD Guidelines.

70 The collision mediating aspects of this mechanism is not overlooked: "The Guidelines are supported by a unique implementation mechanism of National Contact Points (NCPs), agencies established by adhering governments to promote and implement the Guidelines. The NCPs assist enterprises and their stakeholders to take appropriate measures to further the implementation of the Guidelines. They also provide a mediation and conciliation platform for resolving practical issues that may arise" OECD Guidelines, supra, Forward.

71 OECD Guidelines Chapter IV Commentary, para. 38.

custom, declaration, sentiment and the like) from public international organizations as a framing element to those obligations. The transposed obligations of the UNGP to the OECD Guidelines, includes the recognition that the autonomous responsibilities of enterprises arise irrespective of the legal frameworks of states that might otherwise shield a part of an enterprise from some or all of the responsibility to respect human rights. In the Guidelines, this is effectuated through enhanced coverage in the context of supply chain responsibility.[72]

These substantive obligations are supposed to be implemented in part through the National Contact Point (NCP) complaint processes. Though the OECD Guidelines themselves are voluntary recommendations to governments erected to multinational enterprises, the obligation to establish and operate NCPs is mandatory.[73] The role of the NCP is collision minimizing, a focal point of intersections between state legal orders, international obligations and the governance frameworks of societally constituted non-state actors. NCPs are required to further the effectiveness of the OECD Guidelines "in accordance with the core criteria of visibility, accessibility, transparency, and accountability to further the objective of functional equivalence."[74] Among its other functions, the NCP is understood to function as a site for the interpretation of the Guidelines and especially in its application to concrete disputes among parties. "The National Contact Point will contribute to the resolution of issues that arise relating to implementation of the Guidelines in specific instances in a manner that is impartial, predictable, equitable, and compatible with the principles and standards of the Guidelines."[75] It is free to engage in the resolution of these disputes, that is, in fleshing out the implementation of the UNGPs through the OECD Guidelines, through a number of distinct approaches.[76] A jurisprudence of sorts is contemplated by the rules.[77] And this approach has begun to see a measure of elaboration, though still sporadic and tentative.[78]

More importantly, the anarchic character of the space within which this collision-managing device is being developed is also becoming more evident. Application of the framework has been used to establish the

[72] OECD Guidelines Commentary on General Principles, paras. 16–18.

[73] OECD Guidelines, Amendment of the Decision of the Council on the OECD Guidelines, Part I, para. 1.

[74] OECD Guidelines Procedural Guidance Part I. [75] Ibid., Part I. C. [76] Ibid.

[77] Ibid.

[78] For discussion see Backer, "Rights and Accountability in Development," citing in part Queinnec, The OECD Guidelines, p. 8.

utonomy of international norms (applicable to non-state economic ctors in transnational space).[79] That autonomy creates not merely a pace for the development of substantive norms, but also of process orms as well.[80] But its structures have been used strategically as well. Among individuals harmed by the adverse human rights effects of orporate activity, it provides a means of applying a substantial challenge o the monopoly of conflict resolution through the application of domesic legal orders by local courts.[81] Among states, it provides a basis for the xtraterritorial application of nationalized international norms through rivate market investment activities.[82]

The combination of UNGP and OECD structures permits the posibility of constructing a remedial framework beyond the control ither of states (dominated by the interests of their domestic legal rders) or non-state actors, principally enterprises (dominated by their unctional objectives in their spheres of operation). That combination hus permits a measure of self-constitution for the system of human ights related normative principles and the rules developed thereunder vith relation solely to those principles. The self constituting is made ossible not merely because of the possibility of developing an autonomous remedial framework, supported by states, grounded in international substantive norms, and reflecting the customs and social norm structures of enterprises, but because that autonomous remedial framework will be capable of itself elaborating an increasingly deep set of interpretations of these normative structures in the application of the norms to complaints brought to it by stakeholders within each of these autonomous governance communities. In effect, NCPs have the potential to play the role of common law courts in the development, organically, of a customary system of governance rules (not law – law is reserved after all to the state and grounded in the ideology of state legitimacy) that might transform a system of principles (UNGP) and guidelines (OECD Guidelines) into a complex and fully functioning customary rule system autonomous of any of its sources and its constituent parts.

79 Final Statement 09/1373, discussed in Backer, "Governance without Government," pp. 87–123.

80 Initial Assessment by the UK National Contact Point March 27, 2009.

81 Final Statement On Pakistan's Khanewal Factory, 2009; Final Statement On Pakistan's Rahim Yar Khan Factory, 2009.

82 Discussed in Backer, "Sovereign Investing."

This constitution from the ground up might be as useful today in the transnational sphere as it was in medieval England, for the construction not of a singular law-state, but of a heterodox space within which the governance regimes of states and non-state actors collide and couple in ways that produce a sufficient measure of cooperation to produce a somewhat stable system. But it posits, as well, a light touch, especially from those wedded to the notion of either hierarchy or of the formal structures of law (and its legitimating ideology so closely tied to the formalities of states). The OECD Guidelines also play a role in the useful conflict/collision among state and enterprise governance systems, under the aegis of internationalized normative standards.[83] Here we see the possibility of *anarchos*, a rule system without center or principal – amalgamating horizontally arranged rule systems to the extent necessary to permit, via coupling, a modicum of cooperation between systems through an autonomous mechanism of applying custom grounded in principle. This approach is consonant with the logic of global law,[84] one that posits a stable universe of objects of regulation around which governance systems multiply, the inverse of the traditional approach to law grounded on the presumption of a dynamic population of governable objects bound to static and stable governance systems. The UNGP–OECD system serves both as router and as governance norm producer, though what it produces is neither law, nor system, in its conventional monopolistic and hierarchically superior sense.[85]

Taken together, the UNGP–OECD Guidelines framework presents a curious enterprise, one that recognizes the distinct and autonomous character of governance regimes – among them states, international organizations, and non-state actors – that constitutes at least one of them, and provides a framework, centered on itself, for the management of regime collisions. It is a delicate exercise, made plausible only by a balancing of duties, responsibilities, normative standards, and remedial frameworks, that makes plausible coordination (structural coupling of a sort) among autonomous actors, intermeshed through the mediating language and norm legitimating functions of public international organizations tied sufficiently to states to suggest the traditional relationships between them and also tied to non-state actors to suggest a respect for their governance power and behavior cultures. Translating these normative structures

[83] See, e.g., Final Statement on Pakistan's Khanewal Factory.

[84] Cf. Backer, "The Structural Characteristics of Global Law," pp. 177–99.

[85] Cf. Calliess and Zumbansen, *Rough Consensus and Running Code.*

"into legal doctrine is, of course, a difficult task, not least because today's legal vocabulary is usually obsolete, as it is the product of a bygone societal context."[86] In place of translation, the UNGPs posit mediating collision for coordinating activity when such may be necessary.[87]

II. From out of disorder . . .

For all of the exuberance of the preceding section, the UNGP framework is itself still quite fragile. "While numerous relevant actors around the world have already incorporated elements of the Guiding Principles into their work, many continue to express the need for further learning opportunities, explanations, and information."[88] Indeed, although one can theorize a robust polycentric environment from out of the structures of the UNGP and the OECD Guidelines along the lines suggested here, the emerging realities of its operationalization, its glosses applied in the coupling of autonomous organizations, might also suggest regulated self-regulation.[89] In particular, Gunther Teubner's notion of self-constitutionalizing regimes that is founded not on polycentricity as order without a center, but rather as the construct of a network of linkages that produces both self constitution and dependent autonomy.[90] Teubner does find a center, an ordering point within heterodox systems, and one that is located within the web linkages that produce substantive norms. These linkages then have substance; like the Norns spinning the threads of fate at the foot of Yggdrasil, they do not produce order *formally*, but they do have the *functional effect* of ordering relations among autonomous actors based on the effects of their communicative interventions.[91] This is because they link politically posited law and private governance in what could be called an externally regulated self-regulation. From such a perspective, both ways of regulation do not

86 Rödl, "Fundamental Rights." p. 1017.
87 Cf. Teubner, "Legal Irritants," pp. 417–41; Also Cutler, *Private Power And Global Authority,* p. 199.
88 UN Human Rights Council, Forum on Business and Human Rights, A/HRC/FBHR/2013/2, 2.
89 See, e.g., Backer, "Private Actors and Public Governance Beyond the State"; cf. Riles, "The Anti-Network."
90 See, Teubner, "Self-Constitutionalizing TNCs?"; Bernstein, "Merchant Law."
91 The linkages themselves exhibit a peculiar quality that recalls both the initial thrust of comparative law in early twentieth century Europe and the use of translation to bridge and harmonize. See, e.g., Foster, "Critical Cultural Translation."

constitute mutually exclusive forms of regulation; rather, the potential results from the link established between both forms of regulation itself anchors and directs in accordance with its own logic.[92]

Both the fragility of the transformation of theory to fact, and the governance cultures driving powerful elements to gloss polycentrism out of the UNGPs have been made evident during the course of the Second[93] and Third[94] Forums on Business and Human Rights. These Forums are one of the principal consultative mechanisms[95] for the Working Group on the Issue of Human Rights and Transnational Corporations and Other Business Enterprises, established by the UN Human Rights Council to promote their effective and comprehensive dissemination and implementation.[96] The impulse noted in the First Forum, to refocus on the state duty to protect human rights and on traditional and conventional mechanisms of international law to elaborate a mechanics to that end, appeared to accelerate.[97] The effect both reinforces the relationship between the state, law, and the international public organization they created, but may also drive post national and global governance organizations elsewhere – substantially reducing the ability of the UNGP to serve as a collision mediating architecture, and enhancing its network characteristics.[98] And indeed, this may suggest the dichotomy between hierarchical approaches[99] on the one hand and the deregulated variant of social norms production[100] on the other within the socio-legal debates on transnational law in the constitutional sphere.[101]

92 For a judicial variant consider Wiener and Liste, "Lost without Translation?"

93 UN Human Rights Council, Forum on Business and Human Rights, A/HRC/FBHR/2013/2.

94 See Human Rights Council Forum on Business and Human Rights Second session Item 1 of the provisional agenda, Agenda and organization of work December 2–3, 2014, Concept Note, A/HRC/FBHR/2014/2 (September 23, 2014).

95 Human Rights Council resolution 17/4, para. 6. "[T]he Forum aims to serve as a key annual venue for stakeholders from all regions to engage in dialogue on business and human rights, and to strengthen engagement towards the goal of effective and comprehensive implementation of the Guiding Principles." UN Human Rights Council, Forum on Business and Human Rights, A/HRC/FBHR/2013/2, para. 7.

96 Human Rights Council resolution 17/4, para. 6.

97 UN Human Rights Council, Forum on Business and Human Rights, A/HRC/FBHR/2013/2, para. 11.

98 Renner, "Occupy the System!," pp. 941–64.

99 See, e.g., Koh, "Transnational Legal Process"; Anderson, "Societal Constitutionalism"; Also Watt, "Private International Law Beyond the Schism," p. 417.

100 See, e.g., Shamir, "Corporate Social Responsibility"; Fischer-Lescano and Teubner, "Regime-Collisions"; Teubner, "Legal Irritants."

101 Thornhill, "A Sociology of Constituent Power."

The plenary sessions of both the Second and Third Forums developed the framework of inter-linkages suggested by Teubner.[102] Most of the major stakeholders – states, multi-national enterprises (MNEs), and civil society actors – continue to grasp onto those doctrines and approaches that are most advantageous to each. The UNGP has, at least for the moment, succeeded in providing a common language through which these groups can continue to further their interests. But now those interests appear constrained (if only loosely and rhetorically for the moment) by the principles of the Guiding Principles framework. The *idea of the UNGP, rather than its operationalization* as governance structures, appears to be the animating spirit of the third meeting of these estates general. And that is to be regretted, though it may not be surprising. Having worked hard to become the basis for discussion of the range of governance issues that touch on business and human rights, the UNGP now suffers from its success. Thus, for example, the focus on extraterritoriality lends itself to the augmentation of the hegemony of those states, some of which tend to be the most skeptical about the UNGP project. Freeing business from the constraints of social norms and the pressure of key consumer, labor, and investor communities (organized globally), permits the regulatory fracture within which MNE abuse can be strategically compelling and can be practiced with impunity. Leaving civil society to its own devices produces both nihilism and extremism, grounded in principle and passion, that substantially reduces the relevance and effectiveness of civil society efforts, but that is also bounded by the linkages between these self-constituting bodies and the states and business collectives among which they operate.

The organization of the meetings also reinforced the classical division between states, enterprises, and an amalgam of civil society "others." It is a normative organization that incarnates Teubner's self-constitutionalizing regimes producing both self-constitution and dependent autonomy.[103] The great constitutional actors within this inter-linked space, spaces within which normative structures are built and exported back for absorption, was represented physically by the occupation of space within the forums themselves. States, business elements, and a mass of civil society (and others) each spoke through and at each other – creating linkages from protected autonomous spaces. Those linkages could be powerful. For example, at one forum the business

102 These are discussed in Backer, "The 2nd UN Forum," and Backer, "The 3rd UN Forum."
103 Teubner, "The King's Many Bodies"; Teubner, "Societal Constitutionalism."

community renewed their efforts to recognize the constraining authority of national law in their self-constitution under the UNGP responsibility to respect human rights.[104] The interventions of business sought to essentialize the world of governance, and restrict it to its most narrow and traditional jurisdictional bases. Civil society interventions sought to fragment discussion to the listing of a litany of highly particularized wrongs in need (and quite rightly to be sure) of redress. Both looked to law, through and away from the UNGP, at either the national or international level, suggesting a dependent relation between social norm and public law.[105] There is irony here. States have remained unwilling to *describe the extent of their state duty* (except in the most general terms and under the logic of their own constitutional orders) and yet found the forum a useful site for expressing their *willingness to commit their corporations to normative standards they might refuse to adopt within their own legal systems.*

The conceptual weakness of the UNGP's remedial pillar, one that appears to be derivative in nature, is sound but incomplete. It is certainly true that the remedial obligations of states and the autonomous remediation obligations of MNEs are foundational and a critically important consequence of the state duty and MNE responsibility. Yet, those who drive UNGP interpretation may have missed an opportunity to liberate the remedial pillar from its embedding in solely either the judicial apparatus of states or the remedial mechanisms of MNEs. The failure here to ground the substantive element of the remedial pillar in the human dignity interests of individuals and groups makes the UNGP blind to the possibility of the organization of legitimate remedial apparatuses autonomous of states or MNEs. These include remedial mechanisms organized through public international bodies or otherwise through governance collectives. Yet that lacuna is precisely what the OECD Guidelines sought to fill. The resulting network for managing collisions within a substantive framework that embraces a disordered system of governance organizations permit interactions among governance systems, societal and law-based, that makes possible not just conflict but also cooperation.[106] It manages this from structural coupling rather than as a means of forging a unitary and vertically arranged system out of the centerless universe of systems that flow out of a globalized order. This

[104] Joint IOE-ICC-BIAC Comments.

[105] Mollers, "Transnational Governance Without Public Law?"

[106] Cf. Ellis, "Constitutionalization of Nongovernmental Certification Programs," p. 1035.

s a polycentric rather than a legal universe.[107] Andreas Fischer-Lescano has noted: "Globalization is a challenge that rouses the legal system to emancipate itself from a fixation on the institution of the state."[108] The remedial pillar is likewise a challenge that rouses the normative system of rights to emancipate itself from a fixation on the institution of law, and moves toward polycontextuality.[109]

More generally, industry, civil society, and state actors have combined, n their own ways and for their own purposes, to attack the fundamental premises of the UNGPs and OECD Guidelines, to protect their freedom from regulation by championing a re-nationalization of law making.[110] For civil society actors there is the certainty of unified state structures and the familiarities of law – civil society might well prefer the simplicity of state to the disorganization of the market, but one which is likely to produce nothing as states continue to resist any effort to formally internationalize law beyond the state.[111] But there is also a subversive element – resistance to internationalized norms and autonomous norm regimes makes it possible to move from *anarchos* to chaos – by positing the most lawless state of transnational governance, one in which the only law available is that which might be exercised by states through their domestic legal orders, beyond which there is . . . nothing.

The critiques of the UNGP–OECD framework reflect the deep and unrelenting suspicion of non-law based governance systems.[112] That critique poses a challenge to the horizontal nature of the linkages among states, enterprises, and civil society. But it also suggests the corporeality of the space within which these issues are communicated and then reabsorbed within each of these actors. Civil society and states, especially, tend to view the concept of social norms and/or societally constituted communities both as illegitimate and as ineffective against the ideal of law. This may reflect fears of democratic legitimacy[113] and also reflect a view that international public law must sit at the top of a single hierarchy of governance that constrains both the law system of states and the social norm system of non-state actors, and to do so directly.[114] That is a view, though, that states continue to reject in large part, and that non-state

[107] Hamann and Fabri, "Transnational Networks and Constitutionalism."
[108] Fischer-Lescano, "Global Constitutional Struggles," p. 14.
[109] Sand, "Polycontextuality." [110] Cf. Habermas, "A Political Constitution," pp. 322 ff.
[111] See, e.g., Williamson, "Amnesty Criticises UN." For the biting response of John Ruggie see Ruggie, "Bizarre response."
[112] Teubner, "Global Bukowina," p. 3. [113] Watt, "Private International Law," p. 417.
[114] Kumm, "The Legitimacy of International Law."

actors sometimes view as irrelevant. This critique threatens the linkage system itself by suggesting a profound critique of the underlying premises of the UNGP. But this is a general critique of the response to societal constitutions and the globalized anarchy of multiple governance. To reject the premise that such constitutionalization is possible and to view its expression as illegitimate or illogical ignores facticity in favor of an increasingly elegant but empty normative universe in which the state alone is resident.

This leaves open three important questions worth considering, at least in preliminary form: Which role does the law play for the solution of collision problems, and how does it relate to non-legal regimes? Which non-legal approaches to a solution are there, and how do they relate to law? What might concrete solutions look like? With respect to the first question, the UNGP's state duty to protect human rights suggests that law both supports and impedes solutions to collision problems, precisely because, by its nature, it invariably seeks to privilege itself over non-law regimes. Law does not merely trip over itself; as a manifestation of state power, but also trips over public systems resisting any inversion of legal relationship on which domestic legal orders must give way to an international order construct. With respect to the second question, the UNGP's corporate responsibility to respect offers a more horizontal relationship between law and the societally constituted autonomous regulatory regimes of corporations and other non-state actors. But the foundational premises of classical law systems threaten that relationship. The logic of these law system premises would seek to subsume societally constituted systems, and the social norms that animate it, within the domestic legal orders of states, or ignore them altogether to the extent they could not be translated into law or harmonized within existing legal norms. With respect to the third question, the answers might require independence rather coordination; cooperation rather than the construction of a singular system bounded by law and its idiosyncrasies. The solution may, indeed, require the rise of a new class of governance facilitator, something more than a lawyer (bound by the normative cultures of the law-state) and flexible enough to move between governance cultures.

The UNGPs, then, stand at the center of a set of deep divisions among civil society and state actors about the nature and role of regulation of business at the supra-national (above the state) and transnational (beyond the state) levels. But the UNGPs also serve as the thread with which constitutional linkages have been developed among the autonomous self constitutionalized communities of states, business, and civil society. As theory, its *formal structures* suggests anarchic polycentricity; *as implemented it functions* like autonomous systems tethered together through their complex inter-linkages, their intermeshing,[115] that serves as the medium through which norms are generated and each of these autonomous bodies are disciplined[116] within the logic of their structural coupling. A new model emerges.

Conclusion

Poul Kjaer's insight about the nature of transnational normative orders is particularly helpful in contextualizing the UNGP–OECD Guidelines order within a universe of disordered governance communities. He explains: "Constitutions never stand alone, but always emerge in co-evolutionary settings where several orders emerge simultaneously."[117] The constitution of human rights constraints on the activities of governing orders – states, enterprises, and the international community – provide a glimpse of such a constitutional ordering, one that arises as much from out of the space between collisions as from the delineation of collision itself. But it also suggests that societally constituted organizations are essentially polycentric and disorganized.

> To that end, I would argue that the inherent nature of polycentricity embraces the absence of an ordering principle, though not the absence of order. Order without hierarchy in a more complicated governance space in which states serve as one actor, and an important one, among many and not all of a similar sort. One ought to be able to invoke all relevant rule systems simultaneously to push each of these governance units in a direction you want.[118]

They find points of convergence in those areas where they collide – in this case around the normative structures of human rights.

Within this normative order, law is relevant but not central; non-legal approaches produce the possibility of coordination (but not a "solution," which suggests conflict rather than coordination). And the concrete solution is unacceptable to states seeking to preserve the primacy of their old order, to acolytes of public international law, who seek to impose a

115 See, Teubner, "The Corporate Codes of Multinationals."
116 See, e.g., O'Neill, "The Disciplinary Society."
117 Kjaer, "Transnational Normative Orders," p. 797.
118 Backer, "A Conversation about Polycentricity."

primacy of a supra-national order on a community of states within which non-state organizations are understood as derivative authority, and to enterprises who might see in the chaos of open conflict, of collision without order, a means of avoiding law (and social norms) entirely. The resulting framework may not produce unified law, as classically understood, but it may manage ordered interaction among systems in a governance universe without a center (one that in the classical period had been provided by the ideal of "law" and the *Rechtsstaat*). Here, we move from the generative project of occupying a system[119] to co-existence grounded in something like rough consensus,[120] but without the drive toward unifying harmonization. The emerging UNGP–OECD Guidelines framework provides a window onto a procedural framework within which self-constituted bodies collide to shape their respective relations. But rather than order and the privileging of law, the emerging framework suggests a constitutional framework within which fracture and polycentric co-existence, of short duration, appear to be emerging as the stable state.

> The "protect, respect, and remedy" framework lays the foundations for generating the necessary means to advance the business and human rights agenda. It spells out differentiated yet complementary roles and responsibilities for states and companies, and it includes the element of remedy for when things go wrong. It is systemic in character, meaning that the component parts are intended to support and reinforce one another, creating a dynamic process of cumulative progress – one that does not foreclose additional longer-term meaningful measures.[121]

The UNGP–OECD Guidelines framework posits order without hierarchy and the management of collision between three great autonomous governance communities – states, enterprises, and public international organizations – whose interactions produce intermeshing around specific normative challenges, but which necessarily resist the hegemony of law.

Bibliography

Anderson, G. W., "Societal Constitutionalism, Social Movements, and Constitutionalism from Below," *Indiana Journal of Global Legal Studies*, 20 (2013), pp. 881–906.

[119] Renner, "Occupy the System?"

[120] Calliess and Zumbansen, *Rough Consensus and Running Code*, pp. 134–52.

[121] Ruggie, "Opening Remarks," p. 5.

Alston, P., "The 'Not-a-Cat' Syndrome: Can the International Human Rights Regime Accommodate Non-State Actors?" in P. Alston (ed.) *Non-State Actors and Human Rights* (Oxford University Press, 2005), pp. 3–36.

Anghie, A., *Imperialism, Sovereignty and the Making of International Law* (Cambridge University Press, 2004).

Bailey, S., and U. Mattei, "Social Movements as Constituent Power: The Italian Struggle for the Commons," *Indiana Journal of Global Legal Studies*, 20 (2013), pp. 965–1013.

Backer, L. C., "The 3rd UN Forum on Business and Human Rights: Streaming Live With Thoughts on the Forum as Estates General," *Law at the End of the Day*, December 2, 2014, available at http://lcbackerblog.blogspot.com/2014/12/the-3rd-un-forum-on-business-and-human.html.

"The 2nd UN Forum on Business and Human Rights: Live Streaming and Thoughts on Trends in Managing Business Behaviors," *Law at the End of the Day*, December 3, 2013, available at http://lcbackerblog.blogspot.com/2013/12/the-2nd-un-forum-on-busness-and-human.html.

"A Conversation About Polycentricity in Governance Systems Beyond the State," *Law at the End of the Day* November 11, 2013, available at http://lcbackerblog.blogspot.de/2013/11/a-conversation-about-polycentricity-in.html.

"Sovereign Investing and Markets-Based Transnational Rule of Law Building: The Norwegian Sovereign Wealth Fund in Global Markets," *American University International Law Review* 29 (2013), pp. 1–121.

"Transnational Constitutions' Outward Expression of Inward Self-Constitution: The Enforcement of Human Rights by Apple Inc.," *Indiana Journal of Global Legal Studies* 20 (2013), p. 805–79.

"The Structural Characteristics of Global Law for the 21st Century: Fracture, Fluidity, Permeability, and Polycentricity," *Tilburg Law Review* 17 (2012), pp. 177–99.

"Governance without Government: An Overview and Application of Interactions Between Law-State and Governance-Corporate System," in G. Handl, J. Zekoll and P. Zumbansen (eds.) *Beyond Territoriality: Transnational Legal Authority in an Age of Globalization* (Leiden, Netherlands & Boston, MA: Martinus Nijhoff, 2012), pp. 87–123.

"Private Actors and Public Governance Beyond the State: The Multinational Corporation, the Financial Stability Board, and the Global Governance Order," *Indiana Journal of Global Legal Studies* 18 (2011), pp. 751–802.

"Rights and Accountability in Development v. DAS Air and Global Witness v. Afrimex: Small Steps towards an Autonomous Transnational Legal System for the Regulation of Multinational Corporations," *Melbourne Journal of International Law* 10 (2009), pp. 258–307.

"From Moral Obligation to International Law: Disclosure Systems, Markets and the Regulation of Multinational Corporations," *Georgetown Journal of International Law*, 39 (2008), pp. 591–653.

"The Autonomous Global Corporation: On the Role of Organizational Law Beyond Asset Partitioning and Legal Personality," *Tulsa Law Review* 41 (2006), pp. 541–71.

"Retaining Judicial Authority: A Preliminary Inquiry on the Dominion of Judges," *William and Mary Bill of Rights Journal*, 12 (2003), p. 117.

Bernstein, L., "Merchant Law in a Merchant Court: Rethinking the Code's Search for Immanent Business Norms," *University of Pennsylvania Law Review* 144 (1996), p. 1765.

Calliess, G.-P., and P. Zumbansen, *Rough Consensus and Running Code: A Theory of Transnational Private Law* (Oxford University Press, 2010).

Claire Cutler, A., *Private Power and Global Authority: Transnational Merchant Law in the Global Political Economy* (Cambridge University Press, 2003).

Ellis, J., "Constitutionalization of Nongovernmental Certification Programs," *Indiana Journal of Global Legal Studies* 20 (2013), pp. 1035–59.

Falk, R., *Predatory Globalization: A Critique* (Cambridge: Polity Press, 1999).

Final Statement by the UK National Contact Point for the OECD Guidelines for Multinational Enterprises: Complaint from Survival International Against Vedanta Resources Plc, Urn 09/1373. Available at www.oecd.org/investment/mne/43884129.pdf.

Final Statement By The UK National Contact Point for the OECD Guidelines for Multinational Enterprises: Complaint from the International Union of Food, Agricultural, Hotel, Restaurant, Catering, Tobacco and Allied Workers' Associations against Unilever Plc on Pakistan's Khanewal Factory, 2009, (UK). Available at www.oecd.org/daf/inv/mne/44478619.pdf.

Final Statement by The UK National Contact Point for the OECD Guidelines for Multinational Enterprises: Complaint from the International Union of Food, Agricultural, Hotel, Restaurant, Catering, Tobacco and Allied Workers' Associations against Unilever Plc on Pakistan's Rahim Yar Khan Factory, 2009, Urn 09/1221, At 1 (UK). Available at www.oecd.org/investment/mne/44478663.pdf.

Fischer-Lescano, A., "Global Constitutional Struggles: Human Rights between Colère Publique and Colère Politique" in W. Kaleck, M. Ratner, T. Singelnstein and P. Weiss (eds.) *International Prosecution of Human Rights Crimes* (Heidelberg: Springer, 2007), pp. 13–27.

Fischer-Lescano, A., and G. Teubner, 'Regime-Collisions: The Vain Search for Legal Unity in the Fragmentation of Global Law," *Michigan Journal of International Law* 25 (2003–2004), pp. 999–1046.

Foster, L. A., "Critical Cultural Translation: A Socio-Legal Framework for Regulatory Orders," *Indiana Journal of Global Legal Studies* 21 (2014), pp. 79–105.

Habermas, J., "A Political Constitution for the Pluralist World Society?" in J. Habermas (ed.) *Between Naturalism and Religion* (Cambridge: Polity Press, 2008), pp. 312–52.

Iamann, A., and H. R. Fabri, "Transnational networks and constitutionalism,' *International Journal of Constitutional Law*, 6 (2008), pp. 481–508.

Initial Assessment by the UK National Contact Point for the OECD Guidelines for Multinational Enterprises: Survival International and Vedanta Resources Plc, March 27, 2009. Available at www.business-humanrights.org/Links/Repository/969215/jump.

Johns, F. E., "The Invisibility of the Transnational Corporation: An Analysis of International Law and Legal Theory," *Melbourne University Law Review*, 19 (1994), pp. 893–923.

Joint IOE-ICC-BIAC Comments on the Draft Guiding Principles on Business and Human Rights, Geneva, January 26, 2011. Available at www.iccwbo.org/Data/Policies/2011/ICC-IOE-BIAC-joint-recommendations-to-the-UN-Working-Group-on-Business-Human-Rights/.

Kjaer, P., "Transnational Normative Orders: The Constitutionalism of Intra- and Trans-Normative Law," *Indiana Journal of Global Legal Studies*, 20 (2013), pp. 777–802.

Koh, H. H., "Transnational Legal Process," *Nebraska Law Review*, 75 (1996), pp. 181.

Kumm, M., "The Legitimacy of International Law: A Constitutionalist Framework of Analysis," *European Journal of International Law*, 15 (2004), pp. 907–31.

Mollers, C., "Transnational Governance without Public Law?" in C. Joerges, I.-J. Sand and G. Teubner (eds.), *Transnational Governance and Constitutionalism* (Oxford: Hart, 2004), pp. 329–38.

OECD, Guidelines for Multinational Enterprises (2011), OECD Directorate for Financial and Enterprise Affairs. Available at www.oecd.org/daf/inv/mne/48004323.pdf.

OECD, Annual Report on the OECD Guidelines for Multinational Enterprises 2013 Responsible Business Conduct in Action, Executive Summary. Available at http://mneguidelines.oecd.org/MNE-Annual-Report-2013-Summary.pdf

O'Neill, J., "The Disciplinary Society: From Weber to Foucault," *The British Journal of Sociology*, 37 (1986), pp. 42–60.

Peters, A., "Compensatory Constitutionalism: The Function and Potential of Fundamental International Norms and Structures," *Leiden Journal of International Law*, 19 (2006), pp. 579–610.

Queinnec, Y., "The OECD Guidelines for Multinational Enterprises: An Evolving Legal Status" (Association Sherpa Report, June 2007).

Renner, M., "Occupy the System! Societal Constitutionalism and Transnational Corporate Accounting," *Indiana Journal of Global Legal Studies*, 20 (2013), pp. 941–64.

Riles, A., "The Anti-Network: Private Global Governance, Legal Knowledge, and the Legitimacy of the State," *The American Journal of Comparative Law*, 56 (2008), pp. 605–30.

Rödl, F., "Fundamental Rights, Private Law, and Societal Constitution: On the Logic of the So-Called Horizontal Effect," *Indiana Journal of Global Legal Studies*, 20 (2013), pp. 1015–34.

Ruggie, J. G., *Just Business: Multinational Corporations and Human Rights* (New York: W. W. Norton 2013).

Letter, "Bizarre Response by Human Rights Groups to UN Framework Plan," *Financial Times*, January 19, 2011. Available at www.ft.com/cms/s/0/629fbcd0-2361-11e0-8389-00144feab49a.html#axzz2ngb0wGXd.

Opening remarks by UN Special Representative John Ruggie, October 5, 2009. Available at www.business-humanrights.org/Documents/Ruggie-speech-to-Geneva-consultation-Oct-2009.pdf.

Sachs, N., "Beyond the Liability Wall: Strengthening Tort Remedies in International Environmental Law," *University of California Law Review*, 55 (2008), pp. 837–904.

Sand, I.-J., "Polycontextuality as an Alternative to Constitutionalism" in C. Joerges, I.-J. Sand and G. Teubner (eds.), *Transnational Governance and Constitutionalism* (Oxford: Hart Publishing, 2004), pp. 41–66.

Shamir, R., "Corporate Social Responsibility: A Case of Hegemony and Counter-Hegemony" in B. de Sousa Santos and C. A. Rodríguez-Garavito (eds.) *Law and Globalization from Below: Towards a Cosmopolitan Legality* (Cambridge University Press, 2005), pp. 92–117.

Skinner, G., R. McCorquodale, and O. De Schutter, "The Third Pillar: Access to Judicial Remedies for Human Rights Violations by Transnational Business" (ICAR, CORE ECCJ, December 2013).

Special Representative of the Secretary-General, "Guiding Principles on Business and Human Rights: Implementing the United Nations 'Protect, Respect and Remedy' Framework," UN Doc. A/HRC/17/31 (March 21, 2011). Available at www.business-humanrights.org/media/documents/ruggie/ruggie-guiding-principles-21-mar-2011.pdf.

Teubner, G., *Constitutional Fragments: Societal Constitutionalism and Globalization* (Oxford University Press 2012)

"Self-Constitutionalizing TNCs?: On the Linkage of 'Private' and 'Public' Corporate Codes of Conduct," *Indiana Journal of Global Legal Studies*, 18 (2011), pp. 617–38.

"The Corporate Codes of Multinationals: Company Constitutions Beyond Corporate Governance and Co-Determination" in R. Nikel (ed.), *Conflict of Laws and Laws of Conflict in Europe and Beyond: Patterns of Supranational and Transnational Juridification* (Oxford: Hart Publishing, 2009).

"Societal Constitutionalism: An Alternative to State Centered Constitutional Theory" in C. Joerges, I.-J. Sand and G. Teubner (eds.), *Transnational Governance and Constitutionalism* (Oxford: Hart Publishing, 2004), pp. 2–28.

"Legal Irritants: Good Faith in British Law or How Unifying Law Ends Up in New Differences," in P. Hall and D. Soskice (eds.), *Varieties Of Capitalism* (Oxford University Press, 2001), pp. 417–41.

"The King's Many Bodies: The Self-Deconstruction of Law's Hierarchy," *Law & Society Review*, 31 (1997), pp. 763–88.

"Global Bukowina: Legal Pluralism in the World Society," in G. Teubner (ed.), *Global Law without a State* (Aldershot: Dartmouth, 1996), pp. 3–28.

Thornhill, C., "A Sociology of Constituent Power: The Political Code of Transnational Societal Constitutions," *Indiana Journal of Global Legal Studies*, 20 (2013), pp. 551–603.

United Nations Human Rights Council Res. 17/4, 17th Sess., July 6, 2011, UN Doc. A/HRC/RES/17/4 (July 6, 2011). Available at http://daccess-dds-ny.un.org/doc/RESOLUTION/GEN/G11/144/71/PDF/G1114471.pdf?OpenElement.

UN Human Rights Council, Forum on Business and Human Rights, Second session, 3 and 4 December 2013, Background note by the Secretariat A/HRC/FBHR/2013/2 (24 September 2013).

Ward, H., "Securing Transnational Corporate Accountability through National Courts: Implications and Policy Options," *Hastings International and Comparative Law Review*, 24 (2001), pp. 451–74.

Watt, H. M., "Private International Law Beyond the Schism," *Transnational Legal Theory*, 3 (2011), pp. 347–428.

Weissbrodt, D., "Keynote Address: International Standard-Setting on the Human Rights Responsibilities of Businesses," *Berkeley Journal of International Law*, 26 (2008), pp. 373–91.

Wiener, A., and P. Liste, "Lost without Translation?: Cross-Referencing and a New Global Community of Courts," *Indiana Journal of Global Legal Studies*, 21 (2014), pp. 263–96.

H. Williamson, "Amnesty Criticises UN Framework for Multinationals," *Financial Times*, January 17, 2011.

Zürn, M., "Sovereignty and Law in a Denationalised World" in R. P. Appelbaum, W. L. F. Felstiner and V. Gessner (eds.) *Rules and Networks: The Legal Culture of Global Business Transactions* (Oxford: Hart Publishing, 2001).

8

Non-financial Reporting for business enterprises

An effective tool to address human rights violations?

SEBASTIAN EICKENJÄGER

Between 2005 and 2008, world food prices rose by 83 per cent, maize prices almost tripled, wheat prices increased by 127 per cent, and rice prices by 170 per cent.[1] The Food and Agriculture Organization of the United Nations (FAO) estimated that in 2008 more than 40 million additional people were pushed into hunger as a consequence of the food crisis,[2] and in 2009 the FAO stated that for the first time since 1970, more than one billion people in the world were suffering from hunger.[3] In 2011, global food prices reached another peak and in 2013 the FAO declared that there had been progress in the last years but 'it is insufficient overall to achieve the hunger reduction goals'.[4]

At the same time, the financial sector experiences a boom in the trade of raw materials on global financial markets, that is, a boom in the trading in commodity derivatives. The share of agricultural commodities within capital investments in raw materials increased to one fourth, about 100 billion US dollars. From 1998 to 2008 the investment volume in commodity index funds increased from 3 to 174 billion US dollars.[5] In general, the participation of speculators and non-traditional investors (e.g., hedge funds and large banks) at the commodity futures exchanges increased rapidly and turned traditional actors into a minority.[6] Speculation on agricultural commodities leads

[1] Mittal, 'The 2008 Food Price Crisis', p. 1.

[2] Food and Agriculture Organisation of the United Nations (FAO), 'Number of Hungry People Rises to 963 Million'.

[3] FAO, 'The State of Food Insecurity in the World 2009', p. 4.

[4] FAO, 'The State of Food Insecurity in the World 2013', p. 9.

[5] Oxfam Germany, 'Mit Essen Spielt Man Nicht!', p. 7.

[6] For an overview of the participating market actors and the changes at the commodity future exchanges see United Nations Conference on Trade and Development (UNCTAD) and Arbeiterkammer Wien, 'Price Formation in Financialized Commodity Markets: The Role of Information', pp. 18–9.

o a 'financialization'[7] of the agricultural trade markets. Many non governmental organisations (NGOs) and some scientists argue that this 'financialization' is one cause for extreme fluctuations and an increase of food prices that has serious impacts on the urban and rural poor in Low Income Food Deficit Countries (LIFDC) or the poorest development countries.[8] Olivier De Schutter, UN Special Rapporteur on the right to food, stresses the 'negative effects of speculation on basic food commodities' and highlights that 'a significant portion of the increases in price and volatility of essential food commodities can only be explained by the emergence of a speculative bubble'.[9]

The alleged impacts of food speculation on world hunger are exemplary for complex correlations between business and human rights in times of globalisation. Human rights violations often cannot be traced back to a specific business action. They often appear as violations that are systemic or of a structural nature. Therefore, they are to be identified in complex constellations between the economic system and communities or parts of a regional/global population.

With respect to the relation between the global trade of agricultural commodities at the financial markets and world hunger, the 'colliding regimes' shall be explicitly identified: On the one hand there is the urban and rural poor population in the poorest development countries who suffer from a violation of their right to food, and on the other hand there are profit-oriented business enterprises that take part in financial affairs that may have negative impacts on the social, cultural, and economic rights of the affected groups and individuals. Therefore, a conflict can be identified between the economic system and economic, social and cultural rights of communities, groups and individuals.

This paper examines the question whether the voluntary mechanism of Non-financial Reporting (NfR) is able to manage regime collisions between the economic system and global (social, cultural, and economic) human rights. The following sections will introduce this mechanism as it is meant to operate and then look at a practical example in a case study on food speculation. The paper will then address shortcomings of NfR in

7 For a definition of the term/phenomenon 'financialization' see United Nations Conference on Trade and Development (UNCTAD) and Arbeiterkammer Wien, 'Price Formation in Financialized commodity markets: The Role of Information', pp. 13ff.

8 See Oxfam Germany, 'Mit Essen Spielt Man Nicht!', pp. 7, 13ff. For the impacts of high food prices on the rural and urban poor population see Ivanic and Martin, 'Implications of Higher Global Food Prices for Poverty in Low Income Countries'.

9 De Schutter, 'Food Commodities Speculation and Food Price Crises', pp. 1, 8.

practice and outline its potential before concluding with a discussion of ways for further development.

Non-financial Reporting

Because of their complexity, these regime collisions pose an enormous challenge to transnational human rights protection. In the last two decades there has been much effort to establish human rights protection as a core business concern and to tie business actors to human rights obligations. There are many initiatives and approaches on the national, regional, international and transnational level, which aim to make corporations accountable for human rights abuses. Still, besides the question if corporations should be legally bound by human rights, questions regarding the means and extent of a direct obligation remain highly controversial. While the international community failed to implement a UN-based treaty regarding general human rights obligations of private actors,[10] there are many UN-based, state-based or private undertakings that aim to hold corporations accountable[11]. These instruments have in common that they operate on a 'voluntary basis' and that they do not contain legally binding provisions for business enterprises.

One instrument of increasing attention is the concept of NfR.[12] NfR can be best described in contrast to financial Reporting (fR): While fR's

[10] UN Economic and Social Council (ECOSOC), Sub-Commission on Promotion & Protection of Human Rights, Norms on the Responsibilities of Transnational Corporations and Other Business Enterprises with Regard to Human Rights, Draft Norms on the Responsibilities of Transnational Corporations and Other Business Enterprises with Regard to Human Rights, E/CN.4/Sub.2/2003/12/Rev.2 of 26 August 2003. For the drafting process and the reasons for the failure to adopt the 'draft norms' see Backer, 'Multinational Corporations, Transnational Law: The United Nations' Norms on the Responsibilities of Transnational Corporations as a Harbinger of Corporate Social Responsibility in International Law'; Kinley and Chambers, 'The UN Human Rights Norms for Corporations: The Private Implications of Public International Law'; Weißbrodt and Kruger, 'Norms on the Responsibilities of Transnational Corporations and other Business Enterprises with Regard to Human Rights'.

[11] Some of the most prominent instruments are the Guidelines of the Organisation for Economic Co-operation and Development (OECD) regarding the duty of multinational corporations (Guidelines for Multinational Enterprises), the Tripartite Declaration of the International Labour Organization (ILO) concerning multinational enterprises and social policy, the Global Compact program of the UN, and finally the 'Guiding Principles on Business and Human Rights: Implementing the United Nations "Protect, Respect and Remedy" Framework' proposed by the UN Special Representative John Ruggie.

[12] Also known as social accounting, social and environmental accounting, corporate social reporting, corporate social responsibility reporting, and non-financial accounting.

urpose is to deliver financial information of a company in the form of a alance sheet or an annual financial report to shareholders, lenders and he tax authority, NfR can be described as a process of communicating nformation on social and environmental impacts and effects of business onduct to interested stakeholders. The report itself can take the form of n annex to the annual financial report, a sustainability report or a stand-lone human rights report. The European Commission assumes that the lobal number of non-financial reports per year increased from almost ero in 1992 to approximately 4,000 in 2010.[13] Still, while 80 per cent of he world's 250 largest companies report on their sustainability, about 4 per cent of the total nearly 42,000 EU 'large' companies currently do ot disclose non-financial information.[14]

NfR in general has its origin in the concept of Corporate Social Responsibility (CSR) and the traditional fR approaches.[15] There are nany global initiatives that deal with NfR.[16] The best known private nitiative in the field of NfR is the Global Reporting Initiative (GRI).[17] Another initiative that recently gained widespread attention is the Reporting and Assurance Frameworks Initiative (RAFI).[18] All of these eporting initiatives have in common that their aim is to assist companies n the preparation of reports on non-financial information. Therefore, hey offer reporting frameworks – also called reporting standards, reporting schemes or guidelines – that guide the companies in creating

13 European Commission, Impact Assessment, SWD(2013) 127 final, (16 April 2013), p. 10.

14 Ibid.

15 For further information on origin, main actors, and used terminology see v. Wensen, Broer, Klein, and Knopf, 'The State of Play in Sustainability Reporting in the EU', pp. 14ff.

16 On the global level there are initiatives, offered both by non governmental organisations (NGOs) and intergovernmental organisations (IGOs), which are completely voluntary like the OECD Guidelines for Multinational Enterprises, the ISO 26 000, ILO Tri-partite Declaration of Principles concerning Multinational Enterprises and Social Policies, the UN 'Protect, Respect and Remedy' Framework on Business and Human Rights proposed by the UN Special Representative John Ruggie and the Global Reporting Initiative (GRI).

17 For information on aims, structures, and practices of the GRI see the GRI's homepage, www.globalreporting.org. For the history of GRI, internal organisation, and major actors within the GRI framework see Brown, de Jong, and Levy, 'Building Institutions Based on Information Disclosure'.

18 RAFI is a three-year initiative that aims to, inter alia, develop a framework for good reporting on the basis of the UN Guidning Principles. For further information on the participating organisations and RAFIs core drafts and documents see www.ungpreporting.org/.

a report and disclosing relevant information.[19] Most of the initiatives, like the GRI and RAFI, follow a so-called multi-stakeholder approach, i.e., the initiatives create and improve their reporting frameworks by involving all relevant stakeholders, like corporations, investors, rating agencies, auditors, scientists, and NGOs in the process of development.

The frameworks are subdivided into different sections. The different sections usually refer to information regarding, for example, the organisational profile of the organisation, governance and policy aspects, strategies for accessing impacts and to integrate findings of impact assessments into its performance and questions relating to remediation processes concerning affected individuals or communities.[20]

While all of the initiatives dealing with NfR are strictly 'voluntary'[21], there are many countries that have passed more or less mandatory NfR legislation.[22] In October 2014, the EU passed a directive that aims to harmonise existing national NfR legislation and establish it where member states have not yet passed regulation in this field.[23] The EU's

[19] The most used reporting schemes are the Guidelines of GRI and the United Nations Global Compact Communication on Progress (UNGC COP). Beside that, there are many other standards which partially only refer to special business sectors like the Carbon Disclosure Project (CDP) and the Connected Reporting Framework (CRF) (for further initiatives see v. Wensen, Broer, Klein, and Knopf, 'The State of Play in Sustainability Reporting in the EU', Appendix C, pp. 135ff.).

[20] See RAFI, 'Draft UN Guiding Principles Reporting Framework'; GRI, 'G4 Sustainability Reporting Guidelines'.

[21] On the international level there are voices that on the one hand demand universal initiatives and on the other hand strive for legally binding approaches and standards. On the UN level, the outcome document of the UN Conference on Sustainable Development (Rio +20) calls for a universal framework on non-financial-reporting (General Assembly, (2012), UN Doc A/RES/66/288, paragraph 47.). The latest report of the United Nations Secretary General´s High-level Panel on Global Sustainability argues for a mandatory reporting framework (General Assembly, (2012), UN Doc A/RES/66/700, paragraph 166.).

[22] For example The Netherlands, Belgium, Denmark, United Kingdom, Finland, Spain, France, and Sweden. For a brief summary on the recent developments in some of these member states see European Commission, Impact Assessment, SWD(2013) 127 final, (16 April 2013), Annex III, pp. 49ff.; for references to the corresponding legislation see European Coalition for Corporate Justice (ECCJ), 'Principles & Pathways: Legal opportunities to improve Europe's corporative accountability framework', p. 11, fn. 5.

[23] European Parliament and the Council, Directive 2014/95/EU of 22 October 2014 amending Directive 2013/34/EU as regards disclosure of non-financial and diversity information by certain large undertakings and groups, OJ L 330/1 of 15 November 2014. The EU's Directive requests mandatory NfR without providing explicit enforcement or sanctions for violations of the obligations. It also aims to unburden small and medium sized companies. According to this, the new EU's Directive provides that only

directive itself offers no reporting guidelines or standards for the disclosure of non-financial information.[24] It states specific matters that shall be the minimum-content of the reports like environmental, social and employee matters, respect for human rights, anti-corruption and bribery matters. Besides that, it names criteria that shall be subject to the reports:

(a) a brief description of the undertaking's business model;
(b) a description of the policies pursued by the undertaking in relation to the matters, including due diligence processes implemented;
(c) the outcome of those policies;
(d) the principle risks related to those matters linked to the undertaking's operations including, where relevant and proportionate, its business relationships, products or services which are likely to cause adverse impacts to those areas, and how the undertaking manages those risks;
(e) non-financial key performance indicators relevant to the particular business.[25]

To guarantee the disclosure of this information, the Directive instructs the EU Member States to provide that companies rely on national, Union-based or international frameworks like, for example, the GRI.[26]

There is a consensus among civil society, governments, companies and their stake- and shareholders that NfR can be a useful management tool, an important risk management mechanism and a crucial source of information for affected communities, groups, and other shareholders that aim to assess the impacts of business' activities.[27] Furthermore, there is a growing demand of government agencies, investors, stock exchanges, and other financial institutions for transparency regarding a company's

undertakings that are public-interest entities with more than 500 employees should be subject to the new requirements. European subsidiary companies or parent companies, which are also subsidiary companies, shall only be exempt from non-financial reporting obligations if they and their subsidiaries are consolidated in the reports of another company.

24 Under Art. 2 of the Directive, the European Commission is advised to prepare 'non-binding guidelines on methodology for reporting non-financial information' by 6 December 2016.

25 Directive 2014/95/EU of 22 October 2014.

26 Ibid.

27 See European Coalition for Corporate Justice (ECCJ), 'EU Legislation on Non-financial Reporting by Companies', p. 2; Amnesty International, 'Non-Financial Reporting: Amnesty International Position Paper'.

'human rights performance'. That is why, besides the promotion of responsibility and transparency, efficiency of capital markets and the performance of companies are major concerns and objectives of NfR.[28] For these reasons, next to affected communities, groups or individuals, NGOs, the media, consumers, employees and trade unions, it is also investors and analysts who are the most common readers.[29]

The idea of NfR in general is not to create an immediate accountability of enterprises for human rights related actions. NfR does not mainly refer to a compensation for human rights violations, but rather aims to establish human rights protection as a core business concern.[30] Nevertheless, NfR is not just a tool to prepare the way for, for example, civil actions. It is an instrument of strengthening human rights through a process of internal self-reflexion.

The following section will introduce a case study on food speculation to examine NfR's actual shortcomings and its potential for managing regime collisions between the economic system and global (social, cultural, and economic) human rights.

Case study: food speculation, stakeholder engagement and NfR in practice

In 2013, Oxfam Germany accused several German companies, inter alia the Allianz Group, of making profit with financial transactions that bear a significant risk to cause hunger in the world.[31] The Allianz Group appears to be a major player in the field of food commodities speculation. Oxfam Germany states that in 2011 the Allianz Group and its subsidiaries held 5 commodity funds with an overall fixed asset of 18.44 billion euros, of which approximately 6.24 billion euros cover agricultural commodities.[32]

[28] See Human Rights Reporting and Assurance Frameworks Initiative (RAFI), 'Draft UN Guiding Principles Reporting Framework', p. 1.

[29] For further information on the readers' perspectives on sustainability reporting see v. Wensen, Broer, Klein, and Knopf, 'The State of Play in Sustainability Reporting in the EU', pp. 85ff.

[30] Augenstein, 'Study of the Legal Framework on Human Rights and the Environment Applicable to European Enterprises Operating Outside the European Union', p. 75, paragraph 232.

[31] Oxfam Germany, 'Mit Essen Spielt Man Nicht!'; also see Oxfam Germany, 'Oxfam Hintergrundpapier, Hungerroulette'.

[32] Oxfam Germany, 'Mit Essen Spielt Man Nicht!', pp. 30ff.

In March 2012, Oxfam Germany contacted the Allianz Group and asked for a statement on the connection between speculation on agricultural commodities and global food prices.[33] The Allianz Group responded to the request by stating that their investments do not affect the demand on the physical markets and therefore do not jack up prices of agricultural commodities.[34] Furthermore, the Allianz Group and Oxfam Germany held several meetings in which the Allianz Group tried to refute Oxfam's allegations. In an open letter Jay Ralph, member of the board of the Allianz SE and chairman of the Environmental, Social and Governance Board of the Allianz SE, defended his company against persistent criticism.[35] In order to defend itself, the Allianz Group referred to internal audits and investigations that show that their business activities do not have a negative impact on food prices. At the same time, the Allianz Group refused to provide or publish its internal information.[36]

The Allianz Group reports on non-financial information on the basis of the GRI Guidelines. The sustainability report of 2012 reacts to the allegations by several NGOs in the form of an interview with the CEO of the Allianz SE, Michael Diekmann:

Question:

In 2012, NGOs criticized banks, hedge funds and insurance companies for investing in agricultural commodities. Does Allianz view that criticism as an occasion to rethink its investments?'

Answer M. Diekmann:

We did review those investments. We don't invest in agricultural commodities, but serve farmers and buyers as a risk partner in the futures market (where only price risks are traded). In return for a premium, we take on the risk posed by price volatility in the spot markets (where commodities are later traded). In that way, we ensure a reliable income

[33] Ibid. [34] Ibid.

[35] Ralph, 'Offener Brief an Oxfam', (15 October 2013), www.allianz.com/de/presse/news/unternehmen/standpunkte/news_2013-10-14.html.

[36] Schiessl, 'Agrarrohstoffe: Streit über die Spekulations-Studie', *Spiegel-Online*, (3 February 2013), www.spiegel.de/wirtschaft/flassbeck-gegen-agrarspekulation-a-880775.html; Kwasniewski, 'Nahrungsmittelinvestments: Allianz wehrt sich gegen Spekulationsvorwürfe', *Spiegel-Online*, (15 October 2013), www.spiegel.de/wirtschaft/unternehmen/allianz-wehrt-sich-gegen-vorwuerfe-der-nahrungsmittelspekulationen-a-928029.html.

for farmers and reliable prices for buyers. In those operations we don't need to 'bet on high prices', because we can earn our risk premium even if prices are low. We believe the criticism of Allianz on this topic is unjustified. But I must also say that it has raised our awareness of the problem. In dialogue with experts and NGOs, we want to find solutions that will help us address undisputed causes of hunger'.[37]

Oxfam Germany states that until now the Allianz Group has not changed its activities in this field. In November 2013, Foodwatch submitted an analysis in response to studies in favour of the position the Allianz Group and other companies involved in food speculations. It concludes that speculation on agricultural commodities is quite likely to have negative impacts on food prices.[38] Meanwhile, Foodwatch published a 'for internal use only' working paper by the Allianz Group, which concludes that 'taking into consideration the huge influx of funds and non-traditional participants into commodity markets, it cannot be totally dismissed, that speculation at least supports excessive price developments'[39].

Shortcomings of NfR in practice: does NfR improve business behaviour?

The fact that actual NfR initiatives are very praxis orientated makes their frameworks generally a practical tool for companies to disclose non-financial information. There is hardly any doubt that elaborating a report makes companies in some way reflect the impacts of their activities on human rights. To manage writing a report, corporations have to establish a 'task force' or a 'working group' that needs to communicate with every relevant internal actor and has to

[37] Allianz Group, 'Sustainability Factbook 2012', (2013), www.allianz.com/v_1363290088000/media/responsibility/documents/ALLIANZ_Sustainability_Factbook.pdf, p. 3.

[38] On the controversial discussion between foodwatch and Ingo Pies et al. who argue that speculation on agricultural commodities has no impact on food prices, see foodwatch, 'foodwatch-Argumentationspapier zur Studie "Finanzspekulation und Nahrungsmittelpreise" von Prof. Hans-Heinrich Bass'; Bass, 'Finanzspekulation und Nahrungsmittelpreise: Anmerkungen zum Stand der Forschung'; Pies and Will, 'Finanzspekulation mit Agrarrohstoffen'; Pies and Glauben, 'Wissenschaftliche Stellungnahme zum Argumentationspapier von Foodwatch'.

[39] Allianz Group, 'Working Paper: Is Speculation to Blame for Rising Food Prices?', p. 11.

xamine almost all sectors of the company.[40] In addition, the working group has to explore internal structures (governance), supply chains, ubsidiaries and their activities. Therefore, writing a sustainability report necessarily promotes a company's awareness regarding internal structures and partnerships that are relevant for human rights related impacts.

Nevertheless, the case study shows that the current NfR in practice often fails to achieve its objectives. Regarding the allegations made by Oxfam Germany, the Allianz Group reports that they reviewed the allegations and that they do not invest in agricultural commodities. Major questions that are components of common reporting frameworks were left unanswered:

> How did the company assess the alleged impacts?[41] What were the findings of the evitable assessments?[42] How does the company integrate its findings into its decision-making processes regarding its further actions?[43] How does the company address tensions between the identified risks and other business objectives?[44] What exactly has the company done to address the risk?[45] How does the company address individuals, groups or communities concerns and complaints?[46]

The Allianz Group did not address the allegations in detail. Even though it turned out that there were internal studies that delivered explicit results, they did not report how exactly they assessed the alleged impacts

[40] For the internal challenges of CSR measures to a company see Scherer, Palazzo, and Seidl, 'Managing Legitimacy in Complex and Heterogeneous Environments'.

[41] See RAFI, 'Draft UN Guiding Principles Reporting Framework', Part C, pp. 11ff.; GRI, 'G4 Sustainability Reporting Guidelines', G4–pp. 24ff. (Stakeholder Engagement), pp. 29–30, G4–pp. 34ff. (Governance), pp. 36ff., G4–DMA, p. 46, G4–HR9 (Human Rights Assessments), p. 74, G4–HR12 (Human Rights Grievance Mechanisms), p. 75.

[42] See RAFI, 'Draft UN Guiding Principles Reporting Framework', Part B, C, pp. 11ff.; GRI, 'G4 Sustainability Reporting Guidelines', G4–pp. 24ff. (Stakeholder Engagement), pp. 29–30, G4–pp. 34ff. (Governance), pp. 36ff.

[43] Ibid.

[44] See RAFI, 'Draft UN Guiding Principles Reporting Framework', Part C4.2, p. 12; GRI, 'G4 Sustainability Reporting Guidelines', G4–pp. 24ff. (Stakeholder Engagement), pp. 29–30, G4–pp. 34ff. (Governance), pp. 36ff.

[45] See RAFI, 'Draft UN Guiding Principles Reporting Framework', Part C4, p. 12; GRI, 'G4 Sustainability Reporting Guidelines', G4–pp. 24ff. (Stakeholder Engagement), pp. 29–30, G4–pp. 34ff. (Governance), pp. 36ff.

[46] See RAFI, 'Draft UN Guiding Principles Reporting Framework', Part C2, pp. 11–2, C6, p. 13; GRI, 'G4 Sustainability Reporting Guidelines', G4–pp. 24ff. (Stakeholder Engagement), pp. 29–30, G4–pp. 34ff. (Governance), pp. 36ff., G4–HR12 (Human Rights Grievance Mechanisms), p. 75.

(especially regarding the involved sections and departments of the company) and what findings were made. The statement that they reviewed the allegations does not contribute to transparency. It is not comprehensible, if the company actually reviewed the allegations and what impacts these reviews had on further activities and decision-making processes. There was no information on the internal praxis in dealing with the tensions between the identified risks for the increase of food prices and expected profits.

The reporting practice of NfR brings up the question of whether NfR does actually improve business behaviour. Do companies actually take into account human rights in decision-making processes? Rob Gray's answer to these questions is: 'no-one can know – but it is probable'.[47] Because there are no monitoring and evaluation mechanisms and since the reporting requirements are too frail for 'greenwashing' (i.e., that companies often misuse their reports to create a false 'green image') the information given by participating companies cannot be verified and there is no guarantee that the information is comprehensive. Therefore, due to a lack of transparency the grade of the implementation of human rights in the internal structures and processes remains unclear.

Apart from the case study, many stakeholders argue that companies often misuse their reports to create a false 'green image' ('greenwashing'). William S. Laufer states that the emergence of the term 'greenwashing' reflects

> an increasing apprehension that at least some corporations creatively manage their reputations with the public, financial community and regulators, so as to hide deviance, deflect attributions of fault, obscure the nature of the problem or allegation, reattribute blame, ensure an entity's reputation and, finally, seek to appear in a leadership position.[48]

Some companies 'engage in complex strategies and counter strategies that serve to shift the focus and attention away from the firm, create confusion, undermine credibility, criticise viable alternatives, and

[47] Gray, 'Does Sustainability Reporting Improve Corporate Behaviour?', p. 82.

[48] Laufer, 'Social Accountability and Corporate Greenwashing', p. 255; see also Deegan and Rankin, 'Do Australian companies report environmental news objectively?'; e.g. Boiral argues that sustainability reports (in this case under the A and A+ GRI standard, which generally is said to be the strictest scheme in the field of reporting standards) 'can be viewed as simulacra that camouflage real sustainable-development problems, presenting an idealized version of company situations' (Boiral, 'Sustainability Reports as Simulacra?', p. 1061). For deficiencies in the UNGC COP framework also see Deva, *Regulating Corporate Human Rights Violations*, pp. 96ff.

deceptively posture firm objectives, commitments, and accomplishments'.[49] 'Greenwashing', therefore, goes along with the possibility of reporting organisations to decide freely which information to publish and how to design the reports. While common guidelines use specific indicators to guide the participating companies, the frameworks still give companies wide latitude on how to shape the reports with the effect that reports are often designed like advertising brochures or catalogues,[50] containing only selected information or lacking relevant information and serving as a platform for presenting 'green' products or technologies.[51]

For these reasons, stakeholders further criticise that the reports are often low in credibility, comparability, and comprehensiveness and therefore of little use in practice.[52] They tend to be difficult to understand, are highly inconsistent and provide extensive unnecessary information, whilst failing to provide the vital facts.[53] Some potential readers stress that there is a high degree of mistrust of the companies' intentions and that they prefer direct means of communication with companies to obtain the required information.[54] NGOs, affected communities or groups and civil society in general see transparency, standardisation, completeness, external assurance, a mandatory requirement and supervision mechanisms for NfR as major aspects for improving current NfR.[55]

Finally, the current lack of unsustainability and the severe collisions in the relationship 'business and human rights' suggest that either companies are still within a initial phase regarding the internalisation of human rights, or company activities actually do not consider human

[49] Laufer, 'Social Accountability and Corporate Greenwashing', p. 255.

[50] See for example H&M's latest sustainability report. The report is designed like a fashion catalogue and, therefore, contains a lot of pictures, animations, and images of H&M's products or models presenting H&M's products: H&M, 'Conscious Actions – Sustainability Report 2013', (2014), http://sustainability.hm.com/en/sustainability/downloads-resources/reports/sustainability-reports.html.

[51] See e.g. the studies of Skouloudisa, Evangelinosa, and Kourmousis, 'Assessing non-financial reports according to the Global Reporting Initiative guidelines: evidence from Greece'; Chapman and Milne, 'The triple bottom line: how New Zealand companies measure up'; Mahoney, Thorne, Cecil, and LaGore, 'A research note on standalone corporate social responsibility reports: Signaling or greenwashing?'.

[52] Tilt, 'The Influence of External Pressure Groups on Corporate Social Disclosure', p. 63.

[53] European Coalition for Corporate Justice (ECCJ), 'EU Legislation on Non-financial Reporting by Companies', p. 1.

[54] v. Wensen, Broer, Klein, and Knopf, 'The State of Play in Sustainability Reporting in the EU', p. 86.

[55] Ibid., pp. 93ff.

rights matters in their decision making processes at all. If the former is the case, the only way to improve the current (unsatisfactory) situation is to make structures and processes transparent and open to a method that will promote and achieve an internalisation of human rights in business conduct. If the latter is the case, then 'company disclosure needs to reflect this so that we can discount the empty rhetoric' and radically reconstruct the given structures of binding business to human rights.[56]

The potential of NfR

If one considers that even the best reporting standard cannot guarantee that the disclosed information is comprehensive, credible, and misused for 'greenwashing' then what is the future for NfR and can it contribute to tie business to human rights obligations?

Promoting self-reflexion through monitoring and enforcement mechanisms

Taking into account the small number of reporting companies and the vast amount of structural violations of human rights, it can be questioned if voluntary initiatives like the GRI or concepts that promote voluntarism in general, like CSR, are an expression of actual self-restraint in terms of self-constitutionalisation of the economic system.[57]

Anyhow, with reference to systems theory it can be argued that only the economic system or business actors decide whether they adjust their communications in favour of their systems' social environment. Because the systems remain autopoietic[58] and, therefore, internal communications only refer to previous internal communications; the difficult task to reciprocally harmonise the function of a social system with its output in favour of its social environment can only be accomplished by a system-internal reflexion.[59] This system-internal reflexion can be initiated from the outside of a system, but it cannot be replaced.[60] Gunther Teubner states that these initiations can only be successful if they orientate

[56] See Gray, 'Does Sustainability Reporting Improve Corporate Behaviour?', p. 82.

[57] For the concept of self-constitutionalisation of business enterprises see Teubner, 'Selbst-Konstitutionalisierung transnationaler Unternehmen?'; for the conditions and chances of a human rights based self-restraint of economic regimes see Teubner, 'Die anonyme Matrix'.

[58] Luhmann, *Die Gesellschaft der Gesellschaft*, p. 757.

[59] Teubner, *Verfassungsfragmente*, p. 134.

[60] Ibid.

hemselves on the system's ways of self-change and aim to give impulses hat can be translated into inner growth processes.[61] The task would be to combine massive external pressure and irritation with intrinsic changes.[62]

This very much describes the idea of an NfR framework equipped with a proper monitoring and enforcement system. Such a framework could serve to improve the internalisation of human rights matters within the structures of business enterprises. Internal learning effects are combined with external pressure, assistance and guidance. NfR would institutionalise a mandatory framework for self-reflexion within the economic system.[63]

Regarding a company's internal self-reflexion, a reporting procedure with a monitoring and enforcement mechanism would have advantages over common individual complaints procedures in several ways.

First, while individual complaints procedures only cover individual cases, reporting procedures can address structural human rights problems where it is difficult to identify victims of misconduct or to prove causality between misconduct and affected people.[64] Second, decisions or findings only have legal validity for representational facts, and access of a specific conflict to, for example, civil courts, and often depends on contingencies, while in report procedures continuous negotiations can be held on specific cases and/or structural shortcomings that may lead to a process of appropriation and internalisation of human rights matters within the internal structures of an involved company.[65] Third, monitoring and enforcement bodies could have several options on how to react to misconduct: They could react to the reports by expressing concerns about corporate conduct or concrete suggestions/proposals with respect to specific matters. In contrast to individual complaint procedures, reporting procedures are characterised by argumentative debates on social struggles, not by ruling specific problems.[66] Through

[61] Ibid., pp. 134–5 [62] Ibid., p. 135.

[63] See Hess, 'Social Reporting: A Reflexive Law Approach to Corporate Social Responsiveness', who refers to Teubner, 'Reflexives Recht'.

[64] Davy, 'Welche rechtlichen Grundregeln müssen für einen wirksamen Menschenrechtsschutz gelten?', pp. 255–6.

[65] Ibid., pp. 255, 258.

[66] Fischer-Lescano, 'Der Kampf um die Internetverfassung', p. 968.

follow-up procedures,[67] committees could pursue the further implementation of the previously communicated concerns and suggestions.

Because of the lack of evaluation or monitoring mechanisms in actual NfR, a direct response to the single reports within the reporting system is not possible. There is no guarantee that reports are exhaustive and there is no possibility to follow-up and efficiently support further actions. Reporting companies receive no feedback and there is no room for argumentative debates – a specific and individual learning process is not possible. Therefore, it is up to the companies to evaluate, recondition and incorporate report-related findings. The present case study proves that the learning factor for corporations is very low. A reporting procedure directed by a monitoring body could have served as a platform to debate Oxfam Germany's allegations, to evaluate the actions of the Allianz Group that have been taken to assess the alleged impacts and to consult on solutions to settle the present conflict.

On that note, for financial reporting Hong Phu Dao very rightly pointed out that 'a high quality financial reporting requirement . . . requires also a mechanism to oversee the appropriate application of the standards' and it 'depends both on the quality of accounting standards and the effectiveness of regulatory enforcement of these standards' because 'in the absence of adequate enforcement, the accounting rules may remain simply requirements on paper'.[68]

Inclusion of civil society in monitoring and enforcement mechanisms

Another major shortcoming of actual NfR is the fact that it does not deliver a proper forum for stakeholders (especially for civil society) to communicate criticism towards companies. Currently, the only way for NGOs to influence NfR, for example, under the GRI, is to take part in the

[67] For the follow up procedures within the UN state report framework, especially the inclusion of NGOs in this process see Committee on Economic, Social and Cultural Rights (CESCR), 'Report on the Twentieth and Twenty-First Sessions', E/2000/22, E/C.12/1999/11, (2001), paragraph 38ff.; CESCR, 'Substantive Issues Arising in the Implementation of the International Covenant on Economic, Social and Cultural Rights – NGO participation in the activities of the Committee on Economic, Social and Cultural Rights', E/C.12/2000/6 of 7 July 2000, paragraph 25ff.

[68] Dao, 'Monitoring Compliance with IFRS', p. 108.

GRI's 'development process'[69] or the 'monitoring program'.[70] Both ptions have in common that the subject of negotiation is the configur-tion of the Guidelines and not the reports themselves. That is one eason, why in the present case no NGO explicitly referred to the Allianz Group's sustainability report. The report actually played no role in ealing with the conflict.

Experiences from the UN-based state reporting procedures[71] have hown that the inclusion of civil society in the monitoring mechanisms s a very effective tool to address misconduct. The inclusion of civil ociety in the reporting, monitoring and follow-up process would signifi-antly increase the extent of external pressure. By giving civil society a ool to scandalise, directly address and making public misconduct[72] owards the company or group concerned and to import these concerns nto a process of evaluation, specific impacts and incidents as well as ssues of general relevance can be addressed. Institutionalised arenas for hosting conflicts between civil society and business enterprises in general would increase societies' democratic control over the economic system.

The inclusion of civil society as well as other stakeholders can be established by giving NGOs the possibility to submit so-called shadow eports[73] or by incorporating counter-accounting.[74] Thereby, reporting companies could be confronted with specific incidents, negative business impacts or business activities-related issues. In turn, the monitoring

69 See the Hompage of the GRI, www.globalreporting.org/standards/g4/g4-developments/Pages/default.aspx

70 See the Hompage of the GRI, www.globalreporting.org/standards/g4/Pages/G4monitoring.aspx.

71 For an overview of the UN state reporting system see Kretzmer, 'Human Rights, State Reports', with further references; Keller, 'Reporting Systems'.

72 Liese, 'Epistula (non) Erubescit', pp. 59–60.

73 For the role of NGOs in the monitoring system of Human Right Treaty Bodies see Clapham, 'UN Human Rights Reporting Procedures: An NGO Perspective'; Klein, *The Monitoring System of Human Rights Treaty Obligations*; Brett, 'The Role of NGOs – An Overview'.

74 Boiral defines counter-accounting 'as the process of identifying and reporting information on organisations' significant economic, environmental and social issues that comes from external or unofficial sources (expert reports, research papers, online journals, studies from NGOs, government publications, legal proceedings, etc.) in view of verifying, complementing or countering organisations' official reports on their performance and achievements' (Boiral, 'Sustainability Reports as Simulacra?', p. 1037). For the Role of civil society and stakeholders in the field of corporate accounting also see O'Dwyer, 'Stakeholder democracy'; Adams, 'The ethical, social and environmental reporting performance portrayal gap'; Gallahofer, Haslam, Monk, and Roberts, 'The emancipatory potential of online reporting'.

system could respond to the information given by the companies and the NGOs by handing out recommendations or stressing the companies' obligation to report on certain aspects.

Therefore, besides the implementation of monitoring and enforcement mechanisms, a major task for actual NfR is to effectively include civil society by providing a right to claim transparency in specific fields of business activities or the possibility to actively influence the evaluation process. Ingeborg Maus has noted that to avoid replication of factual positions of power in negotiating positions, which can be observed in actual NfR regarding the problem of 'greenwashing', it is essential to empower the underprivileged positions by mandatory legal mechanisms.[75] Spaces of autonomy have to be legally ensured by legally framed negotiating positions.[76]

Legal foundation for introducing monitoring and enforcement mechanisms

To sum up, NfR has the potential to serve as an effective means of identifying and tackling collisions of human rights regimes and the economic system. But what are the odds that NfR will achieve its full potential? Amongst private reporting initiatives there are no plans to bring into focus better monitoring and enforcement of the reporting process. The most significant obstacle for introducing proper NfR legislation is the lack of political will. Some Member States, for example, Germany, have explicitly expressed rejection towards the plans of the EU to pass mandatory NfR:

> The federal government explicitly militates against new legal disclosure on social and ecological information in the context of CSR. Such obligations would be a renunciation of the principle of voluntariness und would be accompanied by an extensive administrative burden, especially for small and medium size companies.[77]

[75] See Maus, 'Perspektiven "reflexiven Rechts" im Kontext gegenwärtiger Deregulierungstendenzen'.

[76] Ibid., p. 404.

[77] Positionspapier der Bundesregierung zur Mitteilung der Europäischen Kommission, 'Eine neue EU-Strategie (2011–14) für die soziale Verantwortung der Unternehmen (CSR)', (KOM 2011) 681 endg., (18 November 2011), (translation by author).

In contrast to this, there are concrete points of contact for the introduction of monitoring and enforcement mechanisms both in the EU's Directive itself and in international law.

To refute the reservations of some states, one could first refer to states' obligations in international law with respect to regulating private actors' activities. The Committee on Economic, Social and Cultural Rights (CESCR) has repeatedly stated that states have an obligation to

> effectively safeguard rights holders against infringements of their economic, social and cultural rights involving corporate actors, by establishing appropriate laws, regulations, as well as monitoring, investigation and accountability procedures to set and enforce standards for the performance of corporations. As the Committee has repeatedly explained, non-compliance with this obligation can come through action or inaction . . . States Parties should also take steps to prevent human rights contraventions abroad by corporations which have their main seat under their jurisdiction, without infringing the sovereignty or diminishing the obligations of the host States under the Covenant.[78]

The UN Guiding Principles on Business and Human Rights,[79] proposed by the UN Special Representative on business & human rights John Ruggie, confirm the practice of the committee. The first Principle clearly stresses that states 'must protect against human rights abuse within their territory and/or jurisdiction by third parties, including business enterprises. This requires taking appropriate steps to prevent, investigate, punish, and redress such abuse through effective policies, legislation, regulations, and adjudication'. Like the CESCR, the Guiding Principles clearly stress the importance of steps to prevent companies from violating human rights. Principle three points out that states should 'provide

[78] Committee on Economic, Social and Cultural Rights (CESCR), 'Statement on the Obligations of States Parties Regarding the Corporate Sector and Economic, Social and Cultural Rights', E/C.12/2011/1 of 11 May 2011; also see CESCR, 'General Comment No. 14', E/C.12/2000/4 of 11 August 2000, paragraph 39; CESCR, 'Concluding Observation: Germany', E/C.12/DEU/CO/5 of 12 July 2011, paragraph 10; The 'Maastricht Principles on Extraterritorial Obligations in the Area of ESC Rights' (De Schutter, Eide, et al., 'Commentary') refer to the practice of the Committee and other human rights bodies when stating a state obligation to regulate private conduct (Principle 24) and states must adopt and enforce measures to protect economic, social, and cultural rights 'as regards business enterprises, where the corporation, or its parent or controlling company, has its centre of activity, is registered or domiciled, or has its main place of business or substantial business activities, in the State concerned' (Principle 25).

[79] UN Office of the High Commissioner on Human Rights, 'UN Guiding Principles on Business and Human Rights', HR/PUB/11/04, (2011).

effective guidance to business enterprises on how to respect human rights throughout their operations' and 'encourage, or where appropriate require, business enterprises to communicate how they address their human rights impacts' to comply with their duty to protect human rights. Reporting procedures, if equipped with a monitoring mechanism, are an effective tool to guide the reporting party to compliance.

In this respect, international human rights law obligates states[80] to take effective legislative steps to regulate corporations' conduct with regard to the progressive realisation of rights, i.e., as recognised in the CESCR. On the one hand, it can be argued that states in some respect have a margin of appreciation in the area of extraterritorial jurisdiction over corporate human rights abuses and, therefore, the boundaries between what is legally binding and what is politically opportune are often blurred.[81] On the other hand, there is obviously a lack of regulation in this field, especially when it comes to monitoring and enforcement. There is no doubt that proper NfR can be rated as an effective tool to improve corporations' behaviour as regards human rights. To date, states such as Germany[82] have not taken adequate legal or political steps to prevent their own citizens and national entities from violating economic, social and cultural rights in other countries. Appropriate and effective legislative steps, for example, proper mandatory NfR, are long overdue.

The Directive supports this assumption. It contains a passage that can only be understood as a request to the Member States to create procedures to monitor and enforce the disclosure of non-financial information:

[80] For the question whether EU is obliged by international human rights codifications see Fischer-Lescano, *Human Rights in Times of Austerity*, pp. 23ff. On the relationship between the EU and member states international human rights obligations see Ahmed and de Jesús Butler, 'The European Union and Human Rights'; The Regional Office for Europe of the UN High Commissioner for Human Rights, 'The EU and International Human Rights Law'.

[81] Augenstein, 'Study of the Legal Framework on Human Rights and the Environment Applicable to European Enterprises Operating Outside the European Union', p. 77, paragraph 240; Krennerich, *Soziale Menschenrechte*, pp. 106, 361–2; CESCR, 'Statement on the Obligations of States Parties Regarding the Corporate Sector and Economic, Social and Cultural Rights', E/C.12/2011/1 of 11 May 2011; also see CESCR, 'General Comment No. 14', E/C.12/2000/4 of 11 August 2000, paragraph 39.

[82] Germanwatch and Miseror demand the German Government to comply with the European Commission's request ('Communication: A renewed EU strategy 2011–14 for Corporate Social Responsibility', COM (2011) 681 final of 25 October 2011) to establish a plan for the implementation of the UN-Guiding Principles on Business and Human Rights (Germanwatch and Miseror, 'Nationaler Aktionsplan zur Umsetzung der UN-Leitprinzipien für Wirtschaft und Menschenrechte').

> Member States should ensure that adequate and effective means exist to guarantee disclosure of non-financial information by undertakings in compliance with this Directive. To that end, Member States should ensure that effective national procedures are in place to enforce compliance with the obligations laid down by this Directive, and that those procedures are available to all persons and legal entities having a legitimate interest, in accordance with national law, in ensuring that the provisions of this Directive are respected.[83]

For the enforcement of the reporting obligation itself it would be sufficient to simply sanction an omission. To ensure that the content and substance of the reports are in accordance with the Directives' obligations, it requires more than that. Therefore, the Directive advises the Member States to introduce 'effective national procedures' to enforce the compliance with the Directives' demands. The previous examination illustrates that to effectively ensure a compliance with the reporting obligations, it is indispensable to implement monitoring and enforcement mechanisms that directly deal with the reports and their content. The EU's Directive also supports the proposal to open monitoring and enforcement mechanisms to affected stakeholders by stating that these national procedures should be available to all persons and legal entities that have a legitimate interest in ensuring the compliance with the reporting obligations.

Perspectives for NfR

NfR is only one strategy within a plethora of approaches that try to advance corporate accountability and therefore generally are aimed at preserving the autonomy of social systems or regimes against the expansive drive of the economic system.[84] Sufficient NfR legislation is an instrument with a unique potential to influence the rationality of the economic system and its actors. It can prepare the ground for countering economic forces that restrain or block the fulfilment of (economic, social, and cultural) human rights.[85] The case study pointed out that reports on non-financial information need to be embedded in a procedure that is open to relevant stakeholders and allows

83 Directive 2014/95/EU of 22 October 2014.

84 For an overview of strategies of implementation on the institutional level (within the economic system), the national level, and the international level see Deva, *Regulating Corporate Human Rights Violations*, pp. 200ff.

85 See Freeman, 'Conclusion: Reflections on the Theory and Practice of Economic and Social Rights', p. 386.

continuous negotiations about business conduct and the internal organisation of dealing with human rights related misconduct.

However, the proposed development of NfR would face considerable challenges that should be considered when interpreting the results presented here. Therefore, this paper should be seen as exploratory – serving as an impetus for further research that will widen the perspective on the development of NfR.

First, the precise arrangement of the proposed monitoring and enforcement mechanisms is a crucial question. Possible solutions vary from national to regional or global forms of organisation. The adjacency of regional actors to 'local' companies speaks in favour of a national or regional solution.

Second, the huge amount of potential reporters would be a major task to manage. The European Commission estimates that there are approximately 42,000 'large' companies operating in the EU. This significant fact raises the question if there could be a monitoring system that would be able to evaluate the huge amount of reports. In this regard, actual practices in fR could serve as a role model or even a point of contact. The practice of, for example, European and German monitoring and enforcement bodies in the field of fR presents an effective way to deal with the problem of the huge amount of potential reporters. A concrete monitoring and enforcement procedure will be launched on two occasions: First, there is an ad-hoc procedure that begins when a stakeholder informs the body about a specific misconduct. Second, there is a progressive proceeding of randomly evaluating reports of the obligated companies. In the case of Germany, there are two bodies that monitor and enforce the reporting obligation. The body of the first instance is competent for the actual monitoring and evaluation process. It is set up as a private association and composed of specialised representatives of all relevant stakeholders in the field of fR. The body of the second instance is governmental and capable of imposing sanctions and other mandatory orders on a reviewed company.[86]

Financial Reporting in practice demonstrates that selective procedures and a smart mix of governmental and private control in NfR can be the key for implementing an effective monitoring and enforcement mechanism.

[86] For the organisation of the German financial supervisory sytem see Bockmann, *Internationale Koordinierung nationaler Enforcement-Aktivitäten*. For the European financial supervisory system see Wymeersch, 'The reforms of the European Financial Supervisory System'.

Bibliography

Adams, C. A., 'The Ethical, Social and Environmental Reporting Performance Portrayal Gap', *Accounting, Auditing & Accountability Journal*, 17 (2004), 731–57.

Ahmed, T., and I. de Jesús Butler, 'The European Union and Human Rights: An International Law Perspective', *European Journal of International Law*, 17 (2006), 771–801.

Allianz Group, Economic Research & Corporate Development, 'Working Paper: Is Speculation to Blame for Rising Food Prices? – A Compilation of Facts and Findings', (18 June 2012), www.foodwatch.org/uploads/media/Allianz_Workingpaper06-2012_ger_01.pdf.

Amnesty International, 'Non-Financial Reporting: Amnesty International Position Paper', (April 2013), www.amnesty.org/en/documents/POL30/001/2013/en/.

Augenstein, D., 'Study of the Legal Framework on Human Rights and the Environment Applicable to European Enterprises Operating Outside the European Union' (University of Edinburgh, 2010).

Backer, L. C., 'Multinational Corporations, Transnational Law: The United Nations' Norms on the Responsibilities of Transnational Corporations as a Harbinger of Corporate Social Responsibility in International Law, *Columbia Human Rights Law Review*, 37 (2006), 287–389.

Bass, H. H., 'Finanzspekulation und Nahrungsmittelpreise: Anmerkungen zum Stand der Forschung', *Materialien des Wissenschaftsschwerpunktes „Globalisierung der Weltwirtschaft"*, 42 (2013).

Bockmann, R., *Internationale Koordinierung nationaler Enforcement-Aktivitäten: Eine kritische Analyse unter besonderer Berücksichtigung der Deutschen Prüfstelle für Rechnungslegung* (Wiesbaden: Gabler Verlag, 2012).

Boiral, O., 'Sustainability Reports as Simulacra? A Counter-Account of A and A+ GRI Reports', *Accounting, Auditing & Accountability Journal*, 26 (2013), 1036–71.

Brett, R., 'The Role of NGOs – An Overview' in G. Alfredsson et al. (eds.), *International Human Rights Monitoring Mechanisms – Essays in Honor of Jakob Th. Möller* (Leiden: Matinus Nijhoff Publishers, 2009), pp. 673–80.

Brown, H. S., M. de Jong, and D. L. Levy, 'Building Institutions Based on Information Disclosure: Lessons from GRI's Sustainability Reporting', *Journal of Cleaner Production*, 17 (2009), 571–80.

Chapman, R., and M. J. Milne, 'The Triple Bottom Line: How New Zealand Companies Measure Up', *Corporate Environmental Strategy: International Journal for Sustainable Business*, 11 (2004), 37–50.

Clapham, A., 'UN Human Rights Reporting Procedures: An NGO Perspective' in P. Alston and J. Crawford (eds.), *The Future of UN Human Rights Treaty Monitoring* (Cambridge University Press, 2000), pp. 175–98.

Dao, T. H. P., 'Monitoring Compliance with IFRS: Some Insights from the French Regulatory System', *Accounting in Europe*, 2 (2005), 107–35.

Davy, U., 'Welche rechtlichen Grundregeln müssen für einen wirksamen Menschenrechtsschutz gelten? Bedeutung gerichtlicher und außergerichtlicher Schutzverfahren' in C. Gusy (ed.), *Grundrechtsmonitoring – Chancen und Grenzen außergerichtlichen Menschenrechtsschutzes* (Baden-Baden: Nomos, 2011), pp. 238–64.

Deegan, C. and M. Rankin, 'Do Australian Companies Report Environmental News Objectively? An Analysis of Environmental Disclosures by Firms Prosecuted Successfully by the Environmental Protection Authority', *Accounting, Auditing & Accountability Journal*, 9 (1996), 50–67.

De Schutter, O., 'Food Commodities Speculation and Food Price Crises: Regulation to Reduce the Risks of Price Volatility', Briefing Note 02, (September 2010), www2.ohchr.org/english/issues/food/docs/Briefing_Note_02_September_2010_EN.pdf.

De Schutter, O., A. Eide, et al., 'Commentary to the Maastricht Principles on Extraterritorial Obligations of States in the Area of Economic, Social and Cultural Rights', *Human Rights Quarterly*, 34 (2012), 1084–1169.

Deva, S., *Regulating Corporate Human Rights Violations – Humanizing Business* (London and New York: Routledge, 2012).

European Coalition for Corporate Justice (ECCJ), 'EU Legislation on Non-financial Reporting by Companies – Position Paper of the European Coalition for Corporate Justice', www.corporatejustice.org/IMG/pdf/position_paper_final-2.pdf.

'Principles & Pathways: Legal Opportunities to Improve Europe's Corporative Accountability Framework', (November 2010), www.corporatejustice.org/IMG/pdf/eccj_principles_pathways_webuseblack.pdf.

European Commission, 'Impact Assessment – Accompanying the document Proposal for a Directive of the European Parliament and of the Council amending Council Directives 78/660/EEC and 83/349/EEC as regards disclosure of non-financial and diversity information by certain large companies and groups', SWD(2013) 127 final of 16 April 2013.

Fischer-Lescano, A., *Human Rights in Times of Austerity – The EU Institutions and the Conclusion of Memoranda of Understanding* (Baden-Baden: Nomos, 2013).

'Der Kampf um die Internetverfassung', *Juristenzeitung*, 69 (2014), 965–74.

Food and Agriculture Organisation of the United Nations (FAO), 'Number of Hungry People Rises to 963 Million', (9 December 2008), www.fao.org/news/story/en/item/8836/.

'The State of Food Insecurity in the World 2009 – Economic Crises – Impacts and Lessons Learned', (2009), www.fao.org/docrep/012/i0876e/i0876e00.htm.

'The State of Food Insecurity in the World 2013 – The Multiple Dimensions of Food Security', (2013), www.fao.org/docrep/018/i3434e/i3434e00.htm.

Foodwatch, 'foodwatch-Argumentationspapier zur Studie "Finanzspekulation und Nahrungsmittelpreise" von Prof. Hans-Heinrich Bass', (21 November 2013), www.foodwatch.org/uploads/media/2013-11-21_Argumentationspapier_Bass-Studie_01.pdf.

Freeman, M., 'Conclusion: Reflections on the Theory and Practice of Economic and Social Rights' in L. Minkler (ed.), *The State of Economic and Social Human Rights – A Global Overview* (Cambridge University Press, 2013), pp. 365–88.

Gallahofer, S., J. Haslam, E. Monk, and C. Roberts, 'The Emancipatory Potential of Online Reporting: The Case of Counter Accounting', *Accounting, Auditing & Accountability Journal*, 19 (2006), 681–718.

Germanwatch and Miseror, 'Nationaler Aktionsplan zur Umsetzung der UN-Leitprinzipien für Wirtschaft und Menschenrechte – Anforderungen an den Umsetzungsprozess in Deutschland', (July 2012), www.germanwatch.org/de/download/6648.pdf.

Global Reporting Initiative, 'G4 Sustainability Reporting Guidelines', (2013), www.globalreporting.org/resourcelibrary/GRIG4-Part1-Reporting-Principles-and-Standard-Disclosures.pdf.

Gray, R., 'Does Sustainability Reporting Improve Corporate Behaviour?: Wrong Question? Right Time?', *Accounting and Business Research*, 36 (2006), 65–88.

Hess, D., 'Social Reporting: A Reflexive Law Approach to Corporate Social Responsiveness', *Journal of Corporation Law*, 21 (1999), 41–84.

Ivanic, M., and W. Martin, 'Implications of Higher Global Food Prices for Poverty in Low Income Countries', *World Bank Policy Research Working Paper No. 4594*, (April 2008), www.elibrary.worldbank.org/doi/pdf/10.1596/1813-9450-4594.

Keller, H., 'Reporting Systems', *Max Planck Encyclopedia of Public International Law*, (June 2009).

Klein, E., *The Monitoring System of Human Rights Treaty Obligations – Colloquium Potsdam, 22/23. November 1996* (Berlin: Berlin Verlag Arno Spitz, 1998).

Kinley, D., and R. Chambers, 'The UN Human Rights Norms for Corporations: The Private Implications of Public International Law', *Human Rights Law Review*, 6 (2006), 447–97.

Krennerich, M., *Soziale Menschenrechte – Zwischen Recht und Politik* (Schwalbach: WochenschauVerlag, 2013).

Kretzmer, D., 'Human Rights, State Reports', *Max Planck Encyclopedia of Public International Law*, (October 2008).

Laufer, W. S., 'Social Accountability and Corporate Greenwashing', *Journal of Business Ethics*, 43 (2003), 253–61.

Liese, A., 'Epistula (non) Erubescit. Das Staatenberichtsverfahren als Instrument internationaler Rechtsdurchsetzung', *Die Friedens-Warte*, 59 (2006), 51–69.

Luhmann, N., *Die Gesellschaft der Gesellschaft* (Frankfurt a. M.: Suhrkamp, 1998).

Mahoney, L. S., L. Thorne, L. Cecil, and W. LaGore, 'A Research Note on Standalone Corporate Social Responsibility Reports: Signaling or Greenwashing?', *Critical Perspectives on Accounting*, 24 (2013), 350–59.

Maus, I., 'Perspektiven "reflexiven Rechts" im Kontext gegenwärtiger Deregulierungstendenzen', *Kritische Justiz*, 19 (1986), 390–405.

Mittal, A., 'The 2008 Food Price Crisis: Rethinking Food Security Policies', *UNCTAD: G-24 Discussion Paper Series*, 56 (2009), www.unctad.org/en/Docs/gdsmdpg2420093_en.pdf.

O'Dwyer, B., 'Stakeholder Democracy: Challenges and Contributions from Social Accounting', *Business Ethics: A European Review*, 14 (2005), 28–41.

Oxfam Deutschland, 'Oxfam Hintergrundpapier, Hungerroulette – Wie viel deutsche Finanzinstitute durch Nahrungsmittelspekulationen einnehmen', (May 2013), www.oxfam.de/files/20130507_hungerroulette.pdf.

'Mit Essen spielt man nicht! Die deutsche Finanzbranche und das Geschäft mit dem Hunger', (2013), www.oxfam.de/sites/www.oxfam.de/files/o_nms_2013_mb_web.pdf.

Pies, I., and T. Glauben, 'Wissenschaftliche Stellungnahme zum Argumentationspapier von Foodwatch', *Diskussionspapier Nr. 2013-26 des Lehrstuhls für Wirtschaftsethik an der Martin-Luther-Universität Halle-Wittenberg*, (2013), http://ethik.wiwi.uni-halle.de/forschung/news199874/.

Pies, I., and M. G. Will, 'Finanzspekulation mit Agrarrohstoffen – Analyse und Bewertung aus wirtschaftsethischer Sicht', *Diskussionspapier Nr. 2013-24 des Lehrstuhls für Wirtschaftsethik an der Martin-Luther-Universität Halle-Wittenberg*, (2013), http://wcms.itz.uni-halle.de/download.php?down=32275&elem=2728397.

The Regional Office for Europe of the UN High Commissioner for Human Rights, 'The EU and International Human Rights Law', (2008), www.europe.ohchr.org/Documents/Publications/EU_and_International_Law.pdf.

Reporting and Assurance Frameworks Initiative (RAFI), 'Draft UN Guiding Principles Reporting Framework', (November 2014), www.business-humanrights.org/sites/default/files/documents/DRAFT_UNGPReporting Framework_11Nov2014.pdf.

Scherer, A. G., G. Palazzo, and D. Seidl, 'Managing Legitimacy in Complex and Heterogeneous Environments: Sustainable Development in a Globalized World', *Journal of Management Studies*, 50 (2013), 259–84.

Skouloudisa, A., K. Evangelinosa, and F. Kourmousis, 'Assessing Non-financial Reports According to the Global Reporting Initiative Guidelines: Evidence from Greece', *Journal of Cleaner Production*, 18 (2010), 426–38.

Tilt, C. A., 'The Influence of External Pressure Groups on Corporate Social Disclosure – Some Empirical Evidence', *Accounting, Auditing & Accountability Journal*, 7 (1994), 47–72.

eubner, G., 'Die anonyme Matrix: Zu Menschenrechtsverletzungen durch "private" transnationale Akteure', *Der Staat*, 44 (2006), 161–87.

'Reflexives Recht – Entwicklungsmodelle des Rechts in vergleichender Perspektive', *Archiv für Rechts- und Sozialphilosophie*, 68 (1982), 13–59.

'Selbst-Konstitutionalisierung transnationaler Unternehmen? Zur Verknüpfung "privater" und "staatlicher" Corporate Codes of Conduct"' in S. v. Grundmann et al. (eds.), *Unternehmen, Markt und Verantwortung: Festschrift für Klaus Hopt* (Berlin: De Gruyter, 2010), pp. 1449–70.

Verfassungsfragmente (Frankfurt a. M.: Suhrkamp, 2012).

Jnited Nations Conference on Trade and Development (UNCTAD) and Arbeiterkammer Wien, 'Price Formation in Financialized commodity markets: The Role of Information. Study prepared by the Secretariat of the United Nations Conference on Trade and Development', (June 2011), www.unctad.org/en/docs/gds20111_en.pdf.

Wensen, K. v., W. Broer, J. Klein, and J. Knopf, 'The State of Play in Sustainability Reporting in the EU', (2011), www.ec.europa.eu/social/BlobServlet?docId=6727&langId=en.

Weißbrodt, D., and M. Kruger, 'Norms on the Responsibilities of Transnational Corporations and other Business Enterprises with Regard to Human Rights', *American Journal of International Law*, 97 (2003), 901–22.

Wymeersch, E., 'The reforms of the European Financial Supervisory System: An Overview', *European Company and Financial Law Review*, 7 (2010), 240–65.

PART III

Collisions otherwise

Law and the collision with non-legal spheres

9

A critical theory of transnational regimes

Creeping managerialism and the quest for a destituent power

KOLJA MÖLLER

'To radically shift regime behaviour we must think clearly and boldly, for if we have learned anything, it is that regimes do not want to be changed'.[1] In his text 'Conspiracy as Governance', the whistle-blower Julian Assange uses the term regime in an irritatingly generalizing manner. The transnational governance of security apparatuses, the exchange of information and digital surveillance technology – in Assange's view all of this seems to characterize an overwhelming 'conspiracy'. Here, different functional logics become blurred, ranging from the power-driven state system to the profit interests of private Internet companies. They amount to a higher-ranking regime of regimes. This use of the term regime stands obviously in sharp contrast to recent academic discussions. In the latter context, it is supposed to illuminate novel political constellations beyond the nation-state. In particular, the term refers to the diversity of legal regimes or specific policy regimes. They cannot be seen as a new super unit but as a fragmented constellation.[2] In normative regards, the debate also involves the questions of how to deal with this diversity; how regimes can be kept responsive; and what coordinative rules are advisable when it comes to regime-collisions. The obvious lacuna in this strand of discussion consists in an under-theorized normative twist. Either all this boils down to a merely descriptive theory that sheds light on transnational regimes without any critical engagement with the fragmented orders; or a normative impulse enters the stage that advocates responsiveness and coordination. This message, however, runs the risk of legitimizing

1 Assange, 'Conspirancy as Governance', p. 1.

2 Cf. Alter and Meunier, 'The Politics of International Regime Complexity'; Koskenniemi, 'The Politics of International Law – 20 Years Later'.

already existing regimes, since the overall idea consists in taming and regulating regime interaction. In that sense, it can lead to a creeping managerialism that tries to create order where disorder reigns. To put it more clearly: Is regime theory a 'party of order' in postmodern guise?[3]

At a minimum, this orderliness leads to a momentous argumentative shortcut. This can be explained when the central remedies to fragmentation are scrutinized. The emphasis on better coordinative rules or intensified dialogue insinuates that an exaggerated process of differentiation causes negative side effects. While the regimes are irrevocable and normatively viable, the process of differentiation must be domesticated. However, this point misses the fact that *regimes themselves* play an active part in the collisions or that they might even cause them in the first place. They offer no neutral third meta-site that would instil world society with deliberation and dialogue.

In contrast, in the following I want to explore whether a critical theory of transnational regimes is conceivable. My main thesis is that we need a perspective sensitive to the role and analysis of power. The landscape of transnational regimes is not only an expression of functional differentiation but also of new hegemonic conditions. This insight opens up scope for critique. Instead of merely restricting the inherent logics of regimes – for example, through conflict of laws rules or power-limiting constitutionalization – I will argue that counter-hegemonic effects only arise when the respective rationalities are exposed to a radical critique and countervailing powers.

First, I scrutinize approaches to transnational regimes in political and legal studies, and reveal the fact that they abstain from a wider critique of their subject. In contrast, the regime analysis as carried out by systems theory emphasized a programme of immanent critique. However, the latter still carries managerialist traces, as I show in a second step. I therefore propose a revision in a third step, which is inspired by theories of hegemony. It is not only able to better illuminate relations of domination, but it also radicalizes the mode of critique significantly: It shifts the constitutional issue to the regimes' outside, namely to the challenge of constitutionalising destituent power(s) on the transnational terrain.

[3] Marx, 'Der 18. Brumaire des Louis Bonaparte (1852)', p. 160.

Creeping managerialism

Regimes have become an important analytical category.[4] This applies especially to novel patterns of order that emerge beyond the nation-state. They can no longer be addressed by the simple juxtaposition of the nation-state and the international community or state and non-state actors. However, a close examination of the different approaches reveals that so far it widely remains open to what extent the concept of regime can be used for critical purposes or whether it ultimately entails a managerialist bias when it comes to the problem of how to generally deal with new patterns of order.

The discipline of International Relations (IR) has so far given the concept of regime the most prominent treatment. Here, it serves to elucidate issue-specific patterns of interstate cooperation. The seminal definition states that regimes rely on an interplay of 'principles, norms, rules and decision-making procedures around which actor expectations converge in a given subject area'.[5] While well into the 1980s, the orthodox view on the international state system stressed nation-states' quest for power, the rather liberal regime theory proposed a different emphasis. Since states are faced with challenges that can only be solved together, in cooperation, they develop issue-specific institutions on the international level.[6] As a result, such regimes do not enforce the narrow interest of particular states. On the contrary, they have a socializing effect on state behaviour. They reshape expectations by incorporating the states in procedures of justification and monitoring. In this way, they may well change behaviour. Insofar as regime theory entails the hope that multilateralism enters the stage, it exerts a civilizing effect on the international community and safeguards normative goods.[7]

The weakness of this approach is that it remains a state-centric one. Regimes seem to be constituted by the state system, but we can observe patterns of cooperation that cannot be solely derived from interstate relations: Liberal IR theory hitherto largely ignores legal regimes, private regimes or aesthetic regimes of visibility. Julian Assange's initial example of the surveillance regime shows, for instance, that especially state and private actors tend to intersect more and more.

[4] For an overview, cf. Dimitrova, Egermann, Holert, Kastner, and Schaffner, *Regime*.
[5] Krasner, 'Structural Causes and Regime Consequences', p. 185.
[6] Cf. Hasenclever, Mayer, and Rittberger, *Theories of International Regimes*.
[7] Keohane, Macedo, and Moravcsik, 'Democracy-Enhancing Multilateralism'; Slaughter, *A New World Order*.

Against this backdrop, the normative aspect of regime theory becomes rather dim. While general hope existed that transnational regimes in different policy arenas would ultimately safeguard normative goods, such as the rule of law and human rights, the orders beyond the nation-state carry out a 'dark' side as well. At least in the case of the surveillance regime, no issue-oriented multilateralism has evolved that would popularize the rule of law worldwide. The surveillance regime does not seem to tame national executives but rather to enhance the power potential of states and multinational companies.[8]

Compared to IR and the idiosyncratic take on the normative force of state cooperation, the legal debate chooses a different starting point. In this context, the concept of regime is meant to identify specific areas of international and transnational juridification. This applies to international environmental law, diplomatic law or commercial law.[9] There is probably no branch of research in which the concept of regime has found such broad reception as in the debate about the transnationalization of law. The latter can draw on confirmatory trends in case law, and the argument often refers to a judgment of the International Court of Justice (ICJ). It took the view in the debate about the treatment of prisoners (Tehran hostage case) that international diplomatic law needed to be interpreted as a so-called 'self-contained regime'.[10] Echoing this line of thought, the transnationalization of law is characterized by multiple legal regimes in diverse areas: 'Contemporary international law ... resembles a dense web of overlapping and detailed prescriptions in subject areas as diverse as environmental protection, human rights and international trade'.[11] The report of the International Law Commission (ILC) on 'The Fragmentation of International Law' had turned special attention to this circumstance. It identifies the differentiation of regimes and a concomitant fragmentation of international law:

> What once appeared to be governed by 'general international law' has become the field of operation for such specialist systems as 'trade law', 'human rights law', 'environmental law', 'law of the sea', 'European law' and even such exotic and highly specialized knowledge as 'investment law' or 'international refugee law', etc. – each possessing their own principles and institutions. The problem, as lawyers have seen it, is that such

[8] See Fischer-Lescano in this volume. [9] Berman, *Global Legal Pluralism.*

[10] ICJ, *Case Concerning United States Diplomatic and Consular Staff in Teheran (United States of America* v. *Iran)* [1980] ICJ Rep 3.

[11] Simma and Pulkowski, 'Of Planets and the Universe', p. 484.

> specialized law-making and institution-building tends to take place with relative ignorance of legislative and institutional activities in the adjoining fields and of the general principles and practices of international law. The result is conflicts between rules or rule-systems, deviating institutional practices and, possibly, the loss of an overall perspective on the law.[12]

his approach has far-reaching consequences as there is no longer just terplay between general international law and special rule-systems; ther, conflictive situations emerge over and over again, where general ternational law and legal regimes collide. The report distinguishes tuations in which different interpretations of international law clash, ternational law stands in tension with specific legal regimes or even ifferent special legal regimes clash.[13]

A normative response to these conflicts suggests itself: To counter ragmentation, a taming process needs to be established that constrains he respective regime-collisions. Here, the legal vocabulary draws on the otion of constitutionalism: While the constitution had the task to limit he exercise of political authority in the nation-state, a similar process is ow to be initiated when it comes to regimes.

In this context, two variants can be identified: The *first* variant per-eives legal regimes as quasi-secondary constitutions that emerge as part f the general constitutionalization of international law.[14] They are ubordinated to international law or at least brought into a relation to t. Hope rests with meta-rules, which aim at regulating the relationship etween regimes and general international law. Metaphorically speaking, his is about the constitutionalization of a network that has its centre still n international public law. Coordination rules are needed which could nanage the different sites of conflict.[15] The other, *second* variant egarding the constitutional issue offers an internal perspective. The eneral trend towards constitutionalization cannot be confined to general nternational law alone. What can be observed is that legal regimes levelop themselves their own internal secondary norms and legal hier-rchies. Alec Stone Sweet, for instance, suggests that treaty regimes, like he European Union (EU), European Convention on Human Rights

2 International Law Commission (ILC), 'Fragmentation of International Law: Difficulties arising from the Diversification and Expansion of International Law. Report of the Study Group of the International Law Commission' (13 April 2006) UN Doc A/CN.4/L.682, p. 11.

13 Ibid., p. 30.

14 Kleinlein, *Konstitutionalisierung im Völkerrecht*, pp. 63ff.

5 See Viellechner in this volume.

(ECHR) and World Trade Organization (WTO), develop a constitutional dimension, since 'they are constituted, like the systems of virtually all nation-states today, by written meta-norms or codified secondary rules'.[16] In this sense, constitutionalism is not bound to states and the international community, but can be identified in different forms:

> Simple power-based balance of power arrangements anchored one extreme, the European Union (EU) occupied the opposite extreme, and other regime forms, including the General Agreement on Tariffs and Trade (GATT) and the then-new World Trade Organization (WTO), occupied the middle ground. The continuum captures three dimensions: the extent of hierarchical primacy and entrenchment of the constituting norms; the degree of precision and formality of legal obligation; and the scope of independent, organizational capacity to monitor compliance with, and to enforce, obligations.[17]

In this way, it becomes possible to envisage an internal constitutionalization. It does not amount to a super-constitution 'from above' but operates through self-restraint 'from below'.

With a view to the existing landscape of transnational regimes, these aspirations about juridification tend to be a dubious endeavour. First and foremost, the transnational regimes that were involved in the great crises of world society have rarely shown a low degree of juridification. The best example is the role of the economic regime. For a long time it has been observed that world trade and the banking sector are highly juridified. But contrary to the emphasis on self-restraint, the legal arrangements facilitated crisis tendencies in the world economy and provided a fertile ground for financial accumulation. We can identify a 'new constitutionalism', which enshrines market-liberal programmes with a focus on free trade, investor protection and austerity in higher-ranking norms.[18] This tendency has contributed significantly to the current crisis tendencies.

As different as the approaches in IR and legal debates might be, it is striking to see that a kind of creeping managerialism shines through. The idiosyncrasies of the respective discipline are paraded in order to insert a normative twist: on the one hand, the rationalizing concomitants of administrative statehood at the international level (IR), and on the other hand, the civilizing force of juridification (legal studies).

16 Sweet, 'Constitutionalism, Legal Pluralism, and International Regimes', p. 631.

17 Ibid., p. 622.

18 See Gill and Cutler, *New Constitutionalism and World Order*; Kennedy, 'Law and the Political Economy of the World'.

Critical systems theory

A more promising perspective stems from critical systems theory approaches.[19] They do not explain the origin of regimes with the internationalization of law or policy alone; instead Niklas Luhmann's thesis about the transition to a world society becomes the starting point. In the 1970s Luhmann had already speculated that functional differentiation does not stop at nation-state borders. He observed a transnationalization of functional social systems. This is associated with a change in leadership. In the transition to a world society, 'a clear prevalence of cognitive, adaptive expectations eager to learn' is striking, 'while normative, morality demanding and prescriptive expectations retreat'.[20] Accordingly, the landscape of transnational regimes is understood as an effect that is caused by an underlying dynamic of functional differentiation. Spelling this out, at least three dimensions of regimes become apparent. First, regimes are not only legal or policy-specific units. The systems-theoretical approach assumes that transnational social spaces emerge: like the world economy, world politics or world science. Special legal matters appear not only as an internal differentiation within the legal system, but also as a surface phenomenon that is nurtured by a more fundamental social evolution. This is why regimes have to be seen as *social regimes* that relate to the entirety of a given social area.[21] To use an expression of the sociologist Saskia Sassen, the communication of different functional systems 'assemble' under the overarching rationality of the respective regime.[22] They provide sites for institutional coagulations (institutions like the World Health Organization (WHO), WTO, United Nations (UN), etc.) and overarching rationalities. These rationalities encompass criteria for assessment, logics, or mind-sets, which always over-determine the internal communication structures. This is the result of a type of secondary encoding: a marker that assigns it to the respective regimes supplements the communicative coding within functional systems. Accordingly, legal communication can play a role within the world economic regime, the environmental regime, the science regime or other regimes; political communication is observable in the international

19 Fischer-Lescano and Teubner, 'Regime-Collisions'; for the critical systems theory approach, cf. Fischer-Lescano, 'Critical Systems Theory'; Amstutz and Fischer-Lescano, *Kritische Systemtheorie*.

20 Luhmann, 'Die Weltgesellschaft', p. 68.

21 Fischer-Lescano and Teubner, 'Regime-Collisions', pp. 1023ff.

22 Sassen, *Territory, Authority, Rights*.

state system, but also in the scientific system and so forth. The central mechanism, which constitutes the inner coagulations, is structural coupling. This is the case 'if a system presupposes certain features of its environment on an ongoing basis and relies on them structurally'.[23] The co-evolution of different functional systems establishes mutual linkages under the umbrella of a broader regime rationality. It is obvious that the relationship between institution and communication becomes fuzzy. It is, for instance, questionable whether the talk about a world economic regime encompasses all communication in world society related to the economy or simply denotes a nucleus of already existing institutions and agreements. Does the world economic regime only consist of the WTO, the International Monetary Fund (IMF) and the World Bank? Does it extend to the private *lex mercatoria*? Or does it bundle – in strict systems-theoretical terms – all economy-related communication in world society, like, for instance, protests in the form of consumer boycotts? We will have to return to the aspect of fuzziness at a later point.

Second, and furthermore, regimes have a legal dimension. In social spheres expectations have to be stabilized. This in turn leads to the trend of juridification. Thereby, law changes its form. It is not necessarily linked to the state's monopoly on the use of force. In transnational regimes non-state legal phenomena gain significance:

> The focus in law-making is shifting to private regimes, that is, to agreements among global players, to private market regulation through multinational enterprises, internal rule-making within international organizations, inter-organizational negotiating systems and worldwide standardization processes. The dominant sources of law are now to be found at the peripheries of law, at the boundaries with other sectors of world society that are successfully engaging in regional competition with the existing centres of law-making – national parliaments, global legislative institutions and inter-governmental agreements.[24]

Regimes develop their own decision-making mechanisms, law-making and dispute resolution. These indicated trends can especially be observed in the world economy. In this area, standardized contracts, private arbitration and common law arrangements constitute the engine of a *lex mercatoria* beyond direct state control.[25] This somewhat hyperbolic emphasis on the private sphere may be exaggerated, but it leads us

[23] Luhmann, *Das Recht der Gesellschaft*, p. 441.
[24] Teubner, 'Privatregimes', p. 439 (English version: Teubner, 'Global Private Regimes').
[25] Cf. Cutler, *Private Power and Global Authority*; Renner, 'Death by Complexity'.

recognize that hybrid structures, where nation-state apparatuses teract with international institutions, multinational companies, non-overnmental organizations, lobby groups and social movements play a ndamental role.[26] The hybrid nature of these patterns of order is gnificant, because an approach based on the private/public distinction isses the subject. Demands for subordinating the regimes to the inter-ational political system ignore, for instance, that state apparatuses are eavily involved.

Third, and finally, regimes are also sites at which politics takes place. et, while many regimes are far away from copying nation-state politics, ey establish relations of power, namely relations of power superiority/ower inferiority, even in distance to the political system: Interests ollide, decisions are made or appealed, durable relations of superordina-ion and subordination are stabilized. This leads to a broadening of the ange of the political: So far, the external relations of regimes were the articular focus of attention, that is, their competitive relationship to ther regimes and respective social environments.[27] In this context, both olitical conflict constellations and discursive strategies were explored hat aim at establishing the primacy of certain regimes – such as the vorld economy or security policy. This approach, however, needs to be omplemented by further dimensions. After all, politics does not only ccur in the external relations of regimes but also on their inside. There is truggle about the actual purpose of the respective regime: How proced-ures and decision-making are designed; or which actors are influential nd which are not. And moreover, the 'hidden' politics of private egimes, which is rarely discussed in public, also needs to be considered. There certainly is an evolutionary 'politics', which is already about to ement internal power positions.[28] However, this kind of politics is omewhat more volatile than it was in the framework of nation-state onstitutionalism. 'Politics' seems here rather to correspond more closely

26 This brings them in proximity to theories of empire, which Michael Hardt and Antonio Negri also conceive as 'mixed constitutions'; for their reception of systems theory, see Hardt and Negri, *Commonwealth*, pp. 373ff.; cf. also the mélange of state and private regimes in Scholz and Wolf, 'Ordnungswandel durch Umkehrung einer Normenhier-archie'.

27 Koskenniemi, 'The Politics of International Law – 20 Years Later', pp. 12ff.

28 The best example for this development is obviously the recent debate about private arbitration, cf. Cutler, 'Legal Pluralism as the "Common Sense" of Transnational Capit-alism'.

to what the recent theoretical discussion has termed 'the political'.[29] The latter comes to the fore when issues of dominance and subordination are addressed, or the logic of a regime is questioned. Thus, politics is at least in part decoupled from the state and located within the regimes.

This triple approach has implications for constitutional prospects. Indeed, they cannot simply be reduced to internal legal hierarchies. The decisive criterion is a double reflexivity:

> Auto-constitutional regimes are defined by their duplication of reflexivity. Secondary rule-making in law is combined with defining fundamental rationality principles in an autonomous social sphere. Making the distinction between such societal constitutions and simple regimes even clearer: regimes dispose of a union of primary and secondary legal norms, and their *primary rule-making* is structurally coupled with the creation of substantive social norms in a specific societal sector.[30]

It is therefore essential that regimes do not only have a social, political and legal dimension; rather, all three dimensions are structurally coupled and thus establish a regime-specific reflexivity, which in turn is stabilized in the medium of higher-ranking law. It refers not only 'reflexively' to law, in the sense of a higher-ranking law of law-making, but also to power relations within the regime, its rationality and relations with its social environments.

Rationality maximization

In the next step, the system-theoretical observation takes an explicitly critical turn. Regimes undergo a momentous process that tries to maximize their inherent rationality. The motif of alienation is invoked. Area-specific rationalities become detached from their social environments. They create their respective 'gods',[31] which they equip with all-round problem-solving competence. The global economic regime is built around the expansionist logic of financial accumulation, the state system around the expansion of power claims in security policy and the science system generalizes a type of rationality that disqualifies traditional bodies of knowledge. Regimes coagulate into 'anonymous matrices' that follow a

[29] Cf. Teubner, *Constitutional Fragments*, pp. 114ff.; Christodoulidis, 'On the Politics of Societal Constitutionalism'.

[30] Fischer-Lescano and Teubner, 'Regime-Collisions', p. 1016.

[31] Following Max Weber's polytheism argument, Fischer-Lescano and Teubner, 'Regime-Collisions', p. 1006.

ɔtalizing logic.[32] They stamp their respective inherent rationalities onto ʳorld society. This invokes a figure that resonates less with Luhmann's ystems theory than Marx's critique of political economy: The productive ɔrces of social evolution collapse into destructive forces. They destroy ther societal conditions for communication or prevent them from ever merging.[33] In this respect, a hegemonic trend exists, an urge towards niversalization:

> . . . the point is that regimes such as the "international trade system", the "climate change system" or the "security system" are all engaged in universalization strategies, trying to make their special knowledge and interest appear as the general knowledge and general interest, a commonplace consciousness.[34]

nstead of praising regimes as embryonic forms of a civilizing adminisrative rule, the question arises of how to put a stop to this trend. How an the alienated regimes be constrained? How it is possible to open hem up for their social environments?

In that regard, the vocabulary of constitutionalism can be mobilized gain. The assumption is that constitutional reflexivity does not necesarily lead to a managerialist praise of order. It can also serve as a gateway o the demands of the social environments. The possibility of a 're-entry' ɔrovides decisive leeway.[35] While no super- or meta-constitution of egimes is conceivable, it might be possible to tame the compulsion to naximize through countervailing powers:

> . . . external social forces, which are not only state instruments of power, but also legal rules, and "civil society" countervailing powers from other contexts, media, public discussion, spontaneous protest, intellectuals, social movements, NGOs or trade union power, etc., should apply such massive pressure on the function systems so that internal self-limitations are configured and become truly effective.[36]

n such a hybrid setting, environmental rationalities can enter the stage nd undermine the hegemonic urge, so some hope.

32 Teubner, 'The Anonymous Matrix'.

33 This can unfold in two steps: 1. Hegemonic regimes colonize their social environments by universalizing their rationality. 2. However, since they in turn live off other systems' functions and their environments, 'death by complexity' can occur (cf. Renner, 'Death by Complexity'), since they cannot ensure their own reproduction.

34 Koskenniemi, 'Hegemonic Regimes', p. 315.

35 Cf. Luhmann, 'Observing Re-entries'.

36 Teubner, 'A Constitutional Moment?', p. 13.

For this constellation, which combines a systems-theoretical approach with a postmodern reconstruction of power-limiting constitutionalism, a price has to be paid, however. It comes in the form of restricted spaces for critique and politicization. All the constitutional prospects are meant to correct functional self-reference in an immanent mode, but offer hardly any space for fundamental questioning – hence, for a critique that does not only ask whether the law of the respective regime is just or whether its political constitution does justice to the general interest,[37] but that also asks whether a particular regime, its law or policies are necessary at all. This restriction in articulating critical concerns is mainly due to a normative reading of functional differentiation. It is assumed that critique and politicization can also trigger a totalizing dynamic, not less destructive than the regimes' universalizing urge.[38] Accordingly, the cycles of counter-power have a relatively a clear and restricted task: They should block colonizing effects on the social environments and thereby allow functional differentiation to play out its normative potential, namely the advent of diverse autonomous social sectors. However, what seems unattractive and even dangerous is to question regimes fundamentally or even to revoke them. With regard to the economic constitution, for example, the abandoning of the economic growth is rejected as potentially de-differentiating. Criticism should only attack 'self-destructive growth-excesses', since 'a functioning monetised economy is reliant on a certain compulsion to grow'.[39] What becomes discernible here is that the hybrid constitutionalization is not meant to revoke the respective regime. It cannot revoke it because this would undermine the evolutionary course of functional differentiation as a sort of 'fall of mankind' (evolutionary argument). And it may not evoke it because this falls prey to de-differentiation (normative argument). Consequently, critique always follows an *a posteriori* logic. The political is, as Luhmann had once polemicized with regard to protest movements, reminiscent of 'vaulting on someone else's horses'.[40] It draws parasitically on system differentiation.

In this respect, critical systems theory provides a link to social theory and opens up room for critique. Nevertheless, the central position of

[37] This point refers to the contingency formula of the respective functional system; with regard to the political system, cf. Luhmann, *Die Politik der Gesellschaft*, pp. 118ff.; with regard to the law, cf. Gonçalves, *Il Rifugio delle Aspettative*.

[38] For the role of social movements, cf. Luhmann, *Protest*, pp. 176ff.

[39] Teubner, *Constitutional Fragments*, p. 99.

[40] Luhmann, *Protest*, p. 188.

functional differentiation allows the 'party of order' to creep in: Functional differentiation appears suddenly not only as an observable reality, but rather as a normative ideal of 'civil societal liberty'.[41] Thus, differentiation is in the end equipped with normative potential. It rejects a totalizing critique, which not only aims at the paradoxes in the application of the respective codes but also at their foundational paradox.[42] This leads to restrictions: System-theoretical regime analysis focuses on hegemonic regimes but has yet to acquire the tools to understand differentiation itself as a part of hegemonic conditions. The scope of critique remains centred on power-limiting constitutionalization. In the next step, I suggest a revision, which is inspired by theories of hegemony. This should make it easier to discern the regime collisions and insert the potential for a radical critique into the theoretical horizon.

Hegemony

It was already alluded to above that transnational regimes tend to carry out a hegemonic dimension. However, the concept of hegemony is too multifaceted to locate it only at the phenomenal level.[43] For this reason, a reconceptualization is required that introduces the concept of hegemony in the theory of transnational regimes.[44]

In the post-Marxist take on the concept of hegemony, as it was developed by Chantal Mouffe and Ernesto Laclau, we find a promising approach in order to reconceptualize the analysis of transnational regimes. Of course, Laclau and Mouffe are no systems theorists; in their first joint publication, they heavily criticize a Marxist functionalism that tries to derive social contradictions directly from the rationality of the economic system.[45] They read Marxist categories, such as hegemony,

41 Teubner, 'Privatregimes', pp. 448ff. 42 Cf. Horst, 'Politiken der Entparadoxierung'.

43 In the 1920s, the Italian communist Antonio Gramsci stressed with his concept of 'hegemony' the point that the bourgeoisie generates its rule in modern society with the help of a complex interplay of coercive and integrative mechanisms. In particular, it seemed to be able to generalize its worldview through intellectual and cultural leadership. By creating a wide civil societal terrain, which opens the cultural space for the generalization of different world views, coercive rule is supplemented by relations of leadership, cf. Gramsci, *Gefängnishefte – Kritische Gesamtausgabe*, Heft 13, § 37, p. 1610.

44 For a similar approach, cf. Stäheli, *Sinnzusammenbrüche*.

45 Laclau and Mouffe, *Hegemony and Socialist Strategy*. The anti-essentialism does not yet recognize sufficiently that it leads back into the economy. After Laclau and Mouffe insist that respective societal formations refer back to discursive articulations, which coagulate into a permanent 'sedimented objectivity' (Laclau, *New Reflections on the Revolution of*

class, or contradiction before the backdrop of contemporary post-structuralism and de-constructivism. This constitutes a fundamentally different approach. They do not locate the concept of hegemony at the level of class struggle. They shift it to the level of discourse.[46] Laclau and Mouffe draw on post-structuralist assumptions about the indeterminacy of the social. Yet, they add another step in their argument that more clearly emphasizes the aspect of meaning construction and unity. Their considerations transcend the point that the social is characterized by a differential mode of meaning-creation. The playing field of discourse only opens up because a 'construction of nodal points which partly fix meaning' takes place.[47] The historically unchangeable priority of particular spheres that determine the social directly (economy, state, law, culture, etc.) vanishes in this perspective. But nevertheless, it is possible to analyse nodal points that shape the respective social formation. This reading of the concept of hegemony re-introduces a distinction that for systems theory actually belonged to the old-European *problématique* of stratified societies. It situates the 'part/whole' distinction in the discursive process. Parts (discursive units) claim to represent the whole but fail to generate unity. The relation of part and whole should not be understood as if a whole pre-existed that would only need to be reassembled; it must be seen as a performative act. Since parts claim to represent the whole, they exert an 'ecological dominance', which can, however, never become 'total'. The logic of hegemony produces an imaginary fullness, which remains out of reach. The whole remains unavailable.[48]

If this perspective is applied to regimes, the previously identified gaps can be addressed. The universalizing trend is given a systematic place. The outlined expansionist urge is thus not a purely negative externality. It is not a degenerated turbo self-reference, which eclipses and corrupts 'actual' functional differentiation. The expansionist urge is simply

Our Time, p. 35), it immediately suggests itself to elucidate how a systemic character and a permanent interaction between the economy, law and the state emerge. So far, the post-Marxist discussion often tends to uncover so-called 'essentialism' instead of using the specific theoretical reservoir, e.g., in view of a post-Marxist theory of capitalism, a theory of law, the state, etc.

46 Laclau and Mouffe, *Hegemony and Socialist Strategy*, pp. 93ff.; for a research programme and some applications, see Howarth, Norval and Stavrakakis, *Discourse Theory and Political Analysis*.

47 Laclau and Mouffe, *Hegemony and Socialist Strategy*, p. 113.

48 Laclau develops this argument in a kind of parallel move to the psychoanalytic theory of Jacques Lacan, which also assumes a constitutive lack as driving force of subject formation, cf. Laclau, *On Populist Reason*, pp. 115ff.

evidence for a logic of hegemony that is always already at work in social relations. In this way, the transition to the world society can be read as a *constellation of fragmented hegemony*. It is not only the site at which regimes differentiate but also where new relations of domination and subordination occur. This has three key consequences.

The *first consequence* is that fragmentation is not only an effect of functional differentiation. Rather, it must be understood as part of contested social change. What we call globalization today was decisively shaped by the crisis of the welfare state and the collapse of real-existing socialism.[49] In this vein, post-Marxist studies outline how the combination of state-regulated market conditions, mass democracies and male breadwinner models drifted into crisis from the 1970s and 1980s onwards and paved the way for a market-liberal turn.[50] This very historical trend has triggered the recent surge of globalization, not functional differentiation alone.

The *second consequence* concerns the relationship of regimes between each other. It is not equality or creative plurality that determines the relation of transnational regimes to their social environments, but hegemonic relations, which can be described as *relations of ecological dominance* in the parlance of systems theory.[51] The fact remains that world society is not only characterized by diversity or new complexity, but also by persistent asymmetries. They are the result of processes of hegemony formation, which are of course always met by counter-forces and blockades.

This suggests a correction. Regimes do not develop their bias *a posteriori*. From the very beginning, they are involved in hegemonic struggles. Consequently, not all regimes are the same. Particular regimes succeed in establishing themselves as a 'nodal point', but others fail to do so. While every regime shows a totalizing aspect, not all of them are equally able to maximize self-rationality. Hence, one has to distinguish among hegemonic, non-hegemonic and even counter-hegemonic regimes. This implies a number of methodological challenges when confronted with the question of how such hegemonic relations can be identified.[52] If we

49 Cox, *Production, Power, and World Order*, pp. 274ff.

50 Jessop, *The Future of the Capitalist State*, pp. 56ff.

51 Cf. the concept of 'ecological dominance' in Jessop, *State Power*, 26ff; for similar attempts to conceptualize functional differentiation as capitalist society, see Bachur, *Kapitalismus und funktionale Differenzierung*; Schimank, 'Die Moderne'.

52 See the works of the so-called 'Essex School of Discourse Analysis': cf. Howarth, Norval and Stavrakakis, *Discourse Theory and Political Analysis*.

draw on the various contributions to the regime debate there is much evidence that the current world economic regime and security regime play such a dominant role, yet not the world health regime or the rights of indigenous peoples.[53] This has far-reaching ramifications for the question from what point hegemonic trends can be criticized or restricted.

The *third consequence* is an expanded perspective on the internal regime-constitution. It is not only that the 'world economy' or 'states' generalize their logics; rather, the relationship between part and whole takes effect, after all the logic of hegemony is also effective within regimes. The best example of this is surely the world economic regime. Recent developments indicate not only a general trend towards economization but also the dominance of specific economic *policies*, oriented towards free trade and the protection of property rights. They are even given the status of higher-ranking constitutional norms in treaties and case law, and are therefore no longer questioned.[54] As part they eclipse the whole of regime-specific rationality. The already mentioned fuzziness – that regimes can be seen as overarching communication structures and as specific ensembles of institutions and treaties – just reveals the fact that specific programmes and projects (and not the 'economy' or the 'security' generally) carry out a hegemonic dimension.

This revision shifts the perspective considerably. Regime collisions or interactions have to be examined for how far they reflect the relationship between hegemony and counter-hegemony. And the internal state of regimes, that is, 'economy', 'environment', 'security', is not simply given but itself the subject of social conflict. Differentiation is consequently not an invisible hand and first mover, it is itself the result of conflicts over hegemony.

Destituent power: from societal to plebeian constitutionalism

This leads to a changed conception of transnational constitutionalism. While the systems-theoretical diagnosis had introduced its normative twist at the point where a constitution-typical reflexivity enables social environments to be taken into account, here a more sceptical approach

[53] Cf. Kennedy, 'Law and the Political Economy of the World'; Schneiderman, *Constitutionalizing Economic Globalization*; Brunkhorst, *Critical Theory of Legal Revolutions*; Streeck, *Gekaufte Zeit*.

[54] Gill and Cutler, *New Constitutionalism and World Order*.

omes to the fore. The point is that the evolutionary emergence of gimes has consequences for the form of constitutionalism. At least in egemonic regimes, a strong tendency exists to back up the substantial ocus on a correct policy with higher-ranking law. Specific projects and ubstantial ideas of a 'good order' eclipse as part the whole of ne regime.[55] They are tied down in the medium of constitutionalism. he distinction between codes and programmes becomes blurred. The urrent world economic regime, for instance, is biased towards free trade nd investment protection. The security regime is not about 'security' in eneral terms but is mainly concerned with monitoring and combating errorism. This superposition of codes and programmes has serious onsequences. It restricts the ability of a regime to respond to external ressure. Systems theory assumed that the particular programmes are the ite where openings vis-à-vis the social environments take place.[56] But if he new form of constitutionalism reduces the scope for social conflicts nd collisions to be processed adequately or to become visible at all, it eals off social sectors from potential alternatives and immunizes them gainst environmental demands. Transnational constitutionalism is thus no guarantor of openness and transcendence, but of closure. Substantive rogrammes restrict juridico-political reflexivity, that is, the regime's elf-referentiality. It cuts them off from inquiry. Thus, fundamental uestions – about the purpose of economic activity or the purpose of he security policies – are relegated to the outside of transnational onstitutionalism.[57]

That does, however, not mean that reflexivity would not matter. On he contrary, transnational regimes make use of reflexivity quite often nd stage openings for the respective environments. In the run-up to the inancial crisis, for example, the drafting of the Basel II guidelines in he area of banking regulation was opened up for comments from civil ociety.[58] In its Blairite market-liberal heyday, the European Union ollowed the principles of a comprehensive citizen dialogue and tested

55 The parallel to the early modern 'Policey' is obvious, see Somek, 'Administration without Sovereignty', p. 273.

56 In systems theoretical parlance: 'Based on the changeability of the code, the program level can be understood at the site at which alternative solutions are tested and different articulations of the code offered. Programs serve as a supplement of the code by specifying its application' (Stäheli, *Sinnzusammenbrüche*, p. 283). For this opening function of programme, cf. also Opitz, *An der Grenze des Rechts*, pp. 50ff.

57 For similar observations, cf. Chimni, 'Between Co-option and Resistance'.

58 Barr and Miller, 'Global Administrative Law'.

this approach in various policy areas.[59] Participation opportunities for civil societal actors have emerged in the WTO.[60] Last but not least, the academic debate has tried to address these processes with the concept of governance steering and stakeholder participation. However, these mechanisms exert no limiting but rather legitimacy-generating functions. They incorporate social environments. They breed their own subject of legitimation, their own 'people' – a trend which the young Karl Marx already saw at work in Hegel's attempt of constitutionalizing the societal estates: 'Here the people [Das Volk] is already dressed out, exactly as required in this particular organism, so as to have no determinate character'.[61] In this regard, Julian Assange's point about the hegemonic character of regimes is quite helpful; unhelpful, however, is his implicit assumption that an overwhelming power enforces its interests only 'from above'. In contrast, constitutionalizing processes in regimes are already about cultivating their version of social environments; they are committed to the protection of human rights or to develop methods of balancing, which nevertheless strengthens their respective 'bias' in the end.[62] Based on the hope of restricting effects on regimes through opening them up for their social environments, transnational societal constitutionalism loses its persuasiveness.[63] In other words: some of its desiderata have already been established without achieving the desired limiting effects. In the light of such sceptical observations, the question of critique arises. If constitutionalism coagulates increasingly into a post-democratic form of rule, how and on what basis can critical concerns then be formulated at all?

This sceptical view is able to highlight the emancipatory challenge, however. The task of pushing back hegemonic regimes can only succeed, if their innermost core, namely the reduction of transnational constitutionalism to specific programmes, is tackled. This raises the issue of effective countervailing powers able to cause such an opening. The desideratum would not be a mere re-entry of social environments, but

[59] European Comission, 'European Governance – A White Paper' COM(2001) p. 428; for the application in the field of employment policy, cf. Möller, 'Gouvernementales Wahrheitsregime oder dezentrales Netzwerk-Regieren?'.

[60] Lang, *World Trade after Neoliberalism*, pp. 88ff.

[61] Marx, 'Kritik des Hegelschen Staatsrechts', p. 273.

[62] Cf. Chimni, 'International Institutions Today'; Maus, 'Verfassung oder Vertrag'; Holmes, 'The Rhetoric of Legal Fragmentation and Its Discontents'; For an attempt to uncover the possibility of internal opposition in international law, cf. Ley, *Opposition im Völkerrecht*.

[63] Teubner, *Constitutional Fragments*.

a *destituent power* that neither aims at a managerialist meta-order nor remains in a mere 'construction of respect',[64] but displaces hegemonic projects of their higher-ranking status, opens them up for revision or withdraws them completely.

The young Marx

This perspective does not stand apart from the constitutional mind-set. But instead of drawing on the power-limiting tradition, it takes the *power-constituting* tradition as its starting point.[65] On the one hand, it may seem ill suited to be applied to fragmented regimes given the absence of a global *demos*. On the other hand, the figure of *pouvoir constituant* implies an element of a radical critique that one cannot simply equate with the population of the political state. The idea that only the people generate the constitution and rules itself within its framework includes not just a positive, law-generating dimension. It also possesses an expressly negative dimension, a latent threat of revoking juridico-political forms in society.[66]

At least, this is the way in which the young Marx understood constituent power in his *Critique of Hegel's Philosophy of Right*.[67] Here Marx sought to defend the constitutional theory of the French Revolution against Hegel's managerialist model of a constitution, in which each estate (each regime?) confined to the right dosage should contribute to a succeeding state as a whole.[68] Marx's praise of the revolutionary democratic principle comes in many formulas. The democratic constitution is depicted as 'the resolved riddle of all constitutions', the 'essence

[64] This is Marx's take on Hegel's corporate constitution, see Marx, 'Kritik des Hegelschen Staatsrechts', p. 288.

[65] Cf. the distinction between 'big C' and 'small c' constitutionalism with regard to world society in Kumm, 'The Cosmopolitan Turn in Constitutionalism'; for the paradox relation of constituting and constituted power, cf. Loughlin and Walker, *The Paradox of Constitutionalism*.

[66] Consequently, Beaud identifies also a 'deconstitutionalizing' moment in constituting power, Beaud, *La Puissance de l'Etat*, pp. 224ff.

[67] Marx, 'Kritik des Hegelschen Staatsrechts', pp. 441ff. Admittedly, Hegel's legal philosophy cannot be reduced to a mere defence of a conservative constitutional model, cf. Honneth, *Freedom's Right*; for an approach that makes use of the young Marx with regard to international law, cf. also Koskenniemi, 'What Should International Lawyers Learn from Karl Marx?'.

[68] Hegel, *Grundlinien der Philosophie des Rechts*, pp. 441ff.

of every political constitution' and even the 'truth of the monarchy'.[69] The revolutionary idea of the democratic constitution appears to be a qualitatively completely different principle, a 'completely opposed concept of sovereignty'.[70] With the figure of *pouvoir constituant*, the constitution contains a sort of tribunal that installs a constant pressure on those who rule. This is the decisive turn: Constituent power always entails a destituent scenario, which subjects all legal and political forms to the permanent threat of revocation.[71]

For Marx, this is the 'truth of democracy'. Legal and political forms emerge out of societal conditions. They are 'made' by people and can therefore be changed. It is not the enthusiasm for the political state that renders Marx a proponent of the French Revolution; Marx rather hopes for a transgression of democracy's boundaries. Since the *pouvoir constituant* raises the question of the extent to which people can be understood as authors of their own *legal conditions*, a dynamic process may occur. The inquiry needs to be extended to the totality of social relations, particularly with regard to the question of whether people can see themselves as authors of their own *living conditions*. In this way, Marx turns his reconstruction of the democratic constitution in the end against the state. In the *Critique of Hegel's Philosophy of Right* and in his essay 'On the Jewish Question' the project of a 'true democracy'[72] is discernable, in which the alienated forms of rule return into society and 'man has recognized and organized his "own powers" as social powers, and, consequently, no longer separates social power from himself in the shape of *political* power'.[73]

The post-democratic nature of regime constitutions has to be positioned at this very point; since they are reshaped by concrete ideas of

69 Marx, 'Kritik des Hegelschen Staatsrechts', pp. 230ff. 70 Ibid., p. 230

71 Especially functionalist inspired analyses of constituent power miss this point (cf. Thornhill, 'Contemporary Constitutionalism and the Dialectic of Constituent Power'). They can certainly show that liberal and republican constitutionalism are intertwined, and both prepare the ground for the centralization of political power. The notion of constituent power, however, cannot be reduced to a mere instrument of rule. Once it has found entrance into constitutional law and once the revolution has become an historical event, this can serve as reference point for those ruled, in case they intend to repeal the existing juridico-political forms. At least an available threat scenario for this repeal exists.

72 Marx, 'Kritik des Hegelschen Staatsrechts', p. 232.

73 Marx, 'Zur Judenfrage', p. 370. Abensour unpacks the young Marx's 'democracy against the state' in detail (cf. Abensour, *Democracy Against the State*), but ignores the fact that Marx in fact distinguishes between constitution and state and does not reject the constitution one-sidedly in the name of genuine democracy.

rder, they remain without a destituent moment. The challenge is herefore to renew the threat of revocation. The constitutional question ncreasingly shifts to the outside of hegemonic regimes. Can transational social movements, counter-hegemonic regimes (such as in the eld of social human rights), or political organizations exert such estituent power? The simple interplay of regimes and social environents is not sufficient. After all, it remains open which social nvironments really possess destituent potential.

Potentia and *potestas*

Consequently, if we understand the challenge not only as responsiveness ut also as a question of transnational countervailing powers, yet another onnection to constitutionalism emerges. If destituent power understood n this way occurs as a temporary placeholder for constituent power, it ecomes much more than a mere active civil society. It aims directly at he substantive core of regimes and needs to maintain its ground in the onstitutional struggles of the transnational. It is therefore not only nexhaustible *potentia* but also *potestas*; not only free-floating communiation but also effective countervailing force. To appear as a permanent ountervailing force, the destituent power will have to undergo a constiutionalizing process. Although it resists full-scale juridification, it still eeds its own form.[74] Only in this way can it become visible and find a vay of dealing with its internal contradictions. This is the reason why it vill turn to legal formalism in order to organize itself and not to collapse nto a mere gesture of total politicization or into an anarchic exodus that mmunizes itself against critique and reflexivity.

Even the primal scene of social countervailing power, namely the struggle between the patricians and plebeians in the Roman Republic suggests this. When the Roman *plebs* seceded to the holy mountain *mons sacer* and turned itself into an antagonist, it did not only engage in a revolt but also stabilized itself in the medium of its own legal (*leges sacratea*) and political forms (tribunate). The plebeian secessions, which according to tradition occurred in 494 BC, 450 BC, and 287 BC, were not only a means of a revolt, but they were also a self-organizing process, which found its expression in a plebeian constitution. The *plebs* forms a

[74] In contrast, cf. Giorgio Agamben's view of an exit from politics and law in Agamben, 'What is a Destituent Power?' and Antonio Negri's endeavor to reduce constituent power to *potentia*: Negri, *Insurgencies*.

parallel order. It protects the plebeian institutions against attacks and constitutes the *plebs* as 'counter-sovereign vis-à-vis the established order'.[75] The plebeians swear on their constitution as *leges sacratae*, as sacred and in this sense higher-ranking law. The latter are a basis for ensuring that it is possible to gradually achieve concessions and introduce the tribunes of the plebs as a constitutional institution of the Roman Republic.[76] This applies to the world society alike: Only a transnational *plebeian constitutionalism* is able to set a destituent power in motion.[77] This would also be an alternative to the interplay of overwhelming conspiracy and individualized counter-conspiracy, which Julian Assange emphasizes. Scandalous revelations about the power of the powerful or the encryption of e-mails with the safest application are important issues, but the challenge is more fundamental: How can destituent constituencies establish a sustainable counterweight to hegemonic regimes?

References

Abensour, M., *Democracy against the State: Marx and the Machiavellian Moment* (Cambridge and Malden: Polity Press, 2011).

Agamben, G., 'What Is a Destituent Power?', *Environment and Planning D: Society and Space*, 32 (2014), pp. 65–74.

Alter, K. J., and S. Meunier, 'The Politics of International Regime Complexity', *Perspectives on Politics*, 7 (2009), pp. 13–24.

Amstutz, M., and A. Fischer-Lescano (eds.), *Kritische Systemtheorie: Zur Evolution einer normativen Theorie* (Bielefeld: Transcript, 2013).

Assange, J., 'Conspiracy as Governance' (2006), http://web.archive.org/web/20070129125831/http://iq.org/conspiracies.pdf.

Bachur, J. P., *Kapitalismus und funktionale Differenzierung* (Baden-Baden: Nomos, 2013).

Barr, M. S., and G. P. Miller, 'Global Administrative Law: The View from Basel', *European Journal of International Law*, 17 (2006), pp. 15–46.

Beaud, O., *La Puissance de l'Etat* (Paris: Presses Universitaires de France, 1994).

Berman, P. S., *Global Legal Pluralism: A Jurisprudence of Law beyond Borders* (Cambridge University Press, 2012).

75 Koschorke, Lüdemann, Frank and De Mazza, *Der fiktive Staat*, p. 27.

76 See also Lorey, *Figuren des Immunen*, pp. 281ff. However, Lorey recoils in her reading of the *leges sacratae* from using the concept of constitution and mainly points to constituent *potentia* as being at work (p. 59); for a similar perspective, cf. Breaugh, *The Plebeian Experience*.

77 For the analogy with struggles for political order in the Roman Republic, see Möller, *Formwandel der Verfassung*.

reaugh, M., *The Plebeian Experience: A Discontinuous History of Political Freedom* (New York: Columbia University Press, 2013).

runkhorst, H., *Critical Theory of Legal Revolutions* (London and New York: Bloomsbury Academic, 2014).

Chimni, B. S., 'Between Co-option and Resistance: Two Faces of Global Administrative Law', *NYU Journal of International Law and Politics*, 37 (2004), pp. 799–827.

'International Institutions Today: An Imperial Global State in the Making', *European Journal of International Law*, 15 (2004), pp. 1–37.

Christodoulidis, E., 'On the Politics of Societal Constitutionalism', *Indiana Journal of Global Legal Studies*, 20 (2013), pp. 629–63.

Cox, R. W., *Production, Power, and World Order: Social Forces in the Making of History* (New York: Columbia University Press, 1987).

Cutler, C., *Private Power and Global Authority: Transnational Merchant Law in the Global Political Economy* (Cambridge University Press, 2003).

'Legal Pluralism as the "Common Sense" of Transnational Capitalism', *Oñati Socio-Legal Series*, 3 (2013), pp. 719–40.

Dimitrova, P., E. Egermann, T. Holert, J. Kastner and J. Schaffner, *Regime: Wie Dominanz organisiert und Ausdruck formalisiert wird* (Münster: edition assemblage, 2012).

Fischer-Lescano, A., 'Critical Systems Theory', *Philosophy & Social Criticism*, 38 (2012), pp. 3–23.

Fischer-Lescano, A., and G. Teubner, 'Regime-Collisions: The Vain Search for Legal Unity in the Fragmentation of Global Law', *Michigan Journal of International Law*, 25 (2004), pp. 999–1046.

Gill, S., and C. A. Cutler, *New Constitutionalism and World Order* (Cambridge University Press, 2014).

Gonçalves, G. L., *Il Rifugio delle Aspettative. Saggio sulla Certezza del Diritto* (Lecce and Rovato: Pensa Multimedia, 2013).

Gramsci, A., *Gefängnishefte – Kritische Gesamtausgabe* (Hamburg: Argument, 1991).

Hardt, M., and A. Negri, *Commonwealth* (Cambridge, MA: Harvard University Press, 2009).

Hasenclever, A., P. Mayer and V. Rittberger, *Theories of International Regimes* (Cambridge University Press, 1997).

Hegel, G. W. F., *Grundlinien der Philosophie des Rechts, Werke Band 7* (Frankfurt am Main: Suhrkamp, 1986 [orig. 1821]).

Holmes, P., 'The Rhetoric of Legal Fragmentation and Its Discontents. Evolutionary Dilemmas in the Constitutional Semantics of Global Law', *Utrecht Law Review*, 7 (2011), pp. 113–40.

Honneth, A., *Freedom's Right: The Social Foundations of Democratic Life* (Cambridge, MA: Polity Press, 2014).

Horst, J., 'Politiken der Entparadoxierung. Versuch einer Bestimmung des Politischen in der funktional ausdifferenzierten Weltgesellschaft' in M. Amstutz and A. Fischer-Lescano (eds.), *Kritische Systemtheorie. Zur Evolution einer normativen Theorie* (Bielefeld: Transcript, 2013), pp. 193–217.

Howarth, D. R., A. J. Norval and Y. Stavrakakis, *Discourse Theory and Political Analysis: Identities, Hegemonies and Social Change* (Manchester University Press, 2000).

Jessop, B., *The Future of the Capitalist State* (Cambridge and Malden: Polity Press, 2002).

State Power (Cambridge and Malden: Polity Press, 2007).

Kennedy, D., 'Law and the Political Economy of the World', *Leiden Journal of International Law*, 26 (2013), pp. 7–48.

Keohane, R. O., S. Macedo and A. Moravcsik, 'Democracy-Enhancing Multilateralism', *International Organization*, 63 (2009), pp. 1–31.

Kleinlein, T., *Konstitutionalisierung im Völkerrecht. Konstruktion und Elemente einer idealistischen Völkerrechtslehre* (Heidelberg and others: Springer, 2012).

Koschorke, A., S. Lüdemann, T. Frank and E. M. De Mazza, *Der fiktive Staat: Konstruktionen des politischen Körpers in der Geschichte Europas* (Frankfurt am Main: Fischer, 2007).

Koskenniemi, M., 'What Should International Lawyers Learn from Karl Marx?', *Leiden Journal of International Law*, 17 (2004), pp. 229–46.

'The Politics of International Law – 20 Years Later', *European Journal of International Law*, 20 (2009), pp. 7–19.

'Hegemonic Regimes' in M. A. Young (eds.), *Regime Interaction in International Law* (Cambridge University Press, 2012), pp. 305–24.

Krasner, S. D., 'Structural Causes and Regime Consequences: Regimes as Intervening Variables', *International Organization*, 36 (1982), pp. 185–205.

Kumm, M., 'The Cosmopolitan Turn in Constitutionalism. An Integrated Conception of Public Law', *Indiana Journal of Global Legal Studies*, 20 (2013), pp. 605–28.

Laclau, E, *New Reflections on the Revolution of Our Time* (London and New York: Verso, 1990)

On Populist Reason (London and New York: Verso, 2005).

Laclau, E., and C. Mouffe, *Hegemony and Socialist Strategy: Towards a Radical Democratic Politics* (London and New York: Verso, 2001 [orig. 1985]).

Lang, A., *World Trade after Neoliberalism: Reimagining the Global Economic Order* (Oxford University Press, 2011).

Ley, I., *Opposition im Völkerrecht. Ein Beitrag zur Legitimation internationaler Rechtserzeugung* (Heidelberg and others: Springer, 2015).

Lorey, I., *Figuren des Immunen: Elemente einer politischen Theorie* (Zurich: Diaphanes, 2011).

Loughlin, M., and N. Walker, *The Paradox of Constitutionalism* (Oxford University Press, 2007).

Luhmann, N., *Das Recht der Gesellschaft* (Frankfurt am Main: Suhrkamp, 1993).

'Observing Re-entries', *Graduate Faculty Philosophy Journal*, 16 (1993), pp. 485–98.

Protest. Systemtheorie und soziale Bewegungen (Frankfurt am Main: Suhrkamp, 1996).

Die Politik der Gesellschaft (Frankfurt am Main: Suhrkamp, 2002).

'Die Weltgesellschaft' in N. Luhmann (ed.), *Soziologische Aufklärung 2. Aufsätze zur Theorie der Gesellschaft* (Wiesbaden: VS-Verlag, 2005 [orig. 1971]), pp. 63–88.

Marx, K., 'Der 18. Brumaire des Louis Bonaparte' in F. Engels and K. Marx (eds.), *Marx-Engels-Werke Band 8* (Berlin, Dietz-Verlag, 1972 [orig. 1852]), pp. 111–207.

'Kritik des Hegelschen Staatsrechts' in F. Engels and K. Marx (eds.), *Marx-Engels-Werke Band 1* (Berlin, Dietz-Verlag, 1972 [orig.1843]), pp. 203–333.

'Zur Judenfrage' in F. Engels and K. Marx (eds.), *Marx-Engels-Werke Band 1* (Berlin, Dietz-Verlag, 1972 [orig. 1843]), pp. 347–77.

Maus, I., 'Verfassung oder Vertrag. Zur Verrechtlichung globaler Politik' in B. Herborth and P. Niesen (eds.), *Anarchie der kommunikativen Freiheit. Jürgen Habermas und die Theorie der internationalen Politik* (Frankfurt am Main: Suhrkamp, 2007), pp. 383–405.

Möller, K., 'Gouvernementales Wahrheitsregime oder dezentrales Netzwerk-Regieren?', *Leviathan*, 37 (2009), 575–601.

Formwandel der Verfassung. Die postdemokratische Verfasstheit des Transnationalen (Bielefeld: transcript, 2015).

Negri, A., *Insurgencies: Constituent Power and the Modern State* (Minneapolis: University of Minnesota Press, 1999).

Opitz, S., *An der Grenze des Rechts. Inklusion/Exklusion im Zeichen der Sicherheit* (Weilerswist: Velbrück, 2012).

Renner, M., 'Death by Complexity – The Crisis of Law in World Society' in P. F. Kjaer, A. Febbrajo and G. Teubner (eds.), *The Financial Crisis in Constitutional Perspective: The Dark Side of Functional Differentiation* (Oxford: Hart, 2011), pp. 93–112.

Sassen, S., *Territory, Authority, Rights: From Medieval to Global Assemblages* (Princeton University Press, 2006).

Schimank, U., 'Die Moderne: Eine funktional differenzierte kapitalistische Gesellschaft', *Berliner Journal für Soziologie*, 19 (2009), pp. 327–51.

Schneiderman, D., *Constitutionalizing Economic Globalization. Investment Rules and Democracy's Promise* (Cambridge University Press, 2008).

Scholz, S., and K.-D. Wolf, 'Ordnungswandel durch Umkehrung einer Normenhierarchie. Der Schutz geistigen Eigentums und das Recht auf Gesundheit', *HSFK-Report*, 5 (2014).

Simma, B., and D. Pulkowski, 'Of Planets and the Universe: Self-contained Regimes in International Law', *European Journal of International Law*, 17 (2006), pp. 483–529.

Slaughter, A.-M., *A New World Order* (Princeton University Press, 2004).

Somek, A., 'Administration without Sovereignty' in M. Loughlin and P. Dobner (eds.), *The Twilight of Constitutionalism?* (Oxford University Press, 2010), pp. 267–78.

Stäheli, U., *Sinnzusammenbrüche. Eine dekonstruktive Lektüre von Niklas Luhmanns Systemtheorie* (Weilerswist: Velbrück, 2000).

Streeck, W., *Gekaufte Zeit. Die vertagte Krise des demokratischen Kapitalismus* (Berlin: Suhrkamp, 2013).

Sweet, A. S., 'Constitutionalism, Legal Pluralism, and International Regimes', *Indiana Journal of Global Legal Studies*, 16 (2009), pp. 621–45.

Teubner, G., 'Privatregimes: Neo-Spontanes Recht und duale Sozialverfassungen in der Weltgesellschaft' in D. Simon and M. Weiss (eds.), *Zur Autonomie des Individuums: Liber Amicorum Spiros Simitis* (Baden-Baden: Nomos, 2000), pp. 437–53.

'Global Private Regimes: Neo-spontaneous Law and Dual Constitution of Autonomous Sectors in World Society?' in K.-H. Ladeur (ed.), *Public Governance in the Age of Globalization* (Aldershot: Ashgate, 2004), pp. 71–87.

'The Anonymous Matrix: Human Rights Violations by "Private" Transnational Actors', *The Modern Law Review*, 69 (2006), pp. 327–46.

'A Constitutional Moment? The Logics of "Hitting the Bottom"' in P. F. Kjaer, G. Teubner and A. Febbrajo (eds.), *The Financial Crisis in Constitutional Perspective: The Dark Side of Functional Differentiation* (Oxford: Hart, 2011), pp. 9–51.

Constitutional Fragments: Societal Constitutionalism and Globalization (Oxford University Press, 2012).

Thornhill, C., 'Contemporary Constitutionalism and the Dialectic of Constituent Power', *Global Constitutionalism*, 1 (2012), pp. 369–404.

10

Materialism of form

*On the self-reflection of law**

CHRISTOPH MENKE, TRANS. JAVIER BURDMAN

I begin with a simple statement: with law, there is only form. That is to say, with law there is no other as opposed to or outside its form – if or given that to say "there is" [*es gibt*], which implies the "thereness" [*Gegebenheit*] of something, in law as in anything else, is in itself a form. All that there is in law is there only through and, therefore, within its form.

To begin with this simple statement, however, necessarily implies to go beyond it. It is the beginning of thinking law, not its end – and therefore not the truth about law and its form. The truth about the legal form is that it carries a contradiction within itself, which manifests itself in certain collisions. The truth of the legal form is that it contains the other of law within itself – or that the law is the other of itself. By taking a traditional term for the other of form, "matter," I call this the *materialism of law.* This materialism is dialectical, as it does not conceive of matter as the other as opposed to form, but rather as the other of form within the form.

I proceed in three steps. The first step explains the thesis of the gap of law. The second step describes the figure of the self-reflection of modern law. The third step outlines how the self-reflection of modern law both grounds and suspends the form of ("subjective") rights. The goal of the considerations on the materialism of law is a critique of bourgeois law.

The gap of law

The determination of the legal form can proceed from two general insights formulated by Niklas Luhmann. The first insight is that law (as a form) is marked by two distinctions (i). The second insight is that these two distinctions are connected in the law (as a system) through its self-referentiality (ii).

* The text is the abbreviated version of an argument which I have developed further in a book entitled *Kritik der Rechte* (Berlin: Suhrkamp Verlag, 2015), esp. part II.

(i) Law – everything it does – is defined through the use of a form that characterizes it specifically. It is defined by the fact that it draws a specific distinction – for "establishing a form is . . . distinguishing."[1] In law, this is the distinction between law [*Recht*] and illegality [*Unrecht*]. Law uses this distinction in order to do what only law can do: to identify something as legal or illegal. There is "no other authority in society which can proclaim: this is law and this is illegality."[2]

To distinguish means to identify something, and therewith to declare something else its "outside": illegality as the outside of law, law as the outside of illegality. Then (or thereby), there is still yet a "second outside": "the outside of the difference between [law] and [illegality]," or "the outside of the unity of this difference, the outside of [law]. This would then be the world."[3] The law constitutes itself through the use of its form "in a certain domain that then becomes an environment *for it*."[4] The distinction between law and illegality is thus complemented by the distinction between the distinction of law and illegality *and* the non-distinction of law and illegality, or the distinction of law and non-law [*Nichtrecht*].

Both distinctions will be found in the legal form. They are, however, fundamentally different. The first one is normative and symmetrical: it distinguishes between two sides that are normatively opposed (as law and illegality), although they are of the same kind – both are "values" (Luhmann). The second distinction is structural and asymmetrical: the two sides that it distinguishes are the form and its use in law, and the world as the exterior of law, non-law – the juridical form and the juridically indifferent, and therefore (from the viewpoint of law) formless matter.

(ii) The first distinction (between law and illegality) exists within law in such a way that one or the other side of the distinction will be used for the identification of something (as law *or* as illegality). The second distinction (between law and non-law), by contrast, encounters law where (and because), in referring to something, it also refers to itself at the same time: law must distinguish between law and non-law, because there is no law without self-reference. For in order to refer to something and to be able to identify it as legal or illegal, law must relate to other acts of juridical distinction, and it must be able to identify them as juridical too. And in order to do this, law must thus use the distinction of law and

[1] Luhmann, "The Paradox of Form," p. 16.
[2] Luhmann, *Law as a Social System*, p. 100 (italics removed; C. M.).
[3] Luhmann, "Sign as Form," p. 57 adapted to the subject of law.
[4] Luhmann, *Law as a Social System*, p. 105.

on-law. Law cannot be defined only through distinguishing law and legality – for then there could have been a single act of law, a once-only se of the distinction between law and illegality. However, each use of the istinction between the law and illegality is the repetition of the use of his distinction. And therefore not only the identification of something as gal or illegal belongs to law, but also the identification of other acts as nes that use or *do not* use the distinction between law and illegality – hus the use of the distinction between law and non-law also belongs to aw. Law always operates on two planes at once: it *uses* the distinction of aw and illegality (for the identification of something as law *or* illegality), nd it *relates to* this distinction (for the identification of something as law nd non-law). Luhmann describes this in such a way that "the distinction etween distinction and indication [i.e., use] is . . . copied into the listinction," or that the "distinction . . . recurs in itself."[5]

The meaning of distinguishing, the meaning of "distinction," is, as we ave seen, radically different in the two planes: between two mutually xclusive but legally defined values, and between law and the "world" as, rom the viewpoint of law, a zone of indetermination. At the same time, however, both distinctions must operate together. The world outside of aw, the non-law, is the "'unmarked space' – . . . what cannot be distinguished but can only be brought into a form by making a distinction."[6] Law does this by establishing the distinction between law and illegality. Law distinguishes itself *from* non-law by distinguishing between law and llegality *within* non-law – and thus transforms it into law.

This means that *for law*, in the use of the distinction between law and llegality, in juridical decision-making, there is no non-juridical [*Nichrechtliches*]. In law, there is no world; that the world as unmarked space of non-law is "brought into a form" (Luhmann) through juridical distinguishing thus does not mean that, in the operating of law, a form is applied from outside to a non-juridical, foreign material. Therein lies the break with a metaphysical "tradition" that "teaches us to conceptualize form as one side of a distinction whose other side can then be designated in various ways – such as form/matter, form/substance, or form/content."[7] *In the* juridical process there is only the juridical, that which is in the legal form: law is juridical from the start, down to its material. Thus, for instance, court proceedings do not refer to events and actors in the "world," but rather to their juridically formed representatives – without

5 Luhmann, "The Paradox of Form," p. 17.

6 Luhmann, "Sign as Form," p. 57.

7 Luhmann, "The Paradox of Form," p. 15.

representation there is no legal proceedings.[8] In each juridical procedure in which a distinction between law and illegality is made, a pre-procedure is resolved, and therefore concluded, in which the juridically processable elements were generated. The accomplishment of law does not consist in deciding about the non-juridical, but rather it begins by "bringing down" its objects. "Thereby the fallen are not destroyed but are in a certain way raised up again – within the limits fixed by the dominating ones."[9] In legal proceedings no pre-juridical material can emerge, which would then still have to be turned into a juridical one – for law it already always is or was. That the world is "brought into form" through law is not therefore a step that is made in actuality, as an act carried out in the present in legal proceedings, but rather it must have been always already carried out, so that there will have legal proceedings.

At the same time however, the absence of the non-juridical world in the operation of the juridical form is never completely given. Or the success, and thereby the conclusion [*Abgeschlossenheit*] (temporally: the past perfect) of the pre-juridical pre-procedure is never secure. In – although here this can only mean: *against* – the juridical procedure, the non-juridical world can always make itself noticeable, opposing its juridical surrogacy: as confusion, chatter, dispersion, disturbance, refusal, violence.[10]

That the non-juridical world *can* make itself noticeable in this way, that the power of juridification in legal proceedings encounters a limit, given that the incrimination of resistance as illegality ("contempt for the court" or so) cannot capture it – this possibility cannot be grounded upon experience. Rather, to the contrary, the possibility of this experience must be established from the concept of law: the reason that non-law can interrupt law lies in law itself. This reason is no other than the distinction between law and non-law. Law uses this distinction in its self-reference in order to ascertain its self. But given that law can only do so by distinguishing itself within itself from non-law, its self-reference carries within it the reference to *what (and where) it is not*. By knowing itself, the law knows of non-law. Therefore it knows (given that this is what non-law *means*) that there is something that eludes its distinguishing. Indeed, law in its procedure can never experience the non-juridical. It can never in its procedure identify something as non-juridical (given that all juridical identification is identification as something juridical).

[8] Cfr. Trüstedt, "*Nomos and Narrative*," pp. 59–78. [9] Heidegger, *Parmenides*, p. 41.
[10] So it goes in Kleist's *The Broken Jug*. See Menke, "Nach dem Gesetz," pp. 97–112.

But because it knows (of) non-law, it knows of the possibility that something defies its procedure that it cannot integrate. It has a concept not of non-law, but of the possibility of non-law. This possibility realizes itself as experience of the limit of experience: in the identification of or as something that it can neither identify as juridical nor as non-juridical – which is precisely *non-juridical* in that it *is* neither juridical nor non-juridical.

If, however, the possibility of non-juridificability is undissolvably inscribed in law through its self-reference, then the existence or presence of juridical decision-making is also insecure. If there are legal proceedings, if juridical distinctions are being made, then this *is* a juridical decision-making about the juridical. *That* there are legal proceedings, that here and now juridical distinguishing takes place, is however not a given fact. "It follows from this paradox that at no time can one say *presently* that a decision is [juridical], purely [juridical]."[11] Given that law uses the distinction of law and illegality in such a way that it relates to this distinction, and thereby distinguishes itself from the non-distinction of non-law, law refers to its outside within itself. The formless world, the world as non-form, whose absence is presupposed in the operating of law, is present in law as absent. In law, the "background noise of the environments" is audible. "In law it is not almost silent, but rather there is a background noise."[12]

The proceedings of law thus stand under two mutually opposing determinations:

- *On the one hand*, in legal proceedings, there is only the juridical, the non-juridical has always already become juridical, so that it is possible to distinguish between law and illegality.
- *On the other hand*, the pre-procedure of juridification is still in progress, because the "infinite otherness" of the non-juridical can never be conclusively brought into the juridical form.

Or the distinction of law and non-law is at once present and absent in law:

- *On the one hand*, it is necessary that the difference between law and non-law be absent in law – there is no such difference in law (or, where and when there is such difference, there is no law).

[11] Derrida, "Force of Law," p. 252. Derrida himself speaks about a decision being "just" (not: juridical).

[12] Hensel, "Klangpotentiale," pp. 89 and 87 [trans. J. B.].

- *On the other hand*, it is possible that the difference between law and non-law is effective in law – that law cannot be secured against its incursion (and therefore it is uncertain whether there is juridical deciding here and now).

It is between this "on the one hand/on the other" that the *gap* of law opens up. Or the paradox of law: "a paradox is a form that contains itself."[13] For what the form of law thus contains within itself is plainly the distinction between law and non-law, *which it cannot contain within itself* – as long as it wants to (or must) be law, that is, the use of the distinction between law and illegality, and thereby deciding. The reentering of the form into the form is formless. The paradox is: the reference of law to its form is necessary or constitutive of law – without it there is simply no law – *and* impossible or disruptive of law – for it relates the law to the non-juridical, for which it has no use.

The gap of thus demonstrates that the question of the other of law does not dissolve itself as easily as the systemic theory of form suggests. By thinking the legal form as distinction of law *and* illegality, this theory rejects the tradition that proceeds from form as *one* side of the distinction – "for instance form/matter, form/substance, form/content." That is the tradition of metaphysics. Against this tradition, Luhmann poses the question: "What happens if the other side of the distinction . . . is simply omitted from consideration and form as such becomes the main focus of reflection and manipulation?"[14] What then happens, however, is *not* (as Luhmann says here also) that the forms or distinctions "only . . . partake in the play of differences among themselves"[15] – it is not indeed the free play of forms, but rather the (gap-opening, paradox-producing) reentry of the distinction of form *from its other* into the form. One cannot "simply omit" the other side of the distinction. One will not get rid of the other side so easily. Rather, it returns in the self-reference of form, that is, in its interior. But as its other side: no longer matter as substance, content, or material, which obtain presence through form as their essence, but rather as the other of form – matter as the unmarked or formless, as non-form (in the form).

But how does law handle its form-gap? The law must presuppose in its normative operation that it is dealing (only) with things juridical, juridical objects and juridical persons. At the same time law knows, in its self-reference, that the other side, the non-juridical, exists and therefore also

[13] Luhmann, "The Paradox of Form," p. 18. [14] Ibid., p. 15. [15] Ibid.

ıat it is itself only the other side of the non-juridical. Law thus knows ›o that its precondition is not secured and given. This creates the ›ossibility of a paradoxical, that is, juridically impossible situation: that ıw finds itself confronted with a situation which for law cannot exist – ıe situation in which law is *suspended* through the effect of the non-ıridical. Carl Schmitt calls this situation the "exception," and "sover-ignty" that position of power which can make of the precondition *Voraussetzung*] (of law) its own premise or positing [*Setzung*]. The overeign, Schmitt thinks, can posit [*setzen*] the precondition [*das Vor-us*] of law. Of course, he can do so only in a non-juridical act of positing. n the melancholy of the monarch, Benjamin exhibited the logic of (self-) verburdening, which this conversion of precondition into positing lenotes,[16] and Giorgio Agamben described the "anomic tendency" in he inside of law that generates it: "the law applies itself to chaos and life nly on the condition of making itself, in the state of exception, life and ving chaos."[17]

The self-reflection of law

The alternative to sovereignty is the self-reflection of law. It is a wiser way f handling the gap of law. (Self-)reflection is, according to Luhmann, the operation by which the system indicates itself in contrast to its environ-nent. This occurs, for example, in all forms of self-presentation that ıssume the environment does not immediately accept the system in the vay it would like itself to be understood."[18] Self-reflection is thus the step n which law expresses (how that happens remains to be shown) that it ːan refer to itself only in such a way (or, that there can only be law in uch a way) that it refers to itself in contrast with non-law, or to non-law ıs the other of law. The self-reflection of law is thus its *self-alteration* or *elf-externalization*. It includes the *precondition* (the exteriority) of non-aw through law. There is non-*law* as *non*-law only through the self-eflection of law – the other of law, the otherness of non-law, is an effect of its self-reflection. Law is form and non-law formless (*relative* to the uridical form). Non-law is the formless that only exists if or because here is law as a self-reflexive form. Or law and non-law are connected hrough *one* process of formation that in generating form also generates hat which precedes it: the formless, which is constantly being "brought

16 Benjamin, "Ursprung des deutschen Trauerspiels," p. 304.

17 Agamben, *State of Exception*, p. 73.

18 Luhmann, *Social Systems*, p. 444.

into a form"[19] and thereby never (in itself or entirely) turns into form. If the other of form can be called matter, then the self-reflection of law consists in the fact that it lets matter as non- or un-form, as counter-effect of formation, become effective in its own formation. Thus the self-reflection of right means nothing other than its *material proceduralization* – for materialism is the insight that all forms are also generated by the driving forces of matter.

Through its self-reflection, the law does not overcome its fate; but it transforms it into its own action. (Self-reflection is therefore the figure of freedom.) The fate of law is its gap: that it can posit itself only by presupposing its other, against which in turn it must assert itself externally. The fate of law is the violence of its positing, insertion and assertion, which the irreducible externality of its form reproduces endlessly. The self-reflection of law begins with the insight that it is its very form that produces its gap. The externality or subsequentness of form is its own deed. Or the shadow of its own deed: the deed of its positing. The first step of the self-reflection of law consists in the insight: *the form of law itself* – and not some powers that obstruct or corrode it from outside – is the postponement of the juridical form. Through the self-reflection of law the law [*Gesetz*] of form becomes thus the form of the law [*Gesetz*]: posited [*gesetzt*] as form of the law [*Gesetzes*]. How is this new, self-reflexive juridical form to be understood?

Not merely in the way that liberalism understands it – that is, not merely negatively, as self-limitation of law. For there is simply no merely negative self-limitation: the delimitation of law in relation to its other is always also the presupposition of the other (and thus positively: position). Namely: (presup-)posing the other in the (self-)positing of law. Max Weber's conclusion from this dialectic of liberalism is: "recognition" of the non-juridical in law or "materialization" of law.[20] Thereby the other of law, non-law, the matter is brought to bear within law. Obviously that cannot be done by deriving law from non-law, establishing it from the non-juridical. In law, also in self-reflexive, materialized law, the juridical distinction of law and illegality can only ever have (intra-) juridical grounds – there is no "excursion of law into the outside world."[21] The materialization opens law for non-law, but it does not ground law upon or through non-law. Or the non-juridical is not valid in law, but rather operational; its presence in self-reflexive law is not

[19] Luhmann, "Sign as Form," p. 57. [20] Weber, *Wirtschaft und Gesellschaft*, p. 506.
[21] Teubner, "Selbstsubversive Gerechtigkeit," p. 18 [trans. J. B.].

normative, but rather effective: a drive or a force, not a, or simply the, ground.[22] Therefore the materialization of law does not stand in contradiction to its autonomy. The materialization is rather precisely the form in which the autonomy of law is self-reflexively performed .

The concept of juridical self-reflection thus outlined links two fundamental moments: the materialization of law means first to understand law as essentially procedural. Self-reflexive law is law that carries itself out as self-generative – materialization means processualization of form. But at the same time, secondly, that means to understand the processuality of law as essentially material. Processualization means materialization of form, and matter in the form-process is not matter, object, or material – that which the form-process affects from outside – but rather impulse: that which is effective in the form-process, that which drives it. The self-reflection of law means not only its processualization, simply as "proceduralization."[23] Self-reflexive processualization means rather its materialization: without the effectiveness of material impulses, of non-law in law, there is simply no autonomous process of its self-generation. The self-generation of law is its self-transformation, and the self-transformation [*Selbstveränderung*] of law is its self-alteration [*Selbstveranderung*]: effectiveness of the other within law.

The self-reflection of law therefore means both *entry of the ground* of law into law: the processualization of law; and *entry of the other* of law into law: the materialization of law. Both processes are two sides of the same coin. The self-grounding and the self-alteration of law are the same.

The form of rights

We have seen that: the self-reflection of law is the self-reflection of its form by contrast to non-law, the matter that eludes and opposes form. This determination of self-reflexive law links two aspects: (i) *Processuality*, that is: the form of self-reflexive law is the self-generating or self-transforming form. (ii) *Materialism*, that is: the matter of non-law is effective in the form of self-generating law.

But how is there, and where, a self-reflection of law in law? How does law perform its self-reflection? Gunther Teubner describes this as "the development of a coherent form of argumentation about the identity of the system." "One can thus speak of reflexive law in the strict sense of the

22 This is the decisive insight in Fischer-Lescano, *Rechtskraft*, chapter III.
23 Cfr. Habermas, *Between Facts and Norms*, pp. 463–90.

term only if legal theory and legal doctrine deal with the prevailing social conditions of law . . . and if it informs decision-making practice in law."[24] However, it is fundamentally and above all a *formal* consequence that law draws from its self-reflection. This consequence is the modern form of rights. Law reflects upon itself through its form. *The form of rights is the self-reflexive form of law.*

Modern rights are processes of juridification that have become form: the legalization of the natural. The modern form of rights implies the opening of law for non-law, the emergence of law from non-law – the process of responsiveness. The discussion of the concept of self-reflection showed *why* and *how* modern law cultivates this form. For this discussion showed that the natural, which is made possible and permitted through rights, is effective in law, in its material processuality. *Therefore* and *in this manner* the modern form of rights legalizes the non-juridical: because (and by means of this) self-reflexive right *lets* the non-juridical be effective within it, that is, affirming it as effective in it. The self-reflection of the juridical form implies the affirmation of the non-juridical matter. The modern form of rights is nothing other than the configuration and determination of this affirmation of non-law in law.

Because the form of rights follows from the self-reflection of law, because the form of rights presents and carries out the self-reflection of law, both determinations of self-reflexive law, its processuality and its materialism, are at once the fundamental determinations of rights. Rights are therefore:

(i) Procedural: rights are the result of processes, and they are the point of departure and the object of processes. Rights are always thus other rights. *Each right is a new right*: a having-become and thus becoming right. The modern form of rights is the form of a transforming and thus historical law.

(ii) Material (or materialistic): rights are the expression of the effectiveness of the matter of non-law in law. *Rights are always thus fought-for rights*: generated from the protest of non-law against the existing state of law. The modern form of rights is the form of the contested, thus political law.

[24] Teubner, *Law as an Autopoietic System*, p. 20.

Therefore the pronouncement of rights, their declaration, also belongs essentially to its form. In their pronouncement, rights are displayed as created, and therein traced back to the experiences (of suffering and of struggle) from which they emerged.[25] Thus it is just another formulation for the fact that the modern form of rights is the form of self-reflexive law, that such form is *the form of revolutionary law*: rights are the permanent revolution of law as form. But therein also lies the contradiction that tears apart this form. The critique of rights consists in the exhibition of this contradiction.

The self-reflection of law is the fundamental operation through which modern law generates itself. This operation constitutes its essence. The essence of modern law is an *act* – law's self-generation through the act of self-reflection. In this self-reflection emerges the fundamental structure that defines all law as law: the relationship of law and nature, of normative and factual. This takes place in and through law itself, and thereby transforms the law. The self-reflection of law implies its transformation.

If this is the essential determination of modern law, then the modern form of rights is their appearance: the essential self-reflection of law appears (manifests and carries itself out) in the modern form of rights. For the essence is the ground of the appearance, the appearance the expression of the essence. The appearance of the self-reflection of law in the modern form of rights is however ambiguous, contradictory really. The modern form of rights is the presentation as much as the *displacement*, the performance as much as the interruption, indeed, the *repression* of the self-reflection of law: the modern form of rights is appearance [*Erscheinung*] as much as illusion [*Schein*]. Or the modern form of rights is self-contradictory: it exists only through the act of self-reflection of law – this act is the essence of the form, the form of rights is its appearance. But at the same time the modern form of rights is the displacement and repression of self-reflection, in which it grounds. The modern form of rights *is* thus essentially self-reflexive, but it *appears*, that is, proceeds un- and indeed anti-reflexively. Or the modern form of rights is in its essence self-reflexive, but positivist in its self-understanding and its performance. Since "[that] we disavow reflection *is* positivism."[26]

[25] See the texts in Menke and Raimondi (eds.), *Die Revolution der Menschenrechte*, part II: "Deklaration"; especially the introduction by Francesca Raimondi (pp. 95–101).

[26] Habermas, *Knowledge and Human Interest*, p. vii.

This defines the only form [*Gestalt*] that modern law has generated until now: the form [*Gestalt*] of bourgeois law. (For the law established by socialist states was not modern law. It is at most the attempt of rehabilitating a configuration of traditional law: a mix from Greek *Paideia* and Roman *Imperium*). The central figure of bourgeois law is that of subjective rights – bourgeois law interprets the modern form of rights as subjective rights. This bourgeois fundamental figure of subjective rights is the contradiction, which has become reality, between essence and appearance. For the figure of subjective rights grounds in the act of self-reflection that defines modern law. One cannot therefore understand what a subjective right is if one does not conceptualize it as the materialization and processualization of law that has become form. It is however the false manner of self-reflection of law: bourgeois law conceptualizes, and thus carries out, its self-reflection falsely. The idea of subjective rights is a mistake. Bourgeois law commits an error in reasoning. That is the (single) error of bourgeois law, but it is a fundamental error with practical, social, and political consequences. Falsely thought means falsely made.

This error of bourgeois law consists in its positivism: bourgeois law (bourgeois right in its praxis, thus not only the bourgeois theory of subjective rights) is positivistic. If positivism is, according to Jürgen Habermas's definition, the disavowal of reflection, then this does not mean its mere, simple absence. The disavowal of reflection is rather itself a way to carry out reflection. But a performance of reflection in which reflection turns against itself disavows, and disrupts *itself*. The fundamental formula of the self-reflection of law is: non-law becomes effective in law, the material becomes effective in the self-generation of form. Bourgeois law understands and carries out this relatedness, which is constitutive of form, in such a way that it turns the material into the foundation and thus into what is given. In its fundamental figure of subjective rights, bourgeois law *positivizes* the material other of law. The error of bourgeois law consists therefore in understanding the materialism of self-reflection as positivism. Or the mistake of bourgeois law consists in repeating the "myth of the given," through which Wilfrid Sellars defined empiricism:

> One of the forms taken by the Myth of the Given is that there is, indeed *must be*, a structure of particular matter of fact such that (a) each fact can not only be noninferentially known to be the case, but presupposes no other knowledge either of particular matter of fact, or of general truths; and (b) such that the noninferential knowledge of facts belonging to this

> structure constitutes the ultimate court of appeal for all factual claims – particular and general – about the world.[27]

The myth of the given is a myth because it gives authorization. Matter as the positively given has the "authority"[28] to delineate the undisputable point of departure for everything that follows, for all generation of form and norm. Theodor W. Adorno describes positivism in this manner: positivism contorts the materialistic "preponderance of the object" into the pre-givenness of an indisputable, impenetrable immediate, which remains as "residue" after the "subjective appendages have been subtracted."[29] But this subtraction was its own deed, the residue is produced. This is, in bourgeois law, the self-reflection that disavows itself in its performance: bourgeois law is the "resignation before individuality,"[30] whose limiting and founding authority it only generated in itself – which it (according to the technical expression) makes "valid" [*in "Geltung" setzt*].

This positivism is inscribed in the bourgeois configuration of rights. That is the figure of *subjective* rights. The figure of subjective rights is thus a derived category. It has its grounds not in the subject, but rather in law, namely in the positivistically contorted self-reflection of bourgeois law – in bourgeois law, its self-reflection is "clothed in the form of subjective rights."[31] The positivism of bourgeois law is subjectifying, or the subjectivism of rights is positivistic. The juridical myth of the given realizes itself through the bourgeois legal subject. That is: the figure of subjective rights *occupies* the empirical position of the given with the subject. Since the given is the position of the "last instance of appeal," the position of the "authority" (Sellars), this defines the subject as an instance of authorization. This grounds the proprietary logic of the bourgeois legal subject: all subjective law is "*ius proprium*."[32] Bourgeois law turns the non-juridical into its pre-given in the last instance, by understanding the given as *the property* [*das Eigene*] of the subject. The properties [*die*

27 Sellars, *Empiricism and the Philosophy of Mind*, pp. 68–9. 28 Ibid., p. 71.
29 Adorno, *Negative Dialectics*, p. 186. 30 Ibid., p. 161.
31 Luhmann, "Subjektive Rechte," p. 84 [trans. J. B.]. Cfr. Luhmann, *Law as a Social System*, pp. 413–4: "If the legal system has to deal with differentiated sub-systems such as money economy, privatized families, politically programmed state organizations, etc. and has to rely on corresponding structural couplings to do that, it must also reformulate its relations with systems of consciousness. … Modern legal development has done that by abstracting general, socially based norms of reciprocity from the legal figure of subjective rights."
32 Esposito, *Immunitas*, pp. 21–8.

Eigenschaften] of the subject are what are proper to it [*sein Eigenes*] To have properties has the objective sense of applying to something – to have what is proper has the subjective sense of being willed by someone The positivism of subjective rights turns the willing of the proper into an authoritative fact: that I will something as my own [*eigenes*] obtains in bourgeois law the authority of the pre-given, from which all normative positings must proceed.

Let us quickly emphasize what the empiricism or positivism of bourgeois law is *not*: it is not a reductionism – the error of bourgeois law is not so simple, not that rapidly solvable and easy to avoid. The emanation of bourgeois law from the authority of an ultimate given is not the same as a reduction of the normativity of its form to, nor its dissolution in, the merely factual. Bourgeois right does not derive ought from is, but rather *constructs the former starting with*, i.e. on the presupposition of, *the latter*. The (empirical or positivistic) error of bourgeois law lies logically *before* the question of whether being can ground ought. Its error is an ontological error. It lies in the determination of the form of being of matter in and for self-reflexive law. The error lies in apprehending the material that is effective in the self-reflexive form-process of law as positively given.

The mistake of bourgeois law is its false materialism. Materialism means: "passing to the object's preponderance" or to apprehend "matter [as] something like a driving force"[33] – namely: in the self-reflection of form. Empiricism understands this in such a way that the object is something immediate, and its immediacy is a primary and ultimate one. This empirical materialism is countered by dialectical materialism. Adorno's objection against positivism states: matter is no ultimate, but rather a moment, and this moment "in the progress . . . must be transcended," "by virtue of the process which apprehends it."[34] There is no primacy of the object as pre-givenness, but only in the mediation. Dialectical mediation turns that which it mediates into a moment. Thus mediation does not mean external unification, but rather inner, ontological transformation. The dialectical process does not realize the object's preponderance by allowing it to be considered as unchangeably given, as positive determinacy, but rather, conversely and in opposition to positivism, by allowing the material to be effective as nothingness, as radically undetermined. Empirical materialism asserts the authority of

33 Adorno, *Negative Dialectics,* pp. 192 and 182 (on "the materialistic moment in Schelling").

34 Adorno et al., *The Positivist Dispute in German Sociology*, pp. 54 and 76.

ie positive. By contrast, dialectical materialism posits the force of egativity: in the dialectical materialism of the self-reflexive legal process, natter is not something, a something, that is pre-given to form, but ather matter is the nothingness of form (or matter is force[35]).

Conclusion

One materialism against the other – the negativity of dialectics against the ositivity of empiricism: that is the figure of contradiction in modern law. This contradiction concerns all the elements of self-reflexive law: the elationship of normativity and facticity, of form and matter; the logic nd the energetics of its processuality; the justice and the politicality of aw; and finally the concept of revolution, which defines self-reflexive law s modern law. *All* modern law is materialistic, processual, just, political, nd revolutionary – otherwise it is not self-reflexive, therefore not modern. It is so in two ways however, which contradict one another point by point and thus stand irreconcilably opposed: bourgeois law *and the other law.*

The contradiction between bourgeois law and the other law is asymmetric: in bourgeois law, the empirical understanding of law's self-eflection has become a configuration of reality – the only real onfiguration of modern law that we know. The other law, by contrast, does not (yet) exist. It is however the true law. It is the truth, the true configuration, of the self-reflection of law. Bourgeois law is untrue a realization of juridical self-reflection that contorts and represses that which it realizes), but it is there: the other law is true, but it is not there *es gibt es nicht*].

In this situation, the task of critique is to unfold the contradiction *between* bourgeois law and the other law. It does not do so by envisioning another law. That is not the primary task of critique. Its primary and most important task is to make evident, and thus to intensify, the contradiction *within* bourgeois law. That happens (only and already) insofar as bourgeois law is comprehended. For to comprehend bourgeois law means to grasp it as appearance of its essence. And to grasp its essence means to grasp that which bourgeois law generates *and* which antagonizes it – that which is at once its ground and its opponent.

35 Cfr. Menke, *Force*, pp. 41–5.

By grasping the essence of bourgeois law, critique degrades bourgeois law to a mere illusion.

That is the idea of "true critique." "Vulgar" or "dogmatic critique" is a critique "that *struggles* with its object." By contrast, "true criticism shows the inner genesis" of false appearances. "It describes [their] birth ... it *explains* them, comprehends their genesis, their necessity."[36] The only true form of critique is the one that exposes the genesis of that which is criticized – genealogical critique, in which consequently critique and explanation, the dissolution and the exhibition of the necessity of illusion, coincide. It is a figure of immanent critique, not because it measures the existing against its own standard, but rather by confronting it with its essence. As genealogical critique illuminates the existing bourgeois law of subjective rights from the essential act of self-reflection, in the recourse to the act in which bourgeois law formed itself breaking with traditional law, the prospect of a new act emerges in which it will dissolve itself. Critique works on intensifying the crisis of bourgeois law.

Bibliography

Adorno, T. W., *Negative Dialectics*, trans. E. B. Ashton (New York: Routledge, 2004).

Adorno, T. W., et al., *The Positivist Dispute in German Sociology*, trans. G. Adey and D. Frisby (London: Heinemann Educational Books, 1977).

Agamben, G., *State of Exception*, trans. K. Attell (University of Chicago Press, 2005).

Benjamin, W., "Ursprung des deutschen Trauerspiels" in R. Tiedemann and H. Schweppenhäuser (eds.), *Gesammelte Schriften*, vol. I (Frankfurt am Main: Suhrkamp, 1977).

Derrida, J., "Force of Law: The Mystical Foundation of Authority" in G. Anidjar (ed.), *Acts of Religion*, (New York: Routledge, 2002), pp. 230–98.

Esposito, R., *Immunitas: The Protection and Negation of Life* (Malden, MA: Polity, 2011).

Fischer-Lescano, A., *Rechtskraft* (Berlin: August Verlag, 2013).

Habermas, J., *Between Facts and Norms. Contributions to a Discourse Theory of Law and Democracy*, trans. W. Rehg (Cambridge, MA: MIT Press, 1996).

Knowledge and Human Interest, trans. J. J. Shapiro (Boston: Bacon Press, 1971).

Heidegger, M., *Parmenides*, trans. A. Schuwer and R. Rojcewicz (Indiana University Press, 1992).

[36] Marx, "Critique of Hegel's Doctrine of the State," p. 158.

Hensel, I., "Klangpotentiale: Eine Annäherung an das Rauschen des Rechts" in C. Joerges and P. Zumbansen (eds.), *Politische Rechtstheorie Revisited. Rudolf Wiethölter zum 100. Semester* (Bremen: ZERP, 2013), pp. 69–99.

Luhmann, N., "Subjektive Rechte: Zum Umbau des Rechtsbewußtseins für die moderne Gesellschaft" in *Gesellschaftsstruktur und Semantik*, Vol. 2 (Frankfurt am Main: Suhrkamp, 1981), pp. 45–104.

Social Systems, trans. J. Bednarz Jr. and D. Baecker (Stanford University Press, 1995).

"Sign as Form" in D. Baecker (ed.), *Problems of Form* (Stanford University Press, 1999), pp. 46–63.

"The Paradox of Form" in D. Baecker (ed.), *Problems of Form* (Stanford University Press, 1999), pp. 15–26.

Law as a Social System, eds. F. Kastner et al., trans. K. A. Ziegert (Oxford University Press, 2004).

Marx, K., "Critique of Hegel's Doctrine of the State" in *Early Writings*, trans. R. Livingstone and G. Benton (London: Penguin, 1992), pp. 57–198.

Menke, C., "Nach dem Gesetz. Zum Schluß des *Zerbrochnen Krugs*" in M. Groß and P. Primavesi (eds.), *Lücken sehen … Beiträge zu Theorie, Literatur und Performance (Festschrift for Hans-Thies Lehmann)* (Heidelberg: Universitätsverlag Winter, 2010), pp. 97–112.

Force: A Fundamental Concept of Aesthetic Anthropology, trans. G. Jackson (New York: Fordham University Press, 2013).

Menke, C., and F. Raimondi (eds.), *Die Revolution der Menschenrechte* (Berlin: Suhrkamp, 2011).

Sellars, W., *Empiricism and the Philosophy of Mind* (Cambridge, MA: Harvard University Press, 1997).

Teubner, G., *Law as an Autopoietic System*, ed. Z. Bankowski, trans. A. Bankowska and R. Adler (Cambridge, MA: Blackwell, 1993).

"Selbstsubversive Gerechtigkeit: Kontingenz- oder Transzendenzformel des Rechts?," *Zeitschrift für Rechtssoziologie*, 29 (2008), 9–36.

Trüstedt, K., "*Nomos and Narrative*. Zu den Verfahren des Orestie" in I. Augsberg and S.-C. Lenski (eds.), *Die Innenwelt der Außenwelt der Innenwelt des Rechts. Annäherungen zwischen Rechts- und Literaturwissenschaft* (Munich: Fink, 2012), pp. 59–78.

Weber, M., *Wirtschaft und Gesellschaft. Grundriß der verstehenden Soziologie*, ed. J. Winkelmann (Tübingen: Mohr [Siebeck], 1980).

11

The dialectic of democracy and capitalism before the backdrop of a transnational legal pluralism in crisis

SONJA BUCKEL

Introduction: from conflict to corruption

The transnationalization of law began during the crisis of Fordism in the mid-1970s and took on the specific form of fragmentation.[1] Regional, national, and international courts as well as quasi-courts dealt with legal issues that found their ground for claims in different sets of rules. In stark contrast to the nation-state era, this led to new conflicts of laws and a 'chaotic coexistence of globally active bodies of conflict resolution',[2] which resisted any hierarchical solution.[3] They were the result of a 'permanent global conflict between different social rationalities'.[4] When analyzing these conflicts it is important not to interpret them simply as a mere manifestation of 'economic' globalization. An essential feature of modern civil law is its obstinacy, which it was able to keep in this new constellation.[5] The modern form of law is particularly characterized by its independent mode of operation, which removes it from *immediate* power relations. It was therefore possible that in the conflict between European human rights with the European border regime, the former were able to prevail before the European Court of Human Rights, or that in the conflict between state social law and European provisions of free movement, the European Court of Justice (ECJ) could strengthen transnational social rights against the declared will of national governments.[6]

This process of transnationalization, however, has faced for several years now a major crisis of capitalist socialization, in which the 'maximization of the inherent rationalities of various global functional

[1] Buckel and Fischer-Lescano, 'Gramsci Reconsidered', pp. 448–9.
[2] Fischer-Lescano and Teubner, *Regime-Kollisionen*, p. 9. [3] Ibid., p. 14.
[4] Ibid., p. 8. [5] Ibid., p. 23. [6] Buckel, '*Welcome to Europe*'.

systems' and the ensuing 'potential hazards for mankind, nature and society'[7] lead to a crisis. This development now threatens both to destroy the very autonomy of law, its relational autonomy and to foster the direct intrusion of political or economic power.

In exceptional circumstances, during 'momentous historical changes and threats', the law is unable to withstand political pressure, according to Luhmann, and absorbs more and more mere 'dummies of legality'. It starts to operate in a 'state of corruption' and allows for 'its opportunist adaptation to powerful elites'.[8] Even if this exception has not occurred yet, a significant trend has become manifest that already displays elements of this corruption. Take, for instance, the field of Union law; here, the first legally encoded anti-crisis measures already entailed significant legal violations: The so-called New Economic Governance, consisting of five European Union (EU) Regulations plus a Directive,[9] as well as the Fiscal Compact,[10] deals with both the regulation of public debt and budget deficits, and contains provisions that undermine basic norms of EU law in a barely concealed fashion. The mere fact that the same policy area is covered by two conflicting sets of norms – on the one hand, European secondary legislation, and on the other hand, an international treaty – is a first indication of tectonic shifts. Both measures are *ad hoc* responses to the crisis, generated partly via non-transparent procedures and under enormous time pressure, and circumventing democratic institutions in different ways. Moreover, they contain procedural standards that according to applicable European constitutional law fundamentally

[7] Fischer-Lescano and Teubner, *Regime-Kollisionen*, p. 28.

[8] Luhmann, *Das Recht der Gesellschaft*, pp. 81–2.

[9] Regulation (EU) 1173/2011 of the European Parliament and of the Council of 16 November 2011 on the effective enforcement of budgetary surveillance in the Euro area, OJ 2011 No. L306/1; Regulation (EU) 1174/2011 of the European Parliament and of the Council of 16 November 2011 on enforcement measures to correct excessive macroeconomic imbalances in the Euro area, OJ 2011 No. L306/8; Regulation (EU) 1175/2011 of the European Parliament and of the Council of 16 November 2011 amending Council Regulation (EC) no. 1466/97 on the strengthening of the surveillance of budgetary positions and the surveillance and coordination of economic policies, OJ 2011 No. L306/12; Regulation (EU) 1176/2011 of the European Parliament and of the Council of 16 November 2011 on the prevention and correction of macroeconomic imbalances, OJ 2011 No. L306/25; Council Regulation (EU) 1177/2011 of 8 November 2011 amending Regulation (EC) no. 1467/97 on speeding up and clarifying the implementation of the excessive deficit procedure, OJ 2011 No. L306/33; Council Directive 2011/85/EU of 8 November 2011 on requirements for budgetary frameworks of the Member States, OJ No. L306/41.

[10] Treaty on Stability, Coordination and Governance in the Economic and Monetary Union (2 March 2012, entered into force on 1 January 2013).

contradict the standardization of standardizing procedures in particular.[11] In doing so, they modify a policy area that was already configured via secondary and primary law by the Treaty of Maastricht (1992).

The Fiscal Compact was initially to be adopted by dint of the ordinary revision procedure laid down in Art. 48 TEU (Treaty on European Union). However, the suggested policies were so contested that no consensus emerged.[12] Therefore, efforts fled the field of European Union law and turned towards an international treaty concluded in accordance with Art. 216ff. TFEU (Treaty on the Functioning of European Union). Even its provisions, however, required the approval of the European Parliament, which was not sought.[13] Furthermore, a 'reverse majority rule' for the Council was introduced by Art. 7 TSCG (Treaty on Stability, Coordination and Governance in the Economic and Monetary Union) in order to grant structural primacy to the enforcement of austerity policies already at the procedural level. However, this procedure contradicts Arts. 121 and 126 TFEU.[14] The partly congruent measures of the 'New Economic Governance', for instance, the introduction of harsh sanctions for budget deficits as well as the shift of decision-making powers to the European Commission under the so-called restructuring procedures, also find no backing in primary law.[15] Lukas Oberndorfer[16] concludes therefore that the decision of the heads of state and government to turn the TSCG into an international treaty with the intent to circumvent in this way the democratic safety guarantees of the European constitution and the fact that the adoption of the New Economic Governance already avoided the actually required treaty change – leaving central parts without legal basis – suggest that 'prevailing anti-crisis measures can only be generated and implemented by violating formal democracy'.

While the increasing autonomy of law in capitalist society poses itself a key problem for the theory of democracy,[17] the weakening of relational autonomy as a result of the bypassing of democratic institutions also sabotages the constitutional protection against arbitrary measures. However, it is important to note, as Alex Demirović[18] suggested, that the fear of linear erosion leading to authoritarianism has so far not found

[11] Fischer-Lescano and Oberndorfer, 'Fiskalvertrag und Unionsrecht', p. 10.
[12] Ibid., p. 10. [13] Ibid., p. 11. [14] Ibid., p. 13.
[15] Oberndorfer, 'Krisenbearbeitung in der Europäischen Union', p. 30.
[16] Oberndorfer, 'Der Fiskalpakt', p. 175.
[17] Buckel, 'Von der Selbstorganisation zur Gerechtigkeitsexpertokratie'.
[18] Demirović, 'Multiple Krisen, autoritäre Demokratie und radikaldemokratische Erneuerung', p. 200.

onfirmation. This is partly due to the fact that every wave of de-emocratization has given rise to new democratic movements. The world-vide Occupy movements and novel social movement parties in Greece nd Spain do not only resist these processes of de-democratization; at the ame time they create new democratic forms of the political.[19] This in turn as an impact on the law.

To analyse these changes, in the following I will draw on an argument f the materialist theory of democracy; it claims to explain the cycles of tates of normalcy and emergency with the structure of capitalist social-zation: the 'dialectic of democracy and capitalism'. I therefore turn to an rgument that doesn't highlight a collision of logics but rather their ialectical relationship. The concept of dialectics, dating back to Hegel ut freed from his historical teleology, assumes a mediation – instead of a lash – of opposites: These opposite moments not only point at each ther mutually, but the analysis of each points 'to the opposite of its mplied meaning'.[20] The thesis here is therefore that the transnational egal pluralism in crisis is not abolished by this dialectic, but is funda-nentally reshaped through the violation of law's relational autonomy. Iowever, this trend threatens to erode those very procedures that organ-ze hegemony so that capitalist socialization undermines its very own reconditions via its immanent contradictions.

I will demonstrate how Marx developed this theoretical figure on the ccasion of the French bourgeois revolution of 1848, unpack its core lements and indicate how Marxist authors pursued this line of argument urther. To this end, I present paradigmatic illustrations that drew on this rgument during the two great crises of the twentieth century: a) the nterwar period, Nazism and the founding phase of the Federal Republic, as well as b) the crisis of Fordism in the mid-1970s. To conclude, I assess nsights for the current crisis.

Democracy and capitalism in *The Eighteenth Brumaire*

The starting point is Marx's *The Eighteenth Brumaire of Louis Bonaparte*, which is an outstanding historical materialist analysis of the politics of the revolution of 1848. The latter had created constitutional bodies in the course of parliamentary democratization, 'which were novel at least in France and Europe at that time, apart from a concurrently democratizing

19 Candeias and Völpel, *Plätze sichern!*; Lorey, 'Demokratie statt Repräsentation'.
20 Adorno, *Philosophische Terminologie*, pp. 141–2.

Switzerland'.[21] This is, following Marx, unpacked by reconstructing the following four key aspects of this tension-ridden constellation.

The 'unavoidable condition of . . . common rule'

The bourgeois class is not a single, coherent one, but deeply divided into its respective class fractions. In 1848, bourgeois landowners pursued a completely different material interest compared to the financial or industrial capital. Each of these fractions competed in turn with each other and relied on different types of intellectuals in the Gramscian sense: high dignitaries of the army, university professors, clergymen and the press.[22] The hitherto existing monarchy represented only the interests of one group; overall, the bourgeoisie had emerged as the leading societal but not political force. This changed with the revolution of 1848, which was hence also a bourgeois one, although initially all classes had jointly fought for the republic against feudal forces. Yet the working class, the republican as well as the petty bourgeoisie, were immediately excluded from political power: through murder, deportation, imprisonment and the loss of political rights. This sowed the seeds of destruction for the bourgeois republic, as Marx demonstrated explicitly and not without a certain malice.

Parliamentary democracy enabled the political rule of the bourgeoisie for the first time, despite its internal divisions. According to Marx, it proved to be 'the sole form of state in which their general class interest subjected to itself at the same time both the claims of their particular factions and all the remaining classes of society';[23] it allowed the factions shared rule.[24] It was therefore 'the unavoidable condition of their common rule'.[25]

Here, parliamentarianism acted as a relay for the universalization of conflicting interests: 'Every interest, every social institution, is here transformed into general ideas'.[26] Parliamentary discussion and voting procedures were instrumental in this regard. The main achievement of the constitutional revolution of 1848 was, however, the rule of egalitarian legitimized parliamentary law.[27] Rational formal law, which emerged at the same time in Europe, for example in the Napoleonic Code or the

[21] Brunkhorst, *Kommentar zu Karl Marx*, p. 229.
[22] Marx, 'Der achtzehnte Brumaire', p. 114. [23] Ibid., p. 159. [24] Ibid., p. 114.
[25] Ibid., p. 159. [26] Ibid., p. 135. [27] Brunkhorst, *Kommentar zu Karl Marx*, p. 135.

adaptation of Roman law in Prussia, caused the same effect: the universalizing of conflicting individual interests in the field of law.[28]

The subsequent failure of this first attempt resulted in a radical breakup of the bourgeois alliance. Not only did the two major groups segregate, they themselves disintegrated. In addition, the unity between representatives and the represented ceased to exist; they 'faced one another in estrangement and no longer understood one another'.[29]

The parliament as a 'regime of unrest'

But for Marx, the parliament had not only the function of enabling the political rule of the bourgeoisie, but also allowed a look at the interface of the dialectic of capitalism and democracy: The bourgeois class needed parliamentary democracy to prevail politically. *At the same time*, however, this regime is a 'regime of unrest':[30]

> The parliamentary regime lives by discussion, how shall it forbid discussion? . . . The struggle of the orators on the platform evokes the struggle of the scribblers of the press; the debating club in parliament is necessarily supplemented by debating clubs in the salons and the bistros; the representatives, who constantly appeal to public opinion, give public opinion the right to speak its real mind in petitions. The parliamentary regime leaves everything to the decision of majorities; how shall the great majorities outside parliament not want to decide?[31]

The large majorities outside of parliament were the workers and small plot farmers, or to use a Gramscian term: the subalterns. And the majority of decisions, parliamentary struggles and discussions in the press and salons stood in blatant contradiction to the 'rule that disappeared behind thick factory walls'.[32] The bourgeoisie hoped to be able to perpetuate its economic domination through its political power. To do so, it had however at the same time to 'embark on the most risky experiment of a politically egalitarian republic'.[33] When this experiment failed, the proletariat was excluded from all political power by restricting its suffrage. This made clear how much the parliament was not a mere instrument of the 'ruling class' but rather a 'battle ground'. Thus the exclusion of the proletariat and the inability of small plot farmers to organize themselves as a class and to be represented at all restored their

[28] Buckel, 'Von der Selbstorganisation zur Gerechtigkeitsexpertokratie'.
[29] Marx, 'Der achtzehnte Brumaire', p. 163. [30] Ibid., p. 135. [31] Ibid., pp. 135–6.
[32] Brunkhorst, *Kommentar zu Karl Marx*, p. 240. [33] Ibid.

pariah status.[34] 'Egalitarian parliamentarianism and capitalist rule are not easily compatible. In the period of 1848, Marx was convinced that they were totally incompatible, and maybe he was historically even right', concludes Hauke Brunkhorst in 2007 at the beginning of the current major crisis.[35]

The 'social republic', the advancing of the democratic constitution, was therefore on the agenda since the beginning of the bourgeois revolution, which had only been able to succeed in alliance with the proletariat. Although it was 'drowned in the blood of the Paris proletariat' through the suppression of the June riots, even before the inauguration of the National Assembly, this only made it reappear as a threating spectre in subsequent years.[36] The *social revolution*, according to Brunkhorst, is therefore the actual meta-narrative of the Marxian revolutionary dramaturgy. With the emergence of autonomous state power rather a shift 'into the wrong direction' took place.[37]

Involution

Within a few years, this contradiction sought an authoritarian solution, which Johannes Agnoli termed 'involution' in 1968; it is a process of turning democracies back into a pre- or anti-democratic state:[38] To keep intact the *social* power of the bourgeoisie, so the central thesis of the *Eighteenth Brumaire*, the latter is ready to sacrifice democratic gains and ultimately even its political power when confronted with a political crisis.[39]

Gradually, the French upper classes drove all lower classes out of the jointly achieved parliament. To do so, they had to use undemocratic and non-legal means: the massive curtailment of suffrage, the use of the state of emergency, manipulation, bribery, threats and violations of the constitution. Yet by doing so 'did it not afflict parliament itself, as against the executive authority and the people, with incurable weakness'?[40] It destroyed its own means of defence against absolutism, once it had become absolute.[41] When it finally – so the dialectic – was in sole possession of

[34] Marx, 'Der achtzehnte Brumaire', p. 139.
[35] Brunkhorst, *Kommentar zu Karl Marx*, p. 241.
[36] Marx, 'Der achtzehnte Brumaire', p. 174.
[37] Brunkhorst, *Kommentar zu Karl Marx*, pp. 198, 226.
[38] Agnoli, *Die Transformation der Demokratie*, p. 24.
[39] Marx, 'Der achtzehnte Brumaire', p. 136. [40] Ibid., p. 128. [41] Ibid., p. 130.

arliament, this was not worth anything. 'This will only work', argues Brunkhorst aptly,

> if the executive is without any doubt bound to parliamentary law; the parliament's only cover against a hostile executive power aiming at a coup is merely the sovereignty of the people and the ability to mobilize the communicative power of the street, in case things become serious. But this only works, if the people can effectively represent themselves in parliament and are not confronted with a hostile parliamentary dictatorship.[42]

And if everything else is exhausted, their own interest even commands – in order 'to restore tranquillity in the country', to further exploit the other classes – that 'it should be delivered from the danger of its own rule' given that all classes are condemned to like political nullity.[43] Due to its own weakness, the bourgeoisie recoils from the 'pure conditions of [its] own class rule' and longed for the underdeveloped and therefore less dangerous forms thereof'.[44] Under the protection of an unrestrained executive, relieved of the 'troubles and dangers of ruling', it aimed to pursue its private affairs.[45]

Nevertheless, the involution is even dangerous for the bourgeois class, because it leads to the erosion of a process of interest mediation. This becomes clear, when Marx summarizes the consequences of the Bonapartist form of rule towards the end of his study: Bonaparte, as the head of the executive, is hopelessly overwhelmed with the very mediation of conflicting interests and 'gropes' to and fro: 'Bonaparte would like to appear as the patriarchal benefactor of all classes. But he cannot give to one without taking from another'.[46] Thus he infuriates everyone and has to arrange 'a coup d'état in miniature every day'. With the ensuing chaos, he plunges the whole bourgeois economy into chaos.[47]

State machinery

The bourgeois class intensified repression to maintain its social power. It waged an 'uninterrupted war against public opinion', tried to 'cripple' the independent organs of the social movements, destroyed the parliamentary rights of the other classes and finally their own and rendered 'irresistible . . . the executive power hostile to it'.[48]

[42] Brunkhorst, *Kommentar zu Karl Marx*, pp. 245–6.
[43] Marx, 'Der achtzehnte Brumaire', p. 136. [44] Ibid., p. 123. [45] Ibid., p. 166.
[46] Ibid., p. 187. [47] Ibid., p. 189. [48] Ibid., p. 133.

In this way, it contributed to the further centralization of the 'executive power with its enormous bureaucratic and military organization, with its wide-ranging and ingenious state machinery', hence to 'a host of officials numbering half a million, besides an army of another half million'.[49] This state machinery, 'whose work is divided and centralized as in a factory',[50] emerged in the era of absolute monarchism and helped to accelerate the end of feudalism with its particularistic powers. In the course of the historical phases of the French Revolution, absolute monarchy, the Revolution of 1848 and subsequent Bonapartism, 'all revolutions perfected this machine instead of breaking it'.[51]

During this process, the state usurps common affairs:

> Every common interest was immediately severed from the society, countered by a higher, general interest, snatched from the activities of society's members themselves and made an object of government activity – from a bridge, a schoolhouse, and the communal property of a village community, to the railroads, the national wealth, and the national University of France.[52]

All parties who were alternately struggling for supremacy thought that they had acquired this incredible edifice of the state as the price of their victory; this is how Marx describes the classical state illusion. However, at least under the second Bonaparte, the state had become so independent vis-à-vis society that no class – not even the bourgeoisie – ruled the state apparatus. The state machinery was becoming so autonomous, 'that the Chief of the Society of 10 December suffices for its head – an adventurer dropped in from abroad, raised on the shoulders of a drunken soldiery which he bought with whisky and sausages and to which he has to keep throwing more sausages'.[53] And when in the crisis the executive gained at last victory over the legislative power, 'all classes, equally powerless and equally mute, fall on their knees before the rifle butt'.[54]

Democracy and capitalism in the materialist theory of the twentieth century

I now reconstruct how these four elements of Marx's argument were advanced during the respective cycles of democratic development: democracy as a condition of bourgeois rule and at the same time as its

[49] Ibid., pp. 116–7. [50] Ibid., p. 178. [51] Ibid., p. 179. [52] Ibid., pp. 178–9.
[53] Ibid., p. 179. [54] Ibid., p. 178.

nmanent danger, the resulting tendency to involution and the expan-ion of the state machinery.

Democracy as a condition for bourgeois rule

> Parliamentarianism is far from being an absolute product of democratic development, of the progress of the human species, and of such nice things. It is, rather, the historically determined form of the class rule of the bourgeoisie and – what is only the reverse of this rule – of its struggle against feudalism.

'his is how Rosa Luxemburg[55] summarized Marx's conclusions in the *ighteenth Brumaire*. Marxist theory, however, quite often overlooked he contradictory starting point: Even the economically dominant class eeds those processes that it does not simply control to arrive at a ommon political strategy. Instead, democracy was considered a mere nstrument of the bourgeois class.

It was above all Gramsci's theory of hegemony in the 1920s that ddressed the need for universalization. The bourgeois class could nly achieve political and cultural leadership if it was able to transcend ts narrow-minded 'corporate interest', that is, if it was able to undergo catharsis. It could only then gain a 'universal degree of hegemony' nd affect the entire fabric of society with its ideology.[56] Since Gramsci n turn devoted all his attention to cultural institutions, he engaged nly little with the political and legal institutions of bourgeois lemocracy.[57]

For his 'theory of the state', Nicos Poulantzas[58] drew on Gramsci and gave particular attention to the division of the bourgeois class.[59] The ong-term interest in capital utilization was dependent on state proced-ures, since individual fractions tended to only pursue their narrow-minded interests. Therefore, a hegemonic class fraction must succeed in merging the conflicting interests by credibly portraying its own eco-nomic and political interests as representative of the public interest. Only then an unstable balance of compromise arises.[60] The representative

55 Luxemburg, 'Sozialdemokratie und Parlamentarismus', p. 449.
56 Gramsci, *Gefängnishefte*, vol. III, notebook 4, § 38, pp. 495–6.
57 Priester, *Studien zur Staatstheorie*, p. 59. 58 Poulantzas, *Staatstheorie*.
59 Ibid., p. 118. 60 Demirović, *Nicos Poulantzas*, p. 79.

democratic institutions of the state enable this process, since they foster 'the organic circulation and reorganization of hegemony and thus hinder the occurrence of fractures in social cohesion'.[61]

Around the same time, Claus Offe argued from a functionalist-Marxist perspective that the 'class-specific selectivity' of the capitalist state was geared towards 'distiling a "class interest" out of the narrow-minded, short-term, conflicting, half-expressed interests of pluralist influence politics'.[62] Because the bourgeoisie was incapable of managing its own political affairs, it was necessary to harmonize the 'overall capitalist interest' even against the sporadic empirical opposition of individual interest groups. Additionally, complementary selectivity against anti-capitalist interests is required.[63] These 'selection effects' were, however, not to reveal their class character. This was to be achieved through the functional requirement 'of establishing the social conditions for the existence of capital in the name of the common good against the empirical resistance of individual capitals ...'[64] In this way, a 'historic congruence emerged between capitalist relations of production and bourgeois democracy', which 'was only disturbed temporarily ... in situations of extreme crisis'.[65] Poulantzas adopts Offe's idea of 'structural selectivity':[66] The 'function' of the state was the organization of the ruling and the disorganization of the dominated classes.

The inherent danger of democratic rule

At the beginning of the twentieth century, Rosa Luxembourg engaged with the question of how social democrats could both utilize the parliamentary system and at the same time work towards its abolishment in a socialist society. They needed to fight for the right to vote, the right of assembly, the freedom of the press, etc., since the parliamentary system itself served the working class as a platform, from which the 'educating of the masses' could be advanced.[67] After the demise of feudalism, the bourgeoisie, however, tended to abolish it altogether.[68] However, parliamentary struggles should not to be mistaken for the central axis of

[61] Jessop, 'Kapitalistischer Staatstyp und Autoritärer Etatismus', p. 55.

[62] Offe, *Strukturprobleme des kapitalistischen Staates*, pp. 101ff. [63] Ibid., pp. 103–4.

[64] Ibid., p. 115. [65] Ibid.

[66] Bob Jessop later turned this into the concept of a 'strategic selectivity': Jessop, *State Theory*.

[67] Haug, 'Rosa Luxemburg', p. 213.

[68] Luxemburg, 'Sozialdemokratie und Parlamentarismus', p. 451.

political life. Only in combination with the general strike and the mobilization of the street, a socialist society – the social republic – could be achieved.[69]

During the Weimar Republic and the rise of National Socialism, the Marxist legal theorist Franz Neumann emphasized in a similar vein that it was essential to defend civil rights and parliamentarianism against the bourgeoisie. After all, the general character of the law hid the true relations of power in society; at the same time, however, it also transcended this function.[70] And this very effect threatened civil rights; since parliament functioned only as long as the property-owning classes dominated it. 'In the very moment, however, in which the working class emancipates itself, gains political consciousness, the bourgeoisie loses its belief in the rule of law';[71] this is how Neumann reformulates the central argument of the *Eighteenth Brumaire*. The Weimar experience of the first parliamentary democracy in Germany rendered the insights of Marx's study highly topical. 'This separation of political and economic command generates the tension characteristic of the present state of capitalist democracy', argued Hermann Heller at the same time.[72] And thus the demand of the labour movement was 'social democracy', that is, the extension of the concept of a substantive rule of law to the organization of labour and property relations.[73]

In the post-war period, after the experiences of a failed Weimar Republic and National Socialism, the social democratic lawyer and political scientist Wolfgang Abendroth returned to this concept of 'social democracy'. At the time, a broad social consensus existed to break the privileges of the old power elites and to follow the path of far-reaching democratization in the economy and society; this became manifest in the various state constitutions and the Basic Law:[74] 'The end of the Weimar Republic has historically proven that democracy is in the long run no longer possible as a merely formal democracy'.[75] Therefore, the initially merely political principle of the democratically organized state should be transferred to society 'and thus to the management of its economic basis'.[76] In case the participation of all could not be secured in the

[69] Haug, 'Rosa Luxemburg', p. 217.
[70] Neumann, 'Der Funktionswandel des Gesetzes', p. 30.
[71] Neumann, *Behemoth*, p. 300. [72] Heller, *Staatslehre*, p. 155.
[73] Heller, 'Rechtsstaat oder Diktatur?'.
[74] Eberl and Salomon, 'Zum Verhältnis von Wirtschaftsdemokratie und sozialer Demokratie', p. 201.
[75] Abendroth, 'Zur Funktion der Gewerkschaften', p. 222. [76] Ibid., pp. 222–3.

planned control of economic processes, 'which decide the fate of society', then a parliamentary state could not maintain the values of democratic integration but would in the end even abandon parliamentary forms.[77]

This 'leitmotif' in Abendroth's studies on the theory of democracy[78] is an obvious reformulation of the *Eighteenth Brumaire*. But again, the old power elites were able to prevail. It was therefore only the debate about establishing certain elements of social democracy that dominated the post-war period.[79] Capitalist socialization was again allowed to solidify in a manner that even the economic crises were deemed unlikely. A combination of processes of capital concentration and unprecedented state interventionism interfered with the 'growing functional gaps of the market'[80] and cushioned them, leaving some Marxist theorists in the 1970s to assume that a systemic crisis was no longer to be expected. Instead, crises of legitimacy and motivation were emphasized, which were triggered by the very strategies that tried to avoid the great economic crisis.[81]

In the given context, associated considerations in democratic theory are of significance, because they led to a shift in Marxist discourse about the dialectic of capitalism and democracy: The inherent dangers of bourgeois parliamentarianism were seemingly mitigated. The fundamental contradiction was not an issue anymore, since the administrative system became 'sufficient autonomous vis-à-vis the constrained will-formation'.[82] The layout of formal democratic procedures ensured that administrative decisions could largely ignore the motives and needs of citizens. 'This occurs through a legitimation process that elicits mass loyalty but avoids participation'.[83] Thus citizens 'enjoy the status of passive citizens with only the right to withhold acclamation'.[84] In such a structurally depoliticized general public the need for legitimation shrunk to a political abstinence coupled with a focus on career, leisure and consumption, that is, 'system-compatible compensation'.

Claus Offe unpacked these procedural mechanisms further and thereby detailed the concept of state selectivity: Institutions that articulate political needs entailed inbuilt disciplinal mechanisms, which 'filter

[77] Abendroth, 'Demokratie als Institution und Aufgabe', p. 415.
[78] Eberl and Salomon, 'Zum Verhältnis von Wirtschaftsdemokratie und sozialer Demokratie', p. 203.
[79] Eberl and Salomon, 'Postdemokratie und soziale Demokratie', p. 418.
[80] Habermas, *Legitimationsprobleme im Spätkapitalismus*, p. 50. [81] Ibid., p. 129.
[82] Ibid., p. 55. [83] Ibid. [84] Ibid.

nd control processes of will-formation'.[85] Parliaments, political arties, and associations had become representative filter systems that orbade expecting that political and administrative action were geared to ccommodate the immediate demands of the population.[86] Regarding ne parliament he stated, for instance, that the majority of legislative nitiatives and key political decisions had been transferred to the jurisiction of the executive, while the political parties were engaged in a ublicist competition in parliament: 'Especially the most costly plenary essions gave rather the impression to be a joint meeting of the "public elations" departments of various parties than a dispute between rational nterests';[87] this is an observation thirty years before the diagnosis of ost-democracy became popular.

In this late-Fordist constellation, the dialectic between democracy and apitalism seemed to be eroded procedurally. Since the institutions of epresentative democracy isolated themselves from subaltern discourses, hey lost their dangerousness for the continued existence of capitalist ocieties. Party apparatuses, even of social democrats, had become utonomous filtering mechanisms. This could resolve the contradicion.[88] Why, so asks Offe therefore, do parties, associations, trade unions, he parliament and even elections not cease to exist; after all, they had ecome largely functionless. The functionalist answer is: They are still necessary to ensure mass loyalty required for overall stability.[89] Hence, ven at this point in time the dialectic between democracy and capitalism s not completely without effect. The filtering mechanisms just keep it atent. And thus the potential for involution also remains active. The atent conflict becomes manifest once the economic vulnerability of capitalism re-emerges.

Involution

t was Franz Neumann in particular who, apart from August Thalheimer, efreshed Marx's Bonapartism theory by using it to analyze the Nazi egime. In doing so, he also drew to some extent on Carl Schmitt's idea of he state of emergency. However, he reversed the relation of normal and emergency state in a critical move: The former is not determined by the atter, but *vice versa*. A predictable bureaucratic state, which is programmed via general, parliamentary legislation and binds the executive

85 Offe, *Strukturprobleme des kapitalistischen Staates*, p. 31. 86 Ibid., p. 42.
87 Ibid., p. 37. 88 Ibid., p. 125. 89 Ibid., pp. 48–9.

power to the legislature, is how he conceptualizes the functional requirements of the capitalist mode of production. 'If it is necessary for the state to coordinate and integrate hundreds and thousands of individual and group conflicts, the process must be accomplished in a universally binding manner', regulated 'through abstract rational law or at least through a rationally operating bureaucracy'.[90]

Predictability and rationality were the central prerequisites for stable capitalist accumulation in Neumann's and Max Weber's accounts; whereas the state of emergency is associated with a crisis of this very socialization.

> In a manifest crisis of this system, however, the "ideal" forms corresponding to capitalist socialization are questioned to the extent to which the economic and political reproduction of class domination is at risk. Therefore, those involutions tend to emerge in which, as it is claimed, the bourgeois society returns to forms of civilization predating those generated by itself.[91]

For Neumann, the state of emergency is therefore a bourgeois form of rule, yet a degenerated one[92] in the immediate sense. What decays is the unity of the legislative, executive and judicial powers, so that under National Socialism, for instance, no particular site of the monopoly of political power could be identified.[93] The various independent apparatuses (army/police, bureaucracy, party, and large-scale industry), deeply separated by internal contradictions, were only kept together by profit gained through the exploitation of foreign countries and the subaltern at home and through the fear of the 'oppressed masses'.[94] This system of rule could therefore no longer be called a state, rather a 'non-state'[95] or 'regime'.[96]

In the crisis of Fordism, Claus Offe[97] drew directly on this argument: As those politico-democratic and constitutional forms are vital for capitalism, they could not simply be overridden. While the abolition of democratic constitutional rules up until the open switch to authoritarian and fascist forms of political rule were present as a tendency, they ultimately caused more problems than they solved. For either the state would fall into the hands of narrow-minded individual capitalist exploitative interests or 'trigger autonomous rule by the state no longer bound

[90] Neumann, *Behemoth*, p. 542. [91] Schäfer, 'Franz Neumanns Behemoth', p. 693.
[92] Ibid., p. 695. [93] Neumann, *Behemoth*, p. 113. [94] Ibid., p. 544.
[95] Ibid., p. 291. [96] Ibid., p. 543.
[97] Offe, *Strukturprobleme des kapitalistischen Staates*, p. 123.

overall capitalist interests',[98] that is, Bonapartism. Precisely because the ourgeois state gained 'relative autonomy' vis-à-vis democratic formal ructures, which allows an enforcement of overall capitalist interests and e establishment of an ideological mechanism at the same time that recisely 'permits to deny' this complicity, all other forms of bourgeois ceptional rule remained far behind this rationale.[99]

Poulantzas clearly follows Marx, Neumann, and Offe when he assumes at the normal form of the capitalist state is based on democratic stitutions and, following Gramsci, hegemonic class leadership. 'It corsponds to conjunctures in which bourgeois hegemony is stable and fe; exceptional states respond to crises of hegemony'.[100] Crises of egemony become manifest in the crises of representation of political arties, the attempt of various social forces to circumvent them and to fluence the state directly, and finally in the 'attempt of state apparatuses enforce the political order regardless of decisions taken through the spective formal channels'.[101]

However, if these crises cannot be overcome by the normal, demoratic interplay of forces, democratic and constitutional institutions ould be repealed. This leads, however, to the fact that contradictions ould no longer be processed by routine and gradual policy adjustments nd new compromises. The apparent strength of the exceptional state erefore masks its real fragility. It is devoid of any specialized politicoleological apparatuses, which could channel and control the support of e masses. Moreover, it displays 'a rigid division of state power between espective political "clans", which are entrenched in the apparatuses'. It lso lacks an ideology that could create national-popular cohesion.[102] xception regimes became entangled in a muddle of inconsistent political actics. They are hence temporary responses to major crises.

With the crisis of Fordism, which Poulantzas also interprets as a ermanent crisis of state interventionism, a shift occurs: Since then, crisis endencies became a permanent feature of capitalism leading to a new egular form of the capitalist type of state, which integrated elements of he state of emergency. Poulantzas called this constellation 'authoritarian tatism'.[103] 'Intensified state control over every sphere of socio-economic ife' led to a 'radical decline of the institutions of political democracy' as

98 Ibid., p. 124. 99 Ibid., p. 125.
100 Jessop, 'Kapitalistischer Staatstyp und Autoritärer Etatismus', p. 54. 101 Ibid., p. 53.
102 Ibid., p. 55. 103 Ibid., p. 56.

well as 'draconian and multiform curtailment of so-called "formal" liberties'.[104]

The main aspects of the decline of bourgeois democracy are: a) a power shift from parliament to the executive, b) the functional decline of law in favour of special regulations, c) the functional decline of political parties as the central organs generating societal hegemony, and d) an increasing shift of this mediating function onto parallel operating power networks that bypass formal procedures.[105] Just like the exceptional state, the rise of authoritarian statism leads to paradoxical consequences: 'While it clearly strengthens state power at the expense of liberal representative democracy, it also weakens its capacities to secure bourgeois hegemony'.[106] After all, shifting the negotiation of compromises to administration implicates considerable disadvantages: It becomes more and more stagnant and secluded. Only taking short-term considerations into account, new haggling occurs case by case. This would contribute 'to the characteristic incoherence of current government policy, to the lack of any clear and long-term strategy' as well as 'short-sighted leadership and also to a lack of any global politico-ideological project or any "societal vision"'.[107] In this way, authoritarian statism itself generated new forms of popular struggles, which demanded the exercise of another, more direct form of democracy. It failed not only to integrate the population but rather produced 'a veritable explosion of democratic demands'.[108]

State machinery

Marx analyzed the development of the capitalist state in France in the nineteenth century as a dual process: the centralization of physical coercive power and the emergence of a bureaucratic apparatus in the process of class struggles. Unlike Marx, his successors in the theory of the state faced a developed Fordist welfare state in the 1970s. They could therefore assume that the state was not only a bundle of repressive state apparatuses, but needed to be understood as 'extended state' in the Gramscian sense, encompassing ideological and economic apparatuses.

[104] Poulantzas, *Staatstheorie*, pp. 231–2.
[105] Kannankulam, *Autoritärer Etatismus im Neoliberalismus*, p. 20.
[106] Jessop, 'Kapitalistischer Staatstyp und Autoritärer Etatismus', p. 60.
[107] Poulantzas, *Staatstheorie*, p. 276. [108] Ibid., p. 277.

They could also easily draw on the argument of an increasingly autonomous machinery by emphasizing that this was the reason that the state ought not to be regarded as a mere instrument of the ruling class. Thus, the authors involved in the so-called state-derivation debate argued that the unimpeded exchange of goods, competition, and 'freedom' of wage labour were only possible when the economically dominant class would not build its internal relations and the relationship with the working class on immediate force. Physical coercion must therefore undergo a process of institutionalization isolated from all social classes.[109]

Offe assumed also that capitalist societies were 'in great part characterized by the fact that the state is particularized'.[110] This meant that the state developed an 'alienated interest in himself',[111] that is, in its own coherence and existence. It was primarily not concerned with preventing unemployment, but tried to avoid the subsequent problems that unemployment posed to the system of state organizational means (e.g., decreasing tax revenue).[112]

Josef Esser subscribed to the notion that the state's self-interest in its own existence needed to be taken seriously; he criticized Offe, however, for taking this as the sole determinant of the practical operation of political rule. How the interest of the state in itself was determined substantially depended on the respective relationship between societal forces.[113]

It was Poulantzas's project to conceptualize the latter: He paid attention to both social struggles and state institutions, which became increasingly autonomous apparatuses. In this vein, the state was, in one of his famous sayings, 'the material condensation of such a relationship among classes and class fractions'.[114] This meant that a social antagonism was inscribed into the state apparatus and generated contradictions in its interior, among and within the apparatuses.[115] Various social forces find their respective bases within these state apparatuses. This resulted in the fact that the policies of individual state apparatuses pointed sometimes in opposite directions and occasionally even contradicted each part fundamentally. Poulantzas apparently drew here on Neumann's analysis

[109] Hirsch, 'Politische Form, politische Institutionen und Staat', p. 166; Esser, 'Reflexionen über ein gestörtes Verhältnis'.
[110] Offe, *Strukturprobleme des kapitalistischen Staates*, p. 139. [111] Ibid., p. 130.
[112] Ibid., p. 131. [113] Esser, 'Reflexionen über ein gestörtes Verhältnis', p. 215.
[114] Poulantzas, *Staatstheorie*, p. 154. [115] Ibid., p. 164.

of the National Socialist state and arrived at his conclusions for the normal state. The unity of the state, which is crucial for its ability to generate social cohesion, that is, both to commit the ruling forces to a common long-term project as well as to integrate the subalterns, is not self-evident. It can only be ensured with the help of specific state projects, which are developed in the various sections of the state.[116]

Exceptional state or social revolution

Finally and on this theoretical basis, I would like to outline some key aspects that should be taken as a starting point for an empirical analysis of the current crisis of legal pluralism. In doing so, it goes without saying that the discussed theoretical premises have to be updated. This has to begin with the theoretical concepts of capitalism inherent in these theories. One is perhaps not mistaken, when one points out that they are all, due to historical circumstances, based on a simplified notion of a 'pure capitalism'; this in turn leads them to exclusively analyze class relations. An empirical analysis should therefore be based on an intersectional analysis of capitalism.[117]

Furthermore, the two central spatio-temporal transformative processes in the past thirty years need also to be taken into account: transnationalization and the transition from Fordism to post-Fordism. Fragmentation and the conflicts of law, I had initially argued, are the main formative changes of transnationalization. This also applies to the transnationalization of state apparatuses: Thus, with the EU, a multi-scalar ensemble of state apparatuses emerged that is composed of both national and supranational apparatuses.[118] The heterogeneity and competition among the apparatuses has multiplied at a European level and thus also the bases for the diverse social forces. From a legal perspective, just think of the conflict between various legal apparatuses, such as the permanent collision of the German Constitutional Court with the ECJ – currently in the context of the announced purchase of government bonds by the European Central Bank.[119] The basic unity of this ensemble, essential for

[116] Jessop, *State Theory*, p. 128. [117] In detail Buckel, 'Dirty Capitalism'.

[118] Forschungsgruppe 'Staatsprojekt Europa', *Kämpfe um Migrationspolitik*.

[119] German Federal Constitutional Court (BVerfG), BVerfGE 134, 366–438, ECLI:DE:BVerfG:2014:rs20140114.2bvr272813; Opinion of Advocate General Cruz Villalón on Case C-62/14, *Gauweiler and Others* v. *Deutscher Bundestag* (14 January 2015) ECLI:EU:C:2015:7.

he generation of cohesion, is still very weak. There are first indications or elements of a European state project.

This also applies to various democratic and constitutional institutions. Thus, the European Parliament is weak despite co-decision competences; in contrast, the executive remains strong. As a result, the shift from the legislative to the executive power has become more pronounced. Finally, in the crisis, 'New Economic Governance' and the Fiscal Treaty have caused 'a massive enhancement of the executive apparatuses' and granted them comprehensive decision-making and sanctioning powers. At the same time, there is a definite weakening of the parliamentary arena – both at national and the European level'[120] – and the adoption of legal dummies.

The democratic and constitutional institutions are infrastructures universalizing competing interests. The fragmented bourgeois class urgently needs them to develop its own long-term project in order to enable social cohesion and thus stability. They must also be of relative autonomy, which allows the project to be enforced. Therefore, the dialectic of democracy and capitalism becomes manifest in the violation of procedures: For in this way policies and legal reactions become inconsistent and short term. There is a lack of a sustainable vision for society, a hegemonic project. Without the latter, the current crisis can, however, not be overcome. This is the conclusion also reached by Stephen Gill and Ingar Solty:

> We believe that the (at least temporary) failure to reform capitalism . . . is due to a lack of democratic forces that could push the neoliberal state to such measures . . . Today viable exit strategies suffer . . . from this weakening of democratic forces.[121]

This development is driven heavily by the second change: the transition to post-Fordism. While the democratic theories of Habermas, Offe and Poulantzas were still based on a criticism of Fordism's massive state interventionism, this situation changed radically when the Fordist class compromise – which was also a gender compromise and migration regime – was revoked in the early 1980s.[122] The privatization of government functions and the dismantling of social infrastructure, which

120 Oberndorfer, 'Vom neuen, über den autoritären zum progressiven Konstitutionalismus?', p. 78; see also Wissel and Wolff '"Staatsprojekt Europa" in der Krise?'.

121 Gill and Solty, 'Die organischen Krisen des Kapitalismus', p. 61.

122 Streeck, *Gekaufte Zeit*, p. 45.

triggered a care crisis, the precariatization and financialization of working and living conditions as well as the weakening of the organizations of the working class massively changed the post-Fordist state. Therefore one might ask whether the concept of authoritarian *statism* is still at all suitable. John Kannankulam[123] argues convincingly that state institutions were not torn down per se, but rather consent-oriented corporatist arrangements, which had to take the interests of the subalterns into account, were. Individual elements of an authoritarian statism had, however, been proven to be compatible with neoliberal changes. Thus, the increasing autonomy of the executive apparatus was quite useful for the rise of ministries of economic affairs and central banks within the ensemble of state apparatuses. With regard to the European scales, Lukas Oberndorfer[124] arrives at the same conclusion: *The* executive is not strengthened *generally*. 'Rather with the upgrading of those national treasuries and the Commission's Directorate General for Economic and Financial Affairs represented in the ECOFIN-Council, those state apparatuses are strengthened that show a particularly neoliberal and masculinist configuration'. What occurs, therefore, is not a deconstruction of 'the state' but a shift and scalar reorientation of individual apparatuses within the ensemble. Oberndorfer consequently proposes the concept of 'authoritarian competitive statism'.[125] It locates the authoritarian statism within the post-Fordist manner of EU integration that rests on the regulatory competition among Member States.

The decreasing relational autonomy of state and law allows private interests to exert direct influence more often through informal networks – such as through massive lobbying – or to penetrate them significantly, such as in the case of financial bureaucracies. This shift towards decentralized power networks also weakens those representative bodies to which women fought for access via quotas. 'The backrooms of negotiated democracy remain closed to them'.[126]

This is one of the reasons why authoritarian competitive statism underwent a massive crisis of legitimacy and motivation, to use Habermas and Offe's terms. Oberndorfer follows Gramsci and Poulantzas and points to a crisis of hegemony. The latter is characterized by the fact that 'the different scale levels of the ensemble of state apparatuses will replace

123 Kannankulam, *Autoritärer Etatismus im Neoliberalismus*, p. 330.

124 Oberndorfer, 'Vom neuen, über den autoritären zum progressiven Konstitutionalismus?', p. 86.

125 Ibid. 126 Sauer, '"Only paradoxes to offer?"', p. 126.

e now brittle consent by means of executive coercion'.[127] Dirk Martin d Jens Wissel[128] argue in a similar vein and identify a 'fragmented gemony'. The latter is no longer geared towards the promise of a neral welfare gain but rather towards certain social groups or regions, ch as in the relation between northern and southern Europe.

Fragmented hegemony, an increase in coercive elements, declining lational autonomy, dummies of legality, a lacking unity of the ensemble apparatuses and a lacking capacity to develop a viable crisis exit rategy – all these are indications of a major crisis, in which the institions of transnational legal pluralism got caught. The dialectic between emocracy and capitalism of the past democratic cycles showed two ings above all: Such a situation is, first, highly unstable and weakens oth the long-term interest in stable capital utilization and excludes the balterns broadly from political decision-making and juridical procedres. Second, this equally leads to an 'explosion' of democratic ovements as well as to a tendency to involutions, of which it is not ertain whether authoritarian competitive statism will turn into an xceptional state – especially if this crisis is not overcome.

Social revolution was the master narrative of the *Eighteenth Brumaire* ecause it allowed an emancipatory exit from the destructive dialectic of apitalism and democracy. One can only leave the spell of the cycles of utonomizing legal operations and dummies of legality if the cause of this ialectic, the lack of a *societal* democracy, is addressed. The hope for the eturn of a 'democratic capitalism', as suggested by Wolfgang Streeck[129] nd Colin Crouch,[130] however, will always end in the same impasse. As ong as the decisions about what is produced and consumed by whom for hat purpose and to what extent and within what division of labour are aken in an oligarchical manner and not democratically, the dialectic will lways be at work. That is why we have to return to those situations in hich 'social democracy',[131] following Abendroth, or the council democacy, following Marx, were on the agenda as counterhegemonic projects. t is essential to revisit the rich knowledge about real societal experinents,[132] although these experiments were always repressed by ruling orces after only a short time. As unrealistic as this may sound given urrent power relations; when even in Rojava, in a war zone, people try to

27 Ibid., p. 77. 128 Martin and Wissel, 'Fragmentierte Hegemonie'.
29 Streeck, *Gekaufte Zeit*. 130 Crouch, *Postdemokratie*.
31 Eberl and Salomon, 'Postdemokratie und soziale Demokratie'.
32 Very instructive: Demirović, 'Rätedemokratie oder das Ende der Politik'.

make possible a council democracy with a feminist outlook,[133] we in northern Europe have probably no reason to settle for pessimism.

References

Abendroth, W., 'Demokratie als Institution und Aufgabe' in M. Buckmiller, J. Perels and U. Schöler (eds.), *Wolfgang Abendroth, Gesammelte Schriften*, vol. II: 1949–1955 (Hannover: Offizin, 2008 [orig. 1954]), pp. 406–17.

'Zur Funktion der Gewerkschaften in der westdeutschen Demokratie' in M. Buckmiller, J. Perels and U. Schöler (eds.), *Wolfgang Abendroth, Gesammelte Schriften*, vol. II: 1949–1955 (Hannover: Offizin, 2008 [orig. 1952]), pp. 221–30.

Adorno, T. W., *Philosophische Terminologie*, vol. II (Frankfurt am Main: Suhrkamp, 1974).

Agnoli, J., *Die Transformation der Demokratie und andere Schriften zur Kritik der Politik* (Freiburg: Ça-ira, 1990).

Brunkhorst, H., *Kommentar zu Karl Marx. Der achtzehnte Brumaire des Louis Bonaparte* (Frankfurt am Main: Suhrkamp, 2007).

Buckel, S., 'Von der Selbstorganisation zur Gerechtigkeitsexpertokratie. Zum Wandel der Prozeduralisierung des Allgemeinen' in O. Eberl (ed.), *Transnationalisierung der Volkssouveränität: Radikale Demokratie diesseits und jenseits des Staates* (Stuttgart: Steiner, 2011), pp. 33–56.

'Welcome to Europe'. Juridische Kämpfe um das Staatsprojekt Europa (Bielefeld: Transcript, 2013).

'Dirty Capitalism' in D. Martin, S. Martin and J. Wissel (eds.), *Perspektiven und Konstellationen kritischer Theorie* (Münster: Westfälisches Dampfboot, 2015), pp. 29–48.

Buckel, S., and A. Fischer-Lescano, 'Gramsci Reconsidered: Hegemony in Global Law', *Leiden Journal of International Law*, 22 (2009), 437–54.

Candeias, M., and E. Völpel, *Plätze sichern! ReOrganisierung der Linken in der Krise. Zur Lernfähigkeit des Mosaiks in den USA, Spanien und Griechenland* (Hamburg: VSA-Verlag, 2014).

Crouch, C., *Postdemokratie* (Berlin: Suhrkamp, 2008).

Demirović, A., *Nicos Poulantzas. Aktualität und Probleme materialistischer Staatstheorie* (Münster: Westfälisches Dampfboot, 2007).

'Rätedemokratie oder das Ende der Politik', *Prokla. Zeitschrift für kritische Sozialwissenschaft*, 39 (2009), 181–206.

'Multiple Krisen, autoritäre Demokratie und radikaldemokratische Erneuerung', *Prokla. Zeitschrift für kritische Sozialwissenschaft*, 43 (2013), 193–215.

133 Graeber, 'Why is the World Ignoring the Revolutionary Kurds in Syria?'.

Eberl, O., and D. Salomon, 'Zum Verhältnis von Wirtschaftsdemokratie und sozialer Demokratie' in A. Fischer-Lescano, J. Perels and T. Scholle (eds.), *Der Staat der Klassengesellschaft: Rechts- und Sozialstaatlichkeit bei Wolfgang Abendroth* (Baden-Baden: Nomos, 2012), pp. 197–214.

'Postdemokratie und soziale Demokratie – Zur Einführung in den Heftschwerpunkt', *Politische Vierteljahresschrift*, 54 (2013), 415–25.

Esser, J., 'Reflexionen über ein gestörtes Verhältnis: Materialistische Staatstheorie und deutsche Politikwissenschaft' in J. Hirsch, J. Kannankulam and J. Wissel (eds.), *Der Staat der bürgerlichen Gesellschaft. Zum Staatsverständnis von Karl Marx* (Baden-Baden: Nomos, 2008), pp. 203–19.

Fischer-Lescano, A., and G. Teubner, *Regime-Kollisionen. Zur Fragmentierung des globalen Rechts* (Frankfurt am Main: Suhrkamp, 2006).

Fischer-Lescano, A., and L. Oberndorfer, 'Fiskalvertrag und Unionsrecht. Unionsrechtliche Grenzen völkervertraglicher Fiskalregulierung und Organleihe', *Neue Juristische Wochenschrift*, 66 (2013), 9–14.

Forschungsgruppe 'Staatsprojekt Europa' (ed.), *Kämpfe um Migrationspolitik. Theorie, Methode und Analysen kritischer Europaforschung* (Bielefeld: Transcript, 2014).

Gill, S., and I. Solty, 'Die organischen Krisen des Kapitalismus und die Demokratiefrage', *juridikum. zeitschrift für kritik | recht | gesellschaft*, 35 (2013), 51–65.

Graeber, D., 'Why is the World Ignoring the Revolutionary Kurds in Syria?', *The Guardian*, (8 December 2014).

Gramsci, A., *Gefängnishefte. Kritische Gesamtausgabe*, vol. III, notebook 4, ed. K. Bochmann and W. F. Haug (Hamburg and Berlin: Argument, 1991).

Habermas, J., *Legitimationsprobleme im Spätkapitalismus* (Frankfurt am Main: Suhrkamp, 1973).

Haug, F., 'Rosa Luxemburg und der Weg, der zu Gramsci führt und über ihn hinaus' in M. Brie and F. Haug (eds.), *Zwischen Klassenstaat und Selbstbefreiung* (Baden-Baden: Nomos, 2011), pp. 208–39.

Heller, H., 'Rechtsstaat oder Diktatur?' in H. Heller, *Gesammelte Schriften*, ed. M. Draht, O. Stammer, G. Niedermeyer and E. Borinski, vol. II (Leiden: Sijthoff, 1971), pp. 443–62.

Staatslehre (Tübingen: Mohr Siebeck, 1983 [orig. 1934]).

Hirsch, J., 'Politische Form, politische Institutionen und Staat' in J. Esser, C. Görg and J. Hirsch (eds.), *Politik, Institutionen und Staat* (Hamburg: VSA-Verlag, 1994), pp. 157–212.

Jessop, B., *State Theory. Putting the Capitalist State in Its Place* (Cambridge and others: Polity Press, 1990).

'Kapitalistischer Staatstyp und Autoritärer Etatismus. Poulantzas' Staatstheorie als moderner Klassiker' in L. Bretthauer, A. Gallas, J. Kannankulam and I. Stützle (eds.), *Poulantzas lesen. Zur Aktualität marxistischer Staatstheorie* (Hamburg: VSA-Verlag, 2006), pp. 48–64.

Kannankulam, J., *Autoritärer Etatismus im Neoliberalismus. Zur Staatstheorie von Nicos Poulantzas* (Hamburg: VSA-Verlag, 2006).

Lorey, I., 'Demokratie statt Repräsentation. Zur konstituierenden Macht der Besetzungsbewegungen' in I. Lorey, J. Kastner, G. Rauning and T. Waibel (eds.), *Occupy! Die aktuellen Kämpfe um die Besetzungen des Politischen* (Vienna and Berlin: Turia und Kant, 2012), pp. 7–49.

Luhmann, N., *Das Recht der Gesellschaft* (Frankfurt am Main: Suhrkamp, 1995).

Luxemburg, R., 'Sozialdemokratie und Parlamentarismus' in R. Luxemburg, *Gesammelte Werke*, ed. A. Laschitza, vol. XII (Berlin: Dietz Verlag, 1988 [orig. 1905]), pp. 447–55.

Martin, D., and J. Wissel, 'Fragmentierte Hegemonie. Anmerkungen zur gegenwärtigen Konstellation von Herrschaft' in D. Martin, S. Martin and J. Wissel (eds.), *Perspektiven und Konstellationen kritischer Theorie* (Münster: Westfälisches Dampfboot, 2015), pp. 220ff.

Marx, K., 'Der achtzehnte Brumaire des Louis Bonaparte', in *Marx-Engels-Gesamtausgabe (MEGA)*, Part I, vol. XI (Berlin: Akademie Verlag, 1975 [orig. 1852]), pp. 96–189.

Neumann, F., 'Der Funktionswandel des Gesetzes im Recht der bürgerlichen Gesellschaft' in F. Neumann (ed.), *Demokratischer und autoritärer Staat. Beiträge zur Soziologie der Politik* (Frankfurt am Main: Europäische Verlagsanstalt, 1967 [orig. 1937]), pp. 7–57.

Behemoth. Struktur und Praxis des Nationalsozialismus 1933–1944, ed. G. Schäfer (Cologne and Frankfurt am Main: Europäische Verlagsanstalt, 1977 [orig. 1942]).

Die Herrschaft des Gesetzes (Frankfurt am Main: Suhrkamp, 1980 [orig. 1936]).

Oberndorfer, L., 'Der Fiskalpakt – Umgehung der "europäischen Verfassung"und Durchbrechung demokratischer Verfahren?', *juridikum. zeitschrift für kritik | recht | gesellschaft*, 34 (2012), 168–81.

'Hegemoniekrise in Europa – Auf dem Weg zu einem autoritären Wettbewerbsetatismus?' in Forschungsgruppe 'Staatsprojekt Europa' (ed.), *Zwischen europäischem Frühling und autoritärem Etatismus. Die EU in der Krise* (Münster: Dampfboot Verlag, 2012), pp. 50–72.

'Krisenbearbeitung in der Europäischen Union. Economic Governance und Fiskalpakt – Elemente einer autoritären Wende?', *Kritische Justiz*, 45 (2012), 26–38.

'Vom neuen, über den autoritären zum progressiven Konstitutionalismus? Pakt (e) für Wettbewerbsfähigkeit und die europäische Demokratie', *juridikum. zeitschrift für kritik | recht | gesellschaft*, 35 (2013), 76–86.

Offe, C., *Strukturprobleme des kapitalistischen Staates* (Frankfurt am Main: Campus, 2006 [orig. 1969]).

Poulantzas, N., *Staatstheorie. Politischer Überbau, Ideologie, autoritärer Etatismus* (Hamburg: VSA-Verlag, 2002 [orig. 1978]).

riester, K., *Studien zur Staatstheorie des italienischen Marxismus: Gramsci und Della Volpe* (Frankfurt am Main: Campus, 1981).

auer, B., '"Only Paradoxes to Offer?" Feministische Demokratie- und Repräsentationstheorie in der "Postdemokratie"', *Österreichische Zeitschrift für Politikwissenschaft*, 40 (2011), 125–38.

chäfer, G., 'Franz Neumanns Behemoth und die heutige Faschismusdiskussion' in G. Schäfer (ed.), *Franz Neumann: Behemoth. Struktur und Praxis des Nationalsozialismus 1933–1944* (Cologne and Frankfurt am Main: Europäische Verlagsanstalt, 1977), pp. 665–776.

treeck, W., *Gekaufte Zeit. Die vertagte Krise des demokratischen Kapitalismus* (Frankfurt am Main: Suhrkamp, 2013).

Vissel, J. and S. Wolff, '"Staatsprojekt Europa" in der Krise?' in H.-J. Bieling and M. Große Hüttmann (eds.), *Europäische Staatlichkeit: zwischen Krise und Integration* (Wiesbaden: Springer, 2016), pp. 223–40.

12

Putting proportionality in proportion

Whistleblowing in transnational law[*]

ANDREAS FISCHER-LESCANO

It is now common sense that whistleblowing can be an effective way to bring unlawful actions and social grievances to public attention. This has spurred numerous international efforts, from corporate compliance governance codes to endeavors in the political realm, to create transnational safeguards to protect whistleblowers against repression and enable protest against unlawful practices:[1] Whistleblowing is central to the G20's anti-corruption plan, measures instituted by the Organization for Economic Cooperation and Development (OECD), the legal policy proposals of Non Governmental Organizations (NGOs), and Transparency International and national initiatives to establish "safe harbors," which, like the Icelandic Modern Media Initiative (IMMI), call for national media regulations to offer the greatest possible protection for whistleblowers.[2] Provisions designed to shield whistleblowers have been included in the UN Convention against Corruption (Articles 8, 13, and 33), the African Union Convention on Preventing and Combating Corruption (Article 5 Paragraph 6), the Organization of American States' (OAS) Inter-American Convention against Corruption (Article III Paragraph 8),

* I am grateful to Isabell Hensel, Johan Horst, Nora Markard, and Gunther Teubner for their constructive criticisms of an earlier version of this chapter.

1 For an overview, see Buckland and Wills, *Blowing in the Wind?*; Bowers et al., *Whistleblowing: Law and Practice;* Schmolke, "Whistle-blowing-Systeme als Corporate Governance-Instrument transnationaler Unternehmen."

2 G20, *Anti Corruption Plan*, Seoul Summit 2010, Annex III (7); Transparency International, *Recommended Draft Principles for Whistleblowing Legislation*; OECD, *Whistleblower Protection*; Ritchie, "Why IMMI matters," pp. 451ff.; and see the survey of the present-day situation in Human Rights Council, Report of the Special Rapporteur on the Promotion and Protection of Human Rights and Fundamental Freedoms while Countering Terrorism (rapporteur: Martin Scheinin), A/HRC/14/46, 17.5.2010, No. 18: "Members of intelligence services who, acting in good faith, report wrongdoing are legally protected from any form of reprisal. These protections extend to disclosures made to the media or the public at large if they are made as a last resort and pertain to matters of significant public concern."

nd the Civil Law Convention on Corruption (Article 9) as well as the riminal Law Convention on Corruption (Article 22) adopted by the ouncil of Europe.[3]

The rise of legal protections for whistleblowing as a major concern ı transnational legal policy responds to the increasingly transnational ature of the phenomenon itself: Whereas the classical forms of expres-ion whistleblowers resorted to were chiefly disseminated by national rint media and intervened in national debates, the impact of twenty-first entury whistleblowing is global. Due to the growing reach of digital nedia, the emergence of worldwide communication networks, and the vork of WikiLeaks, whistleblowers have access to transnational distribu-ion systems that allow them to disseminate information rapidly, effect-vely, and beyond national jurisdictions.[4] Especially in spaces of ransnational and privatized governance, which are largely impervious o democratic control by the authorities of one or another nation, vhistleblowing thus becomes an indispensable source for the generation f attention to breaches of law.

Security policy, where national institutions prize secrecy rather than ransparency,[5] is another domain in which whistleblowing plays an

For a survey of texts and norms see Fischer-Lescano, "Internationalrechtliche Regulierung des Whistleblowing", pp. 4 ff. (part I) and 48 ff. (part II). Even US President-elect Barack Obama issued a full-throated statement in support of whistleblowing in his 2008 transition agenda – at least as long as the whistleblower complies with the logic of the surveillance state rather than turning against it: "Often the best source of information about waste, fraud, and abuse in government is an existing government employee committed to public integrity and willing to speak out. Such acts of courage and patriotism, which can sometimes save lives and often save taxpayer dollars, should be encouraged rather than stifled. We need to empower federal employees as watchdogs of wrongdoing and partners in performance. Barack Obama will strengthen whistleblower laws to protect federal workers who expose waste, fraud, and abuse of authority in government." Barack Obama and Joe Biden, The Obama-Biden Plan, available at http://change.gov/agenda/ethics_agenda (last accessed January 13, 2015).

For a general discussion, see Winter, *Widerstand im Netz.*

The official statement issued by the German Federal Government on August 13, 2013 in reply to a question of the Social Democratic Party of Germany's parliamentary group concerning US wiretapping programs and the extent of the collaboration of German intelligence agencies with their US counterparts (BT-Drs. 17/14456) is symptomatic. "For reasons of the welfare of the state" (ibid., 4), large parts of the government's statement were classified as unsuitable for publication. The sections released for publication contain nothing but truisms such as the assertion that, given the realities of data transmission, it cannot be ruled out that agencies may have access even to purely domestic e-mail communications by tapping "networks or servers abroad" through which such communications are routed (ibid., answer to question 15).

important role, revealing the tendency of transnationally interconnected security services to overreach in their surveillance efforts.[6] Their surveillance-state methods have long slipped the fetters of the rule of law in the nation state. Aided by compliant global players in the information technology business, from Yahoo to Microsoft, which have received monetary compensation for their cooperation,[7] they have dramatically undermined the democratic and participatory structures charged with their oversight. Yet the field of security policy is also where whistleblowers, despite the widespread appreciation of their function as transmitters bringing social norms to bear on economic, scientific, military, and political decision-making, may suddenly find that they have exhausted the tolerance for their actions. When whistleblowers defy the attempts of surveillance states to benefit from what they do, when they turn their critical attention to security policy itself, they quickly confront severe political, economic, and legal repression: sources of funding are cut off and activists face prosecution and defamation. Legal actions taken to prevent the publication of documents and sanction whistleblowers in response to the critical investigation of issues in security policy have long been a "professional hazard" for journalists,[8] as the proceedings against the *New York Times* and Daniel Ellsberg in connection with the publication of the Pentagon Papers (1971), the indictment of Carl von Ossietzky for the work of *Die Weltbühne* during the Weimar Republic (1931), and the investigation against Conrad Ahlers and Rudolf Augstein during the *Spiegel* scandal (1962) in postwar Germany attest. Most recently, the cases of the WikiLeaks spokesman Julian Assange, who sets the whistleblowing platform's strategic direction, the WikiLeaks informant Chelsea Manning, who exposed war crimes in Afghanistan and Iraq, and the American intelligence agency employee Edward Snowden, whose 2013 revelations on Prism, XKeyscore, and the NSA triggered the ongoing surveillance and espionage scandal, demonstrate that the general endorsement of whistleblowing is supposedly limited by putative duties of loyalty and obligations of secrecy, reasons of state, operational interests, and other common good concerns.

In cases of conflict between disclosure and secrecy, the law generally answers the question of which forms of whistleblowing are permissible

[6] Deiseroth, "Whistle-blowing in der Sicherheitspolitik."

[7] MacAskill, "NSA paid Millions," *The Guardian*, August 23, 2013.

[8] von Ossietzky, "Der Weltbühnen-Prozeß," p. 250: "I know any journalist who asks critical questions about the Reichswehr must be prepared to face charges of treason; it's a natural professional hazard."

and which are unlawful through the "application of statutory provisions or regulations that call for adjudicators either to explicitly balance the two interests or to enforce statutes that incorporate this balance in their structure."[9] The judicial method of balancing and its schematic implementation under the principles of proportionality and practical concordance are thus of crucial significance when adjudicators must translate the abstract principle of support for whistleblowing into specific rules and resolutions of collisions, that is, to answer the question of which forms of whistleblowing are permissible when and where.

The focus of the following observations will be on the example of whistleblowing in the field of security policy. I will argue that balancing, proportionality, and practical concordance as they routinely figure in legal discourse are subtle instruments of repression. To disrupt the repressive operation of this legal method, the principle of proportionality will need to be reassessed. Only a tempered proportionality can facilitate rather than repress the exercise of liberties. I will advance this hypothesis in three steps:

First, balancing, proportionality, and practical concordance have become dominant methods in transnational law. As a consequence of this methodological ascendance, civil liberties are subject to a blanket reservation of ad hoc judicial restriction.

Second, the method of balancing and its objective of establishing proportionality and practical concordance, as currently applied, conceals the nature of the conflicts addressed by legal decisions and results in wrongly framing social conflicts in the law that are divorced from reality. Specifically, the conflict over whistleblowing does not pit subjective liberties against individual and collective opposing rights, the objects of legal protection that are conventionally balanced against each other; instead, it is a conflict between impersonal autonomous spaces.

Third, the development of an adequate legal framework for the collision of these autonomous spaces in cases of whistleblowing requires radical depersonalization of the issue. Instead of basing legal policy considerations on the good or bad intentions of whistleblowers from Edward Snowden to Julian Assange and Chelsea Manning, we will need to develop legal rules that do justice to the significance of whistleblowing as a transmitter of social values, as well as to the interests in confidentiality of the transnational spheres of diplomacy, military affairs, business, and so on.

[9] Fenster, "Disclosure's Effects: WikiLeaks and Transparency," p. 783.

Whistleblowing under the balancing reservation

In the *age of balancing*, the methodology of transnational law, like that of other legal fields, is informed by the idea of optimization through balancing.[10] The techniques of balancing and the establishment of proportionality and practical concordance developed in the international legal dialogue[11] have long broken the chains of national law. They have also become the dominant method of judicial decision-making on the level of transnational law. Proportionality, it is argued, is a universal constitutional principle,[12] a primary characteristic of global constitutionalism,[13] or a central proposition of international law.[14] Similarly, the ICANN arbitration courts[15] frequently render decisions on the allocation of Internet addresses that translate the relation between property rights and rights of expression into a matter of balancing:

> There is arguably no unlimited guarantee of the right to freedom of expression, since [the ICANN arbitration courts] ultimately already aim to balance interests in the protection of private rights against the public interest in the safeguarding of basic rights. This replicates a balancing of individual against general interests provided in national law by the interplay of basic rights protections and general laws.[16]

This balancing process subjects the whistleblower's actions to ad hoc restrictions in light of colliding interests. In employment law, for example, it yields a "balancing between the employee's interest in disclosure and the employer's interest in secrecy."[17] Along the same lines, the European Court of Human Rights (ECtHR) has made the permissibility of whistleblowing dependent on a balancing between employees'

[10] Aleinikoff, "Constitutional Law in the Age of Balancing."

[11] See Kennedy, "A Transnational Genealogy of Proportionality," as well as the comparative legal analysis in Knill and Becker, "Divergenz trotz Diffusion?."

[12] Klatt and Meister, "Verhältnismäßigkeit als universelles Verfassungsprinzip."

[13] Stone Sweet and Matthews, "Proportionality Balancing."

[14] Franck, "Proportionality in International Law" and see the critique in Petersen, "How to Compare the Length of Lines."

[15] ICANN (the Internet Corporation for Assigned Names and Numbers) is a private organization that manages the assignment of Internet addresses (domain names).

[16] Renner, *Zwingendes transnationales Recht*, p. 196; Simma, "Foreign Investment Arbitration," p. 591 speaks of "competing obligations" under different regimes.

[17] von Busekist and Fahrig, "Whistleblowing und der Schutz von Hinweisgebern," p. 121; on the collision between the employee's duty of loyalty to his or her employer and the civic duty to comply with prosecutorial requests for information, see BVerfG, 1 BvR 2049/00 of 2 July 2001 (disclosure of information to prosecutors does not constitute sufficient grounds for termination).

ghts to free expression and the affected opposing rights of employers to ıe protection of their reputation and economic interests.[18] It has stipu- ted that the decision to go public with information must be a last resort nd made in the honest belief that the specific allegations have been arefully verified and that the public interest in the information out- veighs the damage caused by disclosure. In assessing the proportionality f an interference with the whistleblower's rights, authorities must con- ider in particular the public interest in the information revealed. In this ontext, the ECtHR has called for a fair balancing between the protection f the employer's reputation and rights on the one hand, and the rotection of the employee's freedom of expression on the other hand. But the balancing process itself remains mysterious: The court has emained silent on which specific entities are to be balanced. A balancing *ensu lato* that seeks to reconcile the interests of employers and employ- es is combined with remarks on the proportionality of the intervention, vhich is in turn said to be determined by the public interest in the nformation to be revealed. Yet the ECtHR has not said how this public nterest is to be gauged and what distinguishes public from private nterests, leaving crucial parameters of the balancing process vague. The court thus retains a free hand in subsequent decisions and the ability o intervene and make inconspicuous adjustments to the judicial practice on a case-by-case basis, but this is detrimental to the establishment of stable legal doctrine and hence to the creation of reliable protections for vhistleblowers. The outcome of the balancing process remains unfore- eeable and whistleblowing is subject to the general and unqualified eservation that property rights – which are conceived as equal-ranking – nust not be infringed.[19]

Similarly, in the field of security policy, many attempts to demarcate he boundaries of permissible whistleblowing consider the relative weight of duties to protect, rights to security, and civil liberties.[20] For example, with regard to the release of information on the whistleblowing platform WikiLeaks, it has been argued that the freedom of expression must be "reconciled with potential opposing rights in the sense of a practical concordance."[21] As a consequence, defenders of whistleblowing and the

18 ECHR, *Heinisch* v. *BRD*, 21.07.2011, Cs. 28274/08, para. 64ff.

19 For a general discussion of the prevailing obsession with balancing, which impedes the formation of stable behavioral expectations, see Ladeur, *Kritik der Abwägung*, pp. 9–10.

20 Fenster, "Disclosure's Effects."

21 Hoeren and Herring, "Urheberrechtsverletzung durch Wikileaks?," p. 146.

exercise of the freedom of expression are frequently called upon to justify the legitimacy of such actions vis-à-vis the public interest in security as an opposing right. In this scenario, however, the practical implementation of the principle of proportionality is often effectively an "assault on human rights."[22] The formula of practical concordance, which demands that in case collisions of constitutional principles by the competing principles must be balanced in a way to realize the maximum effectiveness of each of the principles, also operates in this way. The use of the practical concordance scheme clearly shows that in situations of collision between individual and collective objects of legal protection, community interests may overwhelm civil liberties.[23] The technique of practical concordance, a modified adaptation of Gratian's twelfth-century *Concordia Discordantium Canonum* introduced to twentieth-century constitutional doctrine by Konrad Hesse and Richard Bäumlin, who had been students of Rudolf Smend,[24] is a model of "repressive tolerance," as Bäumlin candidly acknowledged in 1970.[25] Practical concordance allows for a praxis that restricts the exercise of basic and human rights in favor of collective goods even when the constitutional text would demand that these rights be guaranteed without reservation. The fact that concordance knows "no unconditional priority of basic rights over government responsibilities" allows for

> optimum practical concordance to be established between the different elements of the constitution, and specifically between the section on basic rights and the constitutionally prescribed or required government responsibilities, such as schools, the military, and the public administration.[26]

This model quickly defeats mechanisms of constitutional protection for whistleblowers. Considerations of proportionality in constitutional law and the establishment of practical concordances then go hand in hand with anti-espionage provisions and compromise the well-intended transnational

[22] Tsakyrakis, "Proportionality: An Assault on Human Rights?" Rusteberg, "Grundrechtsdogmatik als Schlüssel" p. 19, argues that an imbalance is structurally immanent to case-by-case consideration in such constellations.

[23] For a more extensive discussion, see Fischer-Lescano, "Kritik der praktischen Konkordanz"; on the collision of liberties and government objectives in the US, see Mathews and Stone Sweet, "All Things in Proportion?," p. 116.

[24] The *locus classicus* is in Hesse, "Grundzüge des Verfassungsrechts der Bundesrepublik Deutschland," para. 72: "The resolution of the problem must correlate objects of constitutional protection in such fashion that each of them gains reality."

[25] Bäumlin, "Das Grundrecht der Gewissensfreiheit," p. 19.

[26] Bäumlin, ibid., pp. 18–9.

codes designed to protect whistleblowing.[27] To place the freedom of whistleblowing under a sweeping balancing reservation is to gut it. As soon as whistleblowers address the practices of security services, breaking out of their role as private watchdogs in the service of state-surveillance networks, tolerance for their actions is at an end. Tolerance is then another term for repression. Herbert Marcuse put this succinctly in his essay on "Repressive Tolerance," criticizing that "what is proclaimed and practiced as tolerance today, is in many of its most effective manifestations serving the cause of oppression."[28] Balancing, proportionality, and practical concordance rescind the liberties the transnational law-making process has bestowed by shackling them to colliding individual and community values.

The illusion of proportionality

This repressive substance of the legal method of balancing, which frequently culminates in the establishment of putative proportionality and practical concordance, results from a subjectivist mis-specification that has infected the liberal legal paradigm and its habitual practice of considering the relative weight of subjective rights and opposing rights. Balancing, that is the basis of its methodological ascendance, enables courts and legal workers to administrate justice in individual cases without tying them into an emerging legal doctrine in any further detail – to exert judicial decisionism, as Ernst-Wolfgang Böckenförde put it in a critical essay.[29] The adjudicators retain all freedoms in their decision about colliding freedoms by veiling the principles of political order and legal/policy values that underlie their decision so as to render them unrecognizable: "It is not the dialectical *concordantia discordantium* that makes this mixture so distressing, but the complete renunciation of any reference to reality, which is an original sin of the law."[30] The opiates of the balancing method drown social conflicts of interest in a twilight state of harmonization allegedly governed by a rational and inclusive logic that optimally unites all conflicting points of view.[31] Balancing is a

[27] Khemani, *The Protection of National Whistleblowers*, p. 23.
[28] Marcuse, "Repressive Tolerance," p. 95.
[29] Böckenförde, "Grundrechtstheorie und Grundrechtsinterpretation," p. 1534.
[30] Wiethölter, *Rechtswissenschaft*, p. 74.
[31] Of the many contributions on this point, see only Riehm, *Abwägungsentscheidungen in der praktischen Rechtsanwendung*; Barak, *Proportionality*, pp. 458ff.

dialectical miracle method: It makes the incompatible compatible and the contrarian and fractious pliable.[32] It transforms the philosophy of opposites into judicial method.[33] The balancing method owes its appeal to the fact that it provides a schema that can set argument and counterargument, right and opposing right, in relation to each other without having to disclose the principles of political order to which the resulting decisions conform.

It makes intuitive sense that the permissibility of whistleblowing cannot be unlimited. *So my point is not to criticize the use of balancing to demarcate its boundaries. What needs to be criticized is how this balancing is implemented, that is, what is put on the scales.*[34] The judicial method sets individual goods in relation to collective goods without forming an idea of this relation. It translates social conflicts into conflicts between legally protected rights or principles without taking an interest in where the lines of social collision actually run. This transforms the social conflict into a legal one that can putatively be resolved in accordance with criteria of rationality, optimization, and inclusiveness. Balancing as it is conventionally practiced is the subtle technique of judicial hallucination. Entangled in phantom debates over the optimum implementation of subjectivist principles and values, the law remains blind to the fact that the balancing process does not merely decide questions of law and principle; its particular conception of the situation it balances is already the result of the reframing of a social conflict internal to the law. True, it is an inevitable consequence of the autonomy the law has attained that instances of social conflict must first be translated into the language of law before the law can resolve them. The problem is not that such translation takes place, but how it proceeds. The law's vision of the conflicts it resolves is in no way adequate to their complexity. It has not evolved a sense – this is the point Rudolf Wiethölter's trenchant critique homes in on – for the judicial distortion of social conflict, for the realities that are lost in the transformation into law, and for how the legal

[32] Cf. Heraclitus, *Fragments*, fragment 56, p. 37: "The cosmos works by harmony of tensions, like the lyre and bow"; see also Taubes, *Ad Carl Schmitt*.

[33] See Adam Müller's treatise on opposites: Müller, "Vom Gegensatz. Erstes Buch"; for more on Müller, see Ogorek, "Adam Müllers Gegensatzphilosophie."

[34] This point is made by Reimer, "... und machet zu Jüngern alle Völker?"; Poscher, "Theorie eines Phantoms"; see also the critique of balancing in Webber, "Proportionality, Balancing, and the Cult of Constitutional Rights Scholarship" and Kahn, "The Court, the Community and the Judicial Balance," pp. 4–5.

reframing might translate social questions more adequately into the *quaestio iuris*:

> The legal premise of proportionality, I have sought to argue, is the most influential transformative instrument for the osmosis, for translations, for instances of covariance between law and society, the highest and most general productive principle of a ... justification of rules of collision guiding the decision in cases of competing rights, interests, needs. Legal relations are indeed (in Germany, they have been since Savigny's days!) neither pure objects of assessment nor pure assessments of objects, but always already pre-mediated general decisions concerning the correlative association of facts with a specific law, as a qualification of the legal answers to social questions ... The covert premises implicit in the application of the theory of qualification itself, i.e., in how the principle of proportionality is applied, contain a complete program of social theory (*sub verbo* proportionality, justice, or the like), because it is the theory of qualification (not the norm) that determines the selection of object domains, and because this theory is determined in turn (not by norms, but) by the selection from alternative highest value assessments. What stands in need of explanation (and justification), then, are the mediating definitions (association) of objects of (e.g., commercial) law and a methodology guided by a substantial theory (social purposes, systemic responsibilities, the circumlocutions are of no concern to us: qualifications of proportionality as a theory of/for/in the practice itself). Yet this critical work remains undone. Whether and how it could be done is a question that cannot be answered with the means of law, jurisprudence, and the legal profession.[35]

To summarize this critique: the law has only an inadequate and utterly unreflective concept of what it is that the technique of balancing balances, brings into practical concordance, and sets in relation: interests, rights, principles, objects of constitutional protection – there are many candidates for a definition of the colliding entities. What they have in common, however, is that it is always an individual and subjective position (which may be identified as a right, interest, principle, or value) that allegedly needs to be set in relation to individual or collective counter-norms, -interests, -principles, or -values. This situation is even adduced to justify the principle of proportionality as such in the perspective of a theory of norms: as a dynamic relation between norm and counter-norm based on liberties conceived in subjectivist terms.[36]

[35] Wiethölter, "Sozialwissenschaftliche Modelle im Wirtschaftsrecht," p. 139.

[36] von Arnauld, "Die normtheoretische Begründung des Verhältnismäßigkeitsgrundsatzes," pp. 276ff.

This is exactly the gist of the matter: the law blindly adopts fundamental assumptions of liberalist models in which subjective liberties are set in relation to colliding subjective or collective goods. Especially when it comes to issues relating to whistleblowing, such mis-framing of the conflict engenders absurd results and patterns of argument. For example, the German Federal Ministry of Defense (BMVg) invoked § 97a of the German Copyright Act (UrhG) to argue that intellectual property rights (held, as individual rights, by the BMVg) forbade the publication of leaked papers and that whistleblowers, in publishing them, had violated the author's right to first publication granted by § 12 (1) UrhG.[37] Even if one frames the conflict in these terms with the German Federal Constitutional Court's holding, in the "Germania 3" ruling, that the commitment to practical concordance – that is, to "an equilibrium between the various protected (in some cases, constitutionally protected) interests" – extends to copyright law,[38] or rejects the claim that government ministries are creators in the sense of the Copyright Law,[39] such arguments do not chart a path out of the underlying judicial mis-framing of the issue. Whistleblowing does not represent a simple collision between an individual liberty (the whistleblower's freedom of expression or freedom of the press) and opposing individual rights (copyright law as an expression of property rights) or collective goods (reasons of state, state security, etc.). Couching the conflict in such subjective terms does not do justice to its complexity:[40] protecting whistleblowers is not about resolving the collision between subjective rights or principles and opposing rights in a way that safeguards individual liberties, but about the protection and self-delimitation of impersonal autonomous spaces of communication. The subjective right is then in fact what stands in the way of an adequate approach to the problem of whistleblowing.

The reduction of transnational conflicts such as those ignited by cases of whistleblowing to collisions of subjective rights and putative opposing rights is divorced from reality. Corrections to details of the balancing method such as a waiver of the proportionality test in balancing or a narrow application of scope-of-protection analysis, which is designed to avoid situations of collision, do not cut to the heart of the issue: the

[37] Cf. Freeman, "Protecting State Secrets as Intellectual Property."

[38] BVerfG, 1 BvR 825/98 of 29.6.2000 (Germania 3), para 23. The decision concerned the unauthorized use of passages from Brecht's works in Heiner Müller's play *Germania 3*.

[39] But see Hoeren and Herring, "Urheberrechtsverletzung durch Wikileaks?".

[40] Springer et al., "Leaky Geopolitics," p. 685.

subjective right as such, the scope of protection of the compact individual basic right, the use of personal liberties as the unit of measure, is the problem. True, the subjective right is itself the result of a process of differentiation. The *ius*, as the integral union of rights and obligations toward the community, and the Roman *action*, which identified rights with their procedural enforcement, evolved into the subjective right which is independent of procedural considerations and models of community. Its invention made it possible to shift legal relations from their basis in bilateral reciprocity to a foundation of complementary behavioral expectations – to unmix social relations, as it were:

> Predetermined and judging symbioses of rights and obligations give way to the social empowerment to act. The social reference is reduced to the license granted to something that has its mainspring in the agent himself, in his *libertas intrinsica*, in his will, in his interests.[41]

But the doctrine of subjective rights does not take abstraction far enough. Instead, it has given rise to an empiricism of the law, with grave consequences. This empiricism is not just a naturalistic fallacy: the problem is not that the law refers to what is to draw conclusions concerning what ought to be, as Hans Kelsen criticized in a discussion of Eugen Ehrlich's work.[42] The situation is more dramatic. The fallacy lies in the very fact that the law treats its social environment as existing and conceives it as composed of actual subjects to whom subjective rights are assigned. As Christoph Menke has rightly criticized,[43] this establishes the empiricism of the law as the determining fact in the legal constitution of the bourgeois society it understands to be its natural basis. But rights cannot be grafted onto pre-legal rationally oriented subjects. The subjects do not actually exist in the form the law assigns them. They are merely as-if subjects, projections of the law, an abstracting guise that reduces the human being of flesh and blood to a rational willing entity while also obscuring the social conditioning of the *homo iuridicus*. The critique of empiricism unseats the subject as the alpha and omega of the law. The private autonomous legal subject is not the sun around which the legal planetary system orbits. In a functionally differentiated society, its gravitational pull declines.

41 Luhmann, "Subjektive Rechte," p. 74, trans. by the author.

42 Kelsen, "Eine Grundlegung der Rechtssoziologie," p. 843: "In the field of the law, the rules of is and ought are thus fundamentally different in form."

43 Menke, *Kritik der Rechte*, pp. 99ff.

These observations concur with analyses that have long highlighted the trans-subjective nature of civil rights and liberties and chipped away at the plausibility of the legal form of the subjective right. Niklas Luhmann, who saw this keenly, criticized the judicial distortion of social conflict into a collision of subjective rights, arguing that it had no answer to the contemporary challenges in the system/environment relationships of the global society:

> Yet these are exactly the problems a functionally differentiated society with subsystems that operate in relative autonomy increasingly faces, both in the inter-systemic relationships internal to the society and in the relationship between the social system and its natural and personal environment. So the very social order that was built with the assistance of this subject-centered language may find itself in a situation in which this language is no longer persuasive and becomes implausible.[44]

A law that describes society as made up of "subjects" does not operate at an adequate level of complexity. It is divorced from reality, has no idea of sociality, and distorts social conflicts beyond recognition. Because the rational subject is the cornerstone of its thinking, it has no room for ecological and social questions, no language for institutional conflicts and no conception of human freedom.

Safeguarding impersonal liberties

So to conceive the protection of whistleblowers solely as a protection of subjective rights – and even worse, to make the question of whistleblowing hinge on the whistleblower's good faith – is to misconstrue the trans-subjective dimension of whistleblowing as a specific form of intervention into public spaces. Whistleblowing defends basic forms of democratic participation and control against the encroachments of a transnational security apparatus that resorts to unlawful practices and renders those responsible for them invisible. In WikiLeaks, a global space of communication has emerged that, as envisioned by the "Declaration of the Independence of Cyberspace,"[45] has attained substantial autonomy vis-à-vis

[44] Luhmann, "Subjektive Rechte," p. 80, trans. by the author.

[45] Barlow, "Declaration of the Independence of Cyberspace," February 9, 1996, available at https://projects.eff.org/~barlow/Declaration-Final.html (last accessed November 13, 2015). The declaration begins as follows: "Governments of the Industrial World, you weary giants of flesh and steel, I come from Cyberspace, the new home of Mind. On behalf of the future, I ask you of the past to leave us alone. You are not welcome among us. You have no sovereignty where we gather."

national legal orders.[46] WikiLeaks initially relied on a cloud strategy to safeguard the autonomy of this public space.[47] During the publication of the Iraq Papers, a network of mirror servers ensured the accessibility of the data. With the recent efforts to install its servers offshore in order to stabilize and preserve the autonomous space of free communication, WikiLeaks seeks to permanently elude the grasp of national authorities. Such spaces of free communication that defy the attempts of political and military institutions and powerful businesses to seize, monitor, and control them are the central requirement if democracy and the spontaneous and eruptive expression of opinions are to remain viable. Keeping them free is the only way to counter the totalizing tendencies of the transnational security apparatuses. Therein lies the democratic function of a whistleblowing platform such as WikiLeaks.

The judicial search pattern, which is designed to identify proportional and balanced forms of the exercise of individual liberties, is not even remotely adequate to this fundamental significance of whistleblowing to democracy: To provide effective protection for whistleblowers through safeguards of impersonal liberties while also preventing injurious acts of whistleblowing, the law needs to map the lines of social conflict in the *quaestio iuris*. The spaces of communication created by WikiLeaks are spaces of the impersonal exercise of liberty. Following Helmut Ridder, Karl-Heinz Ladeur has proposed a definition of "impersonal liberty" as "the protection of the self-definition of a process of opinion-formation that is also held to possess the ability to reflect on its own rule-compliance."

> This capacity for self-organization is quite plausibly protected as a liberty whose impersonal nature is apparent in the fact that it is not about the self-definition of individuals but about the distributed generation of an autonomous rule-compliant process.[48]

By focusing on the protection of spaces of personal autonomy, the traditional theory of basic rights reduces the panorama of complex social relations in which humans act in the context of differentiated social spheres to a diminutive detail it then installs as the only world. But society is more than the interaction of subjects endowed with reason,

[46] See Teubner, "Globale Zivilverfassungen."
[47] de Filippi and Belli, "Law of the Cloud v Law of the Land."
[48] Ladeur, "Helmut Ridders Konzeption der Meinungs- und Pressefreiheit," p. 290; and see already Ridder, "Die Meinungsfreiheit."

and so issues of basic rights are not exhaustively addressed by rules that govern intersubjective freedoms. Instead, clear distinctions need to be drawn between threats to the integrity of human beings, legal subjects, and impersonal institutions. Conceived in this perspective, basic rights are social and legal counter-institutions against the expansive tendencies of social systems. They protect not simply subjective rights but, depending on their particular form, human beings in their physical integrity, legal subjects in their freedom, or impersonal and institutional autonomous spaces.[49]

Broadening our view to include trans-subjective liberties allows us to reframe the interwovenness of human and social emancipation in the law: The free development of the individual is possible only in concert with the establishment of social spaces of communication. I would like to sketch the consequences of such a shift toward transpersonal liberty safeguards for the legal situation of whistleblowing in three steps:

Step one – Facilitating the evolution of forces: In a first step, it needs to be understood that the protection of whistleblowers not only safeguards individual personal development, but also protects the autonomous space of communication. Ludwig Raiser urged early on that the perspective of subjective rights must be complemented by a perspective of the emancipation of human forces via social institutions. To protect social institutions means to safeguard space for human development, and so his admonition is more relevant now than ever: "The ability to develop one's own forces and the opportunity to derive economic profit from doing so should not be understood as subjective rights against competitors and customers."[50] In the same vein, Gunther Teubner elaborates on the objective of facilitating individual development through the protection of institutions in his argument in favor of protection for whistleblowers, writing that the deliberate promotion of divergent behavior in social institutions can unleash forces of self-correction that stimulate "dissension, protest, opposition, and moral courage amid the debilitating atmosphere of . . . hierarchies and pressures to conform."[51] The purpose of such a liberation of whistleblowing is then to establish a culture that facilitates divergence. Fritz Bauer, who was the Hessian chief prosecutor at the time of the

[49] Teubner, "Die anonyme Matrix."
[50] Raiser, "Der Stand der Lehre vom subjektiven Recht," p. 472.
[51] Teubner, "Whistleblowing gegen den Herdentrieb?," p. 39.

Spiegel scandal in 1962, saw this clearly when he criticized that, in the cases of Rudolf Augstein and Conrad Ahlers, "non-conformism was vilified as punishable by jail."[52] The urgent need remains to develop effective provisions to protect whistleblowers from sanctions. It is a cynical state of affairs that Edward Snowden, Chelsea Manning, and others are persecuted and prosecuted for security reasons because they have dared to practice whistleblowing not only as watchdogs in the service of the security services, but also as watchdogs over the security services, in a challenge to the security complex. But in addition to shielding individual whistleblowers and their associates and confidants from the grasp of the security complex, we must see the importance of whistleblowing to the democratic process. Whistleblowing is not only about individual emancipation, but also about social emancipation and the unleashing of social forces.[53] Put abstractly, the challenge is to make a situation possible in which transnational security apparatuses are once again subject to, rather than in command of, the imperatives of democratically organized social forces. Nothing less is at stake than society's ability to regain control of security policy and socioeconomic conditions.

Step two – Identifying collisions: The collisions, disputes, conflicts of interest, real contradictions, and antagonisms that arise in this context are not simply collisions between subjective liberties (let alone principles of subjective freedom) and (individual or collective) opposing rights. Instead, they manifest a collision between incompatible social spheres that overwhelm and compromise each other. Karl Marx pioneered the analysis of the destructive potential of economic rationality, whose reach was already global in his day; his observations have been confirmed by many later writers.[54] Max Weber introduced the concept of modern polytheism to highlight the hazards inherent in the economic sphere as well as other areas of life and analyzed the resulting dangerous conflicts between different rationalities.[55] Contemporary analyses often follow Jean-François Lyotard in speaking of discourse collisions.[56] Meanwhile, the larger public has become alive to the social, human, and ecological risks posed by other highly specialized

[52] Bauer, "Schriftliche Stellungnahme von Generalstaatsanwalt Dr. Fritz Bauer," pp. 139–40.
[53] On the concept of force in this context, see Fischer-Lescano, *Rechtskraft*, pp. 115ff.
[54] Most formidably by Polanyi, *The Great Transformation*, pp. 270ff.
[55] Weber, *Gesammelte Aufsätze zur Wissenschaftslehre*, pp. 605ff.
[56] Lyotard, *The Differend: Phrases in Dispute*, pp. xiff.

global systems such as science and technology. The economic, scientific, military, and technological as well as political spheres have become embroiled in a "clash of rationalities" in the global society, with all the attendant destructive tendencies.[57] That has consequences also for whistleblowing, which provokes conflicts of one kind in the context of the economic system and another kind in the context of transnational diplomacy and transnational security. Each area has its own criteria to determine what constitutes the core interests of a transnational public information which must be disseminated even when colliding rationalities suggest otherwise. The judicial task is to identify the precise constellation of spheres in each instance and to develop adequate rules for such collisions that do not merely render justice in individual cases, but lend themselves to generalization. That, in turn, is the condition on which the possibility of the emergence of a stable legal doctrine rests.

Step three – Putting proportionality in proportion: The method of the establishment of proportionality must accordingly submit to a proportionality test. The arbitrary approach to the conflict by means of the unspecific consideration of the relative weight of principles of liberty and their social constraints must be supplanted by the development of norms that adequately protect a given social sphere against the encroachments of other domains seeking to maximize the purview of their own distinctive rationality. It goes without saying that the law must safeguard, for example, the core domain of diplomatic exchange and enable diplomatic confidence-building, even in backrooms; complete transparency would be prejudicial to diplomacy.[58] On the other hand, with regard to security policy whistleblowing, the military-police complex cannot claim unlimited cover from public scrutiny. Yet when secrecy is imperative and when it is impermissible must not depend on the political classification of something as "secret."[59] That would subject the public sphere to politics rather than politics to the public. So norms capable of generalization must instead be developed to govern collisions between the logics of the public interest in disclosure and the particular domain's interest in secrecy. Their goal must be to enable public debate and discussion of sufficient breadth and depth to

57 Luhmann, "The World Society as a Social System."

58 That is the kernel of truth in the demands expressed in Ischinger, "Das Wikileaks-Paradox."

59 Sagar, "Das mißbrauchte Staatsgeheimnis," p. 217.

tie the spheres in question back to the public discourse of society.[60] In the tension between the autonomy of spheres and their responsiveness, the law's mission is to develop norms governing incompatibilities that counter the danger that politics, business, science, and other spheres undermine the instruments of democratic control through the ubiquitous invocation of common good interests such as security, the welfare of the state or the need for secrecy.[61] The function of the law in this context is to defend transnational autonomous spaces of public discussion, opinion formation and debate against interventions and encroachments; that is, in the field of security policy, to allow for democratic oversight and control over transnationally interconnected security policies. As Adolf Arndt rightly pointed out in the early controversies over the concept of the state secret, for defense and security policies to be shaped in a democratic process, the public needs to be "informed about facts that are significant to the formation of the popular will." So in gauging the proportionality of an invasion of the autonomous space of communication, it is vital that military forces and intelligence agencies, too, "must remain subject to public control and criticism; in cases of doubt, the decision must be against the restrictive measure and in favor of the freedom of information."[62] With regard to the protection of and constraints on whistleblowing, this implies that the whistleblower's motivation is thoroughly irrelevant to the assessment of the permissibility of his or her actions. What is determinative, by contrast, is that no protection can be claimed for secrets whose legitimacy is dubitable and in fact an issue under public

60 In a recommendation issued on May 14, 2013, the German Rectors' Conference, an association of public and state-accredited German universities, seeks to forestall public involvement in cases of academic whistleblowing: "For the protection of the sources of information (whistleblowers) and the affected parties, the work of the ombudsperson is subject to strict confidentiality. Such confidentiality is broken when the source shares his suspicion with the public. In so doing, he will frequently be in breach of the rules of good academic practice himself." Yet such a ban on involving the public effectively poses a greater danger to scholarly work, which is based on the free discussion of the formal and substantial qualities of scholarship and its social responsibility, than isolated inquiries into cases of plagiarism; a critical point made by Preuss, "Man darf eine kritische Öffentlichkeit nicht ausschließen," *Süddeutsche Zeitung* of June 6, 2013.

61 On a norm governing cases of incompatibility in another context, see Teubner, "Ein Fall struktureller Korruption?".

62 Arndt, "Umwelt und Recht," pp. 25–6; and cf. the exclusion of "facts which constitute violations of the independent, democratic constitutional order or of international arms control agreements by virtue of having been kept secret from the treaty partners of the Federal Republic of Germany" from secrecy, as provided by § 93 Abs. 2 StGB.

> debate: War crimes and human rights violations are in no way government responsibilities to be shielded from a critical public, nor do they belong to the legitimately secret core of transnational security policy. Similarly, measures that infringe basic rights and rights to integrity and that lack a sufficient legal basis cannot be legitimately confidential. The actions of a whistleblower who discloses war crimes in Iraq and Afghanistan, then, cannot be unlawful any more than the dissemination of information about secret surveillance programs operated in transnational collaboration by intelligence agencies that manifestly infringe the transnational basic and human rights to the protection of personal data.[63]

The goal of whistleblowing, then, is not a completely transparent political sphere; it is not trying to counter the total exposure of the private realm by calling for a total exposure of politics. Whistleblowing aims to allow for a public discussion of illegal and undemocratic practices of transnationally interconnected security services that infringe civil liberties, and to create room for the formation of public opinion. Such debate is a necessity if we are to regain democratic control of central issues in transnational security policy. As national forms of democratic oversight and participation prove manifestly insufficient, WikiLeaks, Edward Snowden, Julian Assange, Chelsea Manning, and all those who venture their lives for our freedom give us reason to hope that we will be able to defend the foundations of our democracy against the transnational network of intelligence agencies and security services.

Bibliography

Aleinikoff, A., "Constitutional Law in the Age of Balancing," *Yale Law Journal*, 96 (1987), pp. 943ff.

v. Arnauld, A., "Die normtheoretische Begründung des Verhältnismäßigkeitsgrundsatzes," *Juristenzeitung*, 55 (2000), pp. 276ff.

Arndt, A., "Umwelt und Recht," *Neue Juristische Wochenschrift*, 1/2 (1963), pp. 24ff.

Barak, A., *Proportionality: Constitutional Rights and Their Limitations* (Cambridge University Press, 2012).

[63] On the challenges of transnational privacy protection, see Hanschmann, "Das Verschwinden des Grundrechts auf Datenschutz"; on the nascent efforts to respond to this situation, see, e.g., Pitz, "Weltweiter Datenschutz."

Barlow, J.P., *Declaration of the Independence of Cyberspace* (February 9, 1996), available at https://projects.eff.org/~barlow/Declaration-Final.html

Bauer, F., "Schriftliche Stellungnahme von Generalstaatsanwalt Dr. Fritz Bauer" in G. Ruge (ed.), *Landesverrat und Pressefreiheit. Ein Protokoll* (Cologne: Kiepenhauer & Witsch, 1963), pp. 135ff.

Bäumlin, R., "Das Grundrecht der Gewissensfreiheit," *Vereinigung der deutschen Staatsrechtslehrer*, 28 (1970), pp. 3ff.

Böckenförde, E.-W., "Grundrechtstheorie und Grundrechtsinterpretation," *Neue Juristische Wochenschrift* (1974), pp. 1529ff.

Bowers, J., et al., *Whistleblowing: Law and Practice* (Oxford University Press, 2010).

Buckland, B., and A. Wills, *Blowing in the Wind? Whistleblowing in the Security Sector* (Geneva: DC-AF-OSF Working Paper, 2012).

v. Busekist, K., and F. Fahrig, "Whistleblowing und der Schutz von Hinweisgebern," *Der Betriebs-Berater*, 68 (2013), pp. 119ff.

de Filippi, P., and L. Belli, "Law of the Cloud v Law of the Land: Challenges and Opportunities for Innovation," *European Journal of Law and Technology*, 3/2 (2012), pp. 1ff.

Deiseroth, D., "Whistleblowing in der Sicherheitspolitik," *Blätter für deutsche und internationale Politik*, 49 (2004), pp. 479ff.

Fenster, M., "Disclosure's Effects: WikiLeaks and Transparency," *Iowa Law Review*, 97 (2012), pp. 753ff.

Fischer-Lescano, A., "Kritik der praktischen Konkordanz," *Kritische Justiz*, 41 (2008), pp. 166ff.

Rechtskraft (Berlin: August-Verlag, 2013).

"Internationalrechtliche Regulierung des Whistleblowing" *Arbeit und Recht*, 64 (2016), pp. 4 ff. (part I) and 48 ff. (part II).

Franck, T., "Proportionality in International Law," *Law & Ethics of Human Rights*, 4 (2010), pp. 231ff.

Freeman, J., "Protecting State Secrets as Intellectual Property: A Strategy for Prosecuting WikiLeaks," *Stanford Journal of International Law*, 48 (2012), pp. 185ff.

Hanschmann, F., "Das Verschwinden des Grundrechts auf Datenschutz in der Pluralität von Rechtsregimen," *Europäische Grundrechte-Zeitschrift* (2011), pp. 219ff.

Heraclitus, *Fragments*, trans. Brooks Haxton (New York: Penguin, 2001).

Hesse, K., *Grundzüge des Verfassungsrechts der Bundesrepublik Deutschland*, 20th edn (Heidelberg: C F. Müller, 1999).

Hoeren, T., and E.-M. Herring, "Urheberrechtsverletzung durch Wikileaks? Meinungs-, Informations- und Pressefreiheit vs. Urheberinteressen," *Multimedia und Recht Zeitschrift für Informations-, Telekommunikations- und Medienrecht*, 3 (2011), pp. 143ff.

Ischinger, W., "Das Wikileaks-Paradox: Weniger Transparenz, mehr Geheimdiplomatie" in H. Geiselberger (ed.), *Wikileaks und die Folgen* (Berlin: Suhrkamp, 2011), pp. 155ff.

Kahn, P. W., "The Court, the Community and the Judicial Balance: The Jurisprudence of Justice Powell," *Yale Law Journal*, 97 (1987), pp. 1ff.

Kelsen, H., "Eine Grundlegung der Rechtssoziologie," *Archiv für Sozialwissenschaft und Sozialpolitik*, 39 (1915), pp. 839ff.

Kennedy, D., "A Transnational Genealogy of Proportionality in Private Law" in R. Brownsword et al. (eds.), *The Foundations of European Private Law* (Oxford: Hart Publishing, 2011), pp. 185ff.

Khemani, M., *The Protection of national Whistleblowers: Imperative but Impossible* (Georgetown University Law Center, 2009).

Klatt, M., and M. Meister, "Verhältnismäßigkeit als universelles Verfassungsprinzip" in M. Klatt (ed.), *Prinzipientheorie und Theorie der Abwägung* (Tübingen: Mohr Siebeck, 2013), pp. 62ff.

Knill, C., and F. Becker, "Divergenz trotz Diffusion? Rechtsvergleichende Aspekte des Verhältnismäßigkeitsprinzips in Deutschland, Großbritannien und der Europäischen Union," *Die Verwaltung*, 36 (2003), pp. 447ff.

Ladeur, K.-H., "Helmut Ridders Konzeption der Meinungs- und Pressefreiheit in der Demokratie," *Kritische Justiz*, 32 (1999), pp. 281ff.

Kritik der Abwägung in der Grundrechtsdogmatik (Tübingen: Mohr Siebeck, 2004).

Luhmann, N., "Subjektive Rechte: Zum Umbau des Rechtsbewusstseins für die moderne Gesellschaft" in N. Luhmann (ed.), *Gesellschaftsstruktur und Semantik*, vol. II (Frankfurt am Main: Suhrkamp, 1993), pp. 45ff.

"The World Society as a Social System," *International Journal of General Systems*, 8 (1982), pp. 131ff.

Lyotard, F., *The Differend: Phrases in Dispute*, translated by Georges Van Den Abbeele (Minneapolis: University of Minnesota Press, 1988).

MacAskill, E., "NSA Paid Millions to Cover Prism Compliance Costs for Tech Companies," *The Guardian*, August 23, 2013.

Marcuse, H., "Repressive Tolerance" in R. P. Wolff, B. Moore Jr., and H. Marcuse (eds.), *A Critique of Pure Tolerance* (Boston: Beacon Press, 1969), pp. 95ff.

Mathews, J., and A. Stone Sweet, "All Things in Proportion? American Rights Review and the Problem of Balancing," *Emory Law Journal*, 60 (2011), pp. 102ff.

Menke, C., *Kritik der Rechte* (Frankfurt a.M.: Suhrkamp-Verlag, 2015).

Müller, A., "Vom Gegensatz. Erstes Buch" in W. Siebert et al. (eds.), *Adam Müller. Kritische, ästhetische und philosophische Schriften*, vol. II (Neuwied: Luchterhand, 1967), pp. 195ff.

Ogorek, R., "Adam Müllers Gegensatzphilosophie und die Rechtsausschweifungen des Michael Kohlhaas" in H. J. Kreutzer (ed.), *Kleist-Jahrbuch 1988/89* (Berlin: Erich Schmidt Verlag, 1988), pp. 96ff.

v. Ossietzky, C. , "Der Weltbühnen-Prozeß," *Die Weltbühne*, December 31, 1931, reprinted in C. v. Ossietzky, *Sämtliche Schriften*, vol. VI (Hamburg: Rowohlt, 1994), pp. 249ff.

Petersen, N., "How to Compare the Length of Lines to the Weight of Stones: Balancing and the Resolution of Value Conflicts in Constitutional Law," *German Law Journal*, 14 (2013), pp. 1387ff.

Pitz, C., "Weltweiter Datenschutz," *Frankfurter Allgemeine Zeitung*, July 31, 2013, p. 19.

Polanyi, K., *The Great Transformation: The Political and Economic Origins of our Time*, 2nd edn (Boston: Beacon Press, 2001 [orig. 1944]).

Poscher, R., "Theorie eines Phantoms. Die erfolglose Suche der Prinzipientheorie nach ihrem Gegenstand," *Rechtswissenschaft*, 1 (2010), pp. 349ff.

Preuss, R., "Man darf eine kritische Öffentlichkeit nicht ausschließen," *Süddeutsche Zeitung*, June 10, 2013.

Raiser, L., "Der Stand der Lehre vom subjektiven Recht im Deutschen Zivilrecht," *Juristenzeitung*, 16 (1961), pp. 465ff.

Reimer, P., ". . . und machet zu Jüngern alle Völker? Von universellen Verfassungsprinzipien und der Weltmission der Prinzipientheorie der Grundrechte," *Der Staat*, 52 (2013), pp. 27ff.

Renner, M., *Zwingendes transnationales Recht. Gemeinwohlinteressen im Recht jenseits des Staates* (Baden-Baden: Nomos, 2011).

Ridder, H., "Die Meinungsfreiheit" in F. L. Neumann, H. C. Nipperdey, and U. Scheuner (eds.), *Die Grundrechte. Handbuch der Theorie und Praxis der Grundrechte* (Berlin: Duncker & Humblot, 1954), pp. 242ff.

Riehm, T., *Abwägungsentscheidungen in der praktischen Rechtsanwendung* (München: C. H. Beck, 2006).

Ritchie, W., "Why IMMI matters: The first Glass Fortress in the Age of Wikileaks," *Suffolk Transnational Law Review*, 35 (2012), pp. 451ff.

Rusteberg, B., Grundrechtsdogmatik als Schlüssel zum Verständnis von Gemeinschaft und Individuum" in D. Burchardt et al. (eds.), *Kollektivität – Öffentliches Recht zwischen Gruppeninteressen und Gemeinwohl* (Baden-Baden: Nomos, 2012), pp. 15ff.

Sagar, R., "Das mißbrauchte Staatsgeheimnis. Wikileaks und die Demokratie" in Geiselberger (ed.), *Wikileaks und die Folgen* (Berlin: Suhrkamp, 2011), pp. 201ff.

Schmolke, U., "Whistle blowing-Systeme als Corporate Governance-Instrument transnationaler Unternehmen," *Recht der internationalen Wirtschaft*, 58 (2012), pp. 224ff.

Simma, B., "Foreign Investment Arbitration: A Place for Human Rights?," *International and Comparative Law Quarterly*, 60 (2011), pp. 573ff.

Springer, S., et al., "Leaky Geopolitics: The Ruptures and Transgressions of WikiLeaks," *Geopolitics*, 17 (2012), pp. 681ff.

Stone Sweet, A., and J. Matthews, "Proportionality Balancing and Global Constitutionalis," *Columbia Journal of Transnational Law*, 47 (2008–09), pp. 72ff.

Taubes, J., *Ad Carl Schmitt. Gegenstrebige Fügung* (Berlin: Merve, 1987).

Teubner, G., "Die anonyme Matrix. Zu Menschenrechtsverletzungen durch private Akteure," *Der Staat*, 44 (2006), pp. 161ff.

"Ein Fall struktureller Korruption? Die Familienbürgschaft in der Kollision unverträglicher Handlungslogiken," *Kritische Vierteljahresschrift für Gesetzgebung und Rechtswissenschaft*, 83 (2000), pp. 388ff.

"Globale Zivilverfassungen: Alternativen zur staatszentrierten Verfassungstheorie," *Zeitschrift für ausländisches öffentliches Recht und Völkerrecht*, 63 (2003), pp. 1ff.

"Whistle blowing gegen den Herdentrieb?" in D. Becker et al. (eds.), *Ökonomie der Werte* (Marburg: Metropolis, 2013), pp. 39ff.

Transparency International, Recommended Draft Principles for Whistleblowing Legislation, November 2009.

Tsakyrakis, S., "Proportionality: An assault on human rights?," *International Journal of Constitutional Law*, 7 (2009), pp. 463ff.

Webber, G., "Proportionality, Balancing, and the Cult of Constitutional Rights Scholarship," *Canadian Journal of Law and Jurisprudence*, 23 (2010), pp. 179ff.

Weber M., *Gesammelte Aufsätze zur Wissenschaftslehre*, 3rd edn (Tübingen: C. J. B. Mohr, 1968).

Wiethölter, R., *Rechtswissenschaft* (Basel: Helbing und Lichterhahn, 1986 – reprint of 1968 publication).

"Sozialwissenschaftliche Modelle im Wirtschaftsrecht," *Kritische Justiz*, 18 (1985), pp. 126ff.

Winter, R., *Widerstand im Netz. Zur Herausbildung einer transnationalen Öffentlichkeit durch netzbasierte Kommunikation* (Bielefeld: Transcript-Verlag, 2010).

13

On the critical potential of law – and its limits

Double fragmentation of law in Chevron Corp. *v.* Ecuador

HANNAH FRANZKI AND JOHAN HORST

Introduction

> The Tribunal hereby orders: the Respondent (whether by its judicial, legislative or executive branches) to take all measures necessary to suspend or cause to suspend the enforcement and recognition within and without Ecuador of the judgment by the Provincial Court Sucumbíos . . . against the First Claimant in the Ecuadorian legal proceedings known as the Lago Agrio Case. . .[1]

> An arbitration award, even though it might be binding for Ecuador, can neither force judges to violate the human rights guaranteed by the constitution, nor can it expect them to disregard obligations emanating from international human rights treaties.[2]

The first statement above was issued by an arbitration panel convened under the rules of the United Nations Commission on International Trade Law (UNCITRAL) to decide a dispute between Chevron Inc. and the State of Ecuador; the second one is a response, published the following day, by the Provincial Court of Justice of Sucumbíos, Ecuador. Both decisions are pieces of a jigsaw puzzle encompassing several legal disputes that followed the oil production of Texaco (now Chevron) in the Ecuadorian rain forest. In February 2011, the Ecuadorian court in Sucumbíos ordered Chevron to pay $18 billion worth in compensation to those affected by the environmental pollution and related health problems, a verdict which was later reduced by the High Court to $9.5

[1] *Chevron Corporation and Texaco Petroleum Corporation* v. *The Republic of Ecuador*, UNCITRAL; PCA Case No. 2009-23 (all further references do documents of this case with full title and PCA Case No. omitted), Second Interim Award, p. 3.

[2] Corte Provincial de Justicia de Sucumbíos, *Aguinda y otros* v. *Chevron*, Statement on Interim Award. p. 3 (our translation).

billion.[3] While the arbitration tribunal claims it has the authority to order the Ecuadorian government to suspend the sentence, the Ecuadorian court, in turn, holds that the government is equally bound by national and international law to protect the human rights of its citizens. To demand that the government must suspend the judgment would not only interfere with the judicial independence, but also result in the violation of the rights of those whose suffering is remedied by the Ecuadorian judgment.

The interim award in *Chevron Corp.* v. *Ecuador* is one of many cases in which arbitration tribunals *de facto* decide upon the situation of a population that is not party to the legal dispute. In this chapter, we discuss the legal disputes emanating from the conflict following Texaco's oil production as an example of a larger set of cases in which investment disputes affect the rights of third parties. These cases usually present themselves as a collision between the rights of those affected by large-scale investment projects on the one hand, and the rights of investors on the other. This collision, we will argue, testifies to a double fragmentation in transnational law, which affects how law frames and decides underlying social conflicts.

The first fragmentation denotes the fragmentation of transnational law into different legal regimes. Rather than constituting a mere collision between conflicting jurisdictions – understood in the traditional way of legal competence – the case of *Chevron Corp.* v. *Ecuador* should be understood as the result of this fragmentation. This perspective focuses on the different logics and rationales underlying the respective legal regimes: with transnational investment law aiming at offering transactional security and shaped by classical and neoclassical notions of free trade and movement of capital on a global scale, it institutionalises a very specific paradigm of political economy which postulates the free market and private property as a basis for economic growth and, related hereto, wealth. While historically human rights law has been closely related to the institution of private property, it has also served to exempt areas of society from the rationale of the market (cf. Sonja Buckel's contribution in this volume). Thus the collision of human rights law and investment law is not a mere conflict of jurisdictions but a collision of different legal rationalities. If transnational human rights law is to remedy the negative consequences of large-scale investment projects, then, to merely include

[3] Barrett, 'Amazon Crusader'.

it into the legal regime of investment protection – as the dominant business and human rights approach seems to suggest – would only make human rights subject to the very logic of investment protection. Rather, a human rights approach to investment arbitration should demand a self-restriction of investment law, that is, arbitration panels should abstain from rendering a decision where rights and interests of third parties are affected.

The second and more fundamental fragmentation manifest in *Chevron Corp.* v. *Ecuador* concerns the relationship between law and its other, the non-law. To understand the suffering of the affected population as human rights violations, or even the idea of the *afectados* as an actually existing group, is already a perspective onto the social as construed by law. In the second part of this chapter we set out to explore this second fragmentation.

We close this chapter arguing that in the face of the double fragmentation, the emancipatory potential of law in the context of social conflict comes to fruition only if it reflects this double fragmentation by what – evoking Walter Benjamin – could be called a double 'deposition' (*Entsetzung*) of law. Before we start with the analytical part of the argument, we advance the central aspects of the legal disputes, which followed the oil drilling activity in Ecuador, in order to set the scene for the analysis.

Chevron Corp. *v.* Ecuador*: the context*

The arbitration dispute under UNCITRAL rules needs to be understood in the context of a lengthy litigation process that started in 1993. US lawyer Stephen Dozinger filed a class action lawsuit in the name of a group of people affected by the oil production of Texaco (the *afectados*), demanding damages suffered by the population in the Ecuadorian Amazon region where Texaco had drilled for oil. He argued that:

> As a direct and proximate result of defendant's breaches of duty, plaintiffs and the class have suffered injuries to their persons and property. Plaintiffs and the class are entitled to recover compensatory and punitive damages in amounts to be ascertained at trial.[4]

One year earlier, in 1992, the concession treaty between the Ecuadorian government and the company had expired, leaving the local population

[4] *Maria Aguinda et al.*, v. *Texaco Inc.*, District Court for the Southern District of New York, Complaint of 3 November 1993, p. 29.

with the remainders of thirty years of oil exploitation – open pits, oil spillages, and health damage. The responsibility of Texaco (which was bought in 2001 by Chevron Corp.) for health and environmental damages is, by now, subject to a range of legal disputes all of which are linked to the class action suit filed in 1993. In 2002, nine years after the suit was first presented, the federal court in New York dismissed its jurisdiction on the grounds of a *forum non conveniens* rationale, arguing that the claim should be brought before an Ecuadorian court, as long as both parties would subject themselves to Ecuadorian jurisdiction. The claimants thus filed a lawsuit with the Court in Lago Agrio (Province of Sucumbíos), which issued a judgment in 2011, obliging Chevron to pay around $10 billion in reparations and compensation.[5] Legal grounds for the claim were, in addition to Ecuadorian tort law and Article 15 of the International Labour Organisation (ILO) Convention No. 169, the Ecuadorian constitution. The latter grants the collective right to a clean and healthy environment, the violation of which enables citizens to file a legal complaint. Furthermore, the bill on environmental management, adopted in 1999, allows any citizen to denounce a breach of its regulations. Thus, one central and contested aspect of the Lago Agrio trial was the degree of the environmental and health damage produced by the oil production. Over the course of the proceedings, more than hundred, often mutually contradicting, expert reports were produced. By the time the judgment was handed down, Chevron had already withdrawn its assets from Ecuadorian soil so that the claimants now seek to enforce the judgment abroad.[6]

Chevron, for its part, embarked on two different legal strategies to fight the decision made by the Ecuadorian court.[7] Based on the 'Racketeer Influenced and Corrupt Organizations Act (RICO-Act)', they filed a claim against the lawyers of the *afectados* in the United States, arguing that the lawyers had conspired to win the claim in Ecuador through illegal practices. In the decision published in March 2014, Judge Kaplan ordered an injunction after finding that the 'decision in the Lago Agrio

[5] Judgment No. 2011-0106, Sala Única de la Corte Provincial de Sucumbios, 3 January 2012 (Spanish). The judgment was approved by the Court of Appeals; see judgment of the Corte Nacional de Justicia, Aguinda, 12 November 2013.

[6] Lawyers for the plaintiffs have sought to enforce the judgment in Brazil, Argentina and Canada, so far without success. For the latest developments see Noronha, 'Ecuadorian Chevron Oil Pollution Case'.

[7] See for an overview of the different legal proceedings: Dhooge, '*Aguinda* v. *Chevron Texaco*'.

case was obtained by corrupt means' and that 'defendants here may not be allowed to benefit from that in any way'.[8] In addition, even before the Ecuadorian court had published its decision, Chevron initiated (in 2009) a UNCITRAL arbitration proceeding against Ecuador with the aim to prevent courts from enforcing the Ecuadorian judgment.[9] The decision in the Lago Agrio case, they argued, violates the rights protected by the bilateral investment treaty between Ecuador and the United States from 1993.[10] In a nutshell, Chevron held that in 1995, Texaco and Ecuador had signed a settlement agreement that released Texaco (and hence now Chevron) from any further claims regarding the environmental pollution caused in Ecuador. By now, the arbitration tribunal has published five decisions and interim measures according to Article 26 (1) UNCITRAL rules,[11] namely four Interim Awards[12] and one Partial Award.[13] In its first Interim Award on Interim Measures, published on 25 January 2013, the tribunal ordered Ecuador to impede the enforcement of the Lago Agrio Judgment in Ecuador. Once the plaintiffs sought to enforce the judgment abroad, the tribunal extended the order so that Ecuador should also impede the enforcement in other countries.[14] The political and legal tensions arising from this decision are at the core of this chapter.

Beyond jurisdiction

Plaintiffs, lawyers and many commentators have celebrated the judgment in the Lago Agrio case as successful precedent to hold companies legally accountable for the negative consequences of their operations.[15] With the pending arbitration proceedings, however, there seems to be the possibility that the panel will decide in favour of Chevron and oblige the Ecuadorian government to prevent the judgment from being enforced. The interim

[8] United States District Court Southern District of New York, *Chevron Corp.* v. *Stephen Donziger, et al.*, 11 Civ. 0691 (LAK), Opinion, 4 March 2014, p. 484.

[9] For a general overview over the various litigations, see Dhooge, '*Aguinda* v. *Chevron Texaco*'.

[10] Treaty between the United States and the Republic of Ecuador concerning the Encouragement and Reciprocal Protection of Investment.

[11] On Article. 26 UNCITRAL Rules cf. Caron and Caplan, *The UNCITRAL Arbitration Rules*, chapter 17.

[12] Fourth Interim Award on Interim Measures, 7 February 2013.

[13] First Partial Award on Track, 17 September 2013.

[14] Second Interim Award on Interim Measures, 16 February 2012; Fourth Interim Award on Interim Measures, 7 February 2013, No. 80.

[15] E.g., Vogt, 'Urteil Ecuador vs. Chevron'.

awards and the first partial award issued so far raise several questions. As indicated earlier, the arbitration panel establishes its own jurisdiction assuming the authority to oblige Ecuador to suspend the local court's judgment. Such a judgment would effectively leave the *afectados* without remedies.

The arbitration tribunal, however, avoids dealing with this contradiction in that it excludes the *afectados* from its jurisdiction. As a result, the fact that the Lago Agrio case and the arbitration proceedings both deal with the same problem while demanding different actions is not perceived as a legal problem for the arbitrators. A close look at the awards reveals the legal reasoning that enables this move. In its submission to the arbitration panel, the Ecuadorian government had pointed out the legal conflicts that would emerge if it were to be obliged to suspend the Lago Agrio judgment. It put forward two central arguments to counter Chevron's demand. First, it argued that if it had to suspend the judgment it would violate the procedural rights of the *afectados* that are granted by international human rights treaties and the Ecuadorian constitution. It demanded that the UNCITRAL tribunal consider the rights of the *afectados* by acknowledging that Ecuador had to comply with international human rights treaties.[16] The second argument put forward by Ecuador is based on the Monetary Gold[17] principle, according to which a court has no jurisdiction where the decision necessarily concerns third parties that are not part to the proceedings before it.[18] This principle has also been applied in investment disputes. Hence, Ecuador held that any decision made by the arbitration panel effectively affected the rights of the *afectados*, which meant that the UNCITRAL tribunal lacked jurisdiction.[19]

As indicated above, the arbitration panel did not follow the Ecuadorian submission but ordered 'the Respondent to take all measures at its disposal to suspend or cause to suspend the enforcement or recognition within and without Ecuador of any judgment against the First Claimant in the Lago Agrio Case'.[20] The legal foundations for the tribunal's position

[16] Track 2 Counter-Memorial on the Merits of the Republic of Ecuador, 18 February 2013, No. 486ff. and No. 493ff.

[17] Ibid., No. 515ff. [18] ICJ Rep. 1954, 19.

[19] Track 2 Counter-Memorial on the Merits of the Republic of Ecuador, 18 February 2013, No. 525.

[20] First Interim Award on Interim Measures, 25 January 2012. This decision was re-affirmed in the 2nd and 4th interim awards, see Second Interim Award on Interim Measures, 16 February 2012, and Fourth Interim Award on Interim Measures, 7 February 2013, No. 80

hat it has jurisdiction to proceed to the merits phase of these arbitration roceedings'[21] are spelled out in the third interim award.[22] In relation to the Ionetary Gold principle referred to by the Ecuadorian government, the rbitrators distinguished several dimensions, two of which are of importnce in the context of this chapter.[23] For one, it affirmed the principle of onsent according to which a tribunal did only have jurisdiction over a party nsofar as it had subjected itself to it. Consequently, it found that in the resent case, the tribunal did not have jurisdiction over the *afectados*. econd, the tribunal agreed that it would not have jurisdiction if its decision ffected an 'indispensable third party'. However, in its view, the *afectados* id not constitute an 'indispensable third party' to the dispute dealt with by he tribunal.[24] This is because it had to decide on the rights and obligations manating from the bilateral investment treaty in general, and in particular whether the 1995 Settlement Agreement between Texaco and Ecuador freed Chevron from any further obligations regarding the damages produced by he oil drilling.[25] While the panel recognised that the arbitration award night indeed affect the rights of the *afectados*, it maintained that this tension vould have to be dealt with by the Ecuadorian government and was not a esponsibility of the tribunal.[26] The tribunal concludes:

> The question for this Tribunal is in essence whether the Respondent has or has not violated rights of the Claimants under the BIT because of the way in which the Respondent has, through its organs, acted in relation to the settlement agreements. The question is one of the rights and obligations existing between the Claimants and the Respondent; and the Lago Agrio plaintiffs, who are not parties to the settlement agreement or to the BIT, do not have rights that are directly engaged by that question. If it should transpire that the Respondent has, by concluding the Release Agreements, taken a step which had the legal effect of depriving the Lago Agrio plaintiffs of rights under Ecuadorian Law that they might otherwise have enjoyed, that would be a matter between them and the Respondent, and not a matter for this Tribunal.[27]

21 Third Interim Award on Jurisdiction and Admissibility, 27 February 2012, 5.2.

22 While in the third interim award the Tribunal applies a prima facie standard that means that the decision is not final, the Tribunal in its first partial award has affirmed the latter. On the prima facie principle, cf. Third Interim Award 4.3ff., on the incorporation of the third interim award in the first partial award see UNCITRAL, *Chevron* v. *The Republic of Ecuador*, 17 December 2013, No. 2.

23 See Third Interim Award 4.59ff.

24 See Third Interim Award 4.65.

25 See Track 2 Counter-Memorial on the Merits of the Republic of Ecuador, 18 February 2013, No. 323ff.

26 Third Interim Award 4.67.

27 Third Interim Award 4.70.

This close look at the doctrinal reasoning of the tribunal allows us to refine our understanding of the way in which the collision presents itself. Rather than colliding interests within one legal regime – that is between rights of the *afectados* on the one hand and the rights of the investors on the other – the *de facto* collision of interests is legally resolved by ignoring what the respective legal regimes find to be beyond their jurisdiction. There is no conflict of interest as far as the rationale of the arbitration tribunal goes, because it does not have jurisdiction over the *afectados*. As a consequence, the rights and interests of the *afectados* are expelled from the arbitration proceedings. At the same time, the Ecuadorian court affirms its jurisdiction over the claims of the *afectados*. At present, there is no legal norm or institution that could decide these competing jurisdictional claims. Rather, each legal forum decides on the scope of its own jurisdiction. What we can observe then is a multipolar conflict of jurisdictions within a heterarchical order.

However, while *legally* there is no hierarchy between these jurisdictions, they are of course embedded within the relationship of forces that characterise the present world order. This is especially true for transnational investment law. Especially post-colonial approaches to international law have pointed out that the legal protection of foreign investment has developed in the context of decolonisation and served primarily the interest of capital exporting countries.[28] In this vein, Kate Miles reminds us that

> it is of fundamental importance to the shape and character of international investment law that the context in which its principles were developed was one of exploitation and imperialism. The rules evolved so as to advance the interests of Western capital-exporting states engaging with the non-European world, and, as such, they protected only the investor.[29]

Furthermore, contributions from the field of (heterodox) international political economy have pointed out that the sedimentation of neoliberal principles in transnational investment law restricts the policy options that can be adopted within nation states.[30] Against this backdrop, we

[28] Anghie, *Imperialism, Sovereignty and the Making of International Law*, pp. 196ff.; Pahuja, *Decolonising International Law*, pp. 95ff.

[29] Miles, 'International Investment Law', p. 10.

[30] See Gill, 'Constitutionalizing Inequality and the Clash of Globalizations', pp. 60–1; Schneiderman, 'Investment Rules and the New Constitutionalism', pp. 757ff.; Schneiderman, *Constitutionalizing Economic Globalization*; Möller, 'Global Assemblages im neuen Konstitutionalismus', pp. 48–9.

have to contextualise jurisdictional conflicts within competing (globalised) economic and political projects.

Jurisdiction otherwise or the problem of double fragmentation

Practitioners and academics have tried to address this problem of conflicting jurisdictions under the heading of 'human rights approaches to investment'.[31] This debate explores doctrinal arguments to consider rights of third parties within investment law.[32] Despite their differences, these proposals essentially attempt to remedy the jurisdictional conflict between arbitration panels and other adjudicatory bodies by developing doctrinal arguments that require arbitration tribunals to take into account the rights of third parties. *Inter alia,* they point out that according to Article 31 of the Vienna Convention on the Law of Treaties, arbitration panels have to consider human rights while interpreting investment treaties[33] or they propose that investment tribunals consider human rights of third parties as part of a balancing or proportionality test.[34] Such proposals are not without merit. However, as we already alluded to in the previous section, the tribunal's jurisdictional considerations in *Chevron Corp.* v. *Ecuador* also point to a collision that is much more fundamental than a conflict of jurisdictions.

First fragmentation: investment law versus human rights law

Traditional jurisdictional thought presents jurisdiction as something that follows from an authority established otherwise (in the present case, the arbitration tribunal claims that its authority is based on the consent of the parties). Within this theoretical framework, conflict, territory and subjects are already there when the law enters the stage. From the margins of jurisdictional thought, however, we are reminded that jurisdiction 'refers first and foremost to the power and authority to speak in

[31] Inter alia: Reiner and Schreuer, 'Human Rights and International Investment Arbitration', pp. 83–4; Simma and Kill, 'Harmonizing Investment Protection and International Human Rights', pp. 695ff.; Simma, 'Foreign Investment Arbitration', pp. 584ff.; Davitti, 'On the Meanings of International Investment Law and International Human Rights Law'; Krommendijk and Morijn, '"Proportional" by What Measure(s)?'.

[32] See Petersmann, 'International Rule of Law and Constitutional Justice'.

[33] Simma and Kill, 'Harmonizing Investment Protection and International Human Rights', pp. 695ff.

[34] Krommendijk and Morijn, '"Proportional" by What Measure(s)?'.

the name of law'.[35] From such a perspective, jurisdiction refers to a double movement of creating and re-affirming authority.[36] 'At the jurisdictional threshold', Bradin Cormack writes, 'the law speaks to itself, and in a mirror *reproduces* as administration the juridical order that it simultaneously *produces*'.[37] To think about jurisdiction as a 'first question of law',[38] that is as a problem of authorisation of legal worlds and not merely as a technical question of competence, enables us to perceive 'how rival forms and accounts of political authority and ways of belonging to law are enacted and performed over the same people and the same places at the same time'.[39] From this perspective, it becomes necessary to revise the doctrinal approaches mentioned above as they fail to account for the fact that the collision at stake involves fundamentally different ways of 'belonging to law'. For the jurisdictional conflict is only the epiphenomenon of a more fundamental collision of different legal regimes, each of which reproduces (in the sense of both to repeat and to produce) the specific logic of a functional system. Only at a first glance does the jurisdictional conflict take place between an international body (the arbitration tribunal) and a national court – defined by territorial parameters. The jurisdiction of international investment law constitutes the juridification of a particular global economic order. It serves the protection of foreign direct investment. To guarantee transaction security by means of legal protection, the story goes, is necessary in order to attract foreign investment, which in turn is required to secure economic prosperity. Transnational investment law thus reproduces a particular economic logic, which has informed wide areas of global economic law. This insight on the relationship between economic law and a particular transnational economic order is by no means original and has been the subject of a number of investigations. In a similar vein, the very basic assumptions on which this economic order is grounded (free trade as means to archive global economic wealth) have been contradicted on an empirical as well as theoretical level.[40]

[35] Rush, 'An Altered Jurisdiction', p. 150.

[36] Matthews, 'From Jurisdiction to Juriswriting', pp. 4–5.

[37] Cormack, *A Power to Do Justice*, p. 9.

[38] Matthews, 'From Jurisdiction to Juriswriting', p. 3.

[39] Pahuja, 'Laws of Encounter', p. 71.

[40] Recently the UNCTAD found for example that 'BITs appear to have no effect on bilateral North-South FDI flows': UNCTAD, Trade and Development Report, 2014 (UNCTAD/TDR/2014), 159. That means that it is rather doubtful whether the signing of Bilateral Investment Treaties has a positive economic effect for so-called developing countries.

The UNCITRAL panel operates within the parameters of this particular economic rationale – the protection of private property, fostering economic development through foreign investment, the maximisation of profit. Accordingly, if it is confronted with the claim that the *afectados* have rights to be protected from the impact of foreign investment, it is confronted with a completely different logic. Any attempt to protect the rights of those affected by foreign investment by means of transnational investment arbitration merely subjects them to the economic rationale that shaped the regime of investment law. They would become mere receivers of law (rights) within a jurisdiction that produces/authorises a world that is centred around the principle of private property and expected profit. The investment arbitration tribunal construes the problem at stake according to its own logic so that other jurisdictional claims are not even perceived. This is epitomised by the following statement:

> . . . from its perspective under international law, this Tribunal is the only tribunal with the power to restrain the Respondent [Ecuador, the authors] generally from aggravating the Parties' dispute and causing irreparable harm to the Claimants [Chevron Corp., the authors] in regard to the enforcement and execution of the Lago Agrio Judgment.[41]

From the perspective of investment law, the rights of those affected by investment projects constitute an obstacle or threat to the smooth functioning of the regimes logic. Human rights of third parties can enter investment treaty arbitration only in the form of a disturbing exception to the rule of investment protection. To address the regime collision by expanding the jurisdiction of the investment arbitration panel over the rights of affected third parties therefore means to frame the conflict in a very specific way: human rights of third parties are only acknowledged within the narrow boundaries of a very specific regime logic. Against this background the call for consideration of human rights in investment treaty arbitration, intended to mitigate the negative effects of investment arbitration proceedings, in fact expands the reach of this regime's logic.[42]

A human rights approach to investment has to take into account that considering rights of third parties within the framework of investment treaty arbitration is not a neutral process. First, investment arbitration panels are not fit to balance human rights with rights of investors because

[41] Fourth Interim Award, No. 82.

[42] See for a similar argument with respect to the lack of transparency and legitimacy of investment arbitration proceedings: Reiner and Schreuer, 'Human Rights and International Investment Arbitration'.

they consider human rights only within the specific and narrow economic rationale of a neoclassical free trade agenda. Second, the delimitation of jurisdiction is also an expression of power asymmetries between the different legal regimes of world law. Thus, including human rights of third parties into investment arbitration proceedings may not lead to a consolidation of those rights in conflicts with investor rights. It would rather mean that a structurally biased adjudicatory body would decide over rights of persons, who have never agreed to such panels and who have no standing in front of them.

A human rights approach to investment arbitration should therefore not demand that arbitration panels consider human rights of third parties as part of their jurisdiction. Instead, the demand should be primarily that arbitration panels abstain from rendering a decision where rights and interests of third parties are affected. This self-restrictive determination of its own jurisdiction would leave it to other forums of world law to deal with the underlying conflicts according to a logic not serving merely the logic of capital. We will discuss this suggestion in more detail in the last section of this chapter. Before doing so, we will turn to what we call the second fragmentation of law which becomes manifest in *Chevron Corp.* v. *Ecuador*.

Second fragmentation: the collision between law and non-law

The intuitive answer to this analysis would be to call upon a different legal regime, such as human rights law or environmental law, to deal with the conflict. While these regimes indeed embody a different social logic than investment law, they are not without their own problems. The process of translating a social conflict into the legal language has its own costs, even for those for whom the protective umbrella of human rights is meant. In addition to the first fragmentation, which concerns the fragmentation of law into different legal regimes, we can identify a second fragmentation affecting the relationship of law to its other, to that which is non-law.[43]

As with the first fragmentation, we take the notion of a second fragmentation of law from Gunter Teubner and Andreas Fischer-Lescano. The second fragmentation of law refers to collisions between modern law and normative concerns emerging from indigenous cultures.[44] From the perspective of systems theory, Teubner and Fischer-Lescano summarise

[43] For an in-depth discussion of this relationship see Menke in this volume.
[44] Teubner and Korth, 'Zwei Arten des Rechtspluralismus'.

the problems arising from strategic litigation with the aim of protecting indigenous knowledge as follows: 'The real problem behind these litigation strategies lies in their issue framing. What are the categories in which politics and law in the centres of modernity perceive the problem of traditional knowledge in peripheral societies?'[45] Still, if the aim is to put limits to the economic exploitation of indigenous knowledge, it is necessary to translate non-legal categories and needs into the language of law.[46] The legal fiction of indigenous 'customary law' is one example, we hold, for how this can be done. Here, the so-called modern law, transforms 'communication from a local culture' into 'formal legal acts', that is, it construes non-law as law. Only through this movement, law perceives the non-law as law and thus can limit itself in a way that leaves space for non-legal communications. Against this backdrop the authors conclude:

> The attempt at understanding how these people see themselves appears to be the only promising chance, in order to reconstruct this understanding as restrictions in the respective language of the fragmented systems. The way in which the producers of traditional knowledge perceive themselves – 'the principle of indigenous self-determination' – should be the normative center of gravitation.[47]

However, in conceptualising the second fragmentation, Fischer-Lescano and Teubner still need to assume that 'indigenous knowledge' exists before and outside modern law. They thus seem to essentialise to a certain extent indigenous identity. This is, however, problematic for several reasons. Most importantly, this notion of indigenous knowledge does not reflect the fact that what they describe as regional and traditional cultures is already the result of a colonial encounter; it is already a description made by 'modern law'.[48] In order to reflect this fact, it is necessary to take the idea of double fragmentation one step further. It is the self-characterisation of modern law as modern and functionally differentiated law that construes that which is non-modern and non-functionally differentiated as its other. Modern law thus produces its other in its self-characterisation. The dichotomy between modern law

[45] Teubner and Fischer-Lescano, 'Cannibalizing Epistemes', p. 19. [46] Ibid.

[47] Ibid., p. 31.

[48] Nelken formulates a similar critique with reference to Teubner's notion of autopoiesis: 'All this suggests that there may be some danger of autopoietic theory being insufficiently reflexive about the extent to which its ideas about legal culture are shaped by the legal culture in which it was created', see Nelken, 'Beyond the Metaphor of Legal Transplants?', pp. 289–90.

and indigenous cultures is the result of modern law's self-characterisation. The non-law is conceived as something that can be translated, captured in law, but not as something that challenges the logic of law itself. This becomes evident also in *Chevron Corp.* v. *Ecuador*.

So far, we have been writing as if the *afectados* were a group of individuals that existed outside the law or before the law, protected by human rights law and which had experienced violations of their rights. However, the very entity of *afectados* is a legal artefact produced by a different jurisdiction – the jurisdiction of social, economic, cultural and environmental rights. Continuing to think jurisdiction in relation to political authority (or legal regimes in relation to differentiated functional systems), the jurisdiction of social, economic and cultural, as well as environmental rights evokes different values or logics than investment law. Here, the basic needs of the individual (or of a group) constitute the basic principle of the world or authority that is invoked. Against this backdrop, the call for human rights might indeed challenge the neo-liberal logic of transnational investment law. To state that the *afectados* have suffered damages and human rights violations (as is done in the Lago Agrio proceedings) authorises a different order or world, a different logic of what is considered important. Still, the human rights regime knows the *afectados* only as receivers of law. The human rights regime gives rights to the *afectados,* who are perceived as some non-legal reality. What is omitted is the fact that the *afectados* as a group exist only through law. To frame the (legal, political, economic) conflict in terms of human rights violations introduces a particular form of representation in which actors 'have rights and culture',[49] but no jurisdiction, that is, no competing authority that would question the human rights language. In this vein, the worldview of the indigenous population that inhabit the territory where the oil drilling took place becomes a cultural good, to be protected by law, but not able to create law itself.

This becomes manifest when the indigenous populations in the affected area are reduced to their 'culture' to bring them under the protective umbrella of rights. Whenever Ecuador invokes the rights of the *afectados* in the UNCITRAL proceedings, it portrays the group in a specific way: the life of the indigenous populations in the area before arrival of the oil companies is described as one led 'in harmony'[50] with the rainforest

[49] Pahuja, 'Laws of Encounter', p. 71.

[50] Track 2 Counter-Memorial on the Merits of the Republic of Ecuador, 18 February 2013, No. 26. ('Before TexPet began its oil activity in the Oriente (East) region of the

and its natural resources. To quote but one example from the Counter Memorial submitted by Ecuador:

> Before TexPet began its oil activity in the Oriente (East) region of the Ecuadorian Amazon, at least eight groups of indigenous peoples lived there in harmony with the rainforest ... Ecuador's indigenous peoples relied on the rainforest for their subsistence through hunting, gathering, and practicing sustainable agriculture. The streams, rivers, and lakes of the rainforest also were inextricably linked with their daily lives because they relied on its waters, groundwater, flora, and fauna for fishing, bathing, cooking, drinking, washing clothes, and transportation. In addition to nutritional and domestic purposes, indigenous peoples used the rainforest's elements in the preparation of traditional medicine. Sustainable agriculture, called 'chacra' or 'swidden agriculture,' also contributed to indigenous groups' ability to survive in low-density populations in the rainforest... Experts praise the indigenous peoples' eco-friendly system as a 'truly sustainable agriculture that is environmentally sound'.[51]

However, rather than actually existing before modern law, the identification with a particular worldview that requires protection is only produced as the 'other' of modernity and modern law. The ecological way of life as characteristic of the inhabitants of the Amazon is the result of their contact with the colonial population:

> What are seen (and they themselves see) today as their traditions, customs and economies are indeed the sedimentation of resistances, survival strategies and adaptive response in the face of mass destruction of their ancestral communal life by modern conquerors and setters of all denominations.[52]

In a similar vein, Bardomiano Hernandez describes the fetishisation of their own culture as a reaction of the affected groups to the threat to their existence.[53] What Sergio Costa und Guilherme Leite Gonçalves write regarding the protection of afro-descendants holds true for the present context as well: the protection of indigenous groups by multicultural

Ecuadorian Amazon, at least eight groups of indigenous peoples lived there in harmony with the rainforest'.).

51 Track 2 Counter-Memorial on the Merits of the Republic of Ecuador, 18 February 2013, No. 28, pp. 14ff.

52 Santos, *Toward a New Legal Common Sense*, p. 238. For the Ecuadorian case see further Rivas and Lara, *Conservación y Petróleo*, and Davidov, 'Aguinda v. Texaco Inc.'.

53 Hernández, 'Cowode'.

rights result in the construction of 'a monolithic identity defined by ancestral traits, which are treated as if they were completely immune and refractory to divisions, internal conflicts and interactions and ties with the surrounding society'.[54] While group rights are necessary, they need to reflect that '... any intervention of the ... law redraws the map of the identity negotiations, intervening in the constitution of the socio-cultural groups'.[55] Hence, the 'cultural characteristics' attributed to the affected population is not a 'reality' translated into the language of law, but the result of a legal strategy.

In her much discussed essay, 'Can the Subaltern Speak', Gayatri Spivak reminds us that in every act of representation there is an aesthetic dimension. To represent denotes both speaking for someone, but also providing an image of something or someone. Whenever I speak for a group I also speak about a group and thereby construe a 'transparent' subject as if it actually existed.[56] Spivak's warning about the structures of power and representation proper to academia is also relevant for the analysis of human rights litigation, something she explores in more depth in a lecture held as part of the Oxford Amnesty Lectures, later published under the title 'Righting Wrongs'. She starts her text with a discussion of the language of 'rights' and 'wrongs'. We can have rights and claim their protection, but wrongs can only be experienced. In order to be able to speak about wrongs, it is always necessary to speak of someone or something else that has produced the damage. Indeed, she observes, 'wrong' is usually used as a verb – to wrong. In relation to 'Human Wrongs' the notion of 'Human Rights' also acquires an active dimension. 'Thus', she concludes, 'Human Rights is not only about having or claiming a right or a set of rights; it is also about righting wrongs, about being the dispenser of these rights'.[57] Spivak refers to a divide that is inscribed into the idea of human rights. In so far as they demand that injustices should be remedied, the grammar of human rights implies a 'friendly social-Darwinist agenda' according to which the fitter population has become active in favour of those who have been wronged but who cannot speak for themselves:[58] 'The work of righting wrongs is shared above a class line that to some extent and unevenly cuts across race and the North-South divide'.[59] The relevance of this comment for

[54] Costa and Gonçalves, 'Human Rights as Collective Entitlement?', p. 68.
[55] Ibid., p. 69. [56] Spivak, 'Can the Subaltern Speak?', p. 271, pp. 276–7.
[57] Spivak, 'Righting Wrongs', pp. 523ff. [58] Ibid., pp. 524–5. [59] Ibid., pp. 525–6.

the present case is probably most obvious with regards to the dispute about the legal representation of the Huoarani people once it became public that Steven Donzinger had sold shares of the legal claim without the knowledge of the plaintiffs.[60]

The juridification of a conflict, that is its translation into a *quaestio iuris* even in the form of subjective rights, produces its own relationships of power – in the form of personal representation as well as the representation of the social conflict at stake. It requires those engaging with the law to define themselves as legal subjects and frame their needs and interests in a way they become understandable in legal terms. In this context, it is worth noting that in Ecuador this form of identity politics around single issues (in this case environmental pollution) has been replacing broader struggles that questioned the development-oriented state politics or demanded redistribution since the 1990s.[61] A tendency which needs to be understood within what Nancy Fraser has called the post-socialist condition:

> an absence of any credible overarching emancipatory project despite the proliferation of fronts of struggle; a general decoupling of the cultural politics of recognition from the social politics of redistribution; and a decentering of claims for equality in the face of aggressive marketization and sharply rising material 'inequality.[62]

The legalisation of the situation as a conflict between the *afectados* and Chevron Corp. is the result of a selective construction of the non-law by law. In this process, a difference between the indigenous population and modern law is created in which the indigenous population is not perceived as a conflicting jurisdiction – capable of producing its own law – but as mere receiver of rights within the structure of a national state. If we draw on social, economic, and cultural rights to counter the neo-liberal jurisdiction of investment law, we have to take into account this violent relationship between law and what it construes as its other.

60 *Chevron* v. *Donziger*, Proposed Intervenors' Memorandum of Law in support of Motion to Intervene; *Huaio* v. *Donziger*.

61 See the contributions in Pineda and Krainer (eds.), *Periferias de la periferia*; see also Lembke, *In the Land of Oligarchs*; Korovkin, 'Between Class and Ethnicity', pp. 331–4.

62 Fraser, *Justice Interruptus*, pp. 3–4, see also Torpey, who states: 'The decline of utopian politics has combined with identity politics to produce "reparations politics"'; Torpey, 'An Avalanche of History', pp. 28–9.

From double fragmentation to the double *Entsetzung* of law

What, then, remains after the analysis carried out thus far? To repeat: with respect to the first fragmentation of law, we have come to the conclusion that the collision of different legal regimes of world law cannot be solved within investment treaty arbitration proceedings. For this would simply expand the reach of the investment regime. Mitigating conflicts between investor rights and human rights of third parties therefore requires that investment tribunals exercise their jurisdiction with self-restraint, when human rights of third parties are affected. The problem of the second fragmentation, that is, the confrontation of the so-called modern law with so-called regional cultures, is that modern law applies the logic of a functionally differentiated law to non-functionally differentiated sectors of society. The double fragmentation of law thus raises the question whether law can have an emancipatory potential[63] at all for the conflicts displayed in *Chevron Corp.* v. *Ecuador*. Against this background it seems as if law has nothing to offer for an emancipatory critique of the underlying conflicts of the case. However, an emancipatory critique of law cannot consist in negating or suspending the law.[64] For the suspension of law would deprive the *afectados* of any chance to receive justice. An emancipatory critique would instead require an enactment of law that does *justice* to its double fragmentation. Drawing on Walter Benjamin's concept of the *Entsetzung* of law[65], and Christoph Menke's studies on law and violence[66] and law and form,[67] we propose that a double *Entsetzung* of the law would allow for an emancipatory enactment of law.

In his essay 'Critique of Violence', Benjamin writes:

> On the breaking of this cycle maintained by mythical forms of law, on the suspension [*Entsetzung*] of law with all the forces on which it depends as they depend on it, finally therefore on the abolition of state power, a new historical epoch is founded.[68]

As Menke points out, the notion of '*Entsetzung*' goes beyond the English translation of suspension.[69]

[63] See Fischer-Lescano, 'Systemtheorie als kritische Gesellschaftstheorie'.
[64] Menke, 'Law and Violence'; Menke, *Recht und Gewalt*, p. 63.
[65] Benjamin, 'Critique of Violence'.
[66] Menke, 'Law and Violence'; Menke, *Recht und Gewalt*.
[67] Menke in this volume.
[68] Benjamin, 'Critique of Violence', p. 300.
[69] Menke, 'Law and Violence', p. 13.

> The German term *Entsetzung* has a double meaning ... For *Entsetzung* means both to depose someone from an office or honour and to lift the military occupation of a town or fortress. *Entsetzung* of law thus means that it is deposed from the office it currently occupies, and *at the same time* released from a power besieging it.[70]

Thus, for Menke, the *Entsetzung* of law does not mean to abolish the law,[71] but deposing and liberating it from its inherent violence.[72] This however would require a different way of enacting the law. Such an enactment of the law would require, according to Menke, a law that becomes self-reflective. A self-reflective enactment of law would reiterate internally the distinction between law and non-law and would be constantly reminded of the fact that that the law itself originates in its distinction from non-law.[73] Thus, the *Entsetzung* of law as deposing and liberating the law from its inherent violence requires a self-reflective enactment of law. When we relate this formal determination of law as a self-reflective enactment, to our analysis of the underlying conflicts of *Chevron Corp.* v. *Ecuador*, we can identify two different forms or instantiations of an *Entsetzung* of law representing the two fragmentations of law.

The Entsetzung *of law I*

As indicated above, investment law enacts the law according to the requirements of its specific internal rationality. It suppresses the interests of the *afectados* and thereby enforces *en passant* certain hegemonic interests against societal resistance. The first deposition (*Entsetzung*) of law would here consist in a self-reflective enactment of investment law according to which investment law would experience its rationality as one among several and potentially equally legitimate rationalities within world law. This would confront an investment panel internally with the question whether it is the legal regime of investment law that should be the judge of the societal conflict at hand or whether it should abstain

[70] Menke, 'Law and Violence', p. 13 (footnotes omitted, italics in the original).

[71] Menke, *Recht und Gewalt*, p. 63.

[72] Menke, 'Law and Violence', p. 13.

[73] This is a rough translation of this passage: 'Die Selbstreflexion des Rechts besteht darin, die Entgegensetzung des Rechts zum Nichtrechtlichen, durch die sich das Recht hervorbringt, im Recht zu wiederholen; das selbstreflexive Recht „weiß"– was das nicht selbstreflexive ... Recht beständig vergisst –, dass es selbst durch seine Unterscheidung das Nichtrechtliche, gegen das es sich durchsetzen muss, erst hervorgebracht hat'. Menke, *Recht und Gewalt*, p. 69.

from judging. The self-reflective enactment of law therefore opens up the option to abstain from judging; that is, to depose itself from its legal authority over the societal conflict. Considering human rights then does not mean to decide a case within the framework of investment law, but rather setting the case free from investment law's rationality. But reflecting on its inherent rationality also bears the potential of an investment law that wants to be different, an investment law that internally opposes its own rationality.[74] For a self-reflective enacting of investment law would also confront investment law internally with its colonial past and its hegemonic position within world law. An enactment of investment law in the face of its inherent violence can thereby develop what Menke calls, with reference to Adorno, *distaste against itself*.[75] Such distaste renders possible internal opposition and internal politicisation of investment law. Without societal pressure, however, such a distaste may not be developed or be without consequences. Never the less, it would serve as a reminder that investment laws' rationality, its design and principles, are not set in stone. A self-reflective inner distaste constantly challenges the current status of investment law and demands a different investment law, an investment law to come.[76] This would be a law that does not serve only to protect investor's rights, but an investment law that would understand the needs of the local population, of environmental protection, of societal interests as realisation of the rationality of investment protection itself.[77] Thus, with reference to the first fragmentation of law in *Chevron Corp.* v. *Ecuador* the *Entsetzung* of investment law would consist in a self-reflective enacting of the law according to which investment law abstains from judging, freeing itself from authority over a societal conflict.

The Entsetzung *of law II*

Parallel to the first fragmentation of law, which demands a reflection on the relationship between different legal regimes, the second fragmentation requires a reflection of law's relationship to the non-law. Here, the suspension of law would consist in an inner legal reflection of law's

[74] See for the notion of self-opposition of law: Fischer-Lescano, *Rechtskraft*.
[75] See Menke, *Recht und Gewalt*, pp. 102–3.
[76] This concept of the 'law to come' draws on Derrida, *Rogues*.
[77] See, for a related concept with reference to the market for OTC Derivatives: Horst, 'Politiken der Entparadoxierung', pp. 193ff.

lationship to non-law. If representing those affected by investment bitration in the form of subjects' human rights seems to be the only ay of recognising them in law at all, to simply abolish human rights oesn't seem to offer any emancipatory way out of the dilemma.[78] We ggested above that, as a strategic decision, translating a social conflict to the *quaestio iuris*[79] can help articulating counter-hegemonic inter- ts. The task for an emancipatory legal practise would be to enact the w in a way that reflects the process of juridification itself, that is the onstruction of something as non-law in the course of the legal process. o paraphrase Christoph Menke, law never refers to events or actors in e 'real world', but only to their legalised representations.[80]

The self-reflection of law we propose here would uncover that, in acting the law, the ascriptions necessary for the legalisation of societal onflicts are made by law itself. This would also mean that law realises at the very distinction between law and non-law is generated only in the rocess of generating the law. Such a self-reflective enactment of law, owever, does not overturn the fissure between law and non-law. There is o immediate reconciliation of law and life.[81] Again, what a self-reflective nactment of law offers is a law where the legal ascriptions and the ridification of social conflicts as well as the distinction between law nd non-law are made visible, and thus can be contested, challenged and pposed. When law's authority over non-law depoliticises a social conflict that it frames it as merely a legal question (and not as a problem of edistribution etc.), a self-reflective law has the potential to bring into elief the politics involved in the depoliticising effects of juridification. self-reflective enactment of law knows of the contingency of its own onstruction of the non-law.

What would this mean in the context of the case discussed in this hapter? The legal proceedings of *Chevron Corp.* v. *Ecuador* translate a ultidimensional conflict encompassing conflicts between different odes of production, different ways of living, different ways of belonging o law, different classes, subjects and regions into a legal language. Yet, his process of framing is not reflected. Rather, the Hourani people are resented as nature-related population that had always been there, the

78 In this vein, Buckel states that critical legal theory shows that the ambivalence of law to simultaneously maintain existing power relations and protect against oppression is characteristic of the form of law: Buckel in this volume.

79 See Fischer-Lescano and Teubner, *Regime-Kollisionen*, p. 87.

80 Menke in this volume.

81 See Menke, 'Law and Violence', p. 14.

problem being the pollution, not the insertion of the rain forest into a global capitalist economy. The legal documents produced in the context of *Chevron Corp.* v. *Ecuador* testify to the tendency of the human rights language to truncate the systematic analysis of the origin of conflict and thereby also the way remedies are thought.[82] While a strategic use of human rights language can of course help to draw attention to certain problems, not to reflect the limits that come with the very concepts of human rights might perpetuate the very relations of power underlying the conflict: economic and colonial.

A self-reflective enactment of law, then, would keep this multidimensionality visible within law. Framing the conflict at hand as a legal conflict between investor rights on the one hand and human and environmental rights on the other, becomes but only one (contestable) translation of the social conflict. Such a law can take into account that the 'othering' of the affected as '*afectados*' and '*indigenas*' in tune with nature is a legal reduction of the underlying conflict under the auspices of a specific legality. The question whether a certain group of '*afectados*' has a legal claim against Chevron for compensation for damages then is only one of many questions the law is confronted with while dealing with the claim.

The representation of the non-legal in and through law always remains a legal construction. However, when law commits itself in its self-reflection to constant irritation it makes its boundaries visible and thereby contestable. This way law can become a medium for the societal negotiation of social conflicts, whose grammar is not predetermined. This would be a law that would transform itself in the face of the social conflict as well as transforming the social conflict.

Bibliography

Anghie, A., *Imperialism, Sovereignty and the Making of International Law* (Cambridge University Press, 2007).

Barrett, P., 'Amazon Crusader. Chevron Pest. Fraud?', *Bloomberg Business Week*, (9 March 2011). Available at www.bloomberg.com/bw/magazine/content/11_12/b4220056636512.htm.

Benjamin, W., 'Critique of Violence' in W. Benjamin, *Reflections, Essays, Aphorisms, Autobiographical Writings* (New York: Harcourt Brace Jovanovich, 1978), pp. 277–300.

[82] Kennedy, 'The International Human Rights Movement'; Marks, 'Human Rights and Root Causes'.

Caron, D., and L. M. Caplan, *The UNCITRAL Arbitration Rules. A Commentary*, 2nd edn. (Oxford University Press, 2013).

Cormack, B., *A Power to Do Justice. Jurisdiction, English Literature, and the Rise of Common Law* (The University of Chicago Press, 2007).

Costa, S., and G. Gonçalves, 'Human Rights as Collective Entitlement? – Afro-Descendants in Latin America and the Caribbean', *Zeitschrift für Menschenrechte*, 5 (2011), pp. 52–71.

Davidov, V., 'Aguinda v. Texaco Inc.: Expanding Indigenous "Expertise" Beyond Ecoprimitivism', *Journal of Legal Anthropology*, 1 (2010), pp. 147–64.

Davitti, D., 'On the Meanings of International Investment Law and International Human Rights Law: The Alternative Narrative of Due Diligence', *Human Rights Law Review*, 12 (2012), pp. 421–53.

Derrida, J., *Rogues: Two Essays on Reason* (Stanford University Press, 2005).

Dhooge, L. J., 'Aguinda v. ChevronTexaco: Discretionary Grounds for the Non-Recognition of Foreign Judgments for Environmental Injury in the United States', *Virginia Environmental Law Journal*, 28 (2010), pp. 241–98.

Fischer-Lescano, A., *Rechtskraft* (Berlin: August Verlag, 2013).

'Systemtheorie als kritische Gesellschaftstheorie' in A. Fischer-Lescano and M. Amstutz (eds.), *Kritische Systemtheorie* (Bielefeld: Transcript, 2013), pp. 13–37.

Fischer-Lescano A., and G. Teubner, *Regime-Kollisionen* (Berlin: Suhrkamp, 2006).

Fraser, N., *Justice Interruptus. Critical Reflections on the 'Postsocialist' Condition* (New York: Routledge, 1997).

Gill, S., 'Constitutionalizing Inequality and the Clash of Globalizations', *International Studies Review*, 4 (2002), pp. 47–65.

Hernández, B., 'Cowode. La imagen waorani del caníbal y la lucha por el territorio en el Yasuní' in J. Pineda and A. Krainer (eds.), *Periferias de la Periferia. Procesos Territoriales Indígenas en la Costa y la Amazonía Ecuatoriana* (Quito: FLACSO, 2012), pp. 165–92.

Horst, J., 'Politiken der Entparadoxierung. Versuch einer Bestimmung des Politischen in der funktional ausdifferenzierten Weltgesellschaft' in A. Fischer-Lescano and M. Amstutz (eds.), *Kritische Systemtheorie* (Bielefeld: transcript, 2013), pp. 189–212.

Kennedy, D., 'The International Human Rights Movement: Part of the Problem?', *European Human Rights Law Review*, 3 (2001), pp. 245–67.

Korovkin, T., 'Between Class and Ethnicity: Encounters of Ecuador's Indigenous People with the Political Left', *Latin American and Caribbean Ethnic Studies*, 5 (2010), pp. 331–4.

Krommendijk, J., and J. Morijn, '"Proportional" by What Measure(s)? Balancing Investor Interests and Human Rights by Way of Applying the Proportionality Principle in Investor-State Arbitration' in P. M. Dupuy, H. U. Petersmann and F. Francioni (eds.), *Human Rights in International Investment Law and Arbitration* (Oxford University Press, 2009), pp. 422–50.

Lembke, M., *In the Lands of Oligarchs: Ethno-Politics and the Struggle for Social Justice in the Indigenous-Peasant Movements of Guatemala and Ecuador* (Stockholm University, 2006).

Marks, S., 'Human Rights and Root Causes', *The Modern Law Review*, 74 (2011), pp. 57–78.

Matthews, D., 'From Jurisdiction to Juriswriting: At the Expressive Limits of the Law', *Law, Culture and the Humanities, published online before print* (20 March 2014), 1–21.

Menke, C., 'Law and Violence', *Law and Literature*, 22 (2010), pp. 1–17.

Recht und Gewalt (August Verlag, Berlin, 2011).

Miles, K., 'International Investment Law: Origins, Imperialism and Conceptualizing the Environment', *Colorado Journal of International Environmental Law & Policy*, 21 (2010), pp. 1–47.

Möller, K., 'Global Assemblages im neuen Konstitutionalismus. Rechtstheoretische Probleme der neo-gramscianischen internationalen politischen Ökonomie (IPÖ)', *Ancilla Iuris*, (2008), pp. 44–56.

Nelken, D., 'Beyond the Metaphor of Legal Transplants? Consequences of Autopoeietic Theory for the Study of Cross-cultural Legal Adaption' in J. Priban and D. Nelken (eds.), *Law's New Boundaries: The Consequences of Legal Autopoiesis* (Aldershot: Ashgate, 2001), pp. 265–302.

Noronha, C., 'Ecuadorian Chevron Oil Pollution Case Goes before Canadian High Court', *Canadian Business*, (11 December 2014). Available at www.canadianbusiness.com/business-news/ecuadorian-chevron-oil-pollution-case-goes-before-canadian-high-court/.

Pahuja, S., *Decolonising International Law* (Cambridge University Press, 2011).

'Laws of Encounter: A Jurisdictional Account of International Law', *London Review of International Law*, 1 (2013), pp. 63–98.

Petersmann, E. U., 'International Rule of Law and Constitutional Justice in International investment Law and Arbitration', *Indiana Journal of Global Legal Studies*, 16 (2009), pp. 513–34.

Pineda J., and A. Krainer (eds.), *Periferias de la periferia. Procesos territoriales indígenas en la Costa y la Amazonia ecuatorianas* (Quito: FLACSO, 2012).

Rivas Toledo, A., and R. Lara Ponce, *Conservación y Petróleo en la Amazonia Ecuatoriana. Un acercamiento al caso huaorani* (Quito: EcoCiencia, 2001).

Reiner, C., and C. Schreuer, 'Human Rights and International Investment Arbitration' in P. M. Dupuy, H. U. Petersmann and F. Francioni (eds.), *Human Rights in International Investment Law and Arbitration* (Oxford University Press, 2009), pp. 82–96.

Rush, P., 'An Altered Jurisdiction: Corporeal Traces of Law', *Griffith Law Review*, 6 (1998), pp. 144–65.

de Sousa Santos, B., *Toward a New Legal Common Sense. Law, Globalization and Emancipation* (London: Butterworths LexisNexis, 2002).

Schneiderman, D., 'Investment Rules and the New Constitutionalism', *Law & Social Inquiry*, 25 (2000), pp. 757–87.

Constitutionalizing Economic Globalization (Cambridge University Press, 2008).

Simma, B., 'Foreign Investment Arbitration: A Place for Human Rights', *International and Comparative Law Quarterly*, 60 (2011), pp. 573–96.

Simma, B., and T. Kill, 'Harmonizing Investment Protection and International Human Rights: First Steps Towards a Methodology' in C. Binder, U. Kriebaum, A. Reinisch and S. Wittich (eds.), *International Investment Law for the 21st Century. Essays in Honour of Christoph Schreuer* (Oxford University Press, 2009), pp. 677–707.

Spivak, G. C., 'Can the Subaltern Speak?' in C. Nelson and L. Grossberg (eds.), *Marxism and the Interpretation of Culture* (Basingstoke: Macmillan, 1988), pp. 271–313.

'Righting Wrongs', *The South Atlantic Quarterly*, 103 (2004), pp. 523–81.

Teubner, G., and A. Fischer-Lescano, 'Cannibalizing Epistemes: Will Modern Law Protect Traditional Cultural Expression?' in C. B. Graber and M. Burri-Nenova (eds.), *Intellectual Property and Traditional Cultural Expression in a Digital Environment* (Cheltenham: Edward Elgar, 2008), pp. 17–45.

Teubner, G., and P. Korth, 'Zwei Arten des Rechtspluralismus: Normkollisionen in der doppelten Fragmentierung der Weltgesellschaft' in M. Kötter and G. F. Schuppert (eds.), *Normative Pluralität ordnen* (Baden-Baden: Nomos, 2009), pp. 137–68.

Torpey, J., 'An Avalanche of History: The "Collapse of the Future" and the Rise of Reparations Politics' in M. Berg and B. Schäfer (eds.), *Historical Justice in International Perspective. How Societies are Trying to Right the Wrongs of the Past* (German Historical Institute, Washington D.C. and Cambridge University Press, 2009), pp. 21–38.

Vogt, J., 'Urteil Ecuador vs. Chevron: Ein Urteil, vielleicht mit Folgen', *taz. Die Tageszeitung*, (4 January 2012). Available at www.taz.de/!84957/.

INDEX

Lightning Source UK Ltd.
Milton Keynes UK
UKHW020226311218
334774UK00017B/277/P

9 781107 5655